Adventure Guide

The
Canadian
Rockies

Brenda Koller

HUNTER

HUNTER PUBLISHING, INC,
130 Campus Drive, Edison, NJ 08818
☎ 732-225-1900; 800-255-0343; fax 732-417-1744
www.hunterpublishing.com

Ulysses Travel Publications
4176 Saint-Denis, Montréal, Québec
Canada H2W 2M5
☎ 514-843-9882, ext. 2232; fax 514-843-9448

Windsor Books
The Boundary, Wheatley Road, Garsington
Oxford, OX44 9EJ England
☎ 01865-361122; fax 01865-361133

ISBN 1-58843-573-3
© 2006 Hunter Publishing, Inc.
Manufactured in the United States of America

This and other Hunter travel guides are also available as e-books through Amazon.com, NetLibrary.com, EBSCO and other digital partners. For more information, e-mail us at comments@hunterpublishing.com.

This guide focuses on recreational activities. As all such activities contain elements of risk, the publisher, author, affiliated individuals and companies disclaim responsibility for any injury, harm, or illness that may occur to anyone through, or by use of, the information in this book. Every effort was made to insure the accuracy of information in this book, but the publisher and author do not assume, and hereby disclaim, liability for any loss or damage caused by errors, omissions, misleading information or potential travel problems caused by this guide, even if such errors or omissions result from negligence, accident or any other cause.

Cover photo: *Mount Robson & Berg Lake,* © Lenard Sanders
Back cover photo *(Jasper)* and spine photo *(Rocky Mountain bighorn sheep)*: Jon Sullivan, PDPhoto.org
All interior color photos, © Brenda Koller,
unless otherwise indicated.

Maps by Toni Carbone, © 2006 Hunter Publishing, Inc.
Index by Nancy Wolff
1   2   3   4

Contents

Kananaskis Country 233

Introduction

What is it about the mountains that lure us in so captivatingly, leave us with a sense of awe and well being, and call us to return time again? Wilderness is the hallmark of Canada and the Rocky Mountains are one of its defining features. Canada is well known the world over for its cherished national and provincial parks and the Rocky Mountain Parks are the most famous of these protected areas.

The Rocky Mountains are a contiguous chain of mountains that stretch from the British Columbia/Yukon border all the way to New Mexico. The provinces of British Columbia and Alberta share the Canadian Rockies with the Continental Divide (the Great Divide) serving as the provincial boundary, a natural divide running along the highest peaks. The western boundary is a great long valley called the Rocky Mountain Trench and to the east are the Interior Plains. Divisions crosswise include: the northern Canadian Rockies, north of the Peace River; the central Canadian Rockies, from the Peace River to the Crowsnest Pass; and the southern Canadian Rockies, south of the Crowsnest Pass to the international border.

This Adventure Guide covers mountain parks of the central Canadian Rockies and the southern Canadian Rockies. Alberta's Jasper National Park, the most northerly Rocky Mountain National Park, and the ever-popular Banff National Park, the first national park in Canada, along with British Columbia's amazing Yoho and Kootenay National Parks, together cover 20,280 sq km (7,800 sq miles) – one of the largest areas of mountain parkland in the entire world. In 1985, these four contiguous national parks (together with the provincial parks of Hamber, Mount Robson and Mount Assiniboine) were declared a UNESCO World Heritage Site. Other Rocky Mountain Parks and areas covered include Kananaskis Country, adjacent to Banff National Park, which incorporates magnificent provincial parks and recreation areas; the distinct and tranquil Waterton Lakes National Park in the southwestern corner of Alberta; and finally, British Columbia's Mount Robson Provincial Park, embodying resplendent Mt. Robson, the highest and one of the most majestic peaks in the Canadian Rockies – and my favorite Rocky Mountain park.

In his classic book *In the Heart of the Canadian Rockies* (London: MacMillan & Co. Ltd., 1906), mountaineer James Outram (1864-1925) compares the splendor of Switzerland's mountains with the United States and concludes that "the wonderous glacial fields, the massing of majestic ranges, the striking individuality of each great peak, the forest areas, green pasture lands, clear lakes, and peaceful valleys, are nowhere found harmoniously blended on the western continent until the traveler visits that section of the Rocky Mountains which lies within the wide domain of Canada."

The Canadian Rockies are one of the world's most popular tourist destinations. About four million people annually visit Canada's Rocky Mountain Parks to experience the essence of Canada's natural and cultural Rocky Mountain heritage. The parks offer a mind-boggling array of year-round choices for the visitor with more and more people venturing off the highways and roads to partake in the landscape and discover some of the most stunning scenery the world has to offer. Easily accessible adventures include walking, hiking and backpacking; mountain biking and bicycle touring; fishing, boating and rafting; horseback riding; skiing, snowboarding and snowshoeing; and so much more. Then, of course, there's wildlife viewing. Visitors to the Canadian Rockies have the opportunity to see some of North America's most spectacular animals, including 69 different species of mammals. And where else but here can you spend your morning hiking into spectacular wilderness areas and by afternoon enjoy high tea in the civilized surroundings of a grand hotel?

I have lived beside the Canadian Rockies all of my life and have been traveling to visit them since I was a child. Much has changed over the years. Along with park development and increased visitation have come environmental awareness and education. Each visit adds an array of new experiences and knowledge that reinforce my passion for the Rockies.

I hope you have the opportunity to experience some of the incredible sights and activities in this guidebook that I'm thrilled to share with you. I'm confident that you will treasure your experiences for a lifetime, as I do.

 "Go, at any cost, and live among the mountains, forgetting that there is anything else in life...." Mary Jobe, an intrepid Rocky Mountain adventurer, ca 1912.

■ My Travel Philosophy

There's a lot you can do to prepare before you even pack a bag or make a single travel arrangement. By reading this guide you may already be gearing up for a trip to the Canadian Rockies. There's much written material available about the Rockies and with the popularity of the Internet, scads of information is available at your fingertips. So I've included plenty of web addresses, as well as suggestions for fascinating further reading. The more you know before you depart, the more enjoyable and safe your trip will be.

In his article "The Mental Training of a Traveler" (*The Geographical Journal*, February, 1915), British historian and statesman Viscount James Bryce (1838-1922) gives some good advice that is just as relevant today as it was back then:

"If a man enters the finest picture-gallery in Europe knowing nothing at all about the painters, whose work is there stored, their dates, the schools they belonged to, or the subjects they painted, he will derive very little benefit, and will carry away a most confused impression; but a little preliminary study will enable him to appreciate and enjoy pictures in a way which will be profitable all the rest of his life. If we start to travel with a certain amount of preliminary knowledge, our travels repay us more and more at every step. First of all, we ought to know what to look for; second, how to observe; and third, how to reflect upon the things we do observe."

There are two ways to arrange your Rocky Mountain visit. You can contact a booking agent, advise them as to when and where you plan to travel, and they can arrange the rest for you: transportation, accommodation, tours and the like. There is usually no fee charged to the traveler for this service and it might save you time, but really you learn very little of your destination in the process. Also, you will be committed to a pre-arranged itinerary. There's nothing wrong with this, but I prefer independent travel for a number of reasons. First, I want to learn about the place I'm going to visit and making all of the arrangements is a learning process. Also, after I arrive at my destination I like the flexibility to change my plans, something that isn't always possible if you're on a prear-ranged schedule.

Every tourist destination has its "canned" attractions, some of which can be quite enjoyable and some of which are best avoided. The Rockies are no exception. I'm pretty good at spot-ting and avoiding tourist traps – overpriced establishments that offer little and charge a lot. Chain stores and chain res-taurants I can frequent at home but I try to avoid them there, too. I'm partial to family-operated businesses as they have a vested interest in treating their customers well and will often "go the extra mile." I embrace places off the beaten path, places a little out of the ordinary, places that many tourists pass by, either because they haven't taken the time to find out about them or because they're simply happy among the hoards at the customary attractions. Realistically, if you're visiting the Rockies during the peak months of July or August, you're going to have to put up with crowds. But there are still some places in the Rockies that few visitors know about and you may well end up with some very satisfying soli-tude.

Most of the activities in this book can be accomplished inde-pendently, but I would like to add a word of caution: if you are not an experienced boater, hiker or backcountry camper and if you are at all hesitant about heading out on the trails, you should sign up for a tour or hire a guide. There are many experienced tour operators and guides to choose from in national and provincial parks and you will learn a great deal from a good tour guide. There are also many interpretive programs and hikes (some of which are free) throughout the parks that are led by Parks Canada and Friends staff and are well worth taking advantage of.

If you have children, don't leave them at home! I often encounter parents who dejectedly state they can't do something because they have their children along. In some instances it's wise – we should all know our limitations. But too often parents assume that children are incapable. Don't erect barriers – break them down! With proper planning, all of the adventures in this guide can be enjoyed with kids in tow, or at least in modified form, depending on the age of your children. My son Oliver first visited Jasper National Park at the tender age of three months and at the age of 10 he backpacked 21 km (13 miles) on the Berg Lake Trail to the base of Mount Robson.

Travel should be accessible to everyone, not just the wealthy. The first tourists to the Canadian Rockies were the privileged class. With the grand hotels open for business, they brought their trunks of belongings and $50,000 lines of credit to spend three or four months in "The Mountain Playground of the World." Providentially, with the development of a national parks system, visionaries set aside regions "for the enjoyment of the whole people." Today, people of all cultures and walks of life enjoy the parks here.

Do you love adventure? Do you like to learn about the places you visit? Do you relish the idea of immersing yourself in Rocky Mountain culture? If you answered yes, yes, yes, then this book will be useful and, I hope, enjoyable for you to read. But please be prepared to follow a strong wilderness code of ethics. Minimizing your impact on the natural environment is essential for preserving this special land for future generations.

Whether you are an armchair traveler or a seasoned adventurer, come with me to this special place.

■ How this Book is Organized

If there is an area or subject beyond the scope of this guide-book that you would like to delve further into, there are plenty of information sources listed that are a mere mouse click away. At the end of the book is a glossary of terms that you may want to familiarize yourself with, as well as many suggestions for further reading – the more you read the more you'll be hooked.

The park chapters are organized in a sort of north-south fashion, starting with Alberta's Jasper National Park, a fine starting point for a Rocky Mountain Parks tour. The exception is British Columbia's Mount Robson Provincial Park, which is northwest of Jasper but listed immediately after Jasper (savvy travelers who visit Jasper will want to make a side-trip from Jasper to Mount Robson).

Heading south from Jasper, the Icefields Parkway provides not only a means to reach Banff National Park, but is one of the most scenic stretches of road in the world. The Icefields Parkway terminates at Lake Louise, which is part of Banff National Park but is itself a separate destination. From Lake Louise, it's a short drive along the scenic Bow Valley Parkway (or the busy Trans Canada Highway) to the cosmopolitan resort town of Banff. Neighbouring Banff National Park (en route to Calgary) is the increasingly popular Kananaskis Country. British Columbia's Yoho and Kootenay National Parks branch west and south from Lake Louise, respectively. And finally, in the extreme southwest corner of Alberta, is Waterton Lakes National Park.

■ Human History in the Rockies

It's difficult for today's tourist to imagine the hardships that early explorers endured in their quest to penetrate the land. Often on the verge of starvation, they bushwhacked through muskeg, forded ice-cold streams and rivers, fought swarms of mosquitoes and black flies, waded deep winter snows and endured freezing temperatures, determined to conquer a daunting land considered impassable. Modern-day travelers can drive the highways and parkways of the Rocky Mountain

Parks from one end to the other in a matter of a few days. Yet much of what we gaze at today has the same view that it did when Aboriginal peoples lived off the land.

Archaeological evidence indicates the presence of Aboriginal peoples 12,000 years ago. Before European explorers and fur traders arrived, four major tribes hunted in the areas now encompassed by Jasper, Banff, Yoho, Kootenay and Waterton National Parks: Kootenays, Shuswaps, Stoneys (Assiniboine) and Blackfoot. These tribes were often at war with each other and with other tribes that occupied the region at intervals – each protecting

Assiniboine Chief Wet It, 1898

their hunting grounds. When the fur traders and explorers arrived, Aboriginal peoples became trading partners and played a major role in early exploration, acting as guides and passing on valuable knowledge. When the railway was constructed and big game hunting depleted, their way of life changed forever and they were obliged to settle on reserves and adapt to white man's society.

In order to satisfy the European demand for furs, the Canadian North West Company and the British-owned Hudson's Bay Company competed to establish trade routes through the Rockies. By 1799 both companies had outposts near Rocky Mountain House (east of the foothills on the North Saskatchewan River). David Thompson, a trader and mapmaker for the North West Company, established the first trade route across the Rockies via Howse Pass in 1807 and in 1811 discovered the Athabasca Pass route. In 1841, Sir George Simpson, governor of the Hudson's Bay Company, crossed the Rockies on a trip around the world and so began the movement of traders, botanists such as David Douglas, missionaries, settlers, artists, writers, sportsmen and adventurers. By the 1850s, the Golden Age of the fur trade began to decline.

In 1858, John Palliser organized an exploratory trip
for the British government
to the western prairies and
mountains. The Palliser
Expedition formed three
groups in which Palliser
ventured over what is today
Kananaskis Country, geolo-
gist and physician Dr.
James Hector crossed Ver-
milion, Kicking Horse, Bow
and Howse Passes and
Thomas Blakiston led a
group to the Waterton area.
In 1859, wealthy Scottish
sportsman James Carne-
gie, Earl of Southesk, was

John Palliser and James Hector

the first "tourist" to the Rockies. Soon gold seekers bound for
the Cariboo country in British Columbia and other tourists
such as the notable Lord Milton and Dr. Cheadle followed.

British Columbia joined the Canadian confederation in 1871
with Prime Minister John A. Macdonald's assurance that it
would be linked to the rest of Canada by railway. Walter
Moberly surveyed Yellowhead Pass as the proposed route for
the Canadian Pacific Railway, but the Kicking Horse Pass
was chosen to keep the tracks close to the international
boundary. The "impossible" was achieved when the costly
Canadian Pacific Railway was completed in 1885, but not
before the discovery of today's well-loved Maligne Lake in
Jasper, Banff Hot Springs and Lake Louise.

The race to be the first to conquer the Canadian Rockies'
unnamed peaks set in motion a half-century of intense exploration. Names synonymous with the Canadian Rockies such
as Tom Wilson, Bill Peyto and Jimmy Simpson began outfitting and guiding in Banff, Canada's first national park. Passenger trains began to roll through the Rockies, the grand
hotels opened for business and the wealthy began their pilgrimage. The Rockies only became accessible to the masses

once roads were built – mainly during the Great Depression and the war years – and the automobile became commonplace. In 1930 Parliament passed the National Parks Act and the boundaries of Jasper, Banff, Yoho and Kootenay Parks were finalized. The Rockies' intriguing human history is reflected in its many mountains, rivers, lakes and valleys that bear the names of Aboriginal peoples, early explorers and visitors to the parks.

■ Geology

This is a simplified overview of how three main forces created the landscape we call the Rocky Mountains. About 1½ billion years ago, particles of sediment lay on the floors of ancient seas. These sediments hardened into sedimentary rock, a process called deposition, which continued over a long period of time until about 1.9 million years ago (so there is a wide variation in the age of the sedimentary rocks found in the Rockies). About 200 million years ago, give or take a few million years, the continental plate began moving northwest and collided with the oceanic plate, moving northeast. The collision caused the horizontal layers of sedimentary rock to fold and fracture, initiating mountain building. (The most common sedimentary rocks in the Rockies are limestone and shale.) This process of mountain building (called uplift) took about 100 million years; the foothills were the last to form, some 65 million years ago. Ever since the mountains were formed, they have been subject to erosion. During the first ice age, about two million years ago, only the highest summits of the Rockies poked through the top of the ice. Glaciers sculpted the range over the last two million years, advancing and retreating over major glacial periods. Sculpting continues today by glaciers and the forces of weather.

The entire Canadian Rockies chain is long and narrow, which geologists separate into four zones. Within the central Canadian Rockies are the following narrow strips, totaling only about 40-50 km (25-31 miles) wide:

■ Foothills – the area between the prairies and the mountains; rock layers have not been greatly uplifted.

- Front Ranges – dramatically rising up above the foothills.
- Main Ranges – the backbone of the Rockies, further subdivided into Eastern Main Ranges and Western Main Ranges.
- Western Ranges – very narrow and not very long, 20 km (12.4 miles) at the widest point and found only between Radium Hot Springs and Golden.

In the southern Canadian Rockies (Waterton National Park) there are foothills 25-40 km wide (15½-25 miles) that are similar to those of the central Rockies; and front ranges (different from the front ranges in the central Rockies), 20-40 km wide (12-25 miles).

Mt. Assiniboine

There are some easily recognizable mountain shapes in the Canadian Rockies. Mt. Assiniboine is an example of a pyramid-shaped mountain, formed by several cirque glaciers that eroded different sides of it simultaneously; Pyramid Mountain in Jasper Park is also a classic example. Castle Mountain in Banff is a castellated type of mountain, typically found in the eastern main ranges and in the front ranges of Waterton Park; the erosion of horizontally oriented rock (featuring near-vertical cliffs) formed these types of mountains. One of the most recognizable mountains in the Canadian Rockies, Banff's Mount Rundle, is often referred to as a "writing desk" shape, which takes its form from thrust sheets that slid upwards and over each other, or overthrust, with layers that tilt mainly

Mount Rundle

downward toward the southwest. Vertically oriented, sawtooth type mountains, such as Banff's Mount Louis, resemble the teeth of a saw. For detailed information on the peaks of the Canadian Rockies, see the searchable database at www.peakfinder.com.

Glaciers

Glaciers are formed where more snow falls than melts each year. Over the centuries, the snow accumulates and is compressed into ice which, pulled by gravity, flows downhill. The lower and upper parts of glaciers advance at different rates and as they move forward, the ice at the lower end or "toe" melts back. When a glacier melts back faster than the forward ice flow (during hot dry summers), the toe retreats. The glacier advances when the rate of melting decreases (during cool summers). Most glaciers in the world are retreating rapidly. Glaciers hold 75% of the world's fresh water.

Glacial Lakes

Glacial lakes are fed by the meltwaters of nearby glaciers. Glacial debris in the form of fine rock material, called glacial flour or mud, is constantly being washed out in the meltwater and lies suspended in the water. The water and glacial flour absorb all colors of the spectrum except green-blue, which it reflects, resulting in the incredible turquoise color of a glacial lake.

Hoodoos

These peculiar-looking geological formations, rather freakish in appearance, easily captivate the imagination. The moniker hoodoo came about as an association with voodoo, characterized by many as "spooky." Bizarre as they appear, hoodoos are simply glacial silt formations caused by erosion. Carved by wind, water and freeze-thaw cycles over the centuries, the caprocks on top are the hardest part, which serves to protect the spire below. Ironically, the

process that creates hoodoos is the same one that destroys them.

Hot Springs

Ahhh.... there's nothing like a hot springs soak after a day of hiking. Sit back, let the warmth surround your tired muscles, enjoy the mountain scenery and free yourself from all your anxieties. Steeped in history, Canadian Rockies hot springs in Jasper, Banff, and Kootenay National Parks were known to Aboriginal peoples and have been revered for generations. Healing properties have long been attributed to hot spring water.

There are over 100 known hot and warm springs in Canada, most of which are in British Columbia. The hot springs in the Rocky Mountains result from rainwater and snow that filters down through rocks and, as it seeps down, becomes heated by the surrounding rocks that are heated by radioactive decay of minerals within the earth's crust. This heated water rises upwards and surfaces as hot springs. The water is piped from its source into soaking pools that are filtered and chlorinated.

 Canadian Rockies hot springs are all **wheelchair-accessible**. Towels, lockers and swimsuits are available for rent. For more information, see www.hotspring.ca.

Life Zones

As a simplified system of classification, there are the three life (elevational) ecozones in the Canadian Rockies:

- **Montane**. Low elevation region, including towns, comprising about 10% of the parks, typically found below 1,500 m (4,900 feet). Characterized by open stands to dense forest as it merges with the subalpine. The greatest variety of wildflowers, trees and shrubs can be found in the montane zone. It also provides the highest quality wildlife habitat. (To put the vastness of the Canadian Rockies into perspective, many visitors only experience 5-10% of the parks, which represents the montane life zone.)

■ **Subalpine**. The largest life zone, comprising about 50% of the parks. The subalpine zone extends from the upper edge of the montane forest to the lower edge of the treeless, alpine zone and is characterized by dense forests, stunted trees (near treeline) and timberline meadows of delicate wildflowers.

■ **Alpine**. The highest life zone comprises about 40% of the parks and is found above 2,200 m (7,200 feet). The cold, windswept alpine zone extends from treeline to the end of vegetation. Alpine plants are small, low-growing and adapted to a very short growing season in their harsh environment.

■ Plants

Lodgepole pine

The Canadian Rockies are rich in plant species, including trees, shrubs, wildflowers, berries, ferns, mosses and much more. Growing environments change dramatically in the Rockies, resulting in thousands of vegetation types. Although there is regional variation, many plant species occur throughout the Canadian Rockies. Common trees include the **evergreens** (conifers) **pine**, **spruce** and **fir**. They're easy to differentiate if you remember pine have long needles in bundles; spruce needles are short, sharp and four-sided; fir needles are short, soft and flat. **Lodgepole pine** is perhaps the most common tree in the Canadian Rockies. The name lodgepole refers to its use by Natives for making tipi poles. Lodgepole pine stands mark areas that have been burned; during a forest fire the heat causes the cones to open much more rapidly than normal, releasing their seeds. The most common deciduous tree in the parks is the **aspen poplar**, which is also known as trembling aspen. You can identify it by its waxy white bark and nearly circular leaves that turn yellow-gold in autumn. The most stunning tree in autumn is the **subalpine larch** (Lyall's larch), found in the upper reaches of the subalpine zone (it does not occur north of Bow Pass). Larch is a coniferous tree (deciduous conifer) that loses its needles after they turn from pale green in summer to yellow-gold in September. **Red paintbrush**, or Indian paintbrush as it's commonly known, is likely the best-known wildflower of the Rockies. But did you know that it's actually the leaves that are colored, not the petals, which are green? The colors range from pale yellow to crimson. Or did you know that black bears, grizzly bears, rodents, deer, elk, sheep and goats eat the **yellow gla-cier-lily**, one of the first plants to bloom as soon as the snow melts? (Bears eat the roots for their high energy value in the spring.)

Red paintbrush

Like birding, identifying and studying wildflowers is a plea-surable pastime. At higher elevations (subalpine meadows) in the Canadian Rockies, wildflowers generally reach their peak from mid-July to early August but blooming times vary according to elevation, weather and site. Some areas are renowned for their prolific wildflower meadows including **Sunshine Meadows** in Banff.

The best way to identify an unfamiliar plant is to bring along a field guide and study the plant carefully. Find the major group to which it belongs, browse through the photos or illustrations, then read the description to see if it matches. Remember, flow-ering plants change in appearance as they mature.

Never pick plants – it's against the law in national parks. When wildflowers are picked, the plant usually dies and some are becoming scarce in many areas. Flowers, trees, shrubs, and mushrooms are part of the park's natural heritage and thus should not be removed or damaged. Leave them as you found them for others to enjoy. Consumption of mushrooms and natu-ral items such as berries is illegal if picked in the park.

■ Weather & Seasons

Quite simply, mountain weather is unpredictable. The daily weather varies from valley to valley and can change quickly. Rain or snow and freezing temperatures can occur at any time of year. The best way to deal with the weather is to prepare for all conditions. During a two-week visit to the Rockies in July, I encountered nothing but 25-30°C (77-86°F) temperatures, but was told that prior to my arrival in Jasper it had rained every day for two weeks. In August I encountered a solid week of socked-in drizzle and it snowed in Waterton Park. The Canadian Rockies have four distinct seasons. Autumn arrives early and spring late, with long winters and plentiful snowfall. Cloudy weather and rain are common. Summer (July and August) is the most popular time to visit the Rockies, when the weather is warmest with typically 20-25°C (68-77°F) temperatures during the long days but cool evenings. Autumn often brings pleasant Indian summer weather. The coldest temperatures usually occur from December to February, when the average low is -15°C (5°F) but cold spells of -30°C (-22°F) are not uncommon; the cold is dry, not damp. Mountain weather is highly variable from year to year.

My favorite time of year in the Rockies is the early fall. The crowds have died down, people in the tourist industry are less busy and more able to take time to chat, accommodations are cheaper, the weather can be lovely with warm sunny afternoons and cool evenings, the fall colors are magnificent and the bugs have all but disappeared. The least desirable times to visit are early winter, when the skiing hasn't started, and late spring, when the skiing is finished and the hiking trails aren't yet accessible.

The weather conditions add an unknown element to travel and often travelers decide to allow inclement weather to, pardon the pun, "cloud" their perspective, when in fact, it can often make a trip that much more interesting – if you are prepared. Understandably, if you're tenting, a steady drizzle day-after-day isn't much fun. But have you ever lain in a tent snug in your sleeping bag, listening to the pitter-patter of the rain and felt an incredible sense of contentment? Have you ever examined the unique shape of ice crystals or listened to the deep crunching sound of your footsteps in the snow when it's freezing cold? And avid photographers know that some of the most interesting photographs are taken in stormy weather.

■ Wildlife

 My most vivid childhood memory of our family's first visit to Jasper Park in the early 1970s would make any park warden cringe. My sister and I giggled with delight as we fed two deer jelly doughnuts from the window of our car. Scads of vehicles stopped on the highway to take photos as tourists attempted to "pet" the deer. We thought this was what the Rockies were all about – a veritable wilderness zoo. We were fortunate not to be harmed, but many others are not so lucky.

It's easy to see how tourists get carried away when it comes to wildlife in the Rockies – the incredible scenery combined with wildlife that may be accustomed to human presence, particularly in town, creates the misconception that these animals are tame. While I was visiting Miette Hot Springs in Jasper, I witnessed a group of young children corner a bighorn ewe and lamb in the parking lot. The parents of the children were nowhere in sight until one little girl was nearly attacked by the ewe and began to yell. Sadly, after years of ongoing public education and awareness initiatives, dangerous wildlife scenarios continue to be played out in the Rockies. Each time we disrupt a wild animal's natural activities we are lessening their chance of survival.

Wildlife Encounters

 All park animals are wild, unpredictable and potentially dangerous. In the spring, cow elk become extremely protective of their calves. They will attack if they perceive you as a threat to their young. In the fall rutting season, male elk, moose and deer are very aggressive. Bears, deer and sheep may forcefully seek food from people. You cannot predict how wildlife will react in any given situation. Remember, not only is it foolish and irresponsible, it is against the law to entice, feed, harass or touch wildlife in the parks.

Bear encounters are rare but there is a great deal of fear of them. Bears are usually more frightened of you than you are of them and pose little threat if you do everything you can to prevent an encounter. Bears will usually run away if they hear people approaching, so it's wise to make lots of noise such as calling out and clapping at regular intervals. (Bear bells are not enough; I personally find them particularly annoying and avoid hiking with any one that uses them.) Bears are not evil or in search of humans for their next meal – as portrayed in many Hollywood movies. Bears exist in the Canadian Rockies and it's unfortunate that because of this fact many people do not venture out on the trails and many who do worry unnecessarily. Bears are fascinating creatures that are to be avoided and treated with respect and caution. Don't let the fear of a bear encounter prevent you from enjoying the outdoors.

Recommended reading: The bear section in *Handbook of the Canadian Rockies* (see bibliography) and *Safe Travel in Bear Country* by Gary Brown. New York: Lyons & Burford, 1996.

To help **avoid bear encounters** while on the trails:

- Make lots of noise to let bears know you're there (even on well-used trails).
- Travel in groups.
- Never cook in or near your tent.
- Store food and garbage correctly and avoid smelly foods such as meat and fish.
- Stay alert and immediately leave the area if you see signs of their presence (tracks, torn-up logs and vegetation, droppings) or if you come across an animal carcass.
- Avoid hiking in obvious feeding areas such as berry patches, cow parsnip thickets or fields of glacier lilies.

If you are not in your vehicle and you **encounter a bear**:

- Stay calm, remain still and talk calmly.
- Do not make direct eye contact.
- Pick up children and stay in a group.
- Do not run, rather back away slowly.

- If possible, leave the area; if not, wait until the bear leaves.
- Try dropping something (not food) to distract the bear but keep your pack for protection.
- If a bear attacks, use pepper spray if you have it; if not, lie face down with your legs apart and cover the back of your neck with your hands.
- Do not move until you are certain the bear has left the area.
- Slowly and quietly get up and walk away.

Cougars are wary animals that naturally keep their distance from people. In the unusual event that you encounter a cougar, you should follow these guidelines:

- Stay calm, remain still and talk calmly.
- Do not make direct eye contact.
- Pick up children and stay in a group.
- Hold your ground or back away slowly, allowing the cougar a way out.
- If necessary, do anything you can to make yourself look bigger, such as spreading your arms.
- Yell, throw rocks or sticks and act aggressively.If you are attacked fight back, do not play dead.

Report all bear, cougar or wolf sightings or aggressive behavior by any wildlife to the nearest Park Warden Office or Visitor Information Center; don't assume that someone else has done it.

There are a number of ways you can limit your impact on park wildlife and prevent conflicts:

- Resist the impulse to approach, reach out or call out to wildlife. Use binoculars and camera lenses to get closer views.
- Keep your distance – Parks Canada guidelines suggest you keep 100 m (328 feet) or 10 bus lengths away from bears, cougars and wolves and 30 m (98 feet) or three bus lengths away from elk, deer, sheep, goats and moose.
- Never leave food attractants out for wildlife, including food scraps, dishwater, dirty dishes or barbecues, garbage or

empty bottles, pet food dishes or toiletries such as tooth-
paste and soap.

■ Always be aware of your surroundings and on the lookout
for signs of animal presence.

■ Carefully supervise children at all times when outdoors.

■ Do not leave pets unattended.

■ If you wish to view roadside wildlife, pull safely out of traffic, remain in your vehicle and move on after a few minutes
or consider not stopping at all.

■ Educate yourself – Parks Canada provides free information brochures (*Bears and People*, *Keep the Wild in Wildlife*) or read one of the many books about animals in the
Rockies.

SETON WATCHING

This method for wildlife viewing is simple: find a
comfortable and safe spot and sit quietly and observe. Within a short time your presence will be accepted and you can watch how creatures go about
their daily lives and interact with each other. Try it.
The method is named for Canadian naturalist Er-
nest Thompson Seton (1860-1946). Seton's simplified philosophy: "Nature is a very good thing."

Wildlife Viewing

Your best chance of observing wild animals is to become as
insignificant as possible while staying safe. Look for wildlife
in a variety of habitats and at different times of the day; many
animals are most active at dawn and dusk. Scan mountain
slopes, slide paths and cliffs with binoculars for mountain
goats, sheep, and grizzly bears. The opportunity to observe
wild animals in their natural habitat is one of the most fascinating experiences the parks offer. Along with this privilege
comes a responsibility to treat wild animals with respect and
caution. Not only is it an important safety issue, it's impera-
tive for their survival.

The following is a brief description of the most commonly
observed mammals in the Rocky Mountain Parks. (Infre-

quently seen wildlife in the Canadian Rockies include caribou, wolves, cougars, lynx, and wolverine.)

Bighorn Sheep

Also called mountain sheep or rocky mountain bighorn sheep. Often confused with mountain goats. Brown to pale tan colored with belly, rump patch and other white patches. Rams (males) have large curled C-shaped horns. Ewes (females) are smaller and have short stubby horns. Offspring are called lambs. Rams head-butt one another during rut, the noise audible for a great distance. They are widespread throughout the Rockies and can be found in alpine meadows and foothills near rocky cliffs and are commonly seen at roadside locations throughout the parks.

Mountain Goats

Yellowish white coat and beard with both sexes having slightly backward curving black horns. Sharp hooves are well adapted for traversing hairline edges. Not frequently seen; they inhabit rocky mountainous areas above timberline where sheep and deer don't normally venture. They sometimes come down to the valley floors to seek out mineral licks. Goats molt in June, losing their winter coats and exposing their purple skin. Males are called billies, females nannies and offspring kids.

White-Tailed Deer

Tan or reddish-brown in summer and greyish-brown in winter with white belly, throat, noseband, eye ring and white inside ears. Often confused with mule deer, which are stockier. The easiest way to differentiate from a mule deer is the tail, which is larger, with a white underside. When alarmed, the tail is raised. Bucks (males) have antlers with  one main beam and several unbranched tines that are shed in late winter or early spring. Females are called does and off-spring fawns. They tend to keep to lower elevations in summer.

Mule Deer

Reddish- or yellowish-brown in summer and greyish in winter with white throat patch, rump patch, inside of ears, inside of legs and lower parts cream-colored. Large mule-like ears. Bucks have antlers branching equally, each a separate beam forking into two tines. Tail is white, tipped with black and hangs straight down even when it runs. Habitat: open montane forests in winter and spring to high subalpine meadows in summer. Commonly seen along roads.

Elks

Correctly called *wapiti*. A large deer with slender legs, thick neck, brownish-reddish with pale rump patch and tail. Stags (males) have dark brown mane on throat and large, many-tined antlers. Herds are commonly found in lower valleys throughout the year as well as Jasper and Banff townsites. Elk  are considered the most dangerous animals in the parks, especially in the spring when the cows are protecting their calves and during the fall rutting season. Stags rub the velvet off their antlers when rutting begins and you can hear them bugling. (Elk were reintroduced in Banff National Park after having been hunted to extinction in the central and southern Rockies in the late 19th and early 20th centuries.)

Moose

Largest deer in the world, second-largest naturally occurring land animal in North America (after bison). Long, dark brown hair, high humped shoulders, long legs, stubby tail, huge muzzle with large dewlap (lobe) under chin and large ears. Bulls (males) much larger than cows (females) with massive antlers that are shed in early winter. Offspring are called calves. Despite their ungainly appearance, they are good swimmers and graceful movers that can run through the forest at speeds up to 56 kph (35 mph)! Habitat: spruce forest, swamps, shallow marshy lakes in summer and aspen and willow thickets mainly in winter. Solitary by nature. Have been known to charge and trample humans if approached.

Black Bears

Black bears also come in brown, cinnamon and blonde. Longer more pointed face than the grizzly bear and shorter claws. Keen sense of smell and hearing. Habitat: montane and lower subalpine forest. Can be found along roadsides and avalanche slopes. Dormant in winter from about November to early April. Sows (females) give birth to cubs in the den in January or February during the hibernation. Males are called boars. Though classed as a carnivore, most of its diet consists of vegetation. Solitary and active day and night in search of food.

Grizzly Bears

Color ranges from blonde to nearly black, often with white-tipped hair. Concave facial profile and a large hump over the shoulders. Front claws are long and straight, sticking out beyond the fur. Usually much larger than black bears but large black bears are larger than small grizzlies – got that? Grizzlies are not true hibernators and can be awakened easily. They normally avoid man and rarely attack humans for food but are considered the most unpredictable and dangerous of all bears, especially when surprised and defending their young. Range from low valleys to alpine meadows.

Coyotes

Grey or reddish-grey with buff, long legs and bushy tail, resembling a medium-sized dog. Patrols meadows and forests in search of rodents. Barks, yelps and howls, often eerily, usually at night.

Columbian Ground Squirrels

Greyish or reddish-brown with bushy tail. Lives underground and can often be seen sitting erect or heard chirping. The common ground squirrel in the mountain parks. They appear tame but may bite or scratch and can pass along ticks and lice.

Red Squirrels

Rust-red to grey-red, the common tree squirrel of the mountain parks. Very chatty, energetic and messy, leaving piles of cone remnants at the bottom of trees. Active throughout the year.

Golden-Mantled Ground Squirrels

Greyish-brown with reddish head and shoulders. Chipmunk-like but with body stripes and no facial stripes.

Least Chipmunks

The most common and smallest chipmunk of the mountain parks. Stripes extend from the nose to the base of tail. Highly active during the summer months, hibernates in winter.

Pikas

Brownish or greyish with small round ears and no visible tail. Not much larger than a mouse but classed with rabbits and hares. Very elusive and well camouflaged in their rocky environment. Highly vocal and social, they communicate in shrill chatters. They are vegetarians that quickly fill their stomach and defecate pellets that they eat and digest again. Active year-round but in winter they stay under the snow in rock piles and feed on stored food that they have dried in the sun during the summer. Totally cute.

Hoary Marmots

Also known as whistlers because of their shrill whistle. Large (3.6-9 kg or 8-20 lbs), silver-grey with brownish rump and whitish belly and black markings. Large bushy tail and small ears. Most often found on talus slopes. Hibernates from Sep-

tember to April. Likes to play-wrestle with other marmots and suntan on rocks. Gotta love 'em.

Beavers

Large rodent (20-27 kg or 45-60 lbs) sometimes up to 49½ kg or 109 lbs, dark brown with small eyes and ears. Large, scaly, flat tail that slaps the water as an alarm signal. Found in rivers, streams, marshes, lakes and ponds and on the Canadian five-cent coin. Active throughout the year; primarily nocturnal but also active in the early morning and evening. Builds dams and lodges. Young are called kits.

ANIMAL TRACKS

 Have you ever seen an animal track and wondered which animal made it? Following in the footsteps of an animal and learning to identify its tracks is a challenging and fun nature activity for adults and children. Pick up a copy of the inexpensive pocket guide *Animal Tracks of the Rockies* by Ian Sheldon (Edmonton, Alberta: Lone Pine Publishing, 1997) and learn some of the secrets of identifying tracks. It's not easy but it's very rewarding when you find a good print and are able to determine which animal it belongs to.

Birding

 Bird watching is considered the fastest-growing outdoor activity in North America. It's no wonder, since birds are a delight to watch and listen to. Nearly 300 species of birds have been recorded in the mountain parks (there are about 650 species in North America) and over 200 are seen fairly frequently. Members of the Corvidae family are the most common, including the **common raven**, **black-billed magpie**, as well as the **gray jay** and **Clark's nutcracker** (shown above) or "camp robbers," as they are also known. Noisy and intelligent,

these scavengers are not leery of people like much of the wild-life in the Rockies.

Spring is the best season for birding and the best time is at dawn but you can enjoy this activity any time of year. Our feathered friends in the Rockies commonly frequent lakes, ponds and marshy areas on the valley bottoms. Ask for a bird checklist at Visitor Information Centers and bring along a good field guide such as *Handbook of the Canadian Rockies*.

■ National & Provincial Parks

Preservation and use of the national parks is governed by the National Parks Act and Regulations. Parks Canada is the federal government agency responsible for the care and operation of Canada's national parks. Attitudes have gradually changed since the early days of the development of the national parks system when the federal government actually encouraged resource extraction. Eventually the government brought in legislation that prevented mining, logging and hunting and protected the parks. Protection and presentation (public understanding, appreciation and enjoyment) remain the two primary components of Parks Canada policy.

Provincial parks are provincially operated and have different objectives than national parks in that their mandate is to provide recreation, while national parks emphasize preservation. The constant challenge in all the parks is maintaining resources in a natural manner while encouraging sustainable park development. The parks are open year-round unless inaccessible due to weather conditions. Entry fees are charged at Canada's national parks (not at provincial parks). Visitors stopping in any national park or traveling on the parkways require a valid **National Park Pass**. Park passes may be purchased at Parks Canada kiosks located at park entrances, from **Visitor Information Centers** in the parks or by mail order by calling ☎ 888-773-8888. (You do not need to purchase your pass in advance; you can buy it when you arrive at the park.) Revenues are used to support visitor services and facilities at the parks. You can purchase **day passes** or, if you spend seven or more days per year in a National Park, the **National Pass** – valid for entry to 28 national parks across Canada – is your best value.

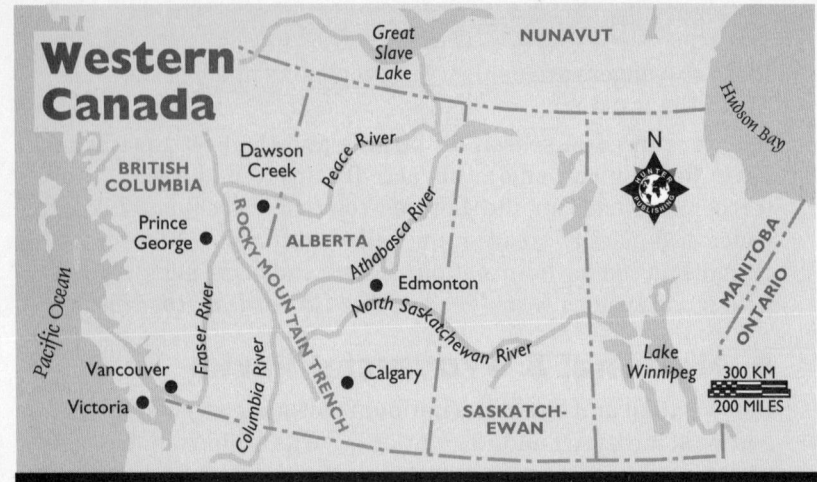

Western Canada

NUNAVUT

Great Slave Lake

Hudson Bay

BRITISH COLUMBIA

Dawson Creek

Peace River

Prince George

ROCKY MOUNTAIN TRENCH

ALBERTA

Athabasca River

Edmonton

North Saskatchewan River

Pacific Ocean

Fraser River

Columbia River

Vancouver

Victoria

Calgary

SASKATCH-EWAN

MANITOBA

ONTARIO

Lake Winnipeg

300 KM
200 MILES

N

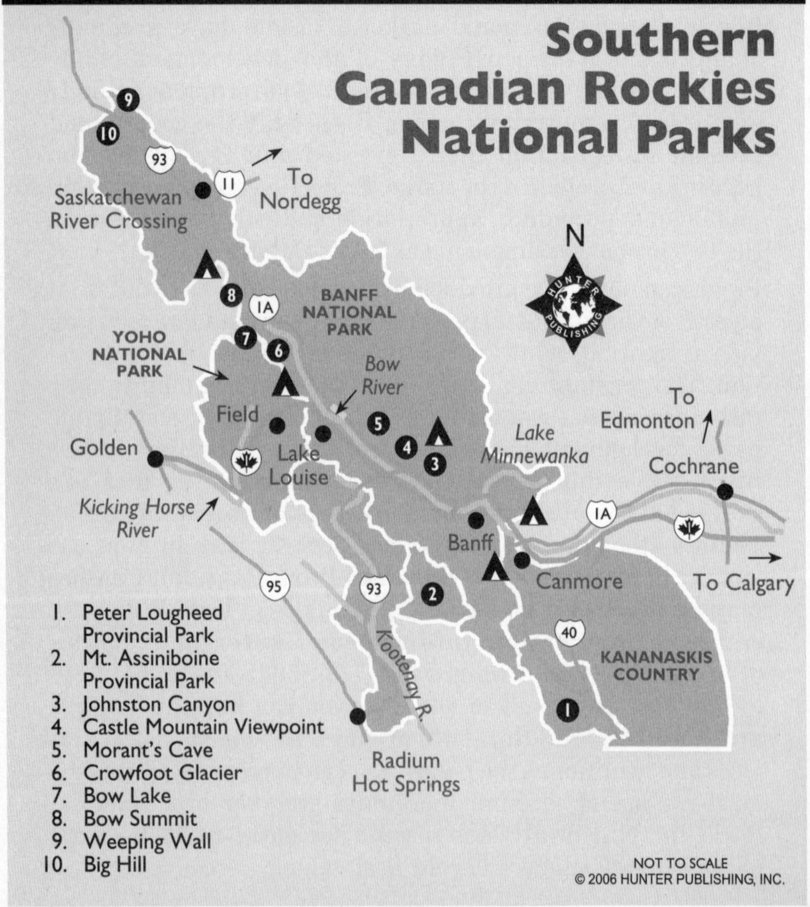

Southern Canadian Rockies National Parks

9

10

93

11

To Nordegg

Saskatchewan River Crossing

N

8

1A

BANFF NATIONAL PARK

YOHO NATIONAL PARK

7

6

Bow River

Field

5

4

To Edmonton

Golden

Lake Louise

3

Lake Minnewanka

Cochrane

Kicking Horse River

Banff

1A

95

93

2

Canmore

To Calgary

Kootenay R.

40

KANANASKIS COUNTRY

Radium Hot Springs

1

1. Peter Lougheed Provincial Park
2. Mt. Assiniboine Provincial Park
3. Johnston Canyon
4. Castle Mountain Viewpoint
5. Morant's Cave
6. Crowfoot Glacier
7. Bow Lake
8. Bow Summit
9. Weeping Wall
10. Big Hill

NOT TO SCALE
© 2006 HUNTER PUBLISHING, INC.

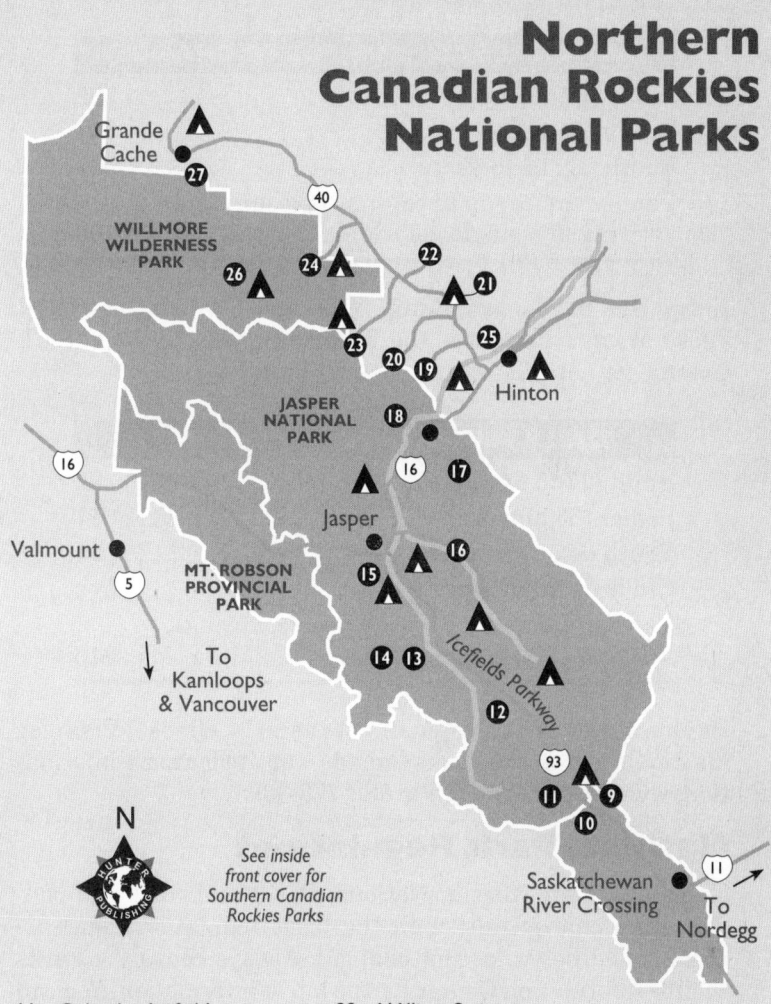

Northern Canadian Rockies National Parks

WILLMORE WILDERNESS PARK

JASPER NATIONAL PARK

MT. ROBSON PROVINCIAL PARK

Grande Cache

Hinton

Jasper

Valmount

To Kamloops & Vancouver

Icefields Parkway

Saskatchewan River Crossing

To Nordegg

N

See inside front cover for Southern Canadian Rockies Parks

11. Columbia Icefield
12. Sunwapta Falls
13. Athabasca Falls
14. Mount Edith Cavell
15. Marmot Basin Ski Area
16. Maligne Lake Road; Maligne Canyon; Medicine Lake, Maligne Lake
17. Miette Hot Springs
18. Pocahontas
19. Athabasca Tower Forestry Lookout & Nordic Centre
20. Kelly's Bathtub
21. Blue Lake Lodge
22. William Switzer Provincial Park
23. Rock Lake Camping
24. Big Berland River Crossing
25. Pierre Grey's Lakes Recreational Area
26. Hinton Natural Resource Interpretive Park; Golf Course; Millennium Park Trailhead
27. Grande Cache Lake & Beach; Griffith Trail; Sulphur Rim Trail; Golf & Country Club

▲ Campgrounds

NOT TO SCALE
© 2006 HUNTER PUBLISHING, INC.

NATIONAL PASS (SUBJECT TO CHANGE)
Adult (17 to 64 years) $55
Senior (65 and over) $47
Youth (six to 16 years) $27
Family/Group (up to seven people, any age, arriving in a single vehicle) $109

Entry fees for Jasper, Banff, Yoho and Kootenay National Parks are as follows (see the Waterton Lakes National Park chapter for entry fees to that park):

DAILY FEES (SUBJECT TO CHANGE)
Adult (17 to 64 years) $8
Senior (65 and over) $7
Youth (six to 16 years) $4
Children (under six) . . . . free
Family/Group (up to seven people, any age, arriving in a single vehicle) $16

Payment may be by cash, traveler's check, Visa, or MasterCard. See the Parks Canada website for more information, www.pc.gc.ca, or call ☎ 888-773-8888.

National Park Regulations

There are many rules in National Parks and rules and policies often change (although the basic regulations, such as those noted below, do not change). Always consult a Parks Visitor Information Center for the latest information. You can call 1-888-WARDENS to report someone that is violating park regulations.

It is unlawful to:

- Collect or remove any natural objects or historical artifacts such rocks, fossils, horns, antlers, wildflowers, nests, mushrooms, berries, etc.
- Collect firewood from the forest or make a fire in a non-designated area.

- Entice, feed, harass or touch wildlife, including birds and ground squirrels.
- Litter or pollute any waters.
- Possess firearms except for the purpose of transporting the them through the park in your vehicle (unloaded and in a case or wrapped securely).
- Not have your pet leashed at all times.
- Camp anywhere other than designated campgrounds.
- Disregard marked closures.

Visitor Information Centers

i One of the first stops on any traveler's itinerary should be at the local Visitor Information Center, the heart of all park activities and services. Staff are "information experts" and will help you to make the most of your visit. If you're already somewhat knowledgeable about the area, you'll better know what to expect and be able to ask more specific questions. The advice and information is free and generally the brochures are free for the taking (some parks have a minimal charge for hiking/skiing trail guide brochures). If you didn't purchase a National Parks Pass at a National Park entrance gate kiosk, you may purchase one at the Visitor Information Center as well as wilderness passes for backcountry camping and national parks fishing licenses. You can make reservations for backcountry camping at the local Visitor Information Center but not for front country (roadside) campsites (see *Camping* section). You can, however, obtain information about them, such as amenities, cost and availability. If you haven't booked accommodations, they can provide assistance.

Visitor Information Centers provide important safety information about wildlife, hazardous activities and conditions and have updated trail, highway, weather, avalanche and bear reports. Parks Canada offers a voluntary safety registration service for people engaging in potentially hazardous activities such as mountaineering, canoeing, kayaking, backcountry skiing and glacier and icefield activities. Registration is also recommended for solo travelers without a local contact. You must provide a comprehensive and accurate description of your route, including any side-trips, and report back immediately upon your return to either the Visitor Information Center or the Warden Office. A safety registration ensures that a search will be initiated on your behalf if you do not return by the date and time recorded. Visitor Information Centers at Jasper, Lake Louise, Banff, Yoho, Kootenay and Kananaskis are also home to Friends shops. They sell topographic maps, books, souvenirs, and gift items. Proceeds from sales support educational programs, research, publications and projects for the parks.

And most Visitor Information Centers have bathrooms, too.

■ Getting There & Getting Around

Enjoy the journey rather than focusing on the destination.

By Road

Getting to wherever you're going in the Canadian Rockies is just as much fun as what you'll do when you arrive, particularly if you're driving. The highways and parkways provide ample pullouts for picnicking, showcasing viewpoints and attractions, viewing wildlife, displaying information about the area or simply for a respite from traveling.

Be prepared for a variety of driving conditions in the mountains. It can snow in the summer, especially at higher elevations. Many cars move along the highways and parkways at top speed. Obey posted speed limits: 90 kph (56 mph) maximum on most major routes and 60 kph (37 mph) maximum on secondary roads. Speed limits of 70 kph (43 mph) are posted in known wildlife collision areas. Be aware of increased traffic during the peak summer months and on the lookout for cyclists – do not drive on the road shoulder. Be patient, as you will inevitably have to slow down for other drivers distracted by the scenery and wildlife.

Road closures occur due to accidents, avalanche control, snow or rockslides, poor driving conditions as well as planned seasonal closures. Road condition reports are available by calling the telephone numbers listed in the individual park chapters or from Visitor Information Centers.

Be cautious of wildlife on the roads, especially during dusk and dawn when many animals are most active and visibility is poor. Pay attention to the posted "wildlife on roads" signs. Scan ahead for movement or shining eyes; if you spot one animal, there may be others. It is very important that you pull off the highways and roads to view wildlife – make sure you slow down, warn other motorists by flashing your hazard lights, pull over in a safe spot and remain in your vehicle (see also *Wildlife* section). Move on after a few minutes or consider not stopping at all. Do not stop along the busy Trans Canada Highway except in an emergency.

Slow down and take extra care when driving in winter conditions. Heavy snowfall can cause havoc for winter motorists, with poor visibility, snow-packed sections and black ice. Check the road reports before you depart. Avoid stopping in posted avalanche zones. Snow tires or all-season radials are required by law for travel on all roads except Highways 1 and 16. It is advisable to carry a winter emergency kit as well as a shovel, plenty of extra clothing and a sleeping bag for each person. There are often few people on the road during extremely cold conditions, so you might have to wait a long time for assistance or walk a long way to a telephone if you break down. (Don't depend on a cell phone because you may not get a signal.)

Driving is on the right side of the road in Canada. Pedestrians in crosswalks have the right of way. US citizens do not need an international driver's license; a valid US license is adequate. AAA members are covered by the CAA while traveling in Canada. The use of seatbelts and baby/child car seats is mandatory.

Motorhome Rentals

 Renting a motorhome or recreational vehicle (RV) is popular with visitors to the Canadian Rockies. Parks Canada operates an excellent network of campgrounds throughout the national parks, while provincial parks also offer lots of camping choices (see *Camping* section). There are many companies that offer RV rentals in Alberta and British Columbia. Here are a few:

- **Go West Campers**, www.gowestcampers.com, ☎ 800-240-1814.

- **Adventure Canada**, www.canada-rv-rentals.com, ☎ 866-672-3572, in the UK and Germany ☎ 800-4267-4267.

- **Cruise America**, www.cruiseamerica.com, ☎ 800-671-8042.

By Bus

 Greyhound provides bus service to all the Canadian Rocky Mountain Parks except Waterton. Students, seniors and Hosteling International members receive a 10% discount and those with an International Student Identity Card (ISIC) get a 25% discount. Greyhound sells bicycle boxes and will accept a bicycle depending on baggage space. ☎ 800-661-8747 for fare and schedule information or www.greyhound.ca.

By Air

 Visitors arriving from outside of Canada usually fly to Calgary or Edmonton International Airports in Alberta or Vancouver International Airport in British Columbia.

By Rail

 The completion of Canada's first transcontinental rail line launched a romantic era of passenger rail travel. With the advent of automobiles and national highway networks after World II, as well as air travel, passenger train service decreased in volume and importance. Today, rail travel seems to be enjoying a resurgence of sorts, with more travelers appreciating this relaxed mode of transportation. **VIA Rail** operates passenger service through Jasper National Park via Edmonton, Vancouver and Prince George, ☎ 888-842-7245, www.viarail.ca. **Rocky Mountaineer Railtours**, ☎ 800-665-7245, www.rocky-mountaineer.com, operates luxury rail tours between Vancouver and Jasper and Calgary/Banff.

■ Where to Eat

Whether it's a hearty breakfast to start your day off right, a packed lunch to take along the trail or an evening of fine dining, you'll find cuisine from around the world in Canada's mountain parks.

DINING PRICE CHART	
Price per person in Canadian $ for an entrée, not including beverage, tax or tip.	
$	Under $10
$$	$10-$25
$$$	Over $25

Choices range from casual to sublime, reasonably priced to "don't ask the price." If it's regional cuisine that gets your taste buds tingling, the Rockies' kitchens are sure to satisfy. Chefs are striving to incorporate locally produced foods in their menu selections. You'll find meats such as the ubiquitous AAA Alberta beef, game selections including buffalo and elk, fish such as salmon and trout, fresh cheeses and grains as well as local produce and herbs. And what would a delectable meal be without a fine bottle of wine? No worries, most fine dining establishments carry a selection of wines sure to please every palate. Tipping is customary in Canada, generally 15-20% for good service.

■ Where to Stay

Singles rates available at some establishments. Don't forget to add the government's share (7% GST plus 8% room tax in British Columbia and 7% GST plus 5% room tax in Alberta).

HOTEL PRICE CHART	
Reflects the price of an average room for two in Canadian $, May-Sept. Rates lower rest of year (except Christmas and New Year's).	
$	Under $50
$$	$50-$100
$$$	$101-$150
$$$$	$151-$250
$$$$$	Over $250

The good news is that there are myriad hotels, motels and lodges to choose from when staying in the Canadian Rockies. The bad news is that mountain living comes at a price as most are in the $150 to $250 range during high season. If you are booking accommodations in advance, a travel agent may be able to get better rates. Typically, lodge-type accommodations are comprised of a cluster of cabins or bungalows, detached or side-by-side, in close proximity to a main lodge and are usually seasonal. Don't expect a great deal of privacy; although often located in scenic environs, cabins are usually clumped close together. And don't be confused by the use of the word "lodge." Quite often a typical hotel or motel will use the term.

 During low season or noticeably slow periods, don't hesitate to ask for a discount off the published rate. Many hosts/innkeepers/hotel clerks – especially privately owned and operated accommodations – are willing to negotiate.

Rental Cottages & Apartments

Private home accommodations (guesthouses) are available in Jasper, Banff (excluding Lake Louise), and Yoho National Parks and in Canmore. As with hotels, rooms run the gamut from tastefully decorated and spacious to tight quarters with a shared bathroom. Private accommodations offer visitors an opportunity to mingle with locals, who will usually take the time to give valuable tourist advice and tend to offer a "personal touch." Some hosts offer breakfast and/or the use of a kitchen and an outdoor sitting area. The level of privacy varies; if you enjoy mingling with the hosts, some generously offer the use of the main kitchen and a common living room as well as a shared entrance or, if you prefer independence, private entrances and separate sitting areas are available. Typically, private homes offer one to three rooms. Many private accommodations do not accept credit cards, taking cash or traveler's checks only. Expect to pay from about $55 to $120 per night and, good news, no room tax.

Hosteling

Hostels were once considered budget accommodation strictly for young people. You might be surprised to know that hostels host travelers of all ages including families from around the world. They are great places to meet like-minded travelers and can feel like a "home-away-from-home." Accommodations usually consist of separate men's

CAMPING/HOSTELS	
Rates in Canadian $, not including taxes.	
$	Under $13
$$	$13-$22
$$$	$23-$30
$$$$	Over $30

and women's dorms and sometimes co-ed dorms. A limited number of family rooms (private rooms) are also available at some hostels, although they are often equivalent in price to staying in a hotel. Most hostels offer kitchens, a common room and various amenities such as a shuttle bus service, lockers, a library, laundry facilities, barbecue, saunas and more. Some have a restaurant, café or pub on site. Staff are often local residents with a wealth of tourist information.

In the Canadian Rockies, there is an excellent network of Hosteling International (HI) Hostels, from Jasper to Waterton, including all along the Icefields Parkway. Hostels are located close to hiking, biking and skiing trails. Rustic hostels are in picturesque (wilderness) settings with no electricity or running water. Many have various daily activities such as guided hikes. They also offer packages such as ski and board, whitewater rafting, women's retreats and more.

Anyone can stay at a HI Hostel but you must be a member of Hosteling International to receive the cheaper members' rates. Hosteling members receive discounts at restaurants, museums, retail shops, and from transportation and tour companies. For example, Hosteling International members receive 15% off single hot pool admission at the Canadian Rockies Hot Springs. To purchase a membership, contact Hosteling International, ☎ 800-663-5777, or check out their website www.hihostels.ca.

Camping

Camping is the ideal way to see the Rockies. More than any other type of accommodation, it allows you to be close to nature – and that's what visiting the Rockies is all about. Camping is an affordable alternative to other accommodations that might be beyond a family's budget. It's a wonderful learning experience as well as being a great family activity. Just pack everything you need in your car or recreational vehicle and hit the road. Even if you don't intend to camp all the time, carrying the necessary gear gives you added flexibility. I also like preparing my own meals, leaving eating in restaurants as a special treat. Children tend to be happier outdoors as well, and there's nothing like roasting wieners and marshmallows around a campfire to please kids and the kid in most adults.

Generally, I don't book campgrounds in advance as I like to be spontaneous and decide where to spend each night as I travel. I drive at a leisurely pace so I don't miss anything and I stop often to take photographs. I don't want to rush in order to get to pre-booked accommodations and meanwhile miss attractions along the way – hurrying, after all, defeats the purpose of a vacation. The price I pay is that I'm sometimes forced to go out of my way to find a campground that has space. I occasionally have to settle for overflow campgrounds. These are are open when all of the other campgrounds in the vicinity are full. Overflow campgrounds are generally quite rudimentary, sometimes only a gravel pit parking area with pit toilets. I don't mind occasionally staying in overflow campgrounds because I'm often only in need of a place to sleep for the night and I depart early the next morning. (These sites are also cheaper than regular campgrounds.) Some overflow campgrounds are surprisingly scenic, such as Silverhorn Creek Campground, used as an overflow for the north end of Banff Park. That said, it is frustrating to be turned away from a full campground in late evening, especially while traveling with children.

 It's the Law: When camping in a National Park you are required to camp in a designated campground. Park Wardens strictly enforce this rule. It is a federal offence to camp illegally and, if caught, it's likely you will be issued a warning notice. However, wardens do have the authority to bring charges, in which case you will have to answer in court.

Lake Annette, Jasper National Park

Above: Angel Glacier, Jasper National Park

Below: Ashlar Ridge, Jasper

Above: Opal Hills

Below: Broad-leafed willow herb grows in abundance on the Sunawapta River flats, Icefield Parkway

Elk grazing, Jasper

Parks Canada operates national park campgrounds through-out the Rockies. (Provincial park campgrounds operate in much the same way as national park campgrounds, although their daily management has mainly been contracted out to independent operators.) **Front country (roadside)** camp-grounds are well signed from highways and usually notices on the signs indicate when a campground is full or closed. National and provincial park front country campgrounds accommodate all types of campers, from bicycle tenting to large recreational vehicles. **Serviced campgrounds** (water, sewer, and electrical hook-ups) are limited. **Primitive or unserviced campgrounds** have no electricity, running water or flush toilets – instead pit toilets and water pumps. Unserviced campgrounds are often more scenic than serviced ones. Some campgrounds have segregated areas for tents and recreational vehicles. Where there is availability, you may be permitted to select your campsite. Try to avoid sites near the washrooms, which may seem convenient but are less private and sometimes smelly.

Some campgrounds in national parks, usually large centrally located ones, are staffed by Parks Canada employees who col-lect fees at entry kiosks. Other campgrounds are **self-register**, which means campers select a site, complete a registration form and deposit fees in an envelope provided at the campground entrance (signs indicate how to register). Certain national and provincial campgrounds have hosts dur-ing the peak season who offer informational assistance.

Payment at national park campgrounds may be made by cash, traveler's check or by credit card (even at self-registration campgrounds). Some provincial park camp-grounds do not accept credit card payments. **Front country camping has traditionally been on a first-come first-served basis but, with recent changes, some national park campgrounds now accept reservations for a fee.** To continue to meet the needs of campers who pre-fer not to reserve in advance, campsites will still be available on a first-come first-served basis.

See **www.pccamping.ca** for the Parks Canada Campground Reservation Service, or ☎ 877-737-3783 (877-RESERVE), teletype (TTY) ☎ 866-787-6221, international calls 905-426-4648. There is an $11 non-refundable reservation fee per reservation and a $9 fee for changes or cancellations made at least 24 hours prior to the reservation. Payment may be made by credit card, certified check or international money order.

You cannot reserve or pay for front country campsites at Visitor Information Centers but you can obtain information about them such as amenities, cost and availability on any given day. Campground opening and closing dates are weather-dependent. Demand is heavy, especially from June through September. If you want to ensure a site and don't have a reservation, arrive early, as campers often line up in the morning. The maximum stay in most provincial and national parks is 14 days. Checkout or re-registration is usually required by 11 am (although I admit I have often stayed until 2 pm without being asked to leave). Park gates usually open at 7 am and close at 11 pm. Quiet hours are from 10 pm to 7 am.

Campfires are permitted at some campsites when a fire permit, which usually includes firewood, is purchased. You should try to keep campfires small and conserve firewood. During hot and dry spells, campfire bans may be in effect. Do not use the fire pit as a garbage disposal.

Most camping sites provide a picnic table. You should never cook inside tents and tent trailers as the scent may be absorbed into the fabric and attract bears. Make sure you lock your food in your vehicle or use provided storage bins/bear poles at night and always maintain a clean campsite. Storing food outside of your vehicle in an insulated cooler is not acceptable as coolers are not bear-proof. Pets must be leashed and never left unattended.

I have never felt unsafe, experienced any harm nor been the victim of theft at any national or provincial park campground. Although I feel comfortable leaving a tent and lawn chairs at my campsite while out exploring, I don't advise leaving other valuables behind.

See individual park chapters for more information on camping and reservations as well as for information on backcountry camping. See *Adventures, Backpacking* section for backcountry (wilderness) camping information.

 It's Free! Free outdoor theater programs are offered during July, August, and early September at many campgrounds throughout the parks. Ask at the Visitor Information Center or check bulletin boards in campgrounds.

■ Photography Tips

 The camera has played a prominent role in recording the history and ever-changing landscape of the Canadian Rockies. Taking professional-looking images is easier than you might think and with rapid advances in the digital realm, improving your photography skills should be... a snap!

You don't have to invest thousands of dollars in state-of-the-art equipment. I get some very good results using my 5.3 megapixel digital point-and-shoot camera with a 7.6mm – 22.8mm zoom lens. A note about children – most kids I know love to photograph. Let them use your camera for the occasional shot and if they don't have their own camera, buy them a disposable so that they can record their own memories. Don't worry if most of the photos are bizarre. It's all part of the fun!

Before your trip, an important step in improving your photography skills is to get to know your camera by thoroughly reading the instruction manual – you'll be amazed at what you learn. You should also take lots and lots of practice shots using all of your camera's features. Keep your camera in a protective padded case along with the manual, plenty of high-quality replacement batteries (rechargeable is best), extra memory cards and any other accessories you may have. Your camera should always be available at a moment's notice, not packed away where it's hard to reach. Many of your best shots will be spontaneous – when the light is changing or for wildlife when you may only have a few seconds to capture a shot.

Here are some easy tips and tricks for improving your photography:

Light – The best light is early in the morning and late in the afternoon, the "golden hours." At dusk, there is a brief window of magical light that photographers get all giddy about, for good reason. Between about 10 am and 2 pm the sun is overhead, creating "flat" light and harsh shadows.

Flash – Use fill-flash (not full-flash) in daylight to eliminate harsh shadows on faces and on backlit subjects.

Balance – Don't get in the habit of placing your subject in the middle of every frame. Try placing the focal point off-center.

Composition – Keep your background clean and avoid trees or the like "growing" out of your subject's head. Take the time to study what's in the frame before you shoot.

Angle – Shoot from different angles. Crouch down, lie on the ground (where it's safe), get up high and shoot down, etc.

Close-ups – Try getting up close and filling the frame with your subject.

Weather – Rainy days can be excellent for photographing close-ups such as wildflowers. Cloud formations add visual interest and heavily clouded skies can bring out a distinctively "gloomy" atmosphere. Overcast days diffuse the light and are best for photographing people outdoors as well as forests.

Technique – Hold your camera steady, elbows at your side and depress the shutter button lightly with your finger.

Framing – Frame your photo with trees, architecture (arches), window frames, etc.

Tripod – Try using a lightweight tripod so that you can shoot in low light situations.

Exposure – Try longer exposures for subjects such as water-falls, using your tripod, of course.

Filters – If your camera accepts filters, there are hundreds to choose from that can enhance your photography. A clear Daylight or UV filter can be used to protect your lenses; a polarizing filter deepens the color and contrast of the sky and other elements and can eliminate glare and reflections.

Experiment – Don't always settle for the familiar. Try shooting vertical instead of horizontal, seeking out bright colors or unusual objects, looking for patterns or interesting shapes – use your imagination.

Software – Photo editing software is becoming mainstream. Any level photographer can accomplish wonders with this tool. Take loads of shots but don't bore your family and friends with every single one – edit them down when you return home and wow them with your best Rockies images.

■ What to Bring

 A visit to the mountains any time of year requires a range of apparel that protects you from wind, cold, rain or snow. Dressing in layers allows you to add or remove clothing as required. To prevent injuries or falls, it's important to wear comfortable, sturdy footwear. See the *Adventures* section and *What to Bring on a Hike* for suggestions if you plan to participate in outdoor activities. Generally, the higher you go, the colder and windier it gets. Ultraviolet radiation is stronger at higher elevations and reflection from snow or ice (not only in winter) can damage your eyes, so be sure to use sunglasses and sunscreen.Other items to bring on your Rocky Mountain vacation include a swimsuit for enjoying the hot springs, a camera and tripod (see *Photography Tips*), binoculars and don't forget your guidebook!

■ Adventures Rockies-Style

Playing it Safe

All outdoor activities involve risk. Although you can never eliminate risk, most accidents can be prevented. The first step in any successful outing is preparation. You or your guide should have knowledge of natural hazards and experience in avoiding and managing them. Caution and self-reliance are essential.

The number one cause of fatal accidents in the parks is swift moving water. Be sure to take the following precautions:

- Wear sturdy, non-slip footwear.
- Stay away from steep riverbanks or edges.
- Heed warning signs and stay behind safety fences (it's very scary how many people I see who don't take this simple precaution).
- Use trail bridges when crossing streams.
- Travel on rivers should only be attempted by well-informed and experienced paddlers.
- Surface water may be contaminated with Giardia, an intestinal parasite that can cause severe health problems. Boiling water for at least five minutes will destroy the organism. Special filters and drops can also be used to purify water.

Backcountry National Park Wardens (Rangers) assist visitors in case of emergency, provide information and ensure that the park's resources are protected. They conduct backcountry patrols throughout the year and will ask to see your Wilderness Pass if you are camping in the backcountry. Since their duties require them to patrol large areas, you should not count on being able to find one in case of emergency. You can check to see if a warden is in the office at one of the warden stations located throughout the parks, but there is no guarantee. Outside radiophones are located at some warden stations and are provided for emergency use only. If you meet a warden, thank him or her for the valuable work they do.

Adventuring with Children

 Family adventures that take us away from our everyday lives challenge adults and children alike. Adventuring teaches us teamwork, adaptability, enables us to develop and practice new skills, builds confidence, stimulates and teaches

us about the environment and the world we live in. The key to any successful outing is largely dependent on preparation. Children are never too young to start adventuring if parents are prepared to accommodate their physical and psychological needs and have faith in their capabilities. Children are natural explorers, curious about the world. Although they often need encouragement, they are usually enthusiastic, energetic and open-minded.

The first step in choosing an appropriate family excursion is assessing your own abilities. How physically fit are you? Most activities require a certain level of physical fitness and the more physically fit you are, the easier and more enjoyable they will be. Do you possess fundamental skills such as basic first aid knowledge? Do you have camping and/or backpacking experience? Are you comfortable carrying babies in a backpack or other carrier? Are you prepared to supervise toddlers constantly? Depending on the type of adventure, certain skills are essential. Then you must assess your children's needs and abilities. Is the activity suitable in duration and difficulty for the specific ages of your children? Adventuring with an infant is quite different from an outing with toddlers or with teenagers.

If you plan on hiking, try nature walks and short hiking trails before tackling major overnight trips. Ensure the hike you select is scenically rewarding enough to keep children motivated. Keep the following in mind:

Preparation – Check and double-check your gear and supplies before you depart. Where adults can go without and endure hardship, children may not.

Endurance – Don't push children. Keep the pace relaxed and be willing to compromise on distances. You will need to take frequent breaks and allow time to play. Accept that you may not reach your destination before you have to turn around. There are no hard and fast rules – each outing and child is unique.

Gear – Children who are old enough should carry their own pack but be prepared to lighten their load if necessary. They enjoy taking responsibility for their own things and especially like to carry a few small toys, snacks and items such as their own water bottle and (disposable) camera or binoculars.

Encouragement – Offer positive words often. I like to bring along surprise rewards such as a small toy, a special treat or promise of a reward when we return (yes, bribery can be effective, but you must follow through with your promises).

Learning – One of the greatest gifts we can teach our children is respect for nature and there is no better way to learn than a family adventure in the outdoors. Allow them to participate in everything, from preparing packs to cooking. Traveling and adventuring with children tends to elicit many reactions. Well-meaning friends and relatives (who rarely travel with children or don't participate in outdoor adventures themselves) often react with disbelief and shock when they hear that children will be participating in "risky" activities. The presence of my son, Oliver, has always elicited warmth and respect from others we encounter (and usually a pat on the back for him) in the outdoors and my experience has been all the more meaningful and enjoyable.

 "We must get beyond textbooks, go out into the bypaths and untrodden depths of the wilderness and travel and explore and tell the world the glories of our journey." *John Hope Franklin*

Tour Operators

All tour operators and guiding companies must be licensed by Parks Canada to offer their services within the national parks. If you are considering hiring a guide, look for those who are accredited by The Mountain Parks Heritage Interpretation Association (MPHIA), www. mphia.org. To hire a mountaineering guide, contact the Association of Canadian Mountain Guides, Box 8341, Canmore, Alberta, T1W 2V1, ☎ 403-678-2885, www.acmg.ca.

Equipment Rentals

Not only do these shops sell and rent sports and camping equipment, they also offer plenty of free advice, from the latest fishing tips to backcountry ski recommendations – it's yours for the asking.

Adventures On Water

Lake Boating

A favorite way to escape the crowds is a peaceful paddle on a scenic lake and the Rockies offer plenty of opportunity to do so. Many of the Rockies' most scenic lakes – Maligne Lake in Jasper, Lake Louise and Moraine Lake in Banff, Emerald Lake in Yoho, Cameron Lake in Waterton – offer canoe and kayak rentals. Lakes are subject to sudden, heavy winds so keep a close eye on the weather. Keep a distance from any waterfowl on the lakes, including loons and their young. Motorboats are prohibited on most park waters.

Canoeing

What is more Canadian than a canoe? Canada is a nation of wilderness, of rivers and lakes. The canoe played a crucial role in the early exploration of Canada. Sir George Simpson, governor of the Hudson's Bay Company's fur empire, made his inspection tours across Canada's river passages in a canoe paddled by skilful Iroquois.

Canoeing is a skill that can easily be acquired with a little instruction and some practice. Forward and backward paddling can be learned in a matter of minutes and, once you have mastered a few additional strokes, you will be ready to tackle almost any lake, as well as some rivers.

Did you know? To be considered a true Canadian, you must have made love in a canoe (on the water that is, and without tipping)?

Swimming

There's no better way to cool down on a hot summer day than a swim in one of the Rockies' gorgeous lakes. Keep in mind that glacial lakes remain very cold year-round; staying in the water for too long can be dangerous due to the risk of hypothermia. Stay close to shore, avoid swimming alone and watch children at all times. There are no lifeguards at the park lakes.

Fishing

 There are many opportunities for angling in mountain rivers, streams and lakes in the Canadian Rockies. There are a variety of tours and guided trips available to suit every type of angler, from fully equipped cabin cruisers to walk-and-wade trips, along with basic instruction and expert tips.

 You will need a **national park fishing permit** for angling in the national parks, $8 per day or $25 per year and a British Columbia or Alberta angling license if you plan on fishing in the provincial parks or other areas of the province. Licenses may be obtained at most Visitor Information Centers and at many commercial outlets.

If you plan to venture out on your own, you'll also need a copy of the latest *Fishing Regulations Summary*. Remember to clean your catch well away from campsites and picnic sites and dispose of entrails properly to reduce the risk of attracting bears. Special regulations, such as closed waters and bans on bait, may be in place to protect park resources. Catch and release fishing is encouraged.

Whitewater Rafting

 Do incredible scenery, wildlife viewing opportunities and exhilarating rapids sound appealing to you? Whether it's whitewater thrills or a smooth water float, rafting the Rockies' spectacular rivers is an activity for everyone. Take advantage of at least one of the many river excursions available throughout the Rockies and you'll see why traveling by river offers a unique perspective that cannot compare with road travel. No rafting experience is necessary and you can paddle along with your guide. Some advanced runs have age and/or weight requirements

with good health mandatory and swimming ability recommended. Wear comfortable, light clothing (swimsuit and shorts) and bring a towel and change of clothes – you will get wet on most rivers. Rafting companies will provide wetsuits, booties, gloves, paddle jackets, life jackets and, when necessary, helmets. This is a "rain or shine" activity with most rafting companies operating from mid-May to September.

Rivers and rapids are rated on an international scale, which ranges from the easiest Class 1 to the near-impossible Class 6. The higher the number, the more difficult and exciting the rapids:

Class 1 & 2 (Novice) – Suitable for families, first-time rafters and those who might be apprehensive; very relaxing; you may get splashed.

Class 3 (Intermediate) – For physically active first-timers or experienced rafters; larger waves and small drops or ledges; you will get wet.

Class 4 & 5 (Advanced) – For physically active first-time rafters or experienced rafters; numerous big waves or holes; you will get soaked.

Class 6 (Unrunnable).

Adventures On Horseback

 Horses were an integral part of the national parks' early development and thankfully today you can still "go out to the West and ride the mountain trails." In the 1920s a saddle horse hired for $4 per day, a pack horse for $2.50 and a guide with a horse for $9. The prices have changed but "blazing the trail" on horseback remains one of the Rockies' best-loved activities. Discover some of the most spectacular scenery in the Canadian Rockies with many opportunities to see wildlife. Trail rides are provided by licensed outfitters and led by qualified guides. No riding experience is necessary; horses and riders are paired based on ability and experience. Relaxing scenic rides range from one hour to all day and multi-day pack trips are offered throughout the Rockies. Options include breakfast rides or mouth-watering barbecue meals. Riders should wear long

pants – preferably jeans, a warm jacket or sweater on cool days, a (cowboy) hat, sunglasses (and sunscreen) and boots with a heel if possible. Reservations are recommended and signed waivers are a requirement.

The riding season generally runs from May to October although a few companies operate year-round and also offer sleigh rides. For non-riders, some outfitters offer carriage or covered wagon rides.

Adventures on Foot

Hiking

 There is no better way to explore the Canadian Rockies than to hit the trails. The Rockies and hiking go together like hot-dogs and mustard, French fries and catsup... well you get the picture. Thousands of miles of maintained trails – from easy to challenging – offer day-hikers some of the most spectacular scenery the world can offer. And it's free! Towering peaks, sheer rock walls and cliffs, cascading waterfalls, alpine lakes, massive glaciers, wildflower-filled meadows and enchanting forests are guaranteed to inspire and exhilarate you. The hikes presented in this guidebook are some of the best in the Canadian Rockies.

Peak hiking season in the Canadian Rockies is from mid-July to mid-August, when the weather is warmest, most trails are free of snow and the wildflowers are in bloom. Hiking is possible by mid-May on some low-elevation trails and by July most trails are open but many are still wet and muddy. Some of the best hiking can be had in September, when the crowds thin out, the foliage begins to change color and, although temperatures start to drop, Indian summer weather can prevail. The best times to avoid the crowds are early morning and late afternoon. These are also the best times to photograph (see *Photography Tips* section).

Hiking can be physically challenging – and spiritually gratifying. The hikes in this guidebook are for those in reasonably good physical condition. On a 13-km (eight-mile) hike in the Yoho Valley we encountered a 72-year old and his sister with four delightful young companions, age five to 14. It's always a pleasure to encounter families with young children and babies in backpacks enjoying an outing. Select a hike that best suits your group's abilities and underestimate your limits rather than over. Use common sense and sound judgment. Be prepared to spend the night in case of emergencies and always check the weather before you go – a storm can change an easy hike into a nightmare.

Map signs at trailheads and trail intersections, as well as numbered trail markers, are intended to help users find their way around designated trails. For safety and park preservation, keep to these marked areas. Help prevent damage by staying on the trail – do not shortcut switchbacks – and obey closure signs. Many trails have steep sections with drop-offs; children should be closely supervised at all times. Some routes may have restricted access – check ahead to avoid disappointment. You may be sharing the trail with other users; hikers should yield to horses, cyclists yield to hikers and horses.

All garbage must be packed out including diapers and personal sanitary products. When you need to urinate, select a spot well away from trails and at least 100 m (100 yards) from water sources, preferably on rocks to help prevent animals from digging up earth. To dispose of human waste, dig a small hole to the active soil layer, about 15 cm (six inches) deep (using a stick, the heel of your boot, etc.), filling the hole with soil afterward. In the alpine, cut out a portion of sod and replace it afterward. Pack out used toilet paper or burn it if the fire hazard is not extreme. Use outhouses at trailheads whenever possible but do not dispose of garbage in them.

Preparation and planning are key ingredients to a successful hike:

■ Obtain the latest local trail information from the Visitor Information Center.

■ For detailed trail descriptions, check trail guidebooks.

■ Check the weather report and be prepared for changing weather conditions by bringing adequate clothing.

■ Hike with companions. If you must hike alone, consider voluntary safety registration.

- Bring enough food and water; at least one litre/quart of water per person, two litres/quarts or more if you are going to be out all day.

- Leave No Trace – pack out what you pack in, as well as any additional litter you may find. For more information on low impact travel, see www.LNT.org.

A Wilderness Code of Ethics

Adopt and practice the following when venturing into the outdoors:

Plan ahead – a well-planned trip means a safer and more pleasurable trip.

Consider others – respect your fellow travelers' privacy by keeping your noise level to a minimum.

Wildlife – do not feed or harass animals or birds.

Plants – do not pick plants or cut trees or tree boughs.

Trails – stay on the trail, avoid shortcuts and respect closures.

Streams, lakes and rivers – keep them pollutant free and pristine.

Pets – keep your pet under control or leave it at home.

Pack it in, pack it out – take your garbage home – all of it.

Human waste – follow proper guidelines for disposal.

Fires – check ahead regarding fire regulations, never chop live trees or branches and better yet, avoid building fires.

Responsibility – leave your campsite cleaner than you found it, increase your knowledge about the outdoors and report unlawful activities to officials.

Insect Pests

Wetter areas are generally worse when it comes to mosquitoes but they can be annoying anywhere. Carry insect repellent throughout the hiking season and avoid wearing scented lotions or perfumes.

Ticks are tiny insects that live in dry grassy areas and are most active from April to June. They attach themselves when animals or hikers brush past the grass or shrubs they inhabit. Once they find a suitable location (on humans they seem to prefer the groin area, armpits, neck and scalp) they bite and begin sucking blood. Although rare, tick bites can cause serious illness. Take precautions to avoid them by walking on cleared trails and avoid rubbing against bushes and tall grass or lounging on grassy areas. Tuck pant legs into socks and check yourself for ticks during and after your hike. If you find an embedded tick, in most cases it can carefully be removed so that the mouthparts do not stay in your skin. Wash the area with soap and water and use an antiseptic. If you cannot remove the tick or if the area becomes infected or a rash develops, see a doctor immediately.

Backpacking

Many of the Rockies' backpacking trails are known the world over. Backcountry travelers have the opportunity to experience natural wonders seen by only a small percentage of visitors. The more popular areas offer maintained trails and campsites with outhouses, tent pads, food storage and covered shelters. Familiarize yourself with the trail you have selected and purchase a topographic map. You must be prepared to be self-sufficient and minimize your impact on the environment. Anyone overnighting in the backcountry must purchase a wilderness pass. See individual park chapters for information on backcountry camping. The use of stoves for cooking is mandatory; campfires are not permitted at every campsite. To help keep water clean, use washbasins and drain pits provided and use biodegradable soap. Pack out all garbage, use food caches and always maintain a clean campsite.

If you plan to do extensive hiking or backpacking, I suggest you purchase and read one of the hiking guides listed in the Bibliography.

So many mountains... so little time.

● A Good Bannock

Meals in the outdoors taste better than anywhere else. During early exploration in the Rockies, it was said that the mark of a true trail cook was his ability to make a light and delicious bannock. If you couldn't make a good bannock you couldn't be a trail cook. There are a few necessary ingredients to make this traditional bread originating with North American Natives: flour, salt, baking powder and water. Apparently, the secret to a good bannock is in the kneading. I've had success with this recipe. Next time you're camping or backpacking, give it a try.

 Making Bannock: Before you leave home, in a resealable plastic bag, mix 1 cup flour, a large pinch of salt, 2 teaspoons baking powder. Once you are in camp, combine the dry ingredients with 1 tablespoon oil and a half-cup water. Add only a little water at a time, especially if you don't have additional flour. The dough should be dry, not wet. Stir and knead the dough into a ball. Pat into a well-greased frying pan (the bannock should not be more than ½ inch thick) and bake over a low fire (or camp stove) until brown, 8 to 10 minutes on each side. Make sure to wiggle the pan occasionally to keep the dough from sticking. You can add dried fruit such as raisins or cranberries. Eat warm with butter and jam.

● **What to Bring on a Hike**

Good quality gear is usually worth the price you pay as it will last a long time and give you less trouble on the trail. Think layers when it comes to clothing and avoid anything made of cotton; select synthetics that wick away moisture from your skin. Invest in high-quality waterproof hiking boots that you've broken in at home. Pack your daypack or backpack with everything you intend to bring on the trail and walk around with it at home; if it's too heavy or not comfortable, rearrange items and remove anything you can live without. Travel light – ease of movement will enhance your trip. Leave anything that isn't necessary behind, including personal music players, make-up and cell phones. You'll be amazed at how little you really need to get by. Double check your pack before you hit the trail.

Climbing Gear: Climbing equipment and clothing remained primitive for many years compared to today's high-tech standards. Footwear, crude nailed boots, clothing and gear were heavy and cumbersome. Women especially look much different since the late 1800s and early 1900s when they climbed in ankle-length skirts. The Swiss guides convinced them to wear knickers (knee-length pants), which proved to be much more practical.

Day Hiking

Each person's daypack should contain:

- waterproof pack cover
- rain gear – shell and pants
- extra socks
- hat and mitts
- bandana
- extra long-sleeved top
- sunglasses
- emergency whistle
- lunch, snacks and emergency power bars
- water – two litres

For the group bring:

- sunscreen
- insect repellent
- waterproof matches or lighter
- flashlight or head lamp with extra batteries
- first-aid kit including moleskin for blisters
- water pump or water purification drops
- duct tape for emergency repairs (see below)
- pocket-knife
- toilet paper
- garbage bag

- map and trail directions
- compass
- extra plastic bags

Backpacking

Each person's backpack should contain the above plus:

- sleeping bag
- insulated pad
- adequate extra clothing for the duration of the trip
- toothbrush and necessary toiletries
- small camping towel and washcloth
- eating utensils and plate/cup

For the group bring:

- wilderness pass
- tent and flycooking pot
- stove and fuel
- biodegradable dish soap and a cloth
- enough food for all meals and snacks (planned in advance)
- two sections of 20-m (20-yard) rope to hang food and other items so they are not within reach of bears and other wildlife

Optional items to bring (necessary for some of us):

- bear spray (highly recommended)
- trekking poles
- camera
- binoculars
- field book
- notebook and pen
- book to read (preferably related to the area you are visiting)
- lightweight sandals or thongs for around camp
- small lightweight toys for children
- collapsible fishing rod and fishing license

Duct Tape: Canadians know the versatility of good old duct tape and outdoor adventurers should not be without it. In an emergency, it is one of the most useful items you can have on hand. From lashing tent poles together or repairing backpacks to helping dress a wound, it's indispensable. You can even fold it lengthwise on itself to make a durable strap that can be used as an arm sling. I used it to hold my cross-country ski boot together while ski touring. Don't pack a whole roll, which might be heavy; rather wrap some around your water bottle and it'll always be handy.

INUKSHUKS

Inukshuks are cairns of stone built by arranging them in a man-like shape. (Inukshuk is an Inuit word meaning "in the shape of man.") Historically they were used by the Inuit as place markers indicating areas to camp, fish and hunt and as navigational aids. They are still used as navigational aids and also as art forms.

Mountain Biking

Mountain biking is a growing sport and recreational activity. No longer on the "fringe," the use of mountain bikes as a means of appreciating and enjoying national parks is a privilege that is gaining in popularity. Designated mountain bike trails range from easy family rides to challenging, with the riding season typically extending from May to October. Choose trails that match your physical condition and skill level.

You must know your intended route as some trails are not clearly marked and signed. Riding non-designated or closed trails is prohibited and riding off-trail destroys vegetation. You should avoid riding on trails that are excessively muddy and cause skidding. The national parks are not suitable for technical riding or downhilling. Be courteous and respectful;

hikers and horses have right-of-way on trails. Guided mountain biking is not permitted on trails in the Rocky Mountain National Parks.

Suggested reading: *Backcountry Biking in the Canadian Rockies* by Doug Eastcott. Calgary, Alberta: Rocky Mountain Books, 1999.

Bicycle Touring

There is no better way to see the world than on a bicycle. If more people parked their cars and hopped on a bicycle, the world would be a healthier place. The general population would be less stressed-out (I've encountered road rage but never bicycle rage), more physically fit and there would be much less pollution (just think, by cycling part of the Rockies instead of driving, you'll actually be helping to slow down the retreat of the glaciers). Unlike driving, you no longer whiz along the highways and roads but, forced to slow down, you become part of the landscape. Areas you may have previously driven become a whole new experience on a bicycle.

Bicycle touring is physically and mentally challenging. Physically, you must be able to cover a reasonable distance each day. Mentally, you must be able to cope with a variety of weather conditions, technical difficulties and other obstacles. Wildlife encounters are of concern, as the cyclist does not have a vehicle to remain in or retreat to; be sure to allow a wide berth. Bicycle touring requires a great deal of preparation and forethought but it is very rewarding.

 Bicycle helmets are mandatory in British Columbia and Alberta.

Winter Adventures

 Winter is indeed a special time in the Rockies. The fast pace of summer dissipates with the crowds and a soothing calmness descends. Attractions that are a hub of activity during the summer months lay quietly blanketed in snow and ice. Imagine the

rushing torrents of waterfalls glistening frozen in the winter sun. Although the parks are quiet, winter brings a whole new scope of exciting adventures. Winter activities and tours include Nordic and alpine skiing, snowboarding, snowshoeing, ice-walks, ice-climbing, outdoor ice skating, ice fishing, horse-drawn sleigh rides and dog-sledding. If you're going to hit the trails, not only are there fewer people to contend with, you might also find it comforting to know that the bears have retired to their dens.

Downhill Skiing & Snowboarding

 The Canadian Rocky Mountain Parks are a winter paradise for downhill enthusiasts. Ski areas in the national parks (Jasper, Banff and Lake Louise) and other areas are operated by licensed business operators. World-class skiing and snowboarding starts in November and extends through May at some mountains. You'll find a good mix of novice to double black diamond runs on incredible snowpacks and some of the best powder anywhere. With facilities that boast such amenities as the world's fastest gondola, you'll have more time to explore the thousands of acres of incredible terrain.

Cross-Country Skiing

 Avid cross-country skiers know that the Canadian Rocky Mountains offer some of the best terrain to explore the parks. Many trails are within a short drive from townsites. Skier and machine track set trails and groomed areas are designated as easy, intermediate or difficult. The ski season on the valley bottom generally extends from December to March. Cross-country trail reports are updated at Visitor Information Centers.

Cross-country ski trails are not regularly patrolled so skiers should take precautions:

- Avoid skiing alone.
- Register your trip with others or at the local Visitor Information Center.
- Use a trail guide map.
- Carry appropriate winter clothing, repair supplies and an emergency kit.
- Carry enough food in case of an emergency.
- Do not stop in areas signed for avalanche danger.

- Be alert for signs of frostbite, hypothermia and fatigue.
- Winter backcountry enthusiasts must be familiar with travel in avalanche terrain.

   Avalanche Hazard, ☎ 800-667-1105, www.avalanche.ca.

Outdoor Ice Skating

 Outdoor ice skating is a quintessential Canadian experience and, combined with the backdrop of the Rocky Mountains, it just doesn't get any better. If the ice is clear, you may be able to see fish swim beneath your feet!

 **Thin ice** is extremely hazardous. Don't venture onto lake, pond or river ice that has not been cleared and checked – ice should be at least 15 cm (six inches) thick. Ice conditions in the parks are not monitored.

■ Useful Information

 US visitors require identification establishing citizenship, such as an original birth certificate as well as picture identification. A passport is not required but is helpful. Single parents must have proof of custody of their children. Citizens of countries other than the United States are required to have a passport and visa (if required). Special restrictions exist on crossing the border with defensive sprays (such as bear spray), firewood, alcohol, firearms and purchases. Tourists may not bring fruits and vegetables into Canada. For specific requirements on crossing the border from the United States into Canada, call ☎ 250-887-3413.

Traveling with Dogs

 Are you a dog owner who would never entertain the thought of leaving your best friend(s) at home? With proper planning, your pooches can come along for the ride without becoming beasts of burden on anyone. Being a responsible dog owner comes with the privilege of owning a canine companion.

Dogs are permitted in the Rocky Mountain National Parks and provincial parks, but they must not be left unattended and they must be on a leash at all times. Owners are required to clean up after their dogs, so be prepared to "stoop and scoop the poop" and do not allow your dog to pollute lakes and streams. Use common sense and practice responsible pet ownership, not allowing your dog to disturb others by barking or allowing them enough lead to jump up on people. Don't allow them on beaches or to swim in lakes where others are swimming. Don't ever leave your pets in a vehicle on a hot day, even for a short time – even with windows rolled down, temperatures inside your vehicle can kill your pet.

Policies on bringing dogs into backcountry (wilderness) campgrounds vary, so be sure to ask at the appropriate park Visitor Information Center before hitting the trails. For example, dogs are permitted on the Berg Lake Trail in Mount Robson Provincial Park on day-hikes but they are not allowed on the trail overnight. Bringing dogs on hiking trails is a contentious issue. Some people are against allowing it and there is merit to this stance. Many dogs are not accustomed to being in the wilderness and their behavior can be unpredictable, especially if encountering wildlife. If a dog runs off on the trail, it's not uncommon for it to chase squirrels and birds, to get spiked by porcupines and, even worse, dogs have been known to lead bears back to their owners. Use your best judgment when it comes to bringing your dog on the trails and, if you are at all in doubt, it's best to leave it at home.

US visitors bringing their dogs into Canada must bring a certificate issued by a licensed American or Canadian veterinarian clearly identifying the pet and certifying that it has been vaccinated against rabies sometime during the previous 36 months.

Public Holidays – British Columbia & Alberta

Government offices, banks and some stores will be closed on these days (or the subsequent work day if the holiday is on a weekend):

New Year's Day. . . . . January 1
Alberta Family Day. . . . . third Monday of February
Good Friday . . . . late March or April

Easter Monday . . . . late March or April
Victoria Day . . . . Monday preceding May 25
Canada Day . . . . July 1
BC Day/Alberta Heritage Day. . . . first Monday of August
Labour Day . . . . first Monday of September
Thanksgiving Day . . . . second Monday of October
Remembrance Day . . . . November 11
Christmas Day . . . . December 25
Boxing Day . . . . December 26

Time Zones

 Most of British Columbia is on Pacific Time, but Yoho National Park and Kootenay National Park are on Mountain Time – one hour ahead of Pacific Time. All of Alberta is on Mountain Time.

Time changes from Mountain Time to Pacific Time (or vice versa) occur at the BC-Alberta border upon entering Mount Robson Provincial Park from Jasper National Park and at Glacier National Park, 75 km (47 miles) west of Golden, BC.

British Columbia and Alberta operate on daylight saving time: clocks are turned forward by one hour on the first Sunday in April and turned back on the last Sunday of October.

The Language

 English speaking travelers shouldn't have any communication difficulties in Canada, but there are a few distinctive words that require some translation:

Eh – A common expression, usually heard at the end of a statement that means, "you understand, right?" Simply pronounced "A."

RCMP – The scarlet-coated men and women of the Royal Canadian Mounted Police or "Mounties."

Z – Canadians typically pronounce the last letter of the alphabet as "zed."

Poutine – Pronounced "poo-teen." Try this delicious combination of French fries, cheese curds and gravy that originated in Quebec.

Toque (pronounced "two-k") – A hat you wear to help keep warm.

Money Matters

 Banks and currency exchanges will exchange foreign funds into Canadian dollars. Some currency exchanges offer better rates than banks. If you have time, shop around as rates vary. Many businesses accept American dollars at fair exchange.

Although credit cards are widely accepted, don't assume they are everywhere.Visa and MasterCard are the most favored credit cards; many businesses do not accept American Express. Automated teller machines (ATMs) are found at banks and retail stores.

Most prices listed in this guidebook do not include taxes. In BC there is a 7% Provincial Sales Tax (PST). There is no PST in Alberta. Taxes for accommodations are 5% in Alberta and 8% in BC.

There is a federal Goods and Services Tax of 7% in all Canadian provinces. Visitors to Canada may claim rebates on GST paid for non-consumable goods and/or accommodation. To be eligible, you must spend a minimum of $200 (before taxes) in total. Each original receipt must show a minimum amount of $50 (before taxes) and be validated (stamped) by Canada Customs upon departure from Canada at border crossings and airport customs. Refund application forms and detailed information are available at www.cra.gc.ca\visitors or by calling ☎ 800-668-4748 or 902-432-5608.

 To avoid being charged a fee to process your claim by a service provider, be sure the form you are using is the government form GST176.

Going Metric

To make your travels in this region easier, we have provided the following chart that shows metric equivalents for the measurements you are familiar with.

GENERAL MEASUREMENTS

1 kilometer = .6124 miles

1 mile = 1.6093 kilometers

1 foot = .304 meters

1 inch = 2.54 centimeters

1 square mile = 2.59 square kilometers

1 pound = .4536 kilograms

1 ounce = 28.35 grams

1 imperial gallon = 4.5459 liters

1 US gallon = 3.7854 liters

1 quart = .94635 liters

TEMPERATURES

For Fahrenheit: Multiply Centigrade figure by 1.8 and add 32.

For Centigrade: Subtract 32 from Fahrenheit figure and divide by 1.8.

Centigrade	Fahrenheit
40°	104°
35°	95°
30°	86°
25°	77°
20°	64°
15°	59°
10°	50°

Telephone Calls

Long distance and toll free calls from Canada dial 1 first, then the area code for long distance. Area codes in Alberta's Rockies are 780 (Jasper area) or 403 (Banff and Waterton area); 250 in BC's Rockies.

Alcohol & Tobacco

Legal drinking age in Alberta is 18, 19 in BC. Legal age for purchase of tobacco is 18.

Information Sources

www.pc.gc.ca
Parks Canada – National Parks of Canada, ☎ 888-773-8888.

www.travelalberta.com
Travel Alberta, ☎ 800-252-3782 or 780-427-4321 outside North America.

www.explorealberta.com
Official Alberta Accommodation Guide, published each year by Travel Alberta. Listings for hotels/motels, resorts, cottages, inns and bed & breakfasts across the province.

www.hellobc.com
Tourism British Columbia, ☎ 800-435-5622 or 250-387-1642 outside North America.

www.env.gov.bc.ca/bcparks
Provincial parks website with information on planning your visit and making campground reservations.

www.ultimaterockies.com
Ultimate Rockies Vacations central reservations for accommodation, activities and tours in the Canadian Rockies, ☎ 877-771-4653.

www.travelcanada.ca
Official travel site of the **Canadian Tourism Commission**.

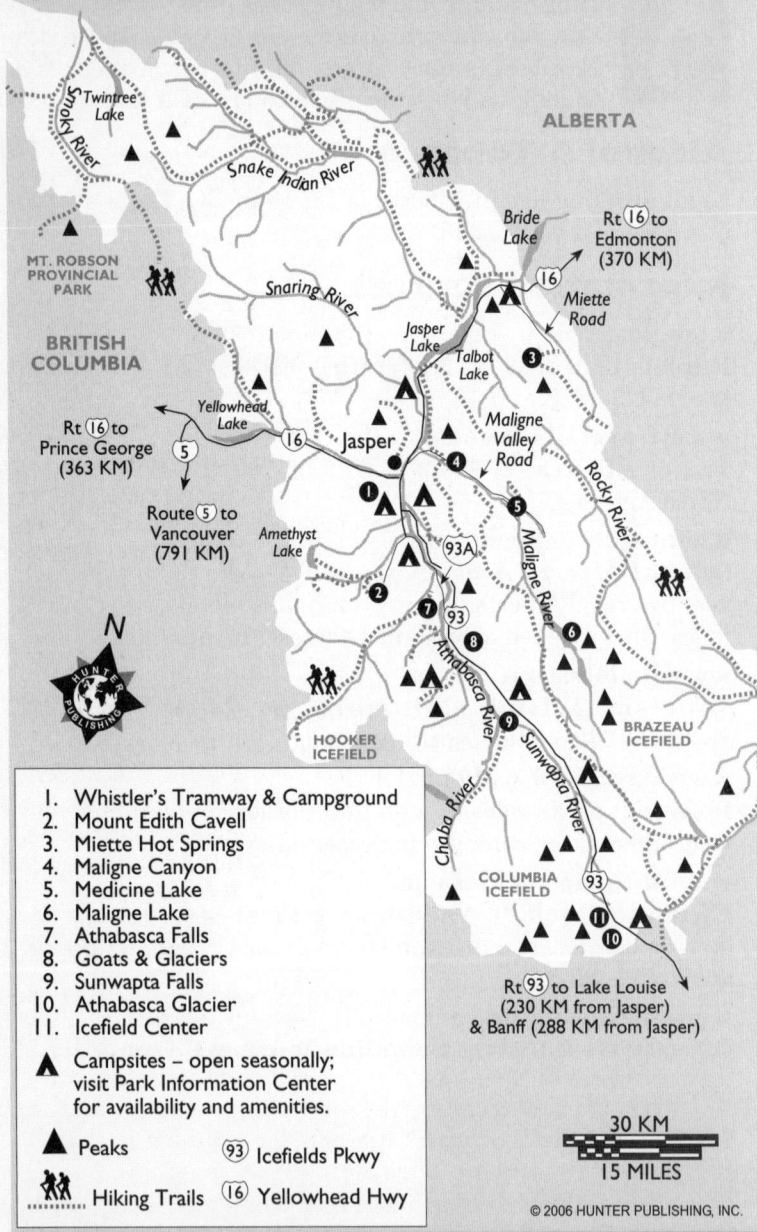

Jasper National Park

ALBERTA

Twintree Lake

Snaky River

Snake Indian River

Bride Lake

Rt 16 to Edmonton (370 KM)

Miette Road

MT. ROBSON PROVINCIAL PARK

Snaring River

Jasper Lake

Talbot Lake

3

BRITISH COLUMBIA

Yellowhead Lake

Rt 16 to Prince George (363 KM)

5

16

Jasper

Maligne Valley Road

Rocky River

4

1

5

Route 5 to Vancouver (791 KM)

Amethyst Lake

93A

Maligne River

2

7

93

8

6

N

Athabasca River

9

Sunwapta River

BRAZEAU ICEFIELD

HOOKER ICEFIELD

Chaba River

COLUMBIA ICEFIELD

93

11

10

Rt 93 to Lake Louise (230 KM from Jasper) & Banff (288 KM from Jasper)

1. Whistler's Tramway & Campground
2. Mount Edith Cavell
3. Miette Hot Springs
4. Maligne Canyon
5. Medicine Lake
6. Maligne Lake
7. Athabasca Falls
8. Goats & Glaciers
9. Sunwapta Falls
10. Athabasca Glacier
11. Icefield Center

▲ Campsites – open seasonally; visit Park Information Center for availability and amenities.

▲ Peaks   ⑨³ Icefields Pkwy

🚶 Hiking Trails   ⑯ Yellowhead Hwy

30 KM

15 MILES

© 2006 HUNTER PUBLISHING, INC.

Jasper National Park

From its humble beginnings in 1811 as the earliest fur-trade post in the central Rockies, to Canada's third-most visited national park, Jasper offers a distinctive Rocky Mountain experience. The largest – 11,228 sq km (4,335 sq miles) – and northernmost Canadian Rockies National Park includes the foothills to the east, the Continental divide to the west along the Alberta/British Columbia

border and extends to the Columbia Icefield in the south. The mighty Athabasca River, a Canadian Heritage River, flows north and east from its origin at the toe of the Columbia Glacier through Jasper Park for 168 km (104 miles) toward the Arctic Ocean.

If, heaven forbid, you are only able to visit one Rocky Mountain Park, I recommend this one. Jasper offers over 1,300 km (808 miles) of superb walking and backpacking trails in the front- and backcountries and excellent opportunities for wildlife viewing. Snow-capped peaks, abundant waterfalls, expansive valleys, sparkling glacial lakes and soothing hot springs fill the landscape. The town is less commercialized than its sister park, Banff, yet it offers a full complement of tourist services, including many restaurants, diverse accommodations and a variety of attractions and shopping.

■ History

Archaeological finds show that Natives were traveling through here 12,000 years ago. The retreat of glaciers permitted the return of plants and animals, which in turn allowed Native groups to occupy the area. Shuswap, Iroquois, Stoneys, Sekani, Beaver, Sarcee and Cree hunted and gathered seasonally.

It was an Iroquois guide named Thomas who led famous Canadian fur-trade explorer David Thompson of the Northwest Company and his party over Athabasca Pass in 1811,

which became the fur trade route to the Columbia Valley for 70 years. While Thompson was the first to successfully cross the Continental Divide, his crew, including one William Henry, built a fur-trading post they called Henry House on the Athabasca River near the location of the present day Jasper Park Lodge. It was the first permanent structure built in the area by non-Natives.

In 1813, the Northwest Company built the post called Rocky Mountain House along the shores of Brûlé Lake. The name was changed to "Jasper's House" after Jasper Hawes took charge of the post. In 1830 the post was relocated to the shores of the Athabasca River near Jasper Lake and became known as Jasper House.

Although a number of travelers and adventurers passed through the area, it remained virtually unchanged until the Grand Trunk Pacific Railway (GTPR) promised to run a transcontinental line through the Rockies via the Athabasca Valley.

In 1907, the government created Jasper Forest Park to protect the precious natural resources in the area. With the arrival of the GTPR in 1911, the railway settlement of Fitzhugh, named after the vice-president of the GTPR, came into development. In 1913 the name was changed to Jasper.

Also in 1913, a second railway was constructed through Yellowhead Pass. The Canadian Northern Railway's lines were only yards apart in some places from those of the GTPR. The government took control of the tracks during World War I and sent duplicate tracks to France. After the war, the government took over both railways and consolidated them into the Canadian National Railway (CNR).

It was the building of the railway that provided the impetus for another Rocky Mountain town to flourish. The railway provided accessibility and Jasper soon became a popular tourist destination. In 1930 the National Parks Act was passed in parliament and Jasper was officially designated a national park.

■ Getting There & Getting Around
By Road

The Yellowhead Highway 16 runs east-west through Edmonton, Prince George and to the coast at Prince Rupert. Branching off Highway 16 at Tête Jaune Cache is Highway 5, which travels south to Kamloops and Vancouver.

The Icefields Parkway (Highway 93) connects Jasper to Lake Louise in Banff National Park. Along this route, Highway 93A starts 7½ km (4.7 miles) south of Jasper. It is the original route of the Icefields Parkway and ends at Athabasca Falls, 33 km (20½ miles) south of Jasper. (Don't confuse Highway 93A with another short section of 93A that follows Hazel Avenue south at its intersection with Connaught Drive – Jasper's main street – and crosses the train tracks and the Yellowhead Highway.)

Distances from Jasper Townsite

Lake Louise . . . . 230 km (143 miles)
Banff. . . . . 286 km (178 miles)
Calgary. 415 km (258 miles)
Hinton . . . . 79 km (49 miles)
Edmonton . . . . 370 km (230 miles)
Mount Robson . . . . 88 km (55 miles)
Prince George . . . . 390 km (242 miles)
Prince Rupert . . . . 1,101 km (684 miles)
Kamloops . . . . 443 km (265 miles)
Vancouver . . via Coquihalla Hwy 805 km (500 miles)
. . . . via Trans Canada Hwy 853 km (530 miles)
. . . . via Rogers Pass 1,074 km (667 miles)

Bus Service

Greyhound, ☎ 780-852-3926 or 800-661-8747 for fare & schedule information, located in the train station on Connaught Drive, www.greyhound.ca. Frequent bus service from/to Edmonton, Prince George, Calgary, Banff and Lake Louise.

Brewster Transportation and Tours, ☎ 877-791-5500 or 780-852-3332, located in the train station, www.brewster.ca. Bus service from Jasper to Lake Louise, Banff and Calgary. Express service to Lake Louise and Banff from May 1 to October 31. Departs Jasper 1:30 pm daily, arrives Lake Louise 5:30 and Banff 7:30 pm. Adults $55/$64, children half-price.

The Mountain Connector, ☎ 888-786-3641 or 780-852-4056, www.mountainconnector.com. Transportation between Jasper, Lake Louise, Banff and Canmore in winter from December to April. Transfers to and from Calgary are also available. Jasper to Banff, $59 adult, $35 child.

Car Rentals

Car rental agencies located in the train station:

National Car Rental, ☎ 780-852-1117, rentacar@telusplanet.net.

Hertz, ☎ 780-852-3888 or 800-263-0600.

Agency one-half block from the train station at the Jasper Shell service station:

Budget Rent-A-Car, ☎ 780-852-3222 or 800-610-3222.

Taxis

Jasper Taxi, ☎ 780-852-3600.

Mountain Express Taxi, ☎ 780-852-8110.

Heritage Cabs, ☎ 780-852-5558.

By Air

 Edmonton, Calgary and Vancouver have international airports and Prince George has a regional airport serviced by national carriers.

By Rail

 **VIA Rail**, ☎ 888-842-7245, www.viarail.ca. The historic train station is downtown on Connaught Drive. VIA Rail operates passenger service through Jasper via Edmonton and Vancouver on "The Canadian" and via Prince George and Prince Rupert on "The Skeena." The Skeena run is a popular and affordable two-day daylight train trip between the west coast town of

Prince Rupert and Jasper, with an overnight in Prince George. From mid-May to October, you can travel in Totem Class and enjoy access to the lounges and observation dome of the park car; meals are available. Via Rail offers various discounts for seniors, children and groups and has promotions for rail passes and low season travel (conditions apply).

See also *Rocky Mountaineer Railtours* under *Guided Tours,* page 89.

See also *Rocky Mountaineer Railtours* under *Guided Tours,* page 89.

THE MAGIC OF TRAIN TRAVEL

Many of my fondest travel memories from childhood include long train rides. Since my seven-year-old son Oliver had never ridden a passenger train, I jumped at the opportunity when I learned Via Rail was offering a special off-season rate.

The Skeena route runs 1,160 km (696 miles) between Jasper and Prince Rupert. During the off-season (from mid-October to mid-May) all passengers ride economy class, so everyone has access to the Park Car – the lounge and domed upper deck with its 360-degree panoramic views. We chose the return trip portion between Prince George and Jasper. This trip wasn't so much about where we were traveling, but about how we were going.

After departing Prince George at 8:30 am, time seemed to stand still as we enjoyed the scenery and wandered about the two train cars. Our first scheduled stop was the historic community of Penny, to drop off passengers and mail. The train pulled into the town of McBride at 12:30 pm for the second scheduled stop and to switch tracks. Passengers disembarked and enjoyed the renovated 1919 train station, home to an inviting café and a gift shop featuring the work of local artists and craftspeople.

Soon the train was passing famous Mount Robson, with low clouds obscuring its peak – the highest in the Canadian Rockies. The famous was infamous on this day, low clouds enveloping the landscape.

Jasper National Park

We arrived in Jasper at 5:30 pm, well rested and relaxed, but an hour late due to a wait for freight
trains. It's a five-minute walk from the train station
through town to the Athabasca Hotel, where we
spent the night after dinner and a stroll around the
town.

The following day, our schedule permitted a relaxing
breakfast and some shopping before departing on
time at 12:45 pm with the same friendly crew.

Part way into the return trip, I finally realized what
was missing from this ride – the familiar clickety-
clack of the rail lines that I was so familiar with. I
was informed that the short branch lines are being
replaced with continuous welded rail (1/4-mile
lengths) on this route.

We pulled back into the Prince George station while
admiring the sunset from the domed upper deck.
Some lucky passengers and the crew would carry on
to Prince Rupert the following morning. For Oliver
and myself, that trip would have to wait, but it's one
I hope we'll make. Riding Via Rail rekindled my af-
fection for train travel and captured the interest of a
young traveler.

■ Special Events

Jasper in January is a two-week winter festival
in the latter part of the month, including a parade,
fireworks, skating parties, snow sculptures, special activities at restaurants, discounted skiing, as
well as accommodations and more.

Celebrate Canada Day, July 1st, with special events
throughout the day, including a parade, pancake breakfast,
entertainment and fireworks. Free admission to Jasper
National Park.

Canada's Parks Day celebrations, held the second or third
Saturday in July. Many outdoor activities including free
guided hikes, special exhibits and children's activities. Stop
by the registration booth at the Visitor Information Center.

The **Jasper Heritage Folk Festival** attracts big-name Canadian musicians, held every second year (2005) on the first weekend of August in Centennial Park. www.jasperfolkfestival.com.

The **Jasper Heritage Rodeo**, a tradition since 1933, is held in August and attracts pro riders from around the world; a dance Saturday night features top Canadian country entertainment.

In October, there's the **Freewheel Biathlon** bike ride to Athabasca Falls and the Jasper Root Romp, a 10-km (six-mile) run along rugged trails.

■ Jasper Townsite

The relaxed town of Jasper – shaped like the letter "J" – is situated on the northwest side of the Athabasca River between the junctions of the Maligne and Miette Rivers. While Jasper has seen its share of growth and commercial development over the years, it still remains less glitzy and more low-key than highly commercialized Banff.

The population of 5,000 (many of whom are employed by the Canadian National Railway) swells to 25,000 or more at any given time during the peak summer months, with annual visitation at approximately two million. Because the town is built in a montane wildlife area, it's not uncommon to see elk and other wildlife wandering about town. **Connaught Drive** is the main street running east-west through town, with most of the businesses and services located on it, as well as **Patricia Street**, one street over. Connaught Drive is named in honor of H.R.H. Prince Arthur, Duke of Connaught, who served as Governor General of Canada from 1911 to 1916. Patricia Street and Patricia Lake are named for his daughter, Princess Patricia.

Jasper offers all of the facilities of a small town including a swimming pool, theater and library. The town and its environs are well suited to exploration on foot or bicycle with many of the most popular attractions just a short drive from the townsite.

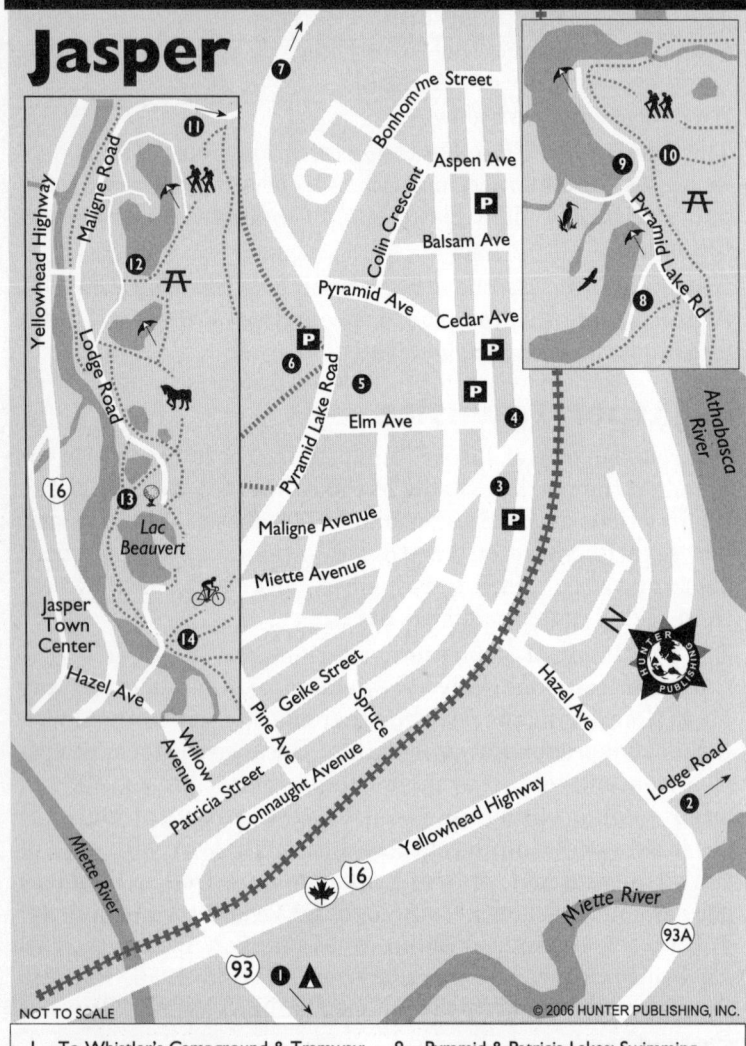

Jasper

Bonhomme Street
Aspen Ave
Colin Crescent
Balsam Ave
Pyramid Ave
Cedar Ave
Elm Ave
Maligne Avenue
Miette Avenue
Geike Street
Hazel Ave
Pyramid Lake Road
Maligne Road
Yellowhead Highway
Lodge Road
Jasper Town Center
Lac Beauvert
Willow Avenue
Patricia Street
Connaught Avenue
Pine Ave
Spruce
Hazel Ave
Yellowhead Highway
Lodge Road
Athabasca River
Miette River
Pyramid Lake Rd
Miette River

NOT TO SCALE

© 2006 HUNTER PUBLISHING, INC.

1. To Whistler's Campground & Tramway; Columbia Icefield; Lake Louise & Banff
2. To Lakes Beauvert, Mildred, Annette, Edith; Old Fort Point; Fairmont Jasper Park Lodge (inset, top left)
3. Whistler's Inn & Den Wildlife Museum
4. Jasper Heritage Railway Station
5. Activity Center; Aquatic Center
6. Jasper Yellowhead Museum
7. To Patricia & Pyramid Lakes (inset, top right)
8. Cottonwood Slough
9. Pyramid & Patricia Lakes: Swimming, Picnic areas, Restaurant, Boating, Ice Skating
10. Pyramid Bench; Scenic Viewpoint; Horseback & Sleigh Rides; Trails
11. To Maligne Canyon & Lake
12. Lake Annette & Lake Edith: Swimming, Playground, Trails, Paved Wheelchair Path
13. Jasper Park Lodge; Golf, Boating, Biking, Horseback & Sleigh Rides, Skating, Skiing
14. Old Fort Point

Distances from Jasper Townsite

Lake Edith & Lake Annette ... 5 km (three miles)
Jasper Park Lodge .... 7 km (four miles)
Maligne Canyon........... 12 km (seven miles)
Maligne Lake................. 48 km (30 miles)
Pocahontas.................. 45 km (28 miles)
Miette Hot Springs .... 78 km (48 miles)
Pyramid Lake .... 7 km (four miles)
Jasper Tramway .... 7 km (four miles
Mt. Edith Cavell .... 29 km (18 miles)
Athabasca Falls.............. 31 km (19 miles)
Sunwapta Falls .... 55 km (34 miles)
Columbia Icefield .... 105 km (63 miles)

The **Visitor Information Center** is a National Historic Site located on Connaught Drive in the center of town. Housed in a rustic building constructed in 1914 as an administration office and home for the first park superintendent, the center is rather small and can become extremely crowded in busy summer months. But there's plenty of room on the surrounding grounds, where visitors can sit and watch the crowds. Unfortunately, there are no public washrooms (they're across the street) but they do provide courtesy phones. ☎ 780-852-6176, jnp_info@pch.gc.ca. **Operating Hours:** Late June to Labour Day, 8:30 am to 7 pm; September, 9 am to 6 pm; October, 9 am to 5 pm; Nov 1 to March 31, 9 am to 4 pm; April 1 to late June, 9 am to 5 pm.

FRIENDS OF JASPER NATIONAL PARK

A non-profit organization whose mandate is "to promote understanding, appreciation and respect for the natural history and cultural heritage of Jasper National Park." Located in the Visitor Information Center, Friends of Jasper National Park offers a variety of free programs in the summer and winter for both adults and children. Take an historical walking tour to learn about Jasper's past, go on a bird walk

Jasper National Park

or a night hike or shop for clothing, gift items, books, maps and tasteful souvenirs in the Friends store. All proceeds are used to support programs, publications, research and projects, including trail restoration. Visit their website, www.friendsofjasper.com, to find the most up-to-date information and check their informative newsletter *Nature Calls*. ☎ 780-852-4767.

■ Attractions

The Jasper Heritage Railway Station

Centrally located on Connaught Drive across from the Visitor Center, the railway station is an example of Arts and Crafts movement-inspired architecture. Built in 1925 by the newly formed Canadian National Railway (CNR), it was the focal point of community activity for many decades. Today, the renovated building houses Via Rail, Rocky Mountaineer Railtours, Greyhound, car rental agencies, a travel agent, and a café and gift shop. If the crowds in town are getting to you, walk across Connaught Drive to the station, where you can sit outside on a nice day and people- or train-watch.

Jasper-Yellowhead Museum

The museum features exhibits that transport visitors through Jasper's history: the fur trade, mountaineering, the arrival of the railway and the creation of the park, early tourism and the warden service. Exhibits in the Showcase Gallery change throughout the year. The museum also contains extensive archives. There's a great little gift shop with an excellent selection of books pertaining to all aspects of the Rocky Mountains as well as jewelry and crafts by local artists. Friendly and helpful staff and minimal admission help make this museum well worth a visit. ☎ 780-852-3013, Pyramid Lake Road.

Summer (Victoria Day to Labour Day) 10 am to 9 pm daily; fall (Labour Day to Thanksgiving) 10 am to 5 pm daily; winter (Thanksgiving to Victoria Day) 10 am to 5 pm, Thursday to

Sunday. Adult $3, student/senior $2, child under 6 free, families $8.

 The old **Jasper Firehall**, next to the Post Office, features exhibits by the Jasper Artists Guild and Jasper Museum in the summer months.

■ **Shopping**

 There's no shortage of shops in Jasper and I always enjoy window-shopping and people-watching along Connaught Drive and Patricia Street. Many shops offer much the same variety of tacky souvenirs (gotta buy at least one), gift items, and fudge (what is it about tourists and fudge?), but you'll also find some unique items such as aboriginal crafts, antiques, and hand-crafted Canadian items. There's a good selection of outdoor clothing and equipment shops, but compare prices as some items tend to be costly. In the summer, most shops are open seven days per week into the evening, with reduced hours in the off-season.

A few of the more notable shops include:

Our Native Land, 601 Patricia Street. A large shop full of native arts and crafts.

Trains & Lattes. A tiny hidden shop and café (and a friendly proprietor) in the railway station that specializes in train memorabilia.

The Niche, 626 Connaught Drive. A fun shop for the ladies, with good-quality clothing, home accessories and unique gift items.

Elysion Florals is tucked away on a walking path between Connaught Drive and Patricia Street. Another one for the ladies, this shop is fun to browse for antiques and giftware among the flowers and plants.

Jasper Camera & Gift, 412 Connaught Drive. Large photographic, book and gift departments.

The Jasper Post Office, 502 Patricia Street. Unique greeting cards, souvenirs and Canadian flags, as well as phone cards and packaging supplies. Stamps make great souvenirs, too.

Mounted Police Gift Shop, 610 Patricia Street. Canadian clothing, gifts and all things "Mountie" – licensed products by the Royal Canadian Mounted Police Foundation. Bring your camera, dress up as a Mountie and have your photo taken for free.

The Beauvert Promenade at The Fairmont Jasper Park Lodge. What to do in the rain? Browse the many upscale shops in the lower level of the main chalet for clothing, gourmet foods, artwork, Christmas decorations, home décor, and much more.

■ Where to Eat

 Although Jasper's townsite is relatively small, you can find excellent cuisine from around the world – Japanese, Greek, Italian, Chinese, Korean, Swiss, French and, of course, North American; from internationally renowned fine dining, to casual cafés and family-style restaurants. Many hotels and lodges offer one or more different eating places.

Jasper has a limited selection of small grocery stores with generally higher prices than larger centers.

Good restaurants in Jasper townsite include:

La Fiesta Tapas, ☎ 780-852-0403, 504 Patricia Street, $$. I tried this restaurant for lunch and desperately wanted to return for dinner. The food was excellent, the service superb and the prices reasonable. I love tapas, little portions of Spanish-influenced food, because you get to try a variety of tastes, as opposed to ordering one entrée. Open for lunch and dinner, this casual restaurant features an intriguing selection of salads and hot tapas, including seafood, pork, chicken, and beef creations, as well as vegetarian fare. How does cornmeal-crusted chicken breast stuffed with smoke tomato

DINING PRICE CHART	
Price per person in Canadian $ for an entrée, not including beverage, tax or tip.	
$	Under $10
$$	$10-$25
$$$	Over $25

risotto and served with a cilantro pesto aioli sound? How about grilled swordfish steak with fennel and fig chutney? During "Tappy Hour" (4:30 to 6:30 and 9:30 to 11 pm) you can order any three items from the Tappy Hour Menu for $18 (it's a fabulous deal; don't know how long it will last). Try the house special red or white sangria. Singles can sit at the bar but it's more fun to go as a group – sharing is what tapas is all about.

Kim Chi House, ☎ 780-852-5022, 407 Patricia Street, $$. I appreciate restaurants that aren't concerned with décor, instead focusing on good food. It was the eccentricity of this restaurant, located in a renovated house, that piqued my interest, plus the fact that I love trying Asian foods. They offer a good selection of flavorful Korean specialties. I ordered the hot & spicy chicken and vegetable hot plate and it was excellent. Open for lunch and dinner.

Caledonia Grill, ☎ 780-852-4070, in the Whistlers Inn on Connaught Drive, $$. Casual contemporary, fresh Canadian cuisine in tastefully (pardon the pun) decorated surroundings. Try one of the many pasta dishes or regional fare such as elk meatballs in a savory tomato sauce, buffalo medallions with peppercorn sauce or wild Canadian duck breast. The fresh food extends to the kids menu. (My son's advice to other kids: be wary when parents snitch French fries off kids' plates – they're the best fries!) Open for breakfast, lunch and dinner.

Tokyo Tom's, ☎ 780-852-3780, 410 Connaught Drive, $$. Excellent Japanese cuisine for lunch or dinner with a very casual atmosphere. This place gets busy so dinner reservations are recommended during July and August.

Fairmont Jasper Park Lodge, ☎ 780-852-6052, $$$. The lodge offers seven choices of dining and lounging from casual to elegant. Fine dining includes the upscale Edith Cavell Dining Room, including Sunday brunch. The Moose's Nook Northern Grill features mountain-themed food, and, if you don't mind paying the likes of $18 for granola, there's Meadows.

Mountain Foods Café, ☎ 780-852-4050, 606 Connaught Drive, $. I've been stopping in at this café as long as I've been visiting Jasper. For lunch, a selection of fresh soups, sandwiches, burgers, salads, wraps, and pitas. The breakfast special includes two eggs, hash browns and toast for $5.50 or you can order bagels, waffles, huevos rancheros, Mexican potato cake, as well as fresh squeezed juices and smoothies. Great for take-out lunches to enjoy on the trail.

Truffles & Trout, ☎ 780-852-9676, Patricia & Hazel Streets, $. A little café in the Jasper Marketplace that offers a selection of beverages, fresh sweets and light meals. Great spot to people-watch.

Scoops & Loops, ☎ 780-852-4333, 504 Patricia Street. Can't leave Jasper without at least one stop for fresh fruit frozen yoghurt. Best selection of ice cream in Jasper. (Sushi also available – what a combination!)

Nutter's, ☎ 780-852-5844, 622 Patricia Street. I always enjoy this interesting little store with its large selection of bulk-buy items such as nuts, snacks, health food, junk food, grocery items and lots more.

Bear's Paw Bakery, ☎ 780-852-3233, corner of Cedar & Connaught. Open daily from 6 am. The proprietor suggests you get your buns down to their bakery to select from the many delectable European-style specialty pastries, tortes, artisan breads, flaky-fresh buttery croissants or hearty muffins – and I concur. (I also suggest you get there early, especially on weekends, before they sell out of bread!) Enjoy with a cup of coffee or tea at one of the few tables inside or benches outside. And don't forget to get a few trail cookies to take along on your hikes. Who can resist?

■ Where to Stay

Downtown

Athabasca Hotel, ☎ 877-542-8422 or 780-852-3386, 510 Patricia Street, www.athabasca-hotel.com, $$ to $$$. The popular "Atha'B," as it's known, offers Jasper's most reasonably priced hotel rooms in a heritage building circa 1929. The renovated rooms are cozy and comfortable. Rooms are basic with less expensive rooms sharing a bathroom but suites are also available. Make sure your room isn't above the pub, as it gets noisy, especially on weekends. When not camping or staying in private accommodations, this busy hotel is a personal favorite.

Park Place Inn, ☎ 866-852-9770 or 780-852-9770, 623 Patricia St, www.parkplaceinn.com, $$$$. Twelve luxuriously appointed heritage-style rooms make up this newer inn. Each room is slightly

HOTEL PRICE CHART

Reflects the price of an average room for two in Canadian $, May-Sept. Rates lower rest of year (except Christmas and New Year's).

$	Under $50
$$	$50-$100
$$$	$101-$150
$$$$	$151-$250
$$$$$	Over $250

different – some with soaker, claw-foot or jetted tubs and gas fireplace. Most rooms sleep four, with one room sleeping up to six. All rooms feature color television, telephone, refrigerator or wet bar, coffee/tea facilities, heritage-style furniture and terry robes. Secure underground parking. One handicap accessible room. Guest book comment: "Great hotel, one of the best I have stayed in anywhere in the world."

Bear Hill Lodge, ☎ 780-852-3209, 100 Bonhomme Street, www.bearhilllodge.com, $$$$. Open May to mid-October. This is the only lodge-type accommodation within easy walking distance of downtown. Chose from tastefully decorated cozy heritage cabins or chalet studios in duplex or fourplex buildings. Deluxe individual suites are also available. Gas or wood burning fireplaces and kitchenettes; breakfast available with some accommodations. Whirlpool, sauna and barbecue facilities. Pets accepted by prior arrangement.

Seventy-nine km (49 miles) east of Jasper is the town of **Hinton**, which offers a cheaper alternative to staying in Jasper Park's hotels, motels and lodges. A number of hotels and motels are right along Highway 16, where you'll also find restaurants and other tourist services.

Near Jasper Townsite

Patricia Lake Bungalows, ☎ 888-499-6848 or 780-852-3560, www.patricialakebungalows.com, $$$ to $$$$. Family-owned and -operated, these lovely cottages and motel are surrounded by immaculate gardens along or near picturesque crystal-clear Patricia Lake, five minutes from town. Located at the end of a private road; the quiet atmosphere is strictly enforced. Some cottages have fully equipped kitchens, gas fireplaces, and TV/VCR/DVD. Amenities include gas barbecue, outdoor hot tub, playground, coin laundry, and satellite television. Also offered: canoe, rowboat and paddleboat rentals ($15 per hour) as well as bicycle rentals ($8 per hour). Handicap accessible accommodations are available. Pets $10 per night. Weekly rates available. Open May to mid-October.

Pyramid Lake Resort, ☎ 888-717-1277 or 780-852-4900, www.pyramidlakeresort.com, $$$$$. This pricey year-round resort is situated above the shores of Pyramid Lake. Rooms and suites each have a gas fireplace, fridge or kitchenette and a balcony with lake/mountain views. Facilities include The Pines Restaurant, gift shop and spa with fitness facilities and a hot tub. Boat rentals are $20 to $35 per hour, bicycle rentals $10 per hour, with a 20% discount for guests. Discounts for CAA/AAA members, senior citizens and corporate clients.

Becker's Chalets, ☎ 780-852-3779, www.beckers-chalets.com, $$$ to $$$$. Family-operated historic lodging with a loyal clientele. Located six km (3.7 miles) south of town along the Athabasca River. Chalets with kitchenettes and fireplaces. Amenities include laundry facilities, gift shop and playground. The facility is home to award-winning Becker's Gourmet restaurant, featuring buffet breakfasts and gourmet dinners with fabulous views. Open May to mid-October.

Pine Bungalows, ☎ 780-852-3491, www.pine-bungalows.com, $$ to $$$. Located two km (1.2 miles) east opposite the northern entrance to town on the Athabasca River. This is one of the best value cabin-type accommodations in Jasper. Choose from basic motel-style units with kitchenettes or rustic one- and two-bedroom bungalows with kitchens and fireplaces. Amenities include laundry facilities, barbecues and picnic tables. Off-season and seniors' rates available. Smoking and non-smoking rooms. Open May to mid-October.

Pocahontas Cabins, ☎ 800-843-3372 or 780-866-3732, www.mpljasper.com, $$$ to $$$$. Located 30 minutes east of town at the bottom of Miette Hot Springs Road. Motel units and nicely appointed cabins with verandas and optional kitchens. Some newly constructed units. Café, convenience store, heated outdoor pool, barbecues and horseshoe pits. Pets welcome at no additional charge. Great family accommodations. I don't recommend the six cabins along noisy Highway 16. Open May to mid-October.

Miette Hot Springs Resort Motel, ☎ 780-866-3750 or 780-852-4039, $$ to $$$. This is an older facility beside the hot springs. Motel units and bungalows are available, some with kitchens and fireplaces. Amenities include playground, barbecue and restaurant. I recommend this facility only if you want accommodation beside the hot springs. Open May to mid-October.

Historic Accommodations – Fairmont Jasper Park Lodge

It's hard to believe that this luxury resort on the shores of Lac Beauvert started out as a tent camp during the burgeoning tourist trade of 1915. "Tent City" consisted of  eight large tents with wooden floors, plus a sizable tent serving as a lounge, dining room and kitchen. The Canadian National Railway completed construction of the Jasper Park Lodge in 1922, a set of log cabins surrounding a main lodge that claimed to be the world's largest log structure. In 1952 the lodge burned down, but was immediately replaced by the present-day structure that accommodates up to 900 guests in 446 rooms. Non-registered guests

may also take part in the resort's many recreational
offerings: horseback riding, golfing on the 18-hole
award-winning course, walking or bicycling the
trails around the resort, or renting a canoe or kayak
and paddling around the lake. Dine in one of the
many restaurants and lounges or browse through
the upscale shops on the lower floor. The price of luxury in 1922: $3 per day. Today, a room will set you
back $479 or more during peak season. ☎
800-441-1414, 780-852-3301, www.jasper-
parklodge.com

Guesthouses & Apartments

Private home accommodations are very popular in Jasper.
There are well over 100 residential homes in Jasper offering
inspected and licensed rooms. If you stroll down the streets of
Jasper townsite you will see signs on some of the homes that
offer rooms for rent. Note that most of these accommodations
do not serve breakfast unless otherwise noted.

> The Visitor Information Center pro-
> vides a Private Home Accommodation
> brochure that is produced annually by
> the Jasper Home Accommodation Associ-
> ation, PO Box 758, Jasper, AB, T0E 1E0.
> See www.stayinjasper.com for detailed
> listings.

The following are all within easy walking distance of downtown:

The Meadows, ☎ 780-852-3474, 302 Aspen Avenue, Host:
Fay McCready, $$. Fay made me feel so much at home at The
Meadows, I didn't want to leave her recently built home with
laundry facilities, barbecue, feather duvets, travel crib, and
cots for extra people. Single and double rooms as well as a
beautiful private family suite with a large sitting area and
kitchen. Private/shared entrances and bathrooms. Discount
for extended stays. These accommodations lend themselves to
reunions and special occasions.

Robin's Nest, ☎ 780-852-1900, 302 Balsam Avenue, $$. A charming older home on a quiet street that offers three bright upstairs rooms with mountain views. Small sitting room with fridge; outside garden area. Shared bathroom; private entrance. Children six or over only. Host: Lee-Anne Mulvihill.

Alberta's Penthouse Suite, ☎ 780-852-3930, 105 Geikie Street, Host: Terry Olsen, $$. A bright and spacious two-bedroom upstairs suite with kitchen and sitting area is immaculate and ideal for families or two couples sharing. Private entrance; TV; off-street parking.

The Gingerbread House, ☎ 780-852-4743, 801 Patricia Street, www.thegingerbreadhouse.ca, $$. Lovely renovated historical home with three units, shared bathroom and entrance. TV/VCR and fridge. Ask about rates for extended stays. Host: Rita Hindle.

Seldom In Guest House, ☎ 780-852-5187, 123 Geikie Street, $$. If you're looking for affordable accommodations and a place to mingle with local residents, this is a good bet. Bright second-floor rooms have private or shared bathrooms and entrance. Common kitchen and living room, along with TV/VCR and lots of books. Hosts: Sherrill & Doug.

Bear's Den, ☎ 780-852-4203, 302 Pyramid Avenue, $$. Rustically decorated room in historical log house on a quiet street. Private bathroom and entrance. Kitchen; laundry; barbecue; TV/DVD/CD; and outside sitting area. German, Swiss and French spoken. Hosts: Lydia & Gerry.

Joe & Sheila's Place, ☎ 780-852-4949, 734 Connaught Drive, $$. Affordable accommodations in a cozy private basement suite. Quiet and comfortable with private bathroom, kitchenette and shared entrance. Hosts: Joe & Sheila.

Camping

 Parks Canada operates 10 campgrounds in Jasper National Park with a total of 1,851 sites. Pocahontas, Whistlers, Wapiti and Wabasso now accept reservations. See www.pccamping.ca for the Parks Canada Campground Reservation Service, or call ☎ 877-737-3783, international calls ☎ 905-426-4648.

Fully serviced sites are very limited and only available at Whistlers and Wapiti, as are showers. Whistlers, Wapiti, Wabasso and Wilcox Creek all offer dumping stations, which can also be found at the Jasper townsite industrial park.

CAMPING/HOSTELS	
Rates in Canadian $, not including taxes.	
$	Under $13
$$	$13-$22
$$$	$23-$30
$$$$	Over $30

Campsites in Jasper National Park

Snaring River, 13 km (eight miles) east of townsite on Celestine Lake Road. 66 primitive sites, $$, overflow $. Mid-May to mid-September.

Pocahontas, 45 km (28 miles) east (closest campground to Miette Hotsprings). 140 unserviced sites, $$$. Mid-May to mid-October. Reservations accepted.

Wabasso, 16½ km (10 miles) south along Highway 93A. 228 unserviced sites, $$$. Disabled access, dumping station, nice setting along the Athabasca River. Late June to early September. Reservations accepted.

Whistlers, 3½ km (two miles) south on Whistlers Road (closest campground to townsite). 781 sites, walk-in $$, unserviced $$$, with power $$$, full hookups $$$$. Showers, disabled access, dumping station, interpretive programs. Closed in winter. Reservations accepted.

Wapiti, 5.4 km (3.4 miles) south along the Icefields Parkway. 365 sites (93 in winter), unserviced $$$, with power $$$. Showers, disabled access, dumping station, nice setting along the Athabasca River. Closed in spring and fall but open in winter. Reservations accepted.

Mt. Kerkeslin, 36 km (22 miles) south along the Icefields Parkway. 42 primitive sites, $$. Mid-May to early September.

Honeymoon Lake, 52½ km (32.6 miles) south along the Icefields Parkway. 35 primitive sites, $$. Mid-May to mid-October.

Jonas Creek, 78 km (48½ miles) south along the Icefields Parkway. 25 primitive sites, $$. Mid-May to mid-September.

Columbia Icefield, 106 km (66 miles) south along the Icefields Parkway. 33 primitive sites, $$, tents only. Mid-May to mid-October.

Above: Wildlife traffic jam, Jasper

Below: Maligne Lake, Opal Hills, Jasper

Stanley Falls, Jasper

Bighorn sheep ewes rest at the end of the Sulphur Skyline trail, Jasper National Park

Valley of the Five Lakes, Jasper

Cavell Meadows, Jasper

Above: Athabasca Glacier Highway (© *Lenard Sanders*)

Below: Maligne Lake boathouse, Jasper (© *Lenard Sanders*)

Above: Overlander Falls, Mount Robson Provincial Park
Below: Kinney Lake, Mount Robson (© Lenard Sanders)

Mount Robson (© Lenard Sanders)

Wilcox Creek, 107½ km (67 miles) south along the Icefields Parkway. 46 primitive sites, $$. Dumping station. Early June to mid-September.

Campgrounds Near Jasper National Park

Folding Mountain Campground, ☎ 780-866-3737. Privately operated camping five km (three miles) east of Jasper Park East Gate on Hwy 16. 96 sites; $$. Full hookups, pull-thru sites, sewage disposal, playground, showers, snack bar, reservations accepted. Open May to October.

Backcountry Camping

There are 100 backcountry campsites in Jasper Park. If you are planning on camping overnight in Jasper's wilderness campgrounds, you must purchase a **wilderness pass**, $9 per person/per night or $63 for an annual permit. You can reserve your camping up to three months in advance in person at the Visitor Information Center or by calling ☎ 780-852-6177. For more information, email: jnp_info@pch.gc.ca.

A $12 non-refundable reservation fee applies and/or a modification fee for changes. Wilderness pass fees, excluding reservation and modification fees, are refundable until 10 am of your date of departure. Reservations are advisable for busy trails during the peak hiking months of July and August; these trails include Skyline, Tonquin, Brazeau Loop and Maligne Lake.

 Be sure to pick up a copy of *Jasper Park's Backcountry Visitor's Guide* from the Visitor Information Center. The brochure explains basic information about planning your trip, safety issues, trail descriptions and a map.

Hosteling

Five hostels operate under the Hosteling International umbrella in Jasper National Park, four of which are rustic cabins with no electricity or running water. None are located in the townsite. Reservations are recommended, essential at Jasper International Hostel. Bookings for accommodations and transportation at any of these hostels can be made through **Jasper International Hostel**, ☎ 780-852-3215, 877-852-0781 or jasper@hihostels.ca.

Jasper International Hostel, seven km (4.3 miles) south on Whistlers Road. 84 beds, men's and women's dorms. Members $$, non-members $$$. Three family rooms; check-in 12 pm-12 am, open year-round. Internet access, shuttle bus. I have stayed at this hostel a number of times, even when it was –50°C/-58°F in January and one of the boilers broke. Staff is accommodating and Ted, the resident dog, is friendly. Great views of Whistlers Mountain.

Maligne Canyon Hostel, 11 km (6.8 miles) east on Maligne Lake Road near the canyon. 24 beds in two cabins. Members & non-members $$. Check-in 5-11 pm, open year-round except Wednesdays, October through April. Rustic cabins in a picturesque setting; shuttle bus. Situated near Maligne Canyon and close to hiking, cycling and cross-country skiing trails.

Mt. Edith Cavell Hostel, 30 km (18.6 miles) south on Edith Cavell Road. 32 beds. Members & non-members $$. Check-in 5-11 pm, mid-June to mid-October. Rustic cabins in a spectacular setting; outdoor wood sauna. Awesome view and ideal base from which to explore the Tonquin Valley, Angel Glacier or Cavell Meadows.

Athabasca Falls Hostel, 32 km (20 miles) south along the Icefields Parkway near Athabasca Falls. 40 beds. Members & non-members $$. Check-in 5-11 pm, open year-round except Tuesdays, October through April. Three rustic cabins; shuttle bus.

Beauty Creek Hostel, 87 km (54 miles) south along the Icefields Parkway. 22 beds. Members & non-members $$; check-in 5-11 pm; mid-May through September. Rustic cabins along the Sunwapta River; shuttle bus. Provides access to excellent hiking trails; extra friendly staff.

■ Wildlife

 In Jasper National Park there are 69 wildlife species, including: 70-90 grizzly bears; 70-90 black bears; 1,300 elk; 80-100 moose; 2,500-3,000 bighorn sheep; 250-300 mountain goats; 20-25 wolves in three-four packs using the Athabasca Valley; 100-120 caribou.

Large herds of elk can commonly be seen throughout the park along highways and roadways and in the townsite. Also commonly seen are mule deer, often along Pyramid Lake Road, and bighorn sheep along Hwy 16 east of the townsite.

Moose are more elusive; try spotting them along the Maligne Lake Road between Medicine Lake and Maligne Lake or at Pocahontas Ponds. Bears can often been seen munching on roadside dandelions almost anywhere in the park.

One of the best places to see playful critters such as hoary marmots, golden-mantled ground squirrels and pika is The Whistlers at the Jasper Tramway.

BEARS & THE PEOPLE OF JASPER

"Not many years ago the population of Jasper townsite was approximately two-thirds people and one-third bears. We all shared the streets of Jasper quite amicably and there were very few confrontations between the two elements of our society. At that time it would be a rare occasion to walk from your home to the downtown area without seeing a bear. The bears respected people and we respected bears. If you happened to meet face to face, it was an unwritten law that you ignored each other. The bears knew it, and we certainly knew it.

The bear's affinity for town was the easy access to food. They preferred the alleys and foraged in every garbage can. We all tried to buy garbage cans with tight-fitting lids, but the bears always outsmarted us. It was part of the daily stint of housekeeping to clean the alley each day, and place garbage back into the garbage cans.

Usually, in the spring, a bear would choose a three-block area to become its home for the summer. If it was a mother bear with cubs, she knew which trees in that area were safe for her cubs while she foraged and fended off dogs.

One year in a particular neighborhood, we had a mother with three cubs. It was most interesting to watch her discipline her family. The cubs played:

they got spanked and boxed by mom, and they learned to be very obedient. They learned never to come down from the tree until their mother told them it was safe. It was great entertainment for all of our guests." From *Jasper A Backward Glance*, by Nora Findlay, 1992 (courtesy Friends of Jasper National Park and Jasper-Yellowhead Historical Society).

■ Adventures

Sports & Camping Equipment Rentals

Jasper Rentals at Totem Ski Shop, ☎ 800-363-3078 or 780-852-3078, 408 Connaught Drive, www.totemskishop.com. Camping equipment rentals including tents $15 per day, backpacks $8 per day, sleep mats, stoves, camp pots, bear spray, and hiking poles as well as baby carriers. Crampons, ice axes, avalanche beacons and probes; snowshoes $10 per day, cross-country skis $9 per day, ski packages $9 to $30 per day.

Edge Control Ski Shop, ☎ 888-242-3343 or 780-852-4945, 614 Connaught Drive. Adult ski packages $22 to $32 per day with discounts for extra days; snowboards $32 per day; telemark equipment, alpine touring equipment, cross country equipment, snowshoes $11 per day.

Jasper Source for Sports, ☎ 780-852-3654, 406 Patricia Street. Mountain bikes for rent, full suspension $12 per hour, $28 per day or $35 per 24 hours. Fishing, boating and camping equipment also available.

On-line Sport, ☎ 780-852-3630, 600 Patricia Street. Backcountry rowboats and canoes $40-$50 per day. Guided fishing tours for rainbow, brook trout and northern pike, as well as fly fishing instruction. Mountain bike rentals $10 per hour, $20 for four hours, $30 per day. Skis, snowboards and snowshoes all available for rent or repair.

Freewheel Cycle, ☎ 780-852-3898, 618 Patricia Street. High-end mountain bike rentals, full suspension $35 half-day, $45 per day; kids' bikes and child carriers; free trail advice.

Guided Tours

Conveniently located in the townsite, booking agents and tour companies can provide details on the recreational opportunities in the park as well as make bookings for accommodations and transportation. Tour operators have a wealth of knowledge and will be pleased to help you with any tourist information you may be seeking.

Do-Travel.com, ☎ 866-857-4545 or 780-852-4545, located in the train station, www.do-travel.com. This booking agent will handle your entire holiday in Jasper, from booking flights, rental cars, activities and tours to complete customized itineraries for individuals and groups, even train packages. Friendly staff, gift shop and an affiliate office based in the UK.

Rocky Mountaineer Railtours, ☎ 800-665-7245, located in the train station, www.rockymountaineer.com. Offers a variety of luxury vacation rail tours from mid-April to mid-October, as well as winter tours. The seven-night/eight-day tour called **The Western Explorer** between Vancouver and Calgary is the most popular, with motorcoach tours of Jasper, the Icefields Parkway, Yoho, and Banff included. Prices start at $1,539 to $4,546, one-way, per person, double occupancy.

Brewster Transportation and Tours, ☎ 877-791-5500 or 780-852-3332, located in the train station, www.brewster.ca. Guided motorcoach tours, May to October. Tours include:

◆ **Discover Jasper** – four hours. Highlights include Jasper townsite, Medicine Lake, Maligne Lake and Maligne Canyon. Adult $46, child (six-15 years) $23.

◆ **Icefields Parkway to Lake Louise or Banff** – 7½ hours to Lake Louise or 9½ hours to Banff, one-way; round-trip overnights in Banff, accommodation not included. Stops at major attractions along the parkway including Athabasca Glacier and a brief stop at Lake Louise before arriving in Banff late afternoon. One-way adult $98 to Lake Louise or $106 to Banff. Round-trip adult $134 to Lake Louise or $148 to Banff; children half-price.

Jasper Adventure Center, ☎ 800-565-7547 or 780-852-5595, 604 Connaught Drive in the lobby of the Chaba

Jasper National Park

Theatre (summer only), 306 Connaught Drive (winter); www.visit-jasper.com/JasAdventureCnt.html. Guided interpretive tours including nature walks, wildlife viewing, and railroad tours. Among their tours are the following:

◆ **Miette Hot Springs Watchable Wildlife Tour** – A four-hour evening drive that provides "the best viewing opportunity for a variety of wildlife in Jasper National Park," as well as a short guided walk to the source of Miette Hot Springs and a soak in the thermal pools. Adult $54, child $25, includes pool admittance.

◆ **Ride the Steel Rails** – A five-hour train ride and van tour along the Fraser River and past Mount Robson. Adult $105, senior $100, youth (12-18 years) $85, child (two-11 years) $55.

◆ **Maligne Canyon Icewalk** – A three-hour winter tour on the frozen floor of the deepest canyon in Jasper Park. Adult $40, child 14 and under $25.

Sundog Tours, ☎ 888-786-3641 or 780-852-4056, 414 Connaught Drive www.sundogtours.com. Nature walks, hikes, rail tours, wildlife tours and more. Booking agents for rafting trips. Winter tours also available.

◆ **Jasper to Banff Sightseeing Tour** – A 10-hour excursion along the Icefields Parkway with stops at the tourist attractions of Athabasca Falls, Columbia Icefield Center, Peyto Lake, Bow Lake, Crowfoot Glacier and Chateau Lake Louise. All interesting stops, but also very crowded. Adult $120, child $85.

Maligne Tours Ticket Office, ☎ 866-625-4463 or 780-852-3370, corner of Patricia and Hazel Streets in The Jasper Marketplace, www.malignelake.com. Bookings for all activities in the Maligne Lake area, including shuttle bus service as well as rafting trips (see *Whitewater Rafting* section).

◆ Maligne Lake **scenic boat cruises** (May to October) depart on the hour from 10 am to 5 pm during peak times. Ninety-minute cruise to Spirit Island, adult $39, child $19.50, five and under free; can also be booked at the lake.

♦ **Guided fishing** that boasts water teeming with rainbow and brook trout. Includes return transportation from Jasper and lunch. Full day $246.60 single, $192.60 per person for two or more.

Walks & Talks Jasper, ☎ 888-242-3343 or 780-852-4994, at Edge Control Ski Shop, 614 Connaught Drive, www.walksntalks.com.

♦ **Secrets of the Mysterious Maligne Valley** – A winter tour that includes a scenic drive, canyon walk, snowshoeing or cross-country skiing. Adult $60, child $35.

♦ **Columbia Icefield Tour** – Includes walks at the icy waterfalls and the icefield. Adult $80, child $45.

Birding Tours in Jasper (On-Line Sport), ☎ 780-852-3630 or online@incenter.net, 600 Patricia Street.

♦ Jasper National Park is home to about 300 species with 82 songbird species that regularly breed in the park. Have you ever seen a bufflehead duck or a magnolia warbler? **Birding tours** consist of a three-hour introduction, a half-day tour or birding by boat. Prices start at $69 per person. All tours include a Parks Canada licensed birding guide, transportation and use of binoculars.

Currie's Guiding, ☎ 780-852-5650, at Jasper Source for Sports, 406 Patricia Street, www.curriesguidingjasper.com.

♦ Offers **guided fishing trips and fly fishing instruction** from April through October, fishing a variety of lakes and rivers in the park. A full day of fly-fishing includes transportation, instruction, equipment and lunch, $189 per person, based on two people. A full-day alpine hike-in trip is the same price.

Horseback Riding

 **Pyramid Riding Stables,** ☎ 780-852-3562, Pyramid Lake Road. Circular trails with spectacular views. Pony, carriage, and wagon rides also available. Winter activities include sleigh rides and dine-and-ride packages.

Jasper National Park

◆ One-hour trail rides with vistas of the Athabasca River Valley, $27-$30 per person.

◆ Two-hour trail rides along the open ridgeline of Cottonwood Creek where you'll see beaver dams, waterfowl and woodland life, $51.

◆ A three-hour ride includes the above as well as a ride through the rolling terrain that overlooks the Pyramid Bench, $70.

◆ The full day ride meanders through the scenic area past Cabin Lake with a picnic lunch at Saturday Night Lake; return via Riley and Mina Lakes, $125.

Skyline Trail Rides, ☎ 888-852-7787 or 780-852-4215, Jasper Park Lodge, www.skylinetrail.com. Pony, wagon and winter sleigh rides as well as horse assisted hiking trips also available.

◆ One or 1½-hour trail rides to Lake Annette $35 or $45.

◆ Two-hour valley view rides $55.

◆ Canyon tours of 4½ hours $99.

◆ Three or four-day pack trips on the Skyline Trail, including accommodation, meals, horses and guide, July through September, $540 per person, four-day $700 per person.

Tonquin Valley Pack and Ski Trips, ☎ 780-852-3909, www.tonquinvalley.com

◆ Horseback trips to the Tonquin Valley Backcountry Lodge, 33 km (20 miles) southwest of Jasper, accessible only by hiking, skiing or horseback riding. Five-day horse trip includes guide, accommodation, meals, boat and canoe use on beautiful Amethyst Lake as well as daily horse rides, $850 per person.

Whitewater Rafting

 Jasper whitewater outfitters run the Athabasca River from May through September with gentle floats and short but lively Class 2+ rapids, good for first-time rafters and families. The more thrilling Sunwapta River (meaning "turbulent river") is run from June through August with Class 3 challenges. For the real

thrill-seekers, the Fraser and Kakwa Rivers offer up to Class 4 rapids.

The following are all members of the Jasper National Park Professional River Outfitters' Association.

Rocky Mountain River Guides, ☎ 780-852-3777, www.rmriverguides.com. All raft trips start and finish at 626 Connaught Drive.

Athabasca River Run, Daily two-hour run provides exceptional vistas of the mountains with Class 2 rapids, suitable for all ages and abilities. Adult $45, child under 12 years $25.

The Canyon Run, a 3-hour trip suitable for everyone over the age of 6. Adult $60, child $30.

◆ The most popular trip and "the best whitewater in Jasper" is a Class 3 intermediate run on the Sunwapta River. No age limit, however children must weigh a minimum of 40 kilos (90 lbs). Twice daily departures, $65 per person.

◆ Multi-day expedition trips start at $500 per person for three days/two nights.

Whitewater Rafting Jasper, ☎ 800-557-7238 or 780-852-7238, www.whitewaterraftingjasper.com. Departures from Jasper townsite, Jasper Park Lodge and near Sunwapta Falls Resort.

◆ **Athabasca Falls** – A 3½-hour, 12-km/7.2-mile run beginning at the base of Athabasca Falls, with numerous Class 2 rapids, departures twice daily. $60 per person, child (six-12 years) $30, third and subsequent children $14.50.

◆ **The Heritage Route** – A six- to seven-hour, 30-km/18-mile customized run with "unparalleled scenery," includes lunch; advance bookings for groups of six or more. $110 per person.

Jasper Raft Tours, ☎ 888-553-5628 or 780-852-2665, www.jasperrafttours.com.

◆ A mellow family-oriented 16-km, 2½-hour run on the Athabasca River with calm stretches and small sets of rapids in large 24-passenger oar rafts. Daily departures from May 15 to September 30 from Jasper Park

Jasper National Park

Lodge and the train station. Adult $47, child under 16 years $15, children under six free.

Maligne Rafting Adventures, 627 Patricia Street, ☎ 866-625-4463 or 780-852-3370, www.mra.ab.ca.

◆ **Fraser Rearguard Run** – A five-hour round-trip through exhilarating rapids and a short portage around Rearguard Falls. $72/person.

Other river trips include gentle floats in large boats for groups of 10 or more, inflatable kayaking for small groups of four or more, and wilderness and overnight trips.

Mountain Biking & Bicycle Touring

 The Jasper region offers ample opportunity to take to the trails on a bicycle, with many of the hiking trails open to cyclists. A number of sports stores in town offer mountain bike rentals, including high-end full suspension bikes (see the *Sports & Camping Equipment Rentals* section).

One of the most popular trail rides begins at **Old Fort Point** and follows the **Athabasca River** to a point below **Maligne Canyon (Trail 7)**.

Pyramid Bench is a tangle of official and unofficial wooded trails that start from the townsite and lead to a bench (plateau) northwest of the townsite. It's studded with more than 20 lakes or tarns (glacially carved basins) with splendid views across the Athabasca Valley.

If touring is your preference, the **Icefields Parkway tour** between Jasper and Lake Louise attracts cyclists from around the world for what is considered to be one of the best short bicycle tours in the world (see the *Icefields Parkway* chapter).

 Stop at the Visitor Information Center for the brochures titled *Summer Trails* and *Other Mountain Biking Trails*, along with excellent advice.

Lake Boating & Fishing

 Boating in rowboats, canoes and kayaks is allowed on most of the ponds and lakes in the park. Boats with electric motors (without on-board generators) are allowed on most road-accessible lakes. Pyramid Lake is the only lake in Jasper where gas-powered motorboats are permitted.

The park has a variety of fish, including pike, rocky mountain whitefish, rainbow trout, lake trout, brook trout and bull trout. They average two to four lbs, although much larger fish are caught, including a 20½-lb rainbow (Alberta record) and a 12.8-lb brook trout.

Maligne Lake is Jasper's best-known fishing hole for record-size rainbow trout, as well as brook trout. In the spring and fall, Medicine Lake also offers good rainbow trout fishing. According to locals, **Talbot Lake**, along Highway 16 east of Jasper, and **Moab Lake**, southwest of town from the Moab Lake Road Junction off of Highway 93A, offer good fishing.

For helpful advice, visit area sports stores. See the *Sports & Camping Equipment Rentals* section for stores in Jasper townsite that rent boats and fishing equipment and offer guided fishing trips. Also see the *Tour Operators & Booking Agents* section for information on guided fishing trips.

Pyramid Lake Boat Rentals, ☎ 780-852-4944. Motorboat, rowboat, kayak, sailboat and fishing rod rentals.

The Boat House at Maligne Lake, ☎ 780-852-3370. Rowboats and canoes for rent, $15/hour or $70/day, kayaks $20/hour or $85/day, canoes with electric motors $90/day, as well as fishing rods. Use caution as Maligne Lake is subject to high winds and waves.

The Jasper Lake Lodge Marina on Lac Beauvert, ☎ 780-852-5708. Canoe, kayak and pedal boat rentals, $20-35 per hour.

VISITOR SITES IN 1945

"When we had guests, the first day we would do the customary circle tour, taking the old road to the Lodge and climbing to read the cairn at Old Fort

Point. This gave our visitors a taste of mountain climbing, as there were no steps or guard rails.Then we would clamber back into the car and drive around Lac Beauvert, stopping to see the breathtaking colors, before driving around Jasper Park Lodge. Usually we included a turn to the right, just past the garages, to the Lodge dump, where the bears foraged for their meals. To our guests, this was frequently the highlight of the trip, because, often there were six or seven bears and occasionally a grizzly.

Then we continued around Lake Annette and around Lake Edith, where there were no barriers to this beautiful drive, eventually coming out to the road that leads to Maligne Canyon. To the left of the turn-in to the fifth bridge, we visited the beaver pond, a little lake with several beavers and their homes. Years later, they were all poached and the pond had dried up.

The road to the canyon was one that thrilled our guests, having some of the sharpest switchbacks that could be handled by a car. Some of our visitors threatened to get out and walk before we arrived at the canyon. That canyon had no guard rails, and certainly we gave the children a good warning and we hung onto their hands fiercely when we walked across the first and second bridges. I was never nervous while there, but sometimes I had nightmares about the trip after the fact.

Following that frustrating but awe-inspiring experience, it was time for a cup of coffee. You could get one in the tea room for 15¢, but that was expensive for a cup of coffee that was just 10¢ downtown – so you brought out the thermos and treated the adults, and got a drink of water from the Maligne River for the children.

On the way down, we stopped where the look-out is now. There was no fence so we had to be careful to view the sheep there. Then we drove the harrowing switchbacks again, before a stop at the fifth bridge, one of the most rustic of the bridges at that time.

The next stop would be at the fish hatchery, now the wardens' headquarters. Millions of fish, mostly trout, of all sizes were cultured and raised in the hatchery. These fish were later planted in the surrounding lakes and made fishing in Jasper a worthwhile sport.

The sixth bridge was always a good spot for a picnic lunch, because, here the children could play in the open field without having to be held back. It was legal to build a bonfire as long as discretion was used and great care was taken in putting it out before leaving.

By this time we had seen an osprey's nest, a lobstick (a tree stripped of all branches except those near the top), some deer, lots of bears and a few sheep if we had been lucky. Quite an outing, for one day." (From *Jasper A Backward Glance*, by Nora Findlay, 1992 (courtesy Friends of Jasper National Park and Jasper-Yellowhead Historical Society).

Jasper National Park

Drives, Sights, Activities & Hikes

Patricia & Pyramid Lakes

Drive: eight km (five miles) from town.

Watchable wildlife: deer, elk, moose, bighorn sheep, bears, beavers, muskrats and a variety of birds at Cottonwood Slough.

The Pyramid Lake Road provides access to Patricia and Pyramid Lakes in an area called the Pyramid Bench. Turn onto Cedar Avenue, which becomes Pyramid

Patricia Lake

Lake Road, from Connaught Drive. The road wanders through a Douglas-fir forest, follows the east shore of Patricia Lake and ends at Pyramid Lake, which is a glacially carved basin called a tarn. A footbridge leads to Pyramid Island (wheelchair-accessible) in the middle of the lake – a fine spot for picnicking – with a dramatic view of Pyramid Mountain, shining orange-red in the sun due to its iron-rich quartzite.

Although Patricia Lake is smaller in size than Pyramid Lake, it is more than twice as deep at 40 m (131 feet). Try the easy 4.8-km (three-mile) walk around the lake. Boat, bicycle and fishing rentals are available at Patricia Lake Bungalows and Pyramid Lake Resort – see Accommodations or Lake Boating & Fishing sections.

Old Fort Point Loop

Hike: 3½-km (two-mile) loop.

Watchable wildlife: bighorn sheep, mule deer, grouse.

To the east of Jasper townsite is a distinctive grassy knoll above the Athabasca River with 360° views of the Athabasca and Miette Valleys, Mt. Edith Cavell to the west and Pyramid Mountain looming over Jasper townsite. The name Old Fort Point is deceiving as a fort is not likely to have been located here. Henry House was located downstream, however. Take Hazel Avenue south at its intersection with Connaught Drive, cross the train tracks and the Yellowhead Highway. Turn left on the Lac Beauvert Road and cross the bridge over the Athabasca River to reach the parking lot. Take the wooden stairs that lead to a cairn, commemorating explorer David Thompson. Follow the sign for Trail No. 1 to the left, which circles back to the parking lot. From here you can also make the loop hike around Lac Beauvert.

The lookout is worthwhile but I found the forest hike boring.

Jasper Tramway

☎ 780-852-3093, www.jaspertramway.com

Drive: seven km (4.3 miles) from town & 2.2 km (1.4 mile) round-trip optional hike.

Watchable wildlife: hoary marmot, golden mantled squirrel, chipmunk, pika, white-tailed ptarmigan, woodland caribou.

The Whistlers, the dome-shaped mountain southeast of the townsite, is named for the whistling sound made by the hoary marmots that inhabit the area. The easiest way to reach the 2,285-m (7,500-foot) ridge summit so you can enjoy the views of the Athabasca and Miette Valleys is to ride the Jasper Tramway for its seven-minute climb up 937 vertical m (3,074 feet). This is Canada's longest and highest aerial tramway.

Make sure you are well dressed, as the tram takes you from forested valley bottom to the alpine level and if you are energetic, you can walk the 1.4-km (.9-mile) trail to the 2,464-m (8,085-foot) summit. Enjoy the vista of six mountain ranges and, on a clear day, views of Mt. Robson 80 km (50 miles) to the northwest.

Tread carefully as the harsh conditions make survival of the plants here a miraculous feat. Vegetation clings closely to the ground to reduce exposure to the wind and blooms are short-lived. Avoid stepping off the trail as a single wayward footstep can destroy in a second a decade of struggle for an alpine plant.

The tramway is three km (two miles) south of the townsite on Highway 93 and four km (2½ miles) up Whistlers Road. The best time to go is early evening (dusk) for photographing as well as for avoiding the crowds at this busy attraction. Restaurant and gift shop at the top.

Open March to October; ask for current first/last departure times. Wheelchair-accessible to the upper terminus. Adult $21, child (five-14 years) $10, family (two adults & two children) $52.

Lake Edith & Lake Annette

Drive: Five km (three miles) from town.

Watchable wildlife: deer, elk, loons.

Drive east on Highway 16 to the Maligne Lake Road and follow the signs towards Jasper Park Lodge. Remnants of a large lake that once covered the valley floor, these two day-use area lakes are popular for picnicking (picnic tables and barbecue grills are available), walking, bird- and wildlife watching. Because they are relatively shallow, they have the warmest waters of any of the lakes in Jasper Park – perfect for swimming and splashing about on a hot day. The wheel-

Jasper National Park

chair-accessible 2½-km (1½-mile) interpretive trail encircling Lake Annette affords good views of the Main Ranges and the Colin Ranges.

You can also access Lake Edith if you bypass the signs to Jasper Park Lodge and take the first subsequent right turn off of the Maligne Lake Road. This leads to a residential area on the lake plus access to the lake and its walking and biking trails.

Lac Beauvert

Walk: 3½-km (two-mile) loop

Watchable wildlife: elk, Canada geese

A leisurely stroll from Jasper Park Lodge around horseshoe-shaped Lac Beauvert – "beautiful green lake." Drive east on Highway 16 to Maligne Lake Road and follow the signs to Jasper Park Lodge. **Trail 4A** leads past the lodge, initially along a paved path then a forest trail, through the golf course and back to the lodge. At the end of the lake, where the trail connects to Old Fort Point, scuba divers enjoy the lake's clear waters.

Maligne Valley

Perhaps the most popular drive in Jasper, this 48-km (30-mile) journey is worth a full day. Explore Maligne Canyon and both Maligne and Medicine Lakes.

 The name Maligne, French for "wicked," was given to the river by Jesuit missionary Pierre Jean de Smet in 1846 when he endured a particularly difficult crossing – "la traverse maligne."

Five kilometres (three miles) east of the townsite, the Maligne Lake Road intersects the Yellowhead Highway and immediately crosses the Athabasca River. At 2.3 km (1.4 miles) a 1.6-km (one-mile) side-road leads to **Sixth Bridge Picnic Area** beside the Maligne River, with the confluence of the Maligne and Athabasca Rivers a short stroll downstream. This picnic area has been a favorite of mine since I was a child. Sixth Bridge, well below the actual canyon, is the final footbridge that spans Maligne Canyon, starting with the First Bridge at the top. (See Maligne Canyon walk and hike below.)

The **Athabasca Valley Viewpoint** at Km 6 (Mile 3.7) is a worthwhile stop for a panoramic view of the valley. Maligne Canyon is about one km farther along the road. The teahouse and gift shop are open from April through October.

For about 11,000 years, the Maligne River has carved a spectacular gorge from limestone bedrock. At two km (1.2 miles) long and 55 m (180 feet) deep, it is the longest and deepest limestone canyon in the Rockies and is being made deeper by about half a centimetre each year.

Winter is a unique time to visit Maligne Canyon. Usually, by late December the Maligne River is frozen solid, creating incredible ice formations throughout the canyon. A number of tour companies offer guided icewalk tours through this magical place.

Maligne Canyon

Walk: .8 km (.5 miles) or

Hike: 3.7 km (2.3 miles) one-way.

For a quick look at the canyon, begin at the lower end of the busy parking lot. The first section to the First Bridge is wheelchair-accessible. The securely fenced interpretive trail follows along the canyon edge. Use extreme caution and closely supervise small children.

You can begin the Maligne Canyon hike in the parking lot at the upper end of the canyon usually overrun with tourists. Or, begin at the lower end at the confluence of the Maligne and Athabasca Rivers and you will be able to walk downhill on your return, enjoying the most peaceful sections of the canyon before encountering the hoards at the upper canyon. On this route you gain a better appreciation of how the canyon was formed. Access from the lower canyon is at Sixth Bridge Picnic Area. It's a gradual climb to Fifth Bridge at 1.6 km (one mile), after which the trail becomes steeper as you climb to Fourth Bridge, the 2.9-km (1.8-mile) mark. Third Bridge at 3.1 km (1.9 miles) is the deepest (55 m or 180 feet) and most unusual section of the canyon. It is incredibly narrow. Third Bridge to First Bridge and the parking lot is usually quite congested and completes the hike.

Jasper National Park

One of the most intriguing features of this journey is **Medicine Lake**, or the disappearing lake, as it is often referred to. With no visible outlet stream, rather an underground drainage system of caves, the level of the lake fluctuates dramatically over the course of the year. In the spring and early summer, the lake level rises due to runoff; by late summer the runoff has slowed and the water level drops. In late autumn all that remains are a few shallow pools on a mud flat. Native legend has it that spirits were responsible for this strange occurrence. Between Maligne Canyon and Medicine Lake, the Maligne River often disappears underground for long stretches, leaving only the dry riverbed visible.

Photo 10: Medicine Lake

Watchable Wildlife

The Maligne Lake Road is one of the best for viewing wildlife in the Rockies. Moose, elk and woodland caribou may be spotted in the mud flats of Medicine Lake when the water level has dropped. Watch for bighorn sheep between Medicine Lake and Maligne Lake as well as moose that frequent the wet roadside meadows. Deer, grizzly bear and black bear are also commonly seen in this area. The Maligne River is easily accessible from the road so birdwatchers can stop anywhere to spot American dippers and harlequin ducks.

Like a pot of gold at the end of a rainbow, Maligne Lake sits auspiciously at the end of the road. The largest glacier-fed lake in the Canadian Rockies (second-largest in the world) stretches 22 km (13.7 miles) through the mountains of the Front Ranges. Its existence is due to a rockslide that created a natural dam about 11,000 years ago. Roughly 15 km (nine miles) to the south end of the lake is **Samson Narrows**, an alluvial fan – a fan-shaped deposit of sediment – that nearly cuts the lake in half. As a result, you cannot see the end of the lake from the visitor complex on the northwest shore.

Maligne Lake is a popular day-use area for all seasons. Non-motorized boating, fishing, hiking and picnicking are enjoyed throughout the summer. Two backcountry campgrounds are accessible from Maligne Lake. **Maligne Tours** offers 90-minute scenic boat tours up the lake (see *Tour Operators & Booking Agents* section) and, unless you are an experienced paddler, it is the only way to see famous Spirit Island. Boat rentals are available at the **Maligne Lake Boathouse** (see *Lake Boating & Fishing* section), built by guide and outfitter Curly Phillips in 1929. Today it is a Provincially Registered Historical Site. A souvenir shop and café (both overpriced) are also part of the busy complex.

Maligne Tours provides an information sheet with a map and overview of the many day-hikes in the Maligne Lake area, including short lake trail walks that permit exploration of the shoreline. The two main parking areas at the lake provide access to the trails.

Women of the Rockies – Mary Schäffer

Only the most tenacious souls dared brave the uncharted wilds of the Canadian Rockies and even fewer women defied convention and ventured down the path of exploration that was considered a man's domain.

Mary Sharples, a bold Quaker woman from Philadelphia, spent summers exploring the Rockies, where she met Dr. Charles Schäffer, a botanist. They married in 1889 and together returned to the Rockies until his death in 1903.

In 1908, using directions from Samson Beaver, a Stoney Native, Schäffer, her guide Billy Warren and a small group, along with 22 horses, made their way from what is now Lake Louise to a mysterious lake Samson called "Chaba Imne," or "Beaver Lake," now known as Maligne Lake. This was only the second recorded visit to the lake and the fist visit by a non-native woman. The group built a makeshift raft and spent several days exploring, mapping and naming the mountains. Schäffer returned again in 1911 for further exploration. In 1913 she moved to Banff and two years later married Billy Warren.

A talented writer, photographer and artist, Schäffer wrote *Old Indian Trails of the Canadian Rockies*, an account of her travels. In 1980, the book was republished as *A Hunter of Peace*.

Mary Schäffer sums up her remarkable determination and the role of privileged women of her day in the following excerpt from *Old Indian Trails* (originally published by G.P. Putnam's Sons, New York, 1911):

"There are few women who do not know their privileges and how to use them, yet there are times when the horizon seems restricted, and we seemed to have reached that horizon, and the limit of all endurance, to sit with folded hands and listen calmly to the stories of the hills we so longed to see, the hills which had lured and beckoned us for years before this long list of men had ever set foot in the country. Our cups splashed over. Then we looked into each other's eyes and said: Why not? We can starve as well as they; the muskeg will be no softer for us than for them; the ground will be no harder to sleep upon; the waters no deeper to swim, nor the bath colder if we fall in.... So we planned a trip."

Opal Hills

Hike: eight-km (five-mile) loop.

Elevation gain: 460 m (1,509 feet).

Watchable wildlife: moose, squirrels, marmots.

If you want to escape the crowds at Maligne Lake and want an excellent overview of the entire Maligne Valley, don't miss this hike. The trailhead is located behind the information board in the upper parking lot at Maligne Lake. Don't be discouraged initially, as the trail climbs very steeply through a forest for 1½ km (.9 miles) to a junction. Then you can take your pick – the trail to the right is steeper but shorter. As the climbing gets easier, the view gets better. In July and August the meadows are filled with wildflowers. You'll see views of the Bald Hills directly across the valley and Maligne Range across Maligne Lake. The unique Opal Hills, named by Mary Schäffer for their pink patches, rise above the trail summit to the east. The view of the hills alone makes this hike worthwhile for me. Bring a sweater, as it gets windy and cold at the top. The trail can be treacherously slippery when wet.

Miette Hot Springs Road

Drive: 17 km (10½ miles).

Watchable wildlife: black bears along the road, bighorn sheep in the pool parking lot area.

The scenic Miette Hot Spring Road – open mid-May to mid-October – is approximately 61 km (38 miles) east of Jasper townsite. At the Hot Springs Road junction, you'll find the Pocahontas Cabins, a trailer drop-off area and the (wheelchair-accessible) trailhead leading to **Old Pocahontas**, the remnants of the abandoned coal mining development, named for the Pocahontas Coalfield in Virginia. The mine operated for 11 years until 1921 when it was shut down after the railway tracks were moved to the other side of the valley and the mine was no longer profitable. The history itself is interesting, but the interpretive trail is not particularly exciting, nor is the view of Punchbowl Falls, 1.3 km (.8 miles) up the road. **Pocahontas Campground** at Km 2.2 (Mile 1.3) is the only campground in the eastern part of Jasper Park. The road follows the **Fiddle River Valley**, where spectacular **Ashlar Ridge**, a sheer 300-m (1,000-foot) wall of limestone, rises from the valley; be sure to stop at the viewpoint at Km 8.9 (Mile 5½).

Miette Hot Springs probably became known to fur traders in the 19th century after local Natives introduced them to the three springs in Sulphur Creek's narrow valley. There is a brief historical reference to an Iroquois/Metis visit to the "volcanic springs" in 1850. In 1910, the year the town of Pocahontas was established, a crude horse trail brought a few people to the squalid springs. Determined to bathe in the healing waters, ironically several people died along the long journey to the springs. In 1919, during a six-week union strike at Pocahontas, the miners built the first log pool at the springs. Proposals to build a sanatorium at the hot springs were not entertained until a road from Pocahontas to the springs was opened in 1935. The now-ruined aquacourt opened in 1938 and the road was upgraded. The present facilities were opened in 1986.

The three hot springs that issue from Sulphur Creek's banks are cooled from a scalding 53.9°C (129°F) – the hottest of the three Canadian Rockies hot springs – to a comfortable 39°C (102°F) as they enter two outdoor soaking pools. There is also one cold plunge pool.

One of the most fascinating attractions at Miette Hot Springs is the short walk to view the source of the springs and the remains of the original aquacourt. From the end of the parking area and picnic area on the right, follow the paved path across Sulphur Creek to the old aquacourt. While standing in the remains of the aquacourt, it's easy to picture a bygone era when bathers basked in the warmth of the sulphurous springs. Two of the springs are not accessible but, to see the third and hottest spring, continue up the trail on the boardwalk about 200 m (656 feet). The hot water issues from cracks in the bedrock and flows into an open cement basin. Interpretive signs explain how the springs work.

If you continue on the trail, it crosses the creek and climbs to Sulphur Pass and beyond on a backpacking trail.

Miette Hot Springs, ☎ 780-866-3939, is open from May 1 to October 11. Summer hours (mid-June to early September) are daily from 8:30 am to 10:30 pm and spring/fall hours are daily from 10:30 am to 9 pm. Single admission adult $6.25, child or senior $5.25, family (two adults, two children) $18.75. Wheelchair-accessible. A gift shop as well as the reasonably priced Ashlar Ridge Café is on site.

Sulphur Skyline

Hike: 9.4 km (5.8 miles) round-trip.

Elevation gain: 700 m (2,296 feet).

Watchable wildlife: golden-mantled ground squirrels, bighorn sheep, ptarmigan.

This is one of the best half-day hikes in Jasper Park and a good early season trail. The 360° panorama overlooking remote wilderness valleys, including the Fiddle River to the southeast, the Miette Range to the south and west and Ashlar Ridge to the north, is well worth the effort to reach the summit. One of the added features of this hike is that you can soak your muscles in the hot springs when you return.

The trail begins on the right side of the hot springs complex entrance and follows a paved path for a short distance. Soon the climb is steady for about two km (1.2 miles) to a junction at Shuey Pass, where you turn right and begin a more serious climb. The trail switchbacks through forest and open slopes before reaching the ridge summit at 2,050 m (6,725 feet).

Bring plenty of water as well as a sweater, since it's very windy at the top. From the summit I've had the pleasure of closely observing herds of bighorn sheep as well as almost stumbling upon flocks of ptarmigan.

Jasper Lake & Talbot Lake Sand Dunes

The Jasper Lake and Talbot Lake Sand Dunes are a well-kept secret despite being in full view; most people never really notice them until they're brought to their attention. I was thrilled to discover this unusual attraction in Jasper Park, especially when my first visit to the dunes was on a hot summer day. My camera did overtime while I explored the dunes and photographed them against the stunning backdrop of mountains and lakes. And, best of all, there were few people around.

Sand dunes are one of the last things you might expect to see in a Canadian Rockies Mountain Park. But, on both sides of the Yellowhead Highway east of Jasper townsite, that is what you will find for a long distance. In fact, the highway is actually built on a natural curving causeway that separates Jasper Lake on the north side and Talbot Lake on the south. Interestingly, Alberta contains half of the dune area in Canada.

Sand dunes, mounds or ridges of sand, are formed by strong winds. The sand actually comes from the site of Jasper Lake, which thousands of years ago was much larger. Over time, the lake drained and sand and silt were exposed to strong winds.

This process of sand and silt settling out continues today as the level of Jasper Lake fluctuates with the melting of glaciers. Jasper Lake is not really a lake, but rather a portion of the Athabasca River, and its level fluctuates with the river.

There are a series of pullouts along the highway where motorists can park and explore the dunes. Be sure to wear your bathing suit to enjoy the shallow waters and keep an eye out for identifying animal tracks in the sand – the area is popular with wildlife and birds.

Highway 93A

This peaceful (and bumpy) stretch of old highway parallels the new highway for 24 km (15 miles) before it rejoins the Icefields Parkway at Athabasca Falls. Winding along the forested west side of the Athabasca Valley, it provides access to many picnic areas and hiking trails as well as the Marmot Basin ski area and Mount Edith Cavell.

Mount Edith Cavell

One of the most accessible, well-known and busy subalpine and alpine areas of the park. At 3,363 m (11,030 feet), classically horn-shaped Mount Edith Cavell is the highest mountain visible from the Jasper townsite. Named for Edith Cavell, a British nurse who remained in Brussels to treat allied wounded soldiers after World War I and was executed as a spy by the Germans in 1915. The fur trade voyageurs called this easily recognized landmark "Great White Mountain" or "La Montagne de la Grande Traverse," (the mountain of the great crossing) in reference to the crossing of the Athabasca River that lay ahead. The Angel Glacier and four other glaciers that at one time clung to her slopes sculpted deep bowl-shaped amphitheatres – known as cirques – on her face. The bottom and right arm of Angel Glacier's robe has diminished considerably.

From Jasper townsite take the Icefields Parkway south seven km (4.3 miles), turn right on Highway 93A and continue on it for 5½ km (3.4 miles) to the Cavell Road junction. The Cavell Road is open late June to October. Vehicles longer than seven m (23 feet) are not permitted to use the road as it is rough, steep and twisting. (There is a parking lot at the junction.) The road climbs 550 m (1,804 feet) along the Astoria River

Valley for 14½ km (nine miles) to the parking area beneath Mount Edith Cavell. To avoid the crowds, visit Mount Edith Cavell before 10 am or after 4 pm. The Cavell Meadows hike can be accomplished in two hours, but I suggest a half-day to fully explore the area.

Cavell Meadows

Hike: 6.1 km (3.8 mile) loop.

Elevation gain: 400 m (1,312 feet).

Begin at the upper edge of the parking area on the paved Path of the Glacier Trail (see below). The trail climbs over a ridge of lateral moraine, marking the farthest extent of the most recent advance of the glacier. Visitors can sit along the moraine ridge and enjoy the close-up views. Cavell Pond, a large emerald-colored pool at the base of Angel Glacier, has only formed in the past 35 years. At Km 2.2 (Mile 1.3) the trail splits for the loop through the meadows; if you stay right the ascent is more gradual. A popular spot to stop for lunch is when you reach the viewpoint for Angel Glacier and Mount Edith Cavell. The trail veers left and climbs to a summit. You can return through the meadows to finish the loop or continue to climb for panoramic views.

Be careful where you tread in Cavell Meadows! The Friends of Jasper National Park have been working very hard over three consecutive summers to reverse the damage caused by years of off-trail hiking. (The project was the winner of an Alberta Tourism award.) Help protect and conserve this special place.

Path of the Glacier

Walk: 1.6-km (one-mile) loop.

An easy interpretive loop that travels through the glacial basin of Cavell Pond. It's a unique vantage point for the Angel Glacier and Mount Edith Cavell.

Hollywood in the Rockies

Since 1919, movie producers have been coming to the Canadian Rockies for much the same reason tourists come today – the dramatic scenery. The Rockies have been the backdrop for hundreds of films that depict such rugged mountain locations as

Jasper National Park

Alaska, Montana and Colorado. In the summer of 1953, two major Hollywood productions with large crews and famous actors descended upon Jasper National Park. *The Far Country* with Jimmy Stewart, Ruth Roman and Walter Brennan was billed as a film about the Klondike gold rush but is more of a typical American Western.

Locations included the Columbia Icefields, along the Athabasca River east of Jasper and Mount Edith Cavell, where Stewart panned for gold in the stream beneath Angel Glacier.

River of No Return with Marilyn Monroe and Robert Mitchum was a Gold Rush Western/musical with locations at Moberly Flats and Maligne Canyon. One review questioned whether it was the scenery of the Canadian Rockies or Monroe that was the greater attraction.

Jasper was also utilized in another 1953 film, the remake of the classic movie *Rose Marie*, starring Howard Keel and Ann Blyth. Filming took place near the townsite and Lac Beauvert.

In those early days, there were few rules and regulations so filmmakers were given exclusive use of an area. Today, policies and regulations limit the use of National Parks so as to minimize impact on park resources and visitors.

Winter Adventures

The not-to-be-missed Maligne Canyon icewalk provides an incredible perspective. **Pyramid Lake** is a popular area for snowshoeing, cross-country skiing and ice skating.

See *Jasper Park's Winter Trails* brochure for details on walking, snowshoeing and cross-country skiing trails in the area. Don't forget to stop in at the Visitor Information Center for up-to-date avalanche-hazard reports and trail conditions.

Alpine Skiing

Marmot Basin, ☎ 780-852-3816, www.skimarmot.com or www.skijaspercanada.com. With a capacity of 11,000 people per hour but with typically only 3,000 to 4,000 people on the slopes, lift-lines are virtually unheard of at Marmot Basin, an underrated world-class ski resort. Nine lifts, including two high-speed quads, one triple, three doubles and three surface lifts service 1,675 acres (678 hectares) with a vertical rise of 914 m (3,000 feet). Eighty-four marked trails – 30% novice, 30% intermediate, 40% expert – provide skiing for every experience level with 100% natural snow. The longest run is 5.6 km (3½ miles). The two main peaks are **Caribou Ridge** and **Marmot Peak**, with new runs developed on **Eagle Ridge**. Three separate lodges on the mountain provide a variety of food services; lessons, rentals, daycare and mountain tours are also available. During the annual "Jasper in January" festival, lift ticket rates are reduced and a number of special events take place.

It's located about 19 km (12 miles) southeast of Jasper townsite on Highway 93A. Most hotels have shuttle service to the hill. The season runs from November to April. Lift tickets: adult $55.14, youth (13-17 years) $43.93, junior (six-12 years) $18.69, senior $39.25. Multi-day lift ticket discounts and ski and stay packages available; ski school. Ask at the front desk of your hotel for discounted lift tickets.

Jasper National Park

Nordic Skiing

Some of Jasper's fabulous hiking trails can also be enjoyed on skis in winter. One of the largest areas for cross-country skiing in Canada, approximately 100 km (62 miles) of groomed trails and 200 km (124 miles) of un-groomed trails are designated for cross-country skiers of all abilities. The **Whistlers Campground Loop** is an easy 4½-km (2.8-mile) trail that is lit for night skiing. Other ski areas include **Maligne Lake**, **Pyramid Bench**, the **Athabasca Falls** area, **Edith Cavell Road** and **The Fairmont Jasper Park Lodge area**.

Outdoor Ice Skating

Lac Beauvert, **Mildred Lake** and **Pyramid Lake** have areas cleared for ice skating.

Travel Reflections – Winter Wanderings

We were hoping the weather might warm up enough to hit the slopes at Marmot Basin but when it hit minus 50°F with the wind chill, and one of the furnaces quit at the hostel, we knew we'd have to adjust our plans. "Jasper in January isn't usually this cold," we were told. Nevertheless, we were booked into the hostel for five days and I wasn't about to cancel all of our plans and head home with my (frozen) tail between my legs, so to speak, just because of a little cold weather. Part of my travel philosophy is "be prepared and don't let the weather stop you," notwithstanding natural disasters, of course. We had packed plenty of warm clothing, our car was winterized and we were happy to be in Jasper, despite the deep freeze.

So off we went to Maligne Canyon. I first visited Maligne Canyon, one of Jasper's most popular attractions, with my photography class in high school and I've returned many times since then, always during the summer months. Watching the rushing torrent of water through the canyon from high above on the viewing bridges is always engrossing but I had never entertained the thought of actually walking along the frozen Maligne River canyon floor. But that's precisely what I was doing and what a thrill it was to look up at the canyon walls instead of looking down! In a state of awe, we cautiously made our way around the ice-clad limestone walls and sparkling ice falls, like slow-motion mice in a frozen maze. Looking skyward at the elusive sun extending its rays down the canyon floor, the icewalk experience was a highlight, it alone making the winter journey worthwhile.

The frigid weather did not deter us from leaving the cozy surroundings of the hostel the following day. Despite the dropping temperatures (yes, it got even colder) the sun shone brilliantly as we drove the Pyramid Lake Road to Pyramid Lake. Bundled up in many layers from head to toe with only our eyes visible, we braved the cold as we walked from the parking lot to Pyramid Island, the only sounds our heavy breathing and the crunch of our boots against the snow. A solitary soul made his way across the lake on snowshoes. Too cold for a picnic on the island, we retreated to the confines of our warm car and peeled away our top layers of clothing.

During the next few days we continued our winter travels in Jasper Park, having the opportunity to see unique winter sights such as Athabasca and Sunwapta Falls, suspended in their frozen winter state. Maligne Lake, a magnet for tourists during the summer months, lay silent under the ice and snow, as if taking a well-deserved rest.

After four days, with skis untouched, we made our way home, stopping only for fuel and to watch a moose that had bedded down in the deep snow. Self-satisfied in being amongst the minority of travelers who avail themselves of popular summer sights during the winter, we returned home with the knowledge that we had survived and thrived.

Jasper National Park

SCENIC MUST-SEE'S

 Here are suggestions for the first-time summer visitor on a four-day schedule. Remember to bring along a camera and binoculars for the many wildlife viewing and photographical opportunities on these adventures.

Day 1: Explore the Maligne Valley with stops at **Maligne Canyon**, **Medicine Lake** and **Maligne Lake**. Bring a picnic lunch to enjoy at any of the stops of interest along the route or at Maligne Lake. Take a boat cruise to **Spirit Island** or, if you're energetic and want to escape the crowds at the lake, hike the **Opal Hills Trail** in the late afternoon and return before dark.

Day 2: Take a scenic morning drive to **Miette Hotsprings**. Hike the **Sulphur Skyline Trail** then soak your muscles in the springs. Afterwards, walk the path to view the old aquacourt and the source of the springs.

Day 3: Delight in the thrills of whitewater rafting on one of Jasper's rivers (pre-book a tour). Select from one of Jasper's many mouth-watering restaurants for lunch and afterwards enjoy some shopping and sights downtown. Take an early evening stroll around the **Valley of the Five Lakes** (see *Icefields Parkway* chapter).

Day 4: Drive to **Mount Edith Cavell** and hike **Cavell Meadows** in the morning when the light on Angel Glacier is best for photographing and before it gets too busy. Spend the afternoon visiting some of Jasper's attractions, such as the **Jasper-Yellowhead Museum** or drive up to **Pyramid Bench** at dusk for wildlife viewing.

If you're not into rafting or hiking, spend a day (or more) driving the **Icefields Parkway** (see *Icefields Parkway* chapter).

DID YOU KNOW?

In the Canadian Rockies, the warmest hot springs are...

- **Miette Hot Springs**, Jasper National Park, 53.9°C (129°F).

The deepest and the longest limestone canyon is...

- **Maligne Canyon**, Jasper National Park, two km (1.2 miles) long and 55 m (180 feet) deep.

The largest glacial-fed lake is...

- **Maligne Lake**, Jasper National Park, 22 km (13.7 miles) long.

The largest body of ice is...

- **The Columbia Icefield**, Jasper National Park, 190 sq km (73 sq miles).

■ To Do List

Next time I visit Jasper National Park I would like to...

■ Backpack the Skyline Trail

Considered one of the exceptional backpacking routes in the Rockies, this 44-km (27-mile), three-day hike is the highest trail in Jasper National Park and provides 25 km (15½ miles) of above treeline meandering. Starting at Maligne Lake and following along the crest of the Maligne Range, the hiker experiences vast wildflower-filled meadows, windswept ridges and breathtaking vistas. This is one of the busiest backcountry trails in Jasper Park with a quota system for its campgrounds, so it is necessary to plan ahead and reserve well in advance. More information is available in Parks Canada's *Backcountry Visitor's Guide to Jasper National Park*.

■ Horseback Ride into the Tonquin Valley

If there's one guided tour I would love to take, it's the five-day horseback trip into the Tonquin Valley. (See *Tonquin Valley Pack and Ski Trips* in the *Horseback Riding* section.) The famous Tonquin Valley is one of the most popular scenic backcountry subalpine areas in the Canadian Rockies and, as a result, it can get busy and the trail muddy. It's infamous for swarming mosquitoes and horseflies as well as bear encounters. As such, an early fall horseback trip would be ideal. **Destination:** the Tonquin Valley Backcountry Lodge at the north end of the Amethyst Lakes, two connected picturesque lakes sitting at the base of The Ramparts, a 1,200-m (3,937-foot) wall of quartzite. From the lodge, daily horse rides venture to numerous destinations vying for attention, including **Moat** and **Tonquin Passes**, as well as **Chrome Lake** and the **Eremite Valley**.

■ Useful Information

Fire, Police, Ambulance, Wardens, Search & Rescue: ☎ 911.

Hospital: 518 Robson Street, ☎ 780-852-3344.

Royal Canadian Mounted Police: ☎ 780-852-4848.

Park Warden Office: ☎ 780-852-6155.

Post Office: 502 Patricia Street (behind Visitor Information Center). Monday to Friday, 9 am to 5 pm, closed weekends and holidays.

Currency Exchange: At Maligne Tours Ticket Office, 627 Patricia Street (Marketplace).

Municipal Library: 500 Robson Street. Monday to Thursday, 11 am to 9 pm, Friday & Saturday, 11 am to 5 pm. Photocopier and fax machine for public use and Internet access.

Jasper Activity Center: 303 Pyramid Avenue, offers racquetball/squash courts, a universal gym, skateboard park, climbing wall, tennis and skating. Weekdays 8:30 am to 11 pm, weekends 9 am to 11 pm.

Jasper Aquatic Center: 401 Pyramid Avenue, has daily public swimming with a waterslide, steam room, whirlpool and wading pool.

Dog-run: Beside the Activity Center.

Internet access:

◆ Library – 500 Robson Street.

◆ Video Stop – 607 Patricia Street.

◆ Soft Rock Café – 632 Connaught Drive.

Laundromats: Offering **showers** as well are on Patricia Street.

Lockers: Available at the bus depot in the train station.

Liquor store: In The Jasper Marketplace, 631 Patricia Street.

Road conditions: ☎ 780-852-3311 or 403-762-1450.

Weather forecast: ☎ 780-852-3185.

Information Sources

www.pc.gc.ca/jasper

Parks Canada website with extensive information about the park, including fees, visitor information, natural wonders, activities, and public safety, such as trail reports, road conditions, and avalanche reports. Jasper National Park, PO Box 10, Jasper, Alberta, T0E 1E0, ☎ 780-852-6176.

www.jaspercanadianrockies.com

Detailed, up-to-date site with comprehensive general tourist information. Jasper Tourism & Commerce, PO Box 98, Jasper, Alberta T0E 1E0, ☎ 780-852-3858,

www.explorejasper.com

Lodging, recreation, coming events, etc.

www.visit-jasper.com

All things relating to Jasper.

www.jaspernationalpark.com

A locally produced travel planner for the Canadian Rockies.

www.discoverjasper.com

A Jasper tourism and travel guide, part of WorldWeb.com.

Jasper National Park

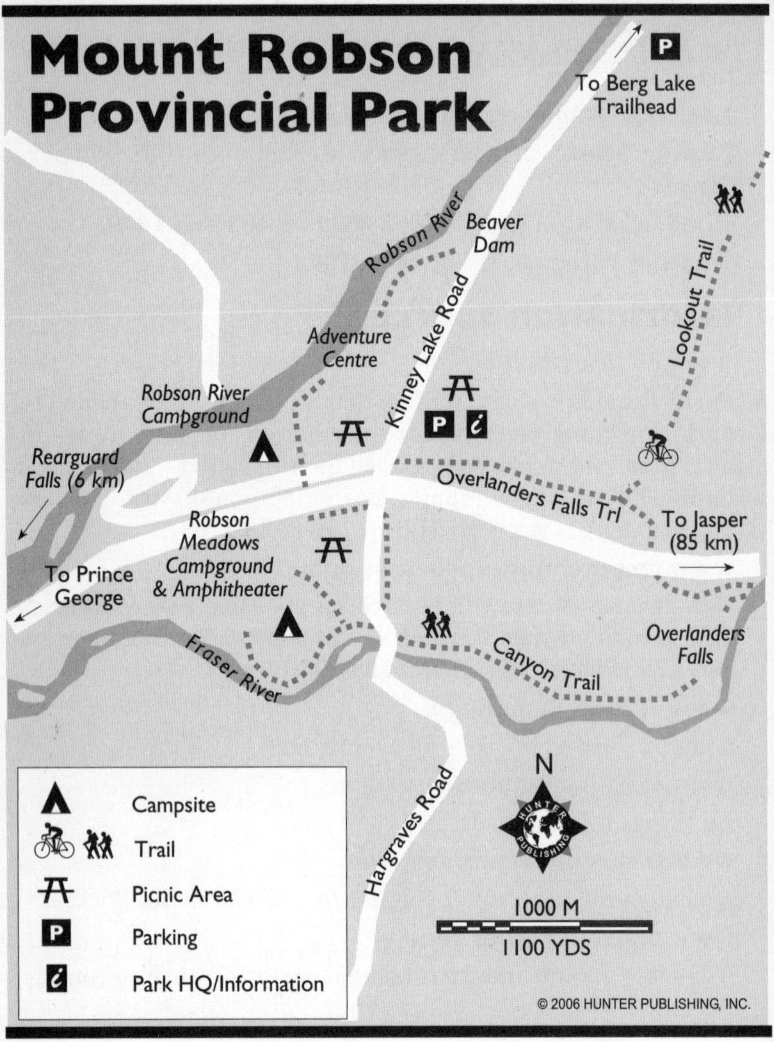

Mount Robson Provincial Park

To Berg Lake
Trailhead

Robson River

Beaver Dam

Kinney Lake Road

Adventure Centre

Lookout Trail

Robson River Campground

Rearguard Falls (6 km)

Overlanders Falls Trl

To Jasper (85 km)

Robson Meadows Campground & Amphitheater

To Prince George

Fraser River

Canyon Trail

Overlanders Falls

Hargraves Road

N

1000 M
1100 YDS

Campsite

Trail

Picnic Area

Parking

Park HQ/Information

© 2006 HUNTER PUBLISHING, INC.

Mount Robson Provincial Park

Many superlatives describe 3,954-m (12,972-foot) Mount Robson, the highest peak in the Canadian Rockies, and justifiably so. This "monarch" of the Canadian Rockies is most certainly an awesome sight and the main attraction of Mount Robson Provincial Park. Towering over the Yellowhead Highway, which

passes by its south face, Robson's sheer size and beauty are monumental. Although the peak is often obscured by cloud, I have seen it as many times free of cloud as I have seen it socked-in. If you happen to be in the park on a clear day, the view alone is worth the drive. Plan to hike the **Berg Lake Trail** to the base of Mount Robson, arguably the most popular and spectacular backpacking trail in the entire Rockies chain.

Situated within the North Continental Range of the Rocky Mountains, adjacent to Jasper National Park along the British Columbia/Alberta border, Mount Robson Provincial Park is truly a jewel.

■ History

Viscount Milton, c. 1864

Shuswap Indians, the earliest known inhabitants of the area, called Mount Robson *Yuh-hai-has-kun*, or *Mountain of the Spiral Road*, in reference to its layered appearance. Exploration for new fur trade routes by the North West Company and the Hudson's Bay Company in the 1800s pushed trading territory farther west. History records do not confirm who Mount Robson was named for, but it could have been Colin Robertson, who was in charge of the Hudson's Bay Company's operations in the area.

The names of the community of Tête Jaune Cache and the Yellowhead Highway, Pass, Mountain and Lake originate from a place along the Fraser River where a blonde mixed-blood Iroquois Indian stored or cached his furs. The French name "Tête Jaune" means "yellow head."

On passing Tête Jaune Cache in 1863 during their Northwest Passage journey, the first tourists, Viscount Milton and his physician Dr. Cheadle, described "a glorious sight, and one which the Shuswaps of the Cache assured us had rarely been seen by human eyes, the summit being generally hidden by clouds... a giant of giants... Robson's Peak."

George Kinney, Conrad Kain and Donald Phillips

While establishing the Alpine Club of Canada (ACC) in 1906, pioneering surveyor and mountaineer A.O. Wheeler proposed the organization's first conquest, the "virgin" Mount Robson. Determined that foreigners not be the first to climb the Canadian Rockies' highest peak, he persuaded three experienced Canadian climbers to attempt the harrowing climb: A.P. Coleman, his brother L.Q., and the Reverend George Kinney. Inclement weather combined with dwindling food supplies forced the climbers to abandon attempted assaults in both 1907 and 1908. Early in 1909, Kinney heard that a group of foreign climbers had plans to make the first assault of Robson. Unable to convince his partners to undertake the trek so early in the season, he hurriedly set out on his own. Along the route he met up with guide Donald "Curly" Phillips and somehow talked the inexperienced but resourceful Phillips into accompanying him. They had few provisions and Phillips' climbing equipment consisted of ordinary rope and a stick in place of an ice axe. But on Friday, the 13th of August, 20 days after making camp at the base of the north side of Robson, Kinney stood on what he considered to be the summit of Mount Robson and declared "In the name of Almighty God, by whose strength I have climbed here, I capture this peak, Mount Robson, for my own country, and for the Alpine Club of Canada."

Although Kinney was well respected, there arose some doubt as to whether he and Phillips had turned back within a few feet of the peak. Wheeler set up a scientific expedition to Mount Robson in 1911, partly to establish an ACC camp near Mount Robson. In 1913 he organized an official first ascent of Robson from the ACC camp at Robson Pass. Led by Austrian-born mountain guide Conrad Kain, along with Albert MacCarthy and William Foster, the team successfully reached the summit. Eventually, both Phillips and Kinney admitted that they had somehow been a few feet short of the summit. Nevertheless, Kinney and Phillips' achievement was given due credit, not only because of the perilous journey they endured just to reach the base of Robson, but because it was also discovered by Kain that the duo had chosen what was likely the most dangerous route to the peak. Curly Phillips went on to become an accomplished guide and outfitter in Jasper. Kinney Lake is the namesake of the Reverend.

Wheeler urged the government of British Columbia to establish Mount Robson as a park and in 1913 it became the second provincial park in British Columbia that today occupies 2,172 sq km (838 sq miles). The park was designated a UNESCO Rocky Mountain Parks World Heritage site in 1990.

■ Getting There

By Road

 The **Yellowhead Highway 16** is the main route running (east-west) through the park. From Jasper to the east, it's a scenic 85 km (53-mile) drive along the Yellowhead Highway to the Visitor Center.

Traveling west, the city of **Prince George**, British Columbia's "Northern Capital," is 305 km (190 miles) from Jasper. The community of **McBride**, which also offers full services to the traveler, is 87 km (54 miles). **Tête Jaune Cache** is at the junction of Highways 16 and 5, 18 km (11 miles) west of the Visitor Center.

Southern access is via Highway 5, 748 km (465 miles) from Vancouver and 338 km (210 miles) from Kamloops or 40 km (25 miles) from Valemount.

THE GEIKIE ROAD

"One of my favorite trips was the road west of Jasper. It bore no resemblance to the Yellowhead Highway which has taken its place. For the most part, this trail was built on the grade of the abandoned Canadian Northern tracks. It was so narrow in spots another vehicle could not be passed. However, there was very little traffic, and no one traveled quickly. In the seven or so miles between Jasper and the Geikie station, there were four or five old, rickety wooden bridges which crossed the Miette River and Meadow Creek.The scenery along this route was spectacularly beautiful. Then we came to a wide, flat, boggy area which was called Moose Flats, where we often watched moose wallowing. Just beyond this flat was a perfect picnic spot.

A little farther is an enclosure that had been an internment camp for some of our Japanese Canadians during the war. The mounds of their huts can still be seen amidst the bridges and pagodas they had made. They had created a garden out of a wilderness.

Now if our guests had not shown signs of fear or boredom, we continued on this same road to Mount Robson. There was one stretch along Moose Lake that was bit terrifying, even to those who were used to it, because where the railroad skirted the lake, there was no room for a car to go. An extremely narrow one-way trail had been carved in between the railroad ties and a very high wall of rock. To get onto this path, we had to cross the railroad track at each end of the half-mile trench. For several years there were no lights to indicate if it was safe to travel without meeting another car. However, all the railroad engineers knew the road and gave the drivers plenty of warning signals.

Having got through that our guests could imagine nothing worse, until the huge hill before Mount Robson and, in poor weather, it was hardly navigable. However, the sight of Mount Robson on a fine day was usually compensation for any amount of hair-raising traveling." (From *Jasper A Backward Glance*, by Nora Findlay, 1992, courtesy Friends of Jasper National Park and Jasper-Yellowhead Historical Society)

■ Touring the Park – Yellowhead Highway 16

Visitor Information Center

A viewpoint is located at the Mount Robson Provincial Park Visitor Information Center, along Highway 16. Unfortunately, during peak season the large parking area is usually jam-packed with cars, recreational vehicles and tour buses. If you can tolerate the crowds, it's a nice place to picnic and there's a playground for children.

The Center is open daily from early May until the end of September, generally from 8 am to 5 pm and to 7 pm during the summer months. You'll find informative displays describing the natural and human history of the park, information and brochures about services and activities within the park, as well as general tourist information, souvenirs and washrooms. The Center also issues backcountry camping permits for backpackers.

A gasoline station/convenience store (with a good little selection of Robson souvenirs) and a café (overpriced) are located next to the Visitor Center.

Mount Terry Fox

In 1981, a courageous young British Columbian lost his life to cancer. But only after he undertook a cross-Canada run that

Mount Robson Provincial Park

raised over $300 million world-
wide for cancer research. Running with one artificial leg,
Terry Fox captured the hearts
of Canadians everywhere
before he was forced to end his
run and finally succumbed to
the disease he fought so hard
against. Terry's spirit lives on.
Every September, communities
around the world raise money
for cancer research by holding

Terry Fox

the "Terry Fox Run." Stop and smell the roses at the viewpoint
of the peak named in Terry Fox's honor, nine km (5.6 miles)
west of the Visitor Center.

Rearguard Falls Viewpoint

Twelve km (7½ miles) west of the Visitor Center is a short
300-m (984-foot) walk to a viewpoint along Rearguard Falls,
the farthest upstream obstacle along the Fraser River for
spawning Chinook salmon. Salmon may be viewed here from
late August to mid-September, after their 11-week migration
from the Pacific Ocean. Mount Robson Provincial Park protects the headwaters and first 100 km (62 miles) of the Fraser
River, BC's longest river and the largest salmon-producing
river in the world, which flows 1,378 km (856 miles) to the
Pacific Ocean.

Overlander Falls Trail

Located 1.6 km (one mile) east of the Visitor Center is a 500-m
(1,500-foot) walk to a view of Overlander Falls. The canyon
trail leads to Robson Meadows Campground.

OVERLANDER FALLS

In the spring of 1862, a group of over a hundred travelers departed Ontario for what was to be a
two-month overland journey to the famous Cariboo
goldfields. The Overlanders – as they came to be
known – were a divergent group, and included the
Schubert family: Francis, Catherine (who was preg-

nant at the time and the only woman on the expedition) and their three children. From Fort Garry (now Winnipeg, Manitoba) the formidable journey west was not what had been expected. With provisions dwindling and increasing hardship as they made their way over the Great Divide, the fortune seekers split-up, with one determined naïve group electing to continue the journey on the Fraser River in makeshift rafts and dugout canoes. Before long, they encountered rapids, waterfalls and the Grand Canyon of the Fraser, where some met their death. But, incredibly, some survived the terror of the mighty Fraser. It wasn't until after further hardship and suffering that 36 of the weary travelers reached Fort Kamloops in mid-October – just in time for Catherine to give birth! Although a few of the courageous souls continued north to seek their fortunes in the goldfields, most opted for a less risky way of life.

Yellowhead Lake & Moose Lake

A sandy beach at Yellowhead Lake makes for an enjoyable swim or sunbathing on a summer's day. Yellowhead Lake also has a 2½-km (1½-mile) interpretive trail as well as other hiking opportunities. Moose Lake is a pleasant rest stop and a great place for travelers to take a cool dip when it's hot. Boat launches are located at both lakes where fishermen can try angling for dolly varden, lake char, rainbow trout and kokanee.

Remember: You must have a valid British Columbia angling license for sport fishing of any kind. Licenses are available from the Visitor Information Center, Mt. Robson Lodge, and several locations in Jasper, Valemount and McBride. A one-day angling license for non-residents of BC costs $20. (Provincial angling licenses are not valid in National Parks.)

Mount Robson Provincial Park

■ Where to Eat

Riverside Café, ☎ 250-566-4099, $$. Located next to the Tête Jaune Lodge, one km (0.6 miles) west of the Tête Jaune Cache junction, along the shores of the Fraser River. With stunning views of the

DINING PRICE CHART	
Price per person in Canadian $ for an entrée, not including beverage, tax or tip.	
$	Under $10
$$	$10-$25
$$$	Over $25

surrounding mountains, this casual café is housed in an historic log cabin built by settlers in 1926. Tête Jaune is said to have had a cache of furs stored below the cabin. On a nice day you can dine on the deck and watch the hummingbirds buzz about. The chef of this family-run restaurant uses fresh ingredients and local products. Open year-round for lunch and dinner.

The Rivers Bar & Grill, ☎ 250-968-4304, $$.

The Terracana Ranch Resort, approximately 25 km (15½ miles) west of the Visitor Information Center, offers casual dining in the cozy main lodge. Meals are served in tastefully decorated surroundings with a view of the resort and the Fraser River. Local ingredients from the ranch and nearby farms are featured on the menu. The wine list boasts an impressive collection. Breakfast 7-11 am, lunch 11 am to 2 pm and dinner 5-9 pm.

■ Where to Stay

Lodging

Mt. Robson Lodge, ☎ 888-566-4821 or 250-566-4821, www.mountrobsonlodge.com, $$ to $$$. Talk about a room with a view. These cozy log cabins five km (three miles) west of the Visitor Center have postcard views of Mount Robson. The cabins are very clean and most have kitchens. Unlike many cabin-style accommodations, these have plenty of room on grassy grounds that afford privacy and room for children to roam. Whitewater rafting excursions are booked and depart from this lodge. You can purchase snacks, souvenirs, and fishing licenses at the tiny coffee shop but the helpful visitor information is free. This is a family operated business open mid-May through September.

Tête Jaune Lodge, ☎ 866-566-9815 or 250-566-9815, www.tetejaune-lodge.com, $$. This motel is one km (.6 mile) west of the Tête Jaune Cache junction and is open year-round. Rooms are very clean; pets

HOTEL PRICE CHART	
Reflects the price of an average room for two in Canadian $, May-Sept. Rates lower rest of year (except Christmas and New Year's).	
$	Under $50
$$	$50-$100
$$$	$101-$150
$$$$	$151-$250
$$$$$	Over $250

are welcome ($5 charge). Facilities include a gas station, store and restaurant. A continental breakfast is included (except in July and August) and they offer a free shuttle to and from the Berg Lake Trailhead.

Terracana Ranch Resort, ☎ 866-968-4304 or 250-968-4304, www.terracana.com, $$$$. Located approximately 25 km (15½ miles) west of the Visitor Information Center, these deluxe riverside cabins with studio, one- or two-bedroom units, including kitchenettes, are luxuriously appointed. Guests can enjoy views of the Fraser River while sitting on their patios nestled hillside. The atmosphere is tranquil, however, cabins (except for the executive cabin) are adjoining, so privacy is somewhat compromised. Amenities include a small bar and dining room in the rustically decorated main lodge, as well as a fitness room, games room, hot tub and sauna. The ranch offers various activities or books activities, such as whitewater rafting, horseback riding, guided hiking and fishing, golfing and offers mountain bike, fishing rod and canoe/kayak rentals. Open year-round except November. Rates include three meals per day.

Camping

 BC Parks operates three seasonal campgrounds in the park. Two campgrounds are near the Visitor Center; both provide large private sites, wheelchair-accessible sites and washrooms with showers. There are no RV hook-ups in the park. Payment may be

Mount Robson Provincial Park

made by cash or travelers
checks only. For more information about BC Parks
campgrounds in Mount
Robson Provincial Park,
☎ 250-566-4811, from late
April to October.

CAMPING/HOSTELS	
Rates in Canadian $, not including taxes.	
$	Under $13
$$	$13-$22
$$$	$23-$30
$$$$	Over $30

**Robson River Camp-
ground**, a personal favorite,
is beside the Visitor Center and nearest the Berg Lake
trailhead. The sites are situated along the river, it's not
crowded and the showers work well, but with only 19 sites it
fills up quickly. Open mid-May to mid-September. $$

Robson Meadows Campground, across from the Visitor
Center, provides 125 sites, group camping, playground facili-
ties, a sani-station ($2 fee) and interpretive programs. This is
the only BC Parks campground in the park that accepts reser-
vations through the Discover Camping system, although res-
ervations are generally not required unless you want a special
site or during busy holiday weekends. (See *Information
Sources* for more information.) Open from the end of April to
early October, with reservations taken from mid-May to early
September. $$

Lucerne Campground is 50 km (31 miles) east of the Visitor Center with 32 sites near the shores of Yellowhead Lake.
Two walk-in/cycle-in campsites are available, one a wheelchair-accessible site. Open from the end of May to
mid-September. $$

Robson Shadows Campground, ☎ 888-566-4821 or
250-566-4821, $$. A privately operated campground at Mt.
Robson Lodge, five km (three miles) west of the Visitor Cen-
ter, with 25 sites (no hook-ups) along the Fraser River.
Showers are included. Open mid-May to mid-October.

Tête Jaune Lodge Campground, ☎ 866-566-9815 or
250-566-9815, $$. A privately operated campground located
one km (.6 miles) west of the Tête Jaune Cache junction.
Riverfront and pull-through sites; water and electrical
hook-ups and showers available. Open mid-April to
mid-October. Rustic sleeping cabins for one to four people also
available. $$$$

■ Wildlife

All wildlife indigenous to the Rocky Mountains can be found in Mount Robson Provincial Park. From a vehicle it is common to see black bears, mule and whitetail deer, moose, elk, and coyotes. Along hiking trails I have seen hoary marmots, pika, chipmunks, and golden-mantled and Columbian ground squirrels. You may also have an opportunity to see grizzly bears, caribou, mountain goats and sheep, wolves, beavers and porcupines. **Moose Marsh**, at the east end of Moose Lake, is touted as one of the best areas for viewing birds and large mammals.

Over 180 species of birds have been identified within the park. Each June, the **"Bird Blitz"** takes place in Mount Robson Park, when bird enthusiasts gather for the opportunity to observe and count the park's feathered population.

■ Adventures

Hiking

Berg Lake Trail

Backpack: 42 km (26 miles) round-trip to Berg Lake, 46 km (28 miles) to Robson Pass Campground (minimum two days).

Elevation gain: 790 m (2,592 feet) to Berg Lake, 796 m (2,610 feet) to Robson Pass.

Watchable wildlife: hoary marmots, pikas, golden-mantled ground squirrels, porcupines, chipmunks, mountain goats, black and grizzly bears.

Many visitors return to hike the world-renowned Berg Lake Trail year after year. Pack-laden hikers are endlessly rewarded with stunning vistas of cascading waterfalls, massive glaciers, pristine lakes and lush valleys, all leading to exquisite glacier-fed Berg Lake at the foot of the north face of Mount Robson. If you are only going to do one backpacking trip in the Rockies, I recommend this one. (I also recommend taking four-five days to fully enjoy this mountain paradise.)

From the **Visitor Center**, the trailhead and parking area is at the end of a two-km (1.2-mile) road leading to the **Robson River Bridge**. The busy trail follows the river through old-growth cedar-hemlock forest for four km (2.4 miles) to **Kinney Lake**. It's another seven km (4.2 miles) to **Whitehorn Campsite**, where there is also a ranger cabin. Whitehorn is a good place to spend the first night on the trail, especially if traveling with children. The shelter is a welcome refuge, especially if it's raining. Firewood is available for the woodstove, which is to be used only during periods of severe weather or emergencies.

After leaving Whitehorn the trail begins a steep ascent into the **Valley of a Thousand Falls**, an elevation gain of 500 m (1,500 feet) over almost five km (three miles). The trail then narrows as it crosses a talus slope above the creek-bed for the first section of the three km (1.8 miles) between **Emperor Falls campsite** and **Marmot campsite**, then descends into the open creek-bed where there are a number of shallow crossings. **Mist** and **Berg Glaciers** come into view; Berg Glacier is one of the few advancing glaciers in the Canadian Rockies. The final two km (1.2 miles) of trail are along the side of Berg Lake.

The **campsite at Berg Lake** is an idyllic base from which to explore some of the other trails in the area, including **Toboggan Falls**, a short, steep route that provides stunning views of Berg Lake and Mount Robson.

Kinney Lake Trail

If you cannot complete the entire Berg Lake Trail, the gentle nine-km (5.6-mile) round-trip hike to the south end of picturesque Kinney Lake will certainly whet your appetite. Take a picnic lunch to enjoy along the shores of the lake before returning to the trailhead. Bicycling is permitted to this popular day-use area.

What You Need to Know about the Berg Lake Trail

The trail is open from May 1 to October 31. Overnight access is on a first-come, first-served basis with a limited number of departures permitted each day. Overnight hikers must register and pay camping fees of $5 per person per night at the Visitor Center (children 12 and under camp free). This must be done from noon to closing time the day prior to departure. Tent pads must be pre-booked for the duration of the hike. (The total number of tent pads is 103.)

Seven **campgrounds** along the trail are: **Kinney Lake** at 7 km; **Whitehorn** at 11 km; **Emperor Falls** at 16 km; **Marmot** at 19 km; **Berg Lake** at 21 km; **Rearguard** at 22 km; and **Robson Pass** at 23 km. Group camping on the trail is available at Whitehorn and Robson Pass campgrounds. (You may change campgrounds en route only if space permits and if you can locate a park ranger to obtain approval.)

A small percentage of departure dates are on the reservation system and for a fee may be reserved in advance through BC Parks' "Discover Camping" Campground Reservations System (see *Information Sources*). Reservations are accepted from June 14 to September 15.

All wilderness camping sites along the trail have tent pads and bear poles or food storage boxes. Pit toilets are located at all campgrounds on the trail; toilet paper is not provided, so come prepared (or be prepared to barter – we traded camp stove fuel for toilet paper). Camping stoves are mandatory for cooking and fires are only permitted in the shelter stoves during periods of extreme weather or emergencies. You must pack out all of your garbage.

Although it is a well-developed, high-use trail, hazardous terrain abounds: steep, uneven and slippery surfaces, cliffs, and fast flowing and glacial waters. Use extreme caution and closely supervise small children. Ranger staff, first aid and emergency radios are located at Whitehorn and Berg Lake.

Dogs must be on a leash at all times and are not permitted overnight on the trail.

Only experienced, properly equipped mountaineers should attempt mountain climbing or venture onto glaciers.

There is backcountry winter camping offered at Berg Lake and along the trail up to Berg. There is no fee collected for winter camping.

Mount Robson Provincial Park

Reflections – Hiking the Berg Lake Trail

The Berg Lake Trail was on my to-do list for a number of years and I was thrilled when I was able to make the trip a reality. Finally, I wouldn't just be driving through the park en route to another destination.

We spent a night at the Robson River Campground but, before departing on the trail, we took advantage of ideal weather to photograph Mount Robson along the Robson River, what was to be the first of many incredible photo opportunities on the trip.

The first few km on the trail were slow going as we adjusted our packs and 10-year-old Oliver got accustomed to his load. Along the shores of Reverend Kinney's aqua-colored lake we ditched our packs and laid out the midday meal. This picturesque site at the base of Mount Robson was but a preview of what we would see in the next 3½ days.

After setting up camp at Whitehorn, we cooked dinner under the shelter, along with a number of other cheerful campers. Our cares and worries over preparing for the trip had now dissipated.

Leaving Whitehorn the next day after a breakfast of hot porridge, the trail began its steep ascent into the Valley of a Thousand Falls and we appreciated the payoff for packing light. "Are there really a thousand falls?" Oliver pondered. There must be; everywhere we looked, cascading water flowed like a bride's veil. The sunshine was brilliant but the heat combined with the elevation gain made the climb challenging.

Like a strategically located rest stop, the spray of mighty Emperor Falls was most welcome. Another steep short grunt to Emperor Falls Campsite and the toughest part of the climb was behind us. We were proud of Oliver for his accomplishment – this was his first major backpacking trip. Hikers along the trail patted him on the back and offered further encouragement.

Robson River (© Lenard Sanders)

Above: Banff Springs Hotel

Below: Bow Falls, Banff

Above: Parker Ridge

Below: Bow Lake

Above: Lake Minnewanka C Level Cirque trail
Below: Mistaya Canyon

An elusive pika darted about the rocks and curious hoary marmots seemed to appear from nowhere as we carefully made our way along the rocky talus. Mist and Berg Glaciers, massive ice serpents with tongues spilling forth moraine, filled the landscape. Our pace quickened as we neared our destination. The final two km of trail along turquoise Berg Lake provided glimpses of floating icebergs that calved from the glacier. We marveled at their shape, one looked like a swan. Click, click, click go the cameras.

When we finally reached Berg Lake Campsite, camp duties were set aside until we had an opportunity to revel in the surroundings and photograph Robson in the setting sun.

The following day we explored some of the other trails in the area, each affording its own unique and stunning views. Our only disappointment was that we didn't book an extra day to explore the area.

We spent our final night at Robson Pass Campground, two km farther along the trail. Despite the change in weather, the rain didn't dampen our spirits. As we prepared for the return hike a rainbow arched over Berg Lake. Although exhausted by the end of the day, we felt exhilarated to have experienced the unique beauty of this Rocky Mountain Park.

The Berg Lake Trail is no longer a "someday I will do it," yet I haven't crossed it off my ever-growing to-do list. I've heard that autumn in Mount Robson Park is splendid... someday.

Whitewater Rafting

 **Mount Robson Whitewater Rafting Co.,** ☎ 888-566-7238 or 250-566-4879, www.mountrobsonwhitewater.com. Based at Mt. Robson Lodge, offering various float trips on the Fraser River, with great opportunities for wildlife viewing, including

black and grizzly bears, moose, deer, bald eagles, beavers and salmon. Trips include a BBQ meal cooked on the most unusual BBQ in the Rockies! Daily departures. Free overnight camping available in the group site at Mount Robson Lodge Campground with the purchase of a rafting trip.

- 2½-hour relaxing interpretive family float, adult $59, child $49 (five and under free).
- Three-hour white-water excursion, $79.
- Day-trip that combines a morning float with thrilling whitewater in the afternoon, $119.

Horseback Riding

Cardinal Ranch, ☎ 866-294-6773 or 250-968-4481, www.rockiesbyhorse.com. A family-operated working horse ranch nine km (5.4 miles) west of Tête Jaune Junction, open May to October. Rides offer potential wildlife viewing and unique vistas of the Robson Valley, Fraser River, Raush Valley and, of course, the Rocky Mountains. If you're like me and you want an opportunity to trot and canter, these guides may be persuaded.

- 1½-hour Lookout Ride, $35.
- Four-hour Valleyview Ride, $80 includes a snack
- Six-hour Day Ride into the heart of the Rockies, $150 includes lunch.
- Two-day Rausch Valley Campout for groups of up to eight, $250.

■ Useful Information

Fire, Police, Ambulance: ☎ 911.

Ranger Station: ☎ 250-566-4325.

Royal Canadian Mounted Police: ☎ 566-4466 (Valemount).

Information Sources

BC Parks, Mount Robson Park Headquarters, located in the Visitor Information Center, Box 579, Valemount, BC V0E 2Z0, ☎ 250-566-4325, www.env.gov.bc.ca/bcparks. Provincial government site that provides detailed information about the park. You can also download the following maps and brochures.

- Location map
- Mount Robson brochure
- Mount Robson Visitor Center/Headquarters area brochure
- Berg Lake area map
- Berg Lake brochure
- Lurcerne Area map
- Mount Fitzwilliam Trail map
- Mount Fitzwilliam Trail brochure
- Robson River and Robson Meadows area map
- Robson River and Robson Meadows brochure

 BC Parks does not regularly update these brochures and some of the information regarding private operators is no longer valid.

Discover Camping Campground Reservation Service, for participating BC Parks campgrounds (Robson Meadows), www.discovercamping.ca, ☎ 800-689-9025. There is a non-refundable reservation service fee of $6.42 per night, to a maximum of $19.26 for three or more nights. If you change or cancel your reservation, there is an additional non-refundable fee of $6.42 per campsite. Reservations can be made up to three months in advance and two days prior to your arrival date at the campground.

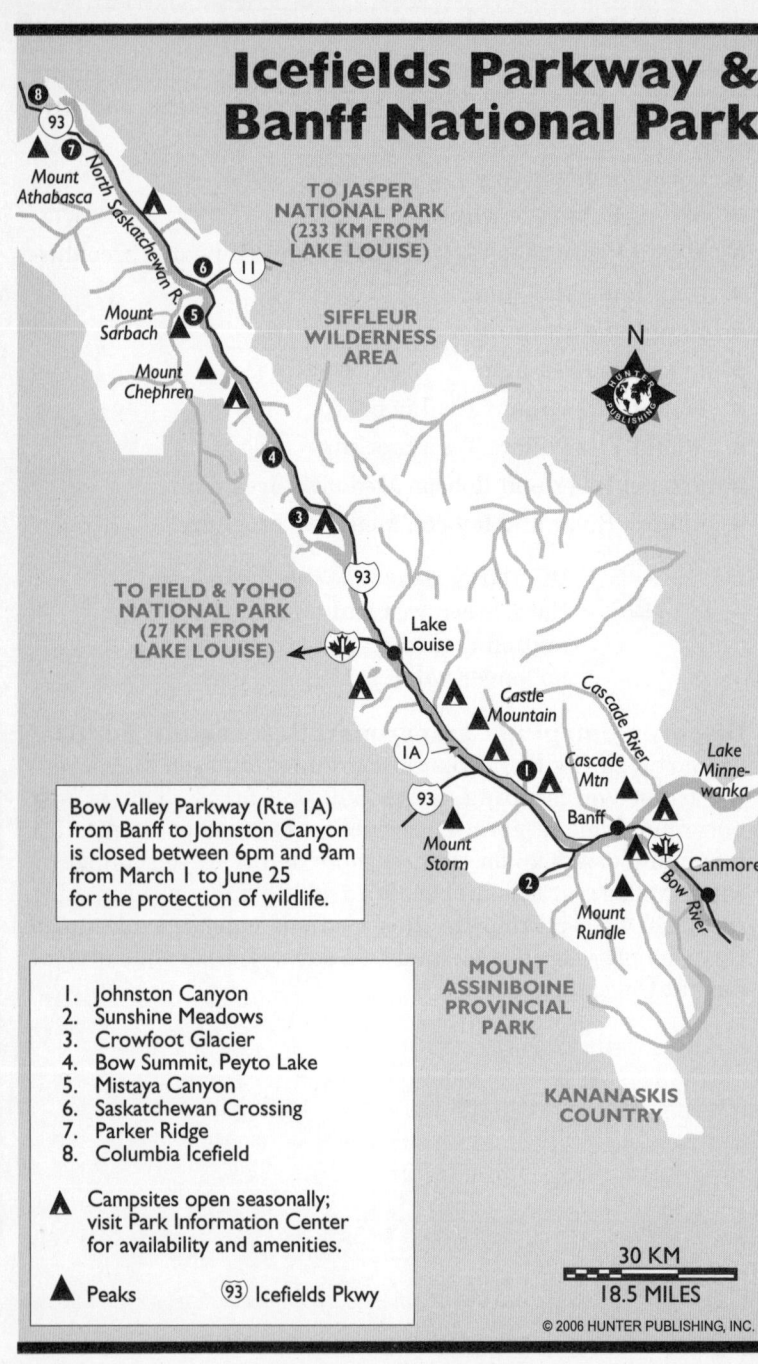

Icefields Parkway & Banff National Park

TO JASPER
NATIONAL PARK
(233 KM FROM
LAKE LOUISE)

Mount
Athabasca

North Saskatchewan R.

SIFFLEUR
WILDERNESS
AREA

Mount
Sarbach

Mount
Chephren

N

TO FIELD & YOHO
NATIONAL PARK
(27 KM FROM
LAKE LOUISE)

Lake
Louise

Castle
Mountain

Cascade River

Cascade
Mtn

Lake
Minne-
wanka

Banff

Canmore

Bow River

Bow Valley Parkway (Rte IA)
from Banff to Johnston Canyon
is closed between 6pm and 9am
from March 1 to June 25
for the protection of wildlife.

Mount
Storm

Mount
Rundle

MOUNT
ASSINIBOINE
PROVINCIAL
PARK

KANANASKIS
COUNTRY

1. Johnston Canyon
2. Sunshine Meadows
3. Crowfoot Glacier
4. Bow Summit, Peyto Lake
5. Mistaya Canyon
6. Saskatchewan Crossing
7. Parker Ridge
8. Columbia Icefield

Campsites open seasonally;
visit Park Information Center
for availability and amenities.

Peaks   93 Icefields Pkwy

30 KM
18.5 MILES

© 2006 HUNTER PUBLISHING, INC.

Icefields Parkway

The Icefields Parkway (Highway 93), connecting Jasper National Park and Lake Louise in Banff National Park, is considered one of the premier mountain drives in the world. The 230-km (143-mile) parkway follows the Continental

Divide north-south, as well as the Athabasca, Sunwapta, North Saskatchewan, Mistaya and Bow Valleys. It gradually climbs from an elevation of 1,000 m (3,280 feet) from Jasper's montane valley floor through subalpine zones at elevations of 1,500-2,200 m (4,900-7,200 feet) to the near-alpine zones of **Sunwapta Pass** and **Bow Summit**.

Glaciers that remain from the Ice Ages dot the landscape, seven icefields within viewing distance of the parkway. The highlight of the drive for many is the **Athabasca Glacier**, the only road-accessible glacier in the parks. The glacier forms part of the **Columbia Icefield**, the largest body of ice in the Rocky Mountains and one of the largest south of the Arctic Circle.

Over half-a-million park visitors travel this route every year. Back in the days when it was a packtrain route, the trip took two weeks on horseback. Today, some traffic zips by at maximum speed, traveling between Jasper and Lake Louise in a matter of hours. Most travelers move at a more leisurely pace, spending several days along the parkway, staying in campgrounds or hostels that line the route. Unlike the transportation corridors of the Yellowhead Highway and the Trans Canada Highway, large transport trucks are not permitted. The maximum speed limits are 70-90 km/hour (43-56 miles/hour). Take your time, stop at the many viewpoints and points-of-interest, be on the lookout for wildlife and explore some of the myriad trails that branch off the highway leading to incredible vistas.

This chapter is organized from north to south, Jasper to Lake Louise. The Icefields Parkway North (to Sunwapta Pass, five km or three miles south of the Icefields Center) is part of Jasper National Park and the Icefields Parkway South is part of Banff National Park.

■ History

Natives and fur traders traveled the valleys along the parkway since the early 1800s. Well-known guide Bill Peyto led the first recorded discovery of the Columbia Icefields in 1898. Mountaineers Norman Collie and Hermann Woolley, along with Hugh Stutfield, came upon a sight they described as "a noble snow-crowned peak, with splendid rock precipices and hanging glaciers." After Collie and Woolley climbed for the better part of a day,

Bill Peyto

they stood on the summit of what they named **Mount Athabasca** – the highest mountain climbed in the Rockies up to that time. Collie later recorded his awe at what they saw: "The view that lay beneath us in the evening light was one that does not often fall to the lot of modern mountaineers. A new world was spread at our feet; to the westward stretched a vast icefield... "

On the occasion of his first visit from Banff to Jasper, mountaineer and surveyor A.O. Wheeler, a strong proponent of a connecting road between Lake Louise and Jasper, declared "through dense primeval forests, muskeg, burnt and fallen timber and along rough and steeply sloping hillsides, a constant flow of travel will demand a broad well-ballasted motor road.... This wonder trail will be world renowned." The forerunner of today's Icefields Parkway was an established pack-train route and, despite those who said it couldn't be done, Wheeler's prophecy came true.

It was a make-work project of the Great Depression. Legions of unemployed began construction in 1931, crews working toward each other from Jasper and Lake Louise. Where explorers had blazed the original trail, with primitive machinery, horses and men labored slowly, season after season. By 1939 it was completed and the one-lane gravel Banff-Jasper Road was opened, ironically during gasoline rationing in war-era 1940. Paving, widening and, surprisingly, little realignment took place in the 1950s and 1960s, ushering in the automobile tourist boom.

 **Recommended Reading:** *Climbs & Exploration in the Canadian Rockies*, by Hugh E.M. Stutfield and J. Norman Collie. Published in 1903 by Longmans, Green and Co., London. Reprinted in 1998, the centennial of the discovery of the Columbia Icefield. Aquila Books, Calgary, Alberta (*Canadian Mountaineering Classics #1*).

■ What You Need to Know

There are few traveler services between Jasper and Lake Louise, especially in winter. The only gas station, The Crossing (at Saskatchewan River Crossing), is seasonal (spring through fall), 153 km (95 miles) south of Jasper or 77 km (48 miles) north of Lake Louise. The parkway is maintained by Parks Canada as a scenic route; all users require a Park Pass.

Parks Canada Visitor Information Centers at Jasper and Lake Louise (see those chapters), as well as at the Icefield Center (see below) can provide trail information, wilderness passes, safety registrations, and general information. Pick up a copy of Parks Canada's *The Icefields Parkway* brochure, which gives general information about the parkway as well as a detailed map indicating points of interest, mountain peaks, trailheads, campgrounds, glaciers and tourist services all along the parkway.

Parks Canada Information, Icefield Center ☎ 780-852-6288. Located 103 km (64 miles) from Jasper, open May 1 to October 15. Operating hours: summer, 9 am to 6 pm; spring and fall, 9 am to 5 pm.

■ Where to Eat

 Restaurants along the parkway are few and far between so, if you are not camping and making your own meals, choices are somewhat limited. Cafeterias and dining rooms are located at

Sunwapta Falls Resort, the **Icefield Center, The Crossing** and **Num-Ti-Jah Lodge**; all are fairly pricey.

■ Where to Stay

The parkway provides an excellent network of campgrounds (including overflow) and hostels. (See *Jasper National Park* chapter and the *Lake Louise* section of the *Banff National Park* chapter for details on campgrounds and hostels along the Icefields Parkway.) Other accommodations include **Sunwapta Falls Resort** (very busy and crowded), **Columbia Icefield Chalet** (see below), **The Crossing** and **Num-Ti-Jah Lodge** (see below).

■ Wildlife

Be prepared to slow down and pull off the parkway for wildlife viewing. Frequently seen throughout the summer along this route: bighorn sheep, mountain goats, elk, moose, mule deer, black bears and coyotes. It is also grizzly bear and wolf habitat.

■ Bicycle Touring

The Icefields Parkway is a world-famous bicycle route. During the summer thousands of cyclists from around the world bike a route that they believe cannot be properly experienced by driving. With many well-spaced campgrounds and hostels along the 230-km (143-mile) parkway, it is well suited for bicycle touring. Easy access from the parkway to trailheads is an added bonus. Cyclists should always use caution, of course. Although some of the parkway has wide paved shoulders, many places have very narrow shoulders. Cyclists must be visible to traffic and alert at all times.

Be sure you pack enough food or plan to spend a fair amount of money in restaurants as the only place to purchase grocery items is from the limited selection at The Crossing.

You can cycle from either direction, but you are more likely to get tailwinds if you travel from Jasper to Lake Louise. I suggest taking at least five days to complete the trip or, better yet, a week, allowing plenty of time for some of the hikes and sights en route.

■ Walks & Hikes

Valley of the Five Lakes

Hike: 4.2 km (2.6 mile) loop.

Watchable wildlife: beavers, muskrats, loons, coyotes, moose.

This is an excellent family hike (or a romantic rendezvous) with five pretty little lakes the highlight of the outing. The trailhead is on the east side of the parkway, nine km (5.6 miles) south of the intersection with Highway 16 at Jasper. The forest trail along the floor of the Athabasca Valley never gets boring like some forest walks. It meanders through forest, across boardwalks, wetlands and meadows. Each lake varies in depth and length – from pond size to about one km (.6 miles) – and is a different beautiful hue of glistening blue-green.

For romantic types, you can rent a rowboat on Lake Five (must be booked in advance from On-line Sport, ☎ 780-852-3630 – See Jasper chapter, *Sports & Camping Equipment Rentals* section). And don't forget a picnic lunch for two!

Athabasca Falls

A testament to the power of fast-moving water, 30 km (19 miles) south of Jasper, Athabasca Falls plunges 30 m (98 feet) into a cloud of mist. Unlike limestone and sandstone canyons of the Rockies, quartzite is the hardest rock in Alberta, extremely resistant to erosion. The force of the Athabasca River has nonetheless carved this broad gorge. The sand and gravel carried by the river has smoothed and potholed the walls of the canyon. Abandoned channels reveal that the river has changed course many times in its search for the path of least resistance. **Mount Kerkeslin**, the Stoney word for wolverine, looms across the parkway to the east.

Visitors to the falls are advised to use extreme caution: the railings at the viewing areas are there for good reason. If you are at the falls on a busy day, in all likelihood you will witness a number of foolhardy people who feel the need to get closer to the canyon for photographs. The smooth, wet and slippery rock has been the site of many fatal accidents. Remain on the viewing platforms!

GOATS & GLACIERS VIEWPOINT

 Approximately six km (3.7 miles) south of Athabasca Falls is the Goats and Glaciers Viewpoint. This picnic area provides an impressive view of the Athabasca Valley and is one of the best places in the Rockies to see mountain goats. Below the viewpoint, the Athabasca River cuts away at the steep bank of glacial till. This exposed glacial till forms a natural mineral lick – mineral salts that attract the goats from the slopes of nearby Mount Kerkeslin.

Sunwapta Falls

 This overrun tourist area is less impressive than Athabasca Falls, yet it's worth a stop for first-time visitors or those of us who might display an "I brake for waterfalls" bumper sticker. It is .6 km (.4 miles) down a paved road that branches from the junction of the Sunwapta Falls Resort, 55 km (34 miles) from Jasper. A short trail leads to the falls where the Sunwapta River is diverted 90 degrees from its northwest course by glacial moraine, then flows southwest a short distance before joining with the Athabasca River approximately three km (1.8 miles) downstream. The falls have eroded deep into the limestone bedrock, with good views of the main falls from the bridge over the gorge.

More interesting, though, are the less crowded lower falls. To access **Lower Sunwapta Falls** – and a bit of solitude – follow the main viewing trail to where the paved trail ends and begins a descent to the lower falls. The trail emerges from the forest at km .6 to open views of the upper Athabasca Valley and Mount Quincy. Continue for another .6 km to a staircase waterfall – three closely spaced waterfalls.

Sunwapta is a Stoney Indian word for "turbulent river." The parkway follows the river to its origin in Sunwapta Lake near the toe of the Athabasca Glacier.

Travel Reflections - Bear Aware

It was lunch hour on a sunny summer afternoon when we arrived at the jam-packed Sunwapta Falls parking area. Visitors were coming and going from their vehicles, families enjoying picnic lunches at the tables along the fringes of the parking lot. We pulled into a parking space immediately beside the main path to the falls, behind a vehicle that had just departed.

We were still sitting in our van when a commotion erupted. A number of people were running from the falls area toward the parking lot. Seconds later, a small agitated-looking black bear sauntered down the trail toward the parking lot, passing beside our van. Picnickers began to flee, people ran toward their vehicles and pandemonium ensued. We stared in amazement as two excited women with cameras quickly followed the bear. Remaining in our seats, we watched them chase the bear across the parking lot to a forested area. The parking lot was full of on-lookers and a man called out to the women, suggesting they back off. By this time they were walking back to the falls, cameras in hand, grins on their faces. Apparently, they had the photos they wanted.

After the bear departed the area and everyone settled down, we spoke to a woman who told us that she was standing on the bridge over the falls when the bear crossed the bridge. Obviously it was accustomed to humans and the scent of lunch may have attracted it to the parking lot.

This scene is a frightening testament to the continued lack of awareness of the dangers that wildlife pose. Although this particular bear was not large, it presented a danger to anyone within close range, especially small children. Everyone involved in this incident was lucky not to be harmed, especially the two bear chasers.

Lessons learned: be aware of the possible presence of bears, even in busy tourist areas where you might not expect them. Maintain a safe distance from all wildlife and certainly don't harass wildlife by following them.

We made sure to bring our pepper spray along before we wandered down to the falls. After we departed the falls we reported the bear sighting to wardens from Sunwapta Falls Resort – no one else had yet reported it.

Beauty Creek Trail to Stanley Falls

Hike: 3.2 km (two miles) round-trip.

Watchable wildlife: American dippers (little grey birds that jump in and out of the water).

No large paved parking lot or signs proclaiming "tourist attraction." I thoroughly enjoy this short hike that was popular during the early days of the Banff-Jasper Highway – before it was rerouted. It gets my vote for a worthwhile "off the beaten path" activity: most parkway tourists bypass it and the trail provides a bit of solitude as well as rewarding scenery after only a short, easy climb.

Look for a small, unmarked pull-off where you can park on the east side of the highway, about two km (1.2 miles) south of Beauty Creek Hostel. The trail initially follows a dike across a wet area; turn right onto the roadbed of the old Banff-Jasper Highway to a bridge abutment, where the trail branches left then climbs through forest along the north side of a narrow limestone canyon. The trail passes about eight pretty cascades, the last and highest being Stanley Falls.

 Use extreme caution, as there are no guardrails along this trail. Jasper Park's *Summer Trails* brochure incorrectly describes the trailhead as being one-half km south of Beauty Creek Hostel. It also shows the trail distance as 6.4 km round-trip, which it likely is, but it becomes indistinct and less interesting after the first 1.6 km.

Along this stretch of highway the Sunwapta River creates endless braided channels across broad alluvial flats – sand, silt and gravel that is washed down from the Columbia Icefield and carried by the river. During the summer months, the showy broad-leaved willow herb – not to be confused with fireweed – bloom profusely along the flats. The large four-petal pink flowers add a striking contrast to the barren flats providing excellent photo opportunities along the highway.

Stutfield Glacier Viewpoint

The Stutfield Glacier is an outlet glacier of the Columbia Icefield. 3,480-m (11,417-foot) **Mount Kitchener** is to the south. Located 94½ km (58.7 miles) from Jasper.

Tangle Falls

Less than two km (1.2 miles) from the Stutfield Glacier, Tangle Falls is opposite a roadside picnic area. Slow down, as the area is a veritable traffic jam. Also watch for bighorn sheep standing in the middle of the road.

Sunwapta Canyon Viewpoint

Just over one km from Tangle Falls, the Sunwapta Canyon Viewpoint affords good views of 3,491-m (11,453-foot) **Mount Athabasca**.

The Columbia Icefield & Athabasca Glacier

On a grand scale, the Columbia Icefield covers an area of 190 sq km (73 sq miles) and in places it is 365 m (1,197 feet) thick. Yet it is but a tiny remnant of an ice sheet that 15,000 years ago covered the area from the Alberta Foothills to the Pacific Coast. It feeds many glaciers, six major glaciers that are named, three of which can be seen from the parkway: **Dome** and **Stutfield Glaciers** and the famous **Athabasca Glacier**, which flows from the icefield's central core. Not only can the Athabasca Glacier be readily viewed, a short road and path lead to its toe, where visitors can touch ice that is hundreds of years old.

The Athabasca Glacier is six km (3.7 miles) long and up to one km (.6 miles) wide but has melted back by 1.6 km (one mile) since 1870. Many scientists believe that the dramatic recession is a result of rapid global warming and that glaciers around the world are disappearing at an alarming rate. Others suggest that, although the recession has been recently abetted by increased carbon dioxide emissions, periods of global warming are a cyclical occurrence and another glacial advance is inevitable.

The 3,451-m (11,322-foot) **Snow Dome**, between the Athabasca and Dome Glaciers, is the highest mountain covered by the Columbia Icefield. It is the only point on the continent where melting snow and ice eventually flow into three oceans: the Atlantic, the Pacific and the Arctic. As such, it is considered the hydrological apex of North America. To the north, water flows into the Sunwapta and Athabasca Rivers and eventually the Mackenzie River and the Arctic Ocean. To the east, water flows into the North Saskatchewan River, across three provinces, into Lake Winnipeg and finally into Hudson Bay and the Atlantic Ocean. To the west, the water flows into the Pacific via the Columbia River system through southern British Columbia and Washington State. The Columbia Icefield is a source of water for millions of people.

 Did You Know? Between the Athabasca and Dome Glaciers you can see a stand of spruce trees, some of which are over 700 years old. These trees are remnants of an ancient forest that was almost destroyed during a period scientists call the Little Ice Age, when the Athabasca Glacier was expanding down the valley.

Directly across from the Icefield Center, date markers along the access road to the Athabasca Glacier indicate how much it has receded since 1844, when the toe was located near today's Icefield Center. Each date marker corresponds to a ridge of rock debris, called a recessional moraine, where the glacier toe remained before continuing its retreat. Spread out over the glacial forefield, rock fragments called glacial till are carried and released by the glacier. Sunwapta Lake is a glacial tarn – a result of melting glacial ice that has formed in a depression carved by the once advancing glacier. It will eventually disappear as mud continues to be deposited in its waters.

Parks Canada has cordoned off an area on the toe of the Athabasca Glacier allowing visitors to walk on the surface. Be extremely careful! Glaciers are always changing. The surface ice can be very slippery and crevasses – deep cracks in the ice – can be fatal. Signs warn of the dangers of falling into crevasses. One sobering sign indicates that nearby a young boy succumbed to hypothermia before he could be rescued from a crevasse. Stay within the boundaries, move slowly and closely supervise small children. Wear a warm jacket, as wind coming off the glacier is very cold.

The Icefield Center

This is across the highway from the Athabasca Glacier, 103 km (64 miles) south of Jasper, at the base of Mount Wilcox in Sunwapta Pass. The Center is open from mid-April to mid-October, 24 hours per day. It is extremely busy during the peak months of July and August, especially during the hours of 10:30 am and 3 pm. The Chalet front desk, tour terminals and the Jasper National Park Information Desk occupy the main floor. A dining room and cafeteria are on the second floor. Note that the Center accepts only cash or traveler's checks.

The Glacier Gallery is a Parks Canada exhibit on the lower floor of the Icefield Center. Large models and interactive displays provide fascinating insight into icefields, glaciers and the river systems they feed. Admission is free of charge.

Columbia Icefield Chalet, ☎ 877-423-7433, $$$$. The chalet occupies the third floor of the Icefield Center, open from May through September. 13 mountain-view rooms, 17 glacier-view rooms and two deluxe rooms are available.

Athabasca Glacier Icewalks, ☎ 800-565-7547 or 780-852-5595, www.icewalks.com. If you would like to safely venture onto the glacier and gain a deeper understanding of icefields and glaciers, sign up for a guided interpretive ice walk. Athabasca Glacier Icewalks operates from June through September, weather permitting. You may book ahead in Jasper at the Jasper Adventure Center (see the *Jasper National Park* chapter) or at the hotel front desk of the Icefields Center.

◆ **Ice Cubed**. Offered daily except Sundays and Thursdays. A three-hour walk explores the lower half of the Athabasca Glacier. Departs at 11 am. $55 adult, $27.50 child seven-17 years.

◆ **Icewalk Deluxe**. Offered Sundays and Thursdays. A five- to six-hour strenuous walk with in-depth discovery of glaciers. Departs 11 am. $60 adult, $30 child.

Brewster Columbia Icefield Glacier Experience, ☎ 877-423-7433 or 403-762-6735, www.brewster.ca/attractions. Brewster operates SnoCoach tours on the Athabasca Glacier, a 90-minute round trip that takes passengers one km onto the glacier from the end of the restricted access road in SnoCoaches, 56-passenger all-terrain vehicles. Passengers may disembark and walk on the glacier at the turnaround point. This is a popular tourist activity. SnoCoaches depart every 15 to 30 minutes from 9 am to 5 pm April to September, as well as in October from 10 am to 4 pm. (I have seen up to eight SnoCoaches operating along the access road and on the glacier at one time – glacier traffic-jams! This from the vantage point of Wilcox Pass – see hike below.) Reservations are not required for individuals. $33.95 adult, $17 child (six-15 years).

Wilcox Pass

Hike: Eight km (five miles) round-trip, 11.2 km (seven miles) one-way to Tangle Falls.

Elevation gain: 335 m (1,099 feet).

Watchable wildlife: bighorn sheep (mature rams).

This is one of the best half-day or day-hikes (to Tangle Falls) in Jasper National Park. If you are anxious to escape the mid-summer crowds at the Icefields Center or the Athabasca

Glacier, the masses are but dots on the landscape from this high alpine valley with its dramatic views of the Athabasca Glacier and its surrounding peaks. The invigorating hike into Wilcox Pass is much more rewarding than dealing with the crowds down below. If you don't want to hike all the way to the pass, hike at least to the viewpoint at Km 2½ (Mile 1½) for a breathtaking reward.

The trailhead is about 50 m (164 feet) along the left side of the short access road to the Wilcox Creek Campground, located three km (two miles) south of the Icefield Center on the east side of the parkway. Snow can remain in the pass area until late July.

The trail climbs steeply for one km (.6 miles) after which you reach an open ridge at Km 2½ (Mile 1.6) and a panorama of Mount Athabasca, Mount Andromeda, the Athabasca Glacier, Snow Dome, Dome Glacier and Mount Kitchener. Although somewhat difficult to recognize, the summit is reached at Km 4 (Mile 2½).

To reach Tangle Falls, continue northward, following along a disappearing boggy trail, keeping left along the base of Wilcox Peak. Continue through the valley of Tangle Creek – a marker indicates where the descent begins – dropping into the forest where a more defined trail is visible, emerging at the parkway 200 m (656 feet) south of Tangle Falls and 10 km (6.2 miles) north of Wilcox Creek Campground.

Wilcox Creek Campground (see *Camping* section, *Jasper National Park*) is a favorite for its accessibility to the Athabasca Glacier and Wilcox Pass. It is the highest campground in the mountain parks. Due to narrow turnarounds and small sites, it is not suitable for large recreational vehicles.

 Did You Know? Less than five km (three miles) south of the Columbia Icefield Center, Sunwapta Pass marks the boundary (since 1930) between Jasper and Banff National Parks. At 2,035 m (6,676 feet), it is the second-highest point on the Icefields Parkway.

Parker Ridge

Hike: 5.4 km (3.3 miles) round-trip.

Elevation gain: 250 m (820 feet).

Watchable wildlife: mountain sheep, mountain goats, pikas, white-tailed ptarmigans, eagles, hawks.

Although this northernmost trail in Banff Park is one of the most heavily used short trails in the Rockies, you won't want to miss the incredible view of the nine-km (5.6-mile) Saskatchewan Glacier – the longest outlet valley glacier of the Columbia Icefield – from the easily accessible alpine zone. The large parking area is just off the west side of the parkway, 8.8 km (5.4 miles) south of the Icefield Center.

The well defined trail switchbacks across an open north-facing slope to the summit. Once you are on the tundra ridge above treeline, the trail veers left and descends slightly to the first viewpoint, then to another a short distance farther along for a better perspective.

Be sure you follow the established route as a number of short-cuts have eroded the trail. Keep in mind that hardy alpine zone flowers bloom in these harsh conditions for only a few weeks each summer so be extra careful where you tread. The trail is closed until it's snow-free, sometimes not until July.

Bridal Veil Falls & Panther Falls

Less than five km (three miles) south of Parker Ridge (two km or 1.2 miles before descending the "Big Hill"), a parking area on the east side of the highway affords a view across the valley to the second-highest waterfall in Banff Park, Bridal Veil Falls. Many tourists pull into the parking area, take a quick look at the falls from their vehicle and carry on their way.

An inconspicuously marked trail at the south end of the parking lot leads to Banff Park's highest waterfall, which is hidden from view – the impressive Panther Falls. The trail descends gradually for about one km to a viewpoint near the base of the falls.

Back at the parking lot and again hidden from view, from the north end you can access the canyon that Nigel Creek has forged before plunging down the falls.

Use extreme caution, especially with small children, since there are no guardrails. The rock along the canyon is slippery, as is the ground near the falls.

North Saskatchewan Valley Viewpoint

This popular pullout is half a km south of Bridal Veil Falls/Panther Falls, with an eagle's eye view down the narrow canyon of the North Saskatchewan River and the parkway. The highway switchbacks along the "Big Bend" in the "Big Hill," with an elevation loss of 425 vertical m (1,394 feet).

Saskatchewan River Crossing

The David Thompson Highway junction at Saskatchewan River Crossing is 153 km (95 miles) south of Jasper or 72 km (45 miles) north of Lake Louise. Three rivers converge here: **Mistaya River** from the south; **Howse River** from the west; and, arising in the Columbia Icefield, **North Saskatchewan River** from the north.

Mistaya Canyon

Yet another impressive limestone canyon. The Mistaya Canyon parking area is on the west side of the parkway 5½ km (3.4 miles) south of Saskatchewan Crossing. To reach the canyon, follow the old roadbed for one km as it descends gradually through the forest. A bridge spans the gorge where you can safely view the deeply cut walls carved by the Mistaya River, which originates in Peyto Lake (see below). *Mistaya* is the Cree word for grizzly bear.

Be careful if you are venturing on the unfenced canyon viewpoints, not advisable when conditions are wet and slippery.

Snowbird Glacier Viewpoint

About 24 km (15 miles) south of Mistaya Canyon on the west side of the parkway, the Snowbird Glacier spreads its wings across the face of Mount Patterson.

Peyto Glacier Viewpoint

About four km (2½ miles) farther south, Peyto Glacier is visible on Mount Thompson to the southwest from the parking area on the east side of the parkway, with Peyto Peak on the right.

Bow Summit

Approximately 190 km (118 miles) south of Jasper (and less than three km or 1.8 miles from Peyto Glacier Viewpoint), 2,069-m (6,788-foot) Bow Summit is the highest point on the Icefields Parkway and the second-highest highway pass in Canada. (The highest stretch of road is the one that traverses Highwood Pass in Kananaskis Country on Highway 40 at an altitude of 2,210 m or 7,250 feet.)

Peyto Lake Viewpoint

An access road branches west from the parkway on Bow Summit, leading to the parking area for the not-to-be-missed viewpoint over brilliant turquoise-colored Peyto Lake.

The .8-km (.5-mile) wheelchair-accessible (careful, it's steep) paved trail leads through subalpine zone forest with its typically stunted spruce and fir trees.

If you enjoy wildflowers, you'll want to explore the meadows surrounding the area. In July and August the ground is a blanket of white, yellow and red heather, western anemone, blue forget-me-nots, white, red, yellow, pink Indian paintbrush... the list goes on. Be sure to stay on the paths as these hardy plants put on a colorful show despite the ground being covered with snow for nine months of the year.

 Be on the lookout for the pesky Clark's nutcrackers noisily flying about. Seems they'll stop at nothing in search of a handout, but remember not to feed them.

Peyto Lake

Hike: 4.8 km (2.9 mile) round-trip.

Leave the crowds behind at the viewpoint and explore the shores of gorgeous Peyto Lake. This trail drops 275 m (902 feet) from the viewpoint to the lake's south end.

Follow the right uphill trail from the viewing platform. The trail to the lake plummets into the forest and switchbacks for two km (1.2 miles), before emerging onto the alluvial flats along the lakeshore.

LEGENDS OF THE ROCKIES - BILL PEYTO

Peyto Lake and Glacier are named for one of the Rockies' most respected pioneer outfitters and guides, Bill Peyto. As with many of the independent characters that made their way to the rough 'n rugged wilds of the fledgling mountain parks, Peyto had a wandering spirit and colorful personality that were trademarks of many successful guides. His legendary reputation as a mountain man was amplified by his outlandish character and wild appearance.

Peyto guided some of the most famous alpinists and hunters of his time and was described as a "guide par excellence, who would not know the meaning of the word defeat."

Recommended Reading: *Diamond Hitch, The Early Outfitters and Guides of Banff and Jasper*, by E.J. Hart. Banff: Summerthought Ltd., 1979.

Simpson's Num-Ti-Jah Lodge

Num-Ti-Jah Lodge was the dream of legendary Rockies outfitter and guide Jimmy Simpson who arrived in Canada from England in 1896. Local natives gave Simpson the name "Nashan-esen," meaning "wolverine-go-quick," due to his speedy ability to travel on snowshoes. For 50 years he led famous mountaineers, scientists, hunters and artists, earning a reputation as a skilful hunter and competent guide with a quick-witted mind and a penchant for tall tales.

In 1898, when he first camped on the shores of Bow Lake, he was immediately enamored with the area and vowed that he would one day make it his home. In 1920 he obtained a lease from the government to build his first cabin, from which he had a base to conduct his outfitting. When the Banff-Jasper highway reached Bow Lake by 1937, Simpson and his family began expanding and in 1950 the lodge in its present form was completed. Simpson named the lodge Num-Ti-Jah, a Stoney Indian word for pine marten, a small animal similar to a sable, prevalent in the area during his trapping days.

After Simpson's death in 1972, his son Jimmy Jr., who also did outfitting , managed the lodge until seven years before his own death in 2003.

Today, the Simpson family no longer operates the lodge but visitors can enjoy the idyllic setting that Jimmy Simpson was so taken with as well as the unique 25-room lodge. Step inside and you'll be transported back in time. The tasteful rustic surroundings include Simpson family photographs and animal trophies that hang from the walls. Spend some time examining Simpson's incredible rock, mineral and fossil collection – 70 years worth of treasures. A ledge along an outside wall of the lodge is adorned with beautiful quartz crystals.

Num-Ti-Jah Lodge is open year-round except October. Amenities include a gourmet dining room and lounge, gift shop and excellent hiking and skiing trails from the site. This is a wonderful summer or winter escape – there are no telephones or televisions. If you are going to splurge on high-end accommodations, why not stay in a place that oozes heritage and character?

Rustic lake-view and mountain-view rooms with private washrooms, as well as four rooms with a shared washroom. All-inclusive packages available. Reserve in advance as the lodge is often full throughout the summer with guests on bicycle tours along the parkway. ☎ 403-522-2167, www.num-ti-jah.com, $$$$ to $$$$$.

 **Recommended Reading:** *Jimmy Simpson, Legend of the Rockies*, by E.J. Hart, Canmore: Altitude Publishing, 1991.

Crowfoot Glacier Viewpoint

Located less than three km (1.8 miles) south of Num-Ti-Jah Lodge (33 km or 20½ miles north of the Trans-Canada Highway). Early in the 20th century the Crowfoot Glacier resembled the foot of a crow with its three large toes clutching the cliff. By the middle of the century the glacier retreated so that the lowest toe is no longer visible.

Helen Lake

Hike: 12 km (seven miles) or 13.8 km (8½ miles) round-trip.

Elevation gain: 550 m (1,804 feet).

Watchable wildlife: hoary marmots.

This is one of my favorite half-day hikes along the Parkway. I love the open meadows filled with wildflowers, the castellated peaks, the whistling hoary marmots whose appearance, I think, is solely for the amusement of hikers, and, of course, the pretty alpine lakes. The road to the trailhead is on the opposite side of the highway from the Crowfoot Glacier viewpoint.

It's a steady climb east for the first three km (1.8 miles), then the trail switchbacks and after one km follows along the foot of a recent rockslide. At km 5 (mile 3) you hop across Helen Creek. Helen Lake sits beneath Cirque Peak, a wonderful spot to relax and watch the fish jump, but don't forget your mosquito repellent.

For views of Katherine Lake and Dolomite Pass, it's worth the hike of another .9 km (.6 miles), skirting the right side of the lake and up along a switchback to a rocky ridge.

Oh... oh... oh... the echoes in the cirque are great – try it!

Banff Townsite

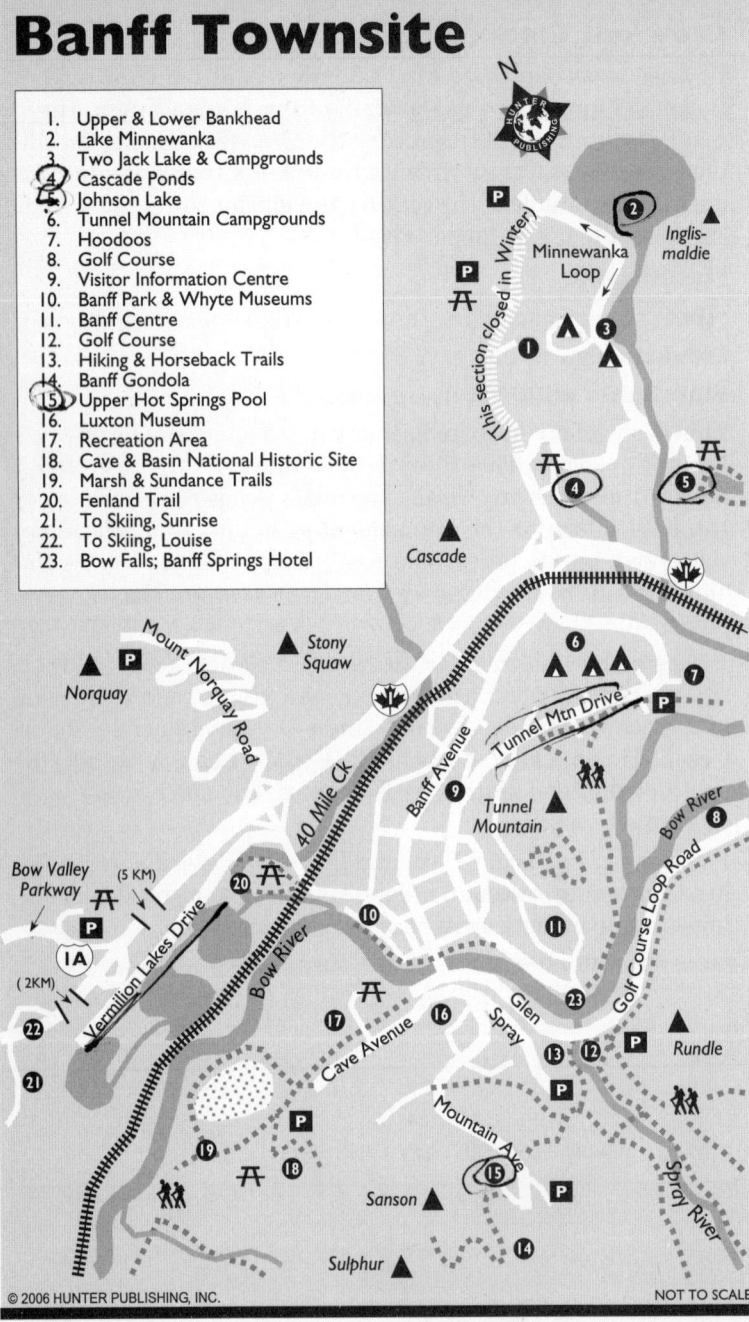

1. Upper & Lower Bankhead
2. Lake Minnewanka
3. Two Jack Lake & Campgrounds
4. Cascade Ponds
5. Johnson Lake
6. Tunnel Mountain Campgrounds
7. Hoodoos
8. Golf Course
9. Visitor Information Centre
10. Banff Park & Whyte Museums
11. Banff Centre
12. Golf Course
13. Hiking & Horseback Trails
14. Banff Gondola
15. Upper Hot Springs Pool
16. Luxton Museum
17. Recreation Area
18. Cave & Basin National Historic Site
19. Marsh & Sundance Trails
20. Fenland Trail
21. To Skiing, Sunrise
22. To Skiing, Louise
23. Bow Falls; Banff Springs Hotel

N

Minnewanka Loop

Inglis-maldie

This section closed in Winter

Cascade

Mount Norquay Road

Stony Squaw

Norquay

Tunnel Mtn Drive

Bow River

Banff Avenue

40 Mile Ck

Tunnel Mountain

Bow Valley Parkway

(5 KM)

Vermilion Lakes Drive

Bow River

1A

(2KM)

Cave Avenue

Glen

Spray

Golf Course Loop Road

Rundle

Mountain Ave

Sanson

Sulphur

Spray River

© 2006 HUNTER PUBLISHING, INC.

NOT TO SCALE

Banff National Park

Banff is one of the most renowned tourist destinations in Canada and the most popular in the Canadian Rockies. It is the oldest national park in Canada, the second in North America (following Yellowstone in Wyoming) and the third-oldest park in the world (following Royal in Australia). It encompasses 6,641 sq kilometres (2,564 sq miles), including the Lake Louise area and part of the Icefields Parkway.

Over eight million people enter Banff Park each year, of which over three million are considered park visitors – the highest visitation of any Canadian National Park.

Most of Banff's natural attractions are easily accessible from its scenic roads and highways. Popular sites around Banff townsite include the **Cave and Basin National Historic Site**, **Upper Hot Springs Pool**, **Cascade Gardens**, **Tunnel Mountain Drive**, **Vermilion Lakes**, **Johnson Lake** and **Lake Minnewanka**. The townsite exudes a cosmopolitan atmosphere with an expansive array of tourist services as well as cultural attractions such as the **Whyte Museum**, the **Banff Park Museum** and the **Banff Center**. The Bow Valley Parkway, Lake Louise and the Icefields Parkway also present countless opportunities for sightseeing and wildlife viewing. Banff National Park maintains 1,500 km (932 miles) of trails and 50 backcountry campgrounds. In winter, three downhill ski areas serve the area.

In the early days of the Rocky Mountain Parks it was thought that, because the extent of the Rockies was so tremendous, there was no danger of them becoming overcrowded. This has, unfortunately, proved to be untrue. Commercial development combined with a global appeal has created a tremendous strain on Banff National Park's wilderness and heritage sites. The pace of development has been curtailed in an effort to ensure the balance between use and preservation. If you are one of the many fortunate enough to experience Banff's unmistakable beauty, embrace it wholeheartedly but please remember to tread lightly.

■ History

The thermal springs at the foot of Sulphur Mountain, known today as the Cave and Basin National Historic Site, are recognized as the "birthplace of Canada's national parks system." Stoney Indians knew of the springs, believing them to have special healing powers. Receiving directions from Stoneys, two American hunters were the first to record a visit to the hot springs in 1875.

By 1883 the Canadian Pacific Railway (CPR) had arrived in the Bow Valley and three railway workers, Frank McCabe and brothers William and Tom McCardell, rediscovered the springs. With dollar signs dancing in their eyes, the three laid claim to the springs. Brought to the public's attention, a number of other claims and counterclaims were filed, with the government finally settling the dispute in 1885 by setting aside as a federal reserve the area around the springs, declaring it "of great sanitary advantage to the public."

The CPR route through the mountains crossed some of the most scenic terrain in North America. But it was clear that construction, maintenance and operating expenses of the route would exceed profits. William Cornelius Van Horne, Vice-President and General Manager of the CPR, a strong supporter of establishing a national park, rose to the challenge of making the mountain section of the railway profitable. "We can't export the scenery; then we will import the tourists!" Van Horne declared. Proclaiming the Canadian Rockies as "the Mountain Playground of the World," he recruited the wealthy, including royalty. They came and stayed at small inns at Siding 29, later renamed Banff for Banffshire, Scotland, and birthplace of CPR President George Stephen. Under Van Horne's direction, the Banff Springs Hotel opened in 1888.

In 1887 the Hot Springs Reserve was expanded and designated as Rocky Mountain National Park. The area around Lake Louise was added to the park in 1902 and in 1930 the park boundaries were fixed and the park renamed Banff National Park.

With the establishment of the luxury Banff Springs Hotel and the increasing number of visitors from around the world, other hotels and businesses opened in the townsite. Soon outfitters were leading excursions farther and farther into the mountains, assisting mountaineers in the race to be first to conquer the summits. To help promote mountaineering, the CPR (Canadian Pacific Railway) imported guides from Switzerland. Banff and Lake Louise became the major Rocky Mountain tourist centers.

■ Getting There & Getting Around

By Road

 Automobiles were not permitted in Banff Park until 1915. Today there are 320 km (200 miles) of paved roads traversing the park, with many visitors arriving from Calgary, a 1½-hour drive. Alberta's most traveled highway, the **Trans Canada Highway (Highway 1)** is wide and well maintained, but this is not a sightseeing highway. It is the major east-west thoroughfare, with traffic moving at maximum speed. To minimize the potential for collisions with wildlife, the Trans Canada around Banff has been fenced off and wildlife corridor underpasses have been installed.

 Try to avoid driving between Lake Louise and Banff or Banff and Calgary on Sundays or on Mondays during holiday weekends, between about 3 and 8 pm, as many Calgarians are heading home from weekend escapes.

The **Bow Valley Parkway 1A** begins one km (.6 miles) from Lake Louise village on the road to the ski area or six km (3.7 miles) west of the town of Banff. Paralleling the busy Trans Canada Highway and the Bow River for approximately 50 km (31 miles), it is the preferred tourist route for scenic appeal and travel at a leisurely pace (maximum 60 km/hr or 37 mph). It's also a very popular bicycle route.

 To protect wildlife, from March 1 to June 25, from 6 pm to 9 am, the Bow Valley Parkway is closed between Johnston Canyon and Banff; use the Trans Canada Highway instead.

Connecting Lake Louise and Jasper, the 230-km (143-mile) **Icefields Parkway (Highway 93)** joins Jasper and Banff National Parks. Visitors should take a few days or longer to fully enjoy the many scenic opportunities along this world-renowned route. (See the *Icefields Parkway* chapter for detailed information.)

Distances from Banff Townsite

Castle Junction . . . . 30 km (19 miles)

Lake Louise . . . . 58 km (36 miles)

Jasper. . . . . 286 km (178 miles)

Field (Yoho) . . . . 90 km (56 miles)

Golden . . . . 130 km (81 miles)

Radium (Kootenay) . . . . 132 km (82 miles)

Canmore. 25 km (15 miles)

Calgary. . . . . 128 km (80 miles)

Edmonton . . . . 424 km (263 miles)

Vancouver . . . . 933 km (580 miles)

Bus Service

 **Banff Public Transit**. Buses run every 40 minutes through the main areas of town during summer. Adult $2, senior or child six-12 years $1, child under six free. Schedules available at the Visitor Information Center.

Greyhound, ☎ 403-762-6751 or 403-522-3870 in Lake Louise or 800-661-8747 for fare and schedule information, 100 Gopher Street (Brewster Terminal) in Banff, Samson Mall in Lake Louise, www.greyhound.ca. Frequent bus service from/to Calgary, Edmonton, Lake Louise and Jasper.

Brewster Transportation and Tours, ☎ 800-760-6934 or 403-760-6934, 100 Gopher Street, www.brewster.ca. Brewster Airporter daily bus service from/to Calgary International Airport year-round. Departures to/from Lake Louise, Banff and Calgary. Calgary to Banff $48, Calgary to Lake Louise $56, Banff to Jasper $64, Lake Louise to Jasper $55, Banff to Lake Louise $15; children half-price. Service from Red Deer and Edmonton also.

The Mountain Connector, ☎ 888-786-3641 or 403-762-4343, www.mountainconnector.com. Transportation between Banff, Lake Louise, Jasper and Canmore in winter from December to April. Transfers to and from Calgary are also available. Banff to Jasper $59 adults, $35 children.

Rocky Mountain Sky Shuttle, ☎ 888-762-8754 or 403-762-5200, www.rockymountainskyshuttle.com. Transportation between the Calgary International Airport and Banff, Lake Louise and Canmore in summer (May to November) and Banff, Lake Louise, Canmore, Sunshine Village, Panorama and Fernie in winter (December to April). Door-to-door service; reservations strongly recommended.

Car Rentals

Avis, ☎ 403-762-3222, Cascade Plaza.

Budget, ☎ 403-762-4565, 202 Bear Street.

Hertz, ☎ 403-762-2027, Fairmont Banff Springs Hotel.

National, ☎ 403-762-2688, Lynx Street & Caribou Avenue.

National (Lake Louise), ☎ 403-522-3870, Samson Mall.

Taxis

Banff Taxi, ☎ 403-762-4444.

Taxi Taxi, ☎ 403-762-3111.

Banff Limousine, ☎ 403-762-5466.

Alpine Limousine, ☎ 403-762-5558.

Banff Airporter, ☎ 403-762-3330.

Banff National Park

By Air

Calgary International Airport, ☎ 403-735-1200.

By Rail

More than 30 freight trains per day cross the park via the CPR line. There is no passenger train service in Banff, but **Rocky Mountaineer Railtours**, ☎ 800-665-7245, www.rocky-mountaineer.com, offers luxury vacation tours through the Rockies and Banff. (See *Jasper* chapter, *Tour Operators & Booking Agents* section, for more information.)

■ Special Events

Canada Day, July 1st festivities include various entertainers, live music, food booths, parade and fireworks; free entrance to Banff National Park.

Canada's Parks Day celebrations, held the second or third Saturday in July. Join a Parks Canada Interpreter for a free three-hour interpretive hike to the top of Sulphur Mountain and Sanson Peak. The Friends of Banff also organize events throughout the day.

Banff Summer Arts Festival at the Banff Center, held in July/August. A huge line-up of fabulous arts events.

Melissa's Road Race, held annually in September with 3-, 10- or 22-km events.

Annual Festival of Wine and Food, held in October/November at the Fairmont Banff Springs Hotel.

The **Banff Mountain Film and Book Festivals** are annual world-renowned weeklong festivals that take place in late October/early November at the Banff Center. They feature mountain/adventure films from around the world, presentations by famous mountaineers, book signings, launches, readings, slide shows and a book fair.

Winterstart, a month-long promotion celebrating winter in the Canadian Rockies, with many events and activities through November and December.

The **Santa Claus Parade** welcomes Santa to Banff at the end of November.

It's a **Rocky Mountain White Christmas** from the end of November through New Year's. Celebrate the season with hotel discounts, special shopping, Christmas carollers and more.

Ice Magic International Ice Sculpture Competition and Exhibition, January in Lake Louise.

Banff/Lake Louise Winter Festival, a tradition since 1916, held in January/February, with sports races, a parade, family winter carnival, town party, Artwalk, pancake breakfast and more.

The **Whyte Museum** and **Banff Center** organize a number of special events throughout the year. Contact them (see *Attractions* section) for a schedule of events.

BANFF INDIAN DAYS

Indian Days **BANFF**
CANADIAN ROCKIES
CANADIAN PACIFIC

It was not unusual for CPR trains to be delayed a number of days during flood season or from avalanches along the lines. During June of 1894 high water on the Bow River washed out part of the railway track along its banks, causing visitors to be stranded at the Banff Springs Hotel. Desperate hotel staff contacted guide Tom Wilson, who had previously performed other public relations activities for the CPR, for suggestions to entertain guests while they waited for the line to be repaired. He approached the Stoney Indians, with whom he had an excellent rapport, and asked them to participate in games and demonstrations for the guests.

The following day, donned in regalia and painted faces, the Stoneys paraded through town to the Banff Springs, where they pitched their tipis, staged horse races and bucking and roping contests and demonstrated their culture. The guests were thrilled and it was decided to stage the event annually.

Wilson helped organize Banff Indian Days for many years thereafter, and it remained a popular event until 1978.

■ Banff Townsite

The townsite of Banff is unique in that it was planned as a resort town from its beginnings. Situated in the Bow Valley at the confluence of the Bow and Spray Rivers at the base of Tunnel and Sulphur Mountains, the Bow River flows between Mount Rundle and Tunnel Mountain with the Spray River flowing into the Bow at the falls.

Some of the best panoramas of the townsite and the valley can easily be had from the summit of **Sulphur Mountain** (to which you can ride the gondola), from the Mount Norquay Road or from Tunnel Mountain Drive. One of Banff townsite's signature scenes, forever photographed and painted **Mount Rundle** dominates the view to the south, the prominent wedge-shaped peak rising to 2,949 m (9,700 feet) and reflected in the **Vermilion Lakes**. As you look northeast up the main street of Banff Avenue, **Cascade Mountain** rises majestically to 2,998 m (9,836 feet), the highest mountain overlooking the townsite.

The town of Banff's resident population is 7,700, of which approximately 400 are summer park employees. During peak visitation in the summer, upwards of 30,000 people can be found in and around the townsite.

Wandering about town, you will find an eclectic mix of restaurants and pubs, shops and boutiques, as well as many cultural attractions, services, accommodations and scenic attractions.

Distances from Banff Townsite

Mount Norquay . . . . 6.6 km (four miles)
Sunshine Village . . . . 16 km (10 miles)
Vermilion Lakes . . . . 4.8 km (three miles)
Tunnel Mountain Hoodoos . . . . . 6.2 km (3.9 miles)
Cave and Basin. . . . . 12 km (.7 miles)
Upper Hot Springs Pool . . . . 4.2 km (2.6 miles)
Banff Gondola . . . . 4.2 km (2.6 miles)
Bow Falls . . . . 1½ km (.9 miles)
Johnson Lake. . . . . 3½ km (2.2 miles)
Lake Minnewanka . . . . 12 km (seven miles)
Bow Valley Parkway Junction . . 5.6 km (3½ miles)

The Visitor Information Center, ☎ 403-762-1550, 224 Banff Avenue, Banff.VRC@pc.gc.ca. Located downtown, the center houses Parks Canada and Banff Tourism advisors as well as a Friends of Banff retail shop. Courtesy phones, public washrooms and free films in the downstairs theater at 8:30 pm during the summer. Operating Hours: June 25 to September 6, 8 am to 8 pm; September 7 to 26, 8 am to 6 pm; September 27 to May 20, 9 am to 5 pm; May 21 to June 24, 8 am to 6 pm.

The Banff Lake Louise Tourism Bureau can also provide assistance with to visitor services, ☎ 403-762-8421, www.bannflakelouise.com.

FRIENDS OF BANFF NATIONAL PARK

A non-profit charitable organization "committed to increasing awareness and appreciation of the natural and cultural heritage of Banff National Park." The Friends operate retail shops at the Visitor Information Centers in Banff and Lake Louise, offering a selection of books, trail guides, maps and gift items. Pick up their *Events Guide* for information on free educational programs offered each summer, including the "Junior Naturalist Program" and guided walks. Rent a "Discovery Backpack," which contains binoculars, field guides, maps and more, $10 for 24 hours. ☎ 403-762-8918, www.friendsofbanff.com.

Banff National Park

Banff Historical Walking Tour

History buffs will enjoy the Banff Historical Walking Tour, highlighting 57 of Banff's first residences, commercial buildings, churches and historic sites. The detailed brochure – available free of charge from the Visitor Information Center – makes a great souvenir. The old **Banff Cemetery**, at the south end of Grizzly Street, is one of the historic sites along the walking tour. It is the final resting place of many of Banff's prominent pioneer residents such as Mary Schäffer Warren, Tom Wilson, Bill Peyto, Byron Harmon and A.O. Wheeler.

■ Attractions

Whyte Museum of the Canadian Rockies, ☎ 403-762-2291, 111 Bear Street, www.whyte.org. Each year's Calendar of Events of the Whyte Museum is jam-packed with interesting exhibitions and programs, some of which are free. The art collection features historical and contemporary works that reflect the nature and development of the visual arts in the Rockies as well as the overall culture of the area. The collection contains approximately 4,000 works, including paintings, drawings, photographs, sculptures, prints, mixed media works, and objects of fine craft. The heritage collection contains material relating to recreation (climbing, skiing, hiking, riding), commerce (outfitting, guiding, packing, surveying), pioneer household and Stoneys First Nations. The museum also operates seven heritage homes including the Whyte home, Bill Peyto's cabin and the Luxton home and garden; guided home tours and historic walks daily June 1 to September 1. Online exhibitions, Museum Shop, archives and library. Open 10 am to 5 pm daily, closed Christmas and New Year's Day. Adult $6, student/senior $3.50, family $15.

Women of the Rockies – Catharine Whyte

Catharine Robb was born into a life of privilege in Massachusetts in 1906. A Boston debutante, her childhood ambition was to help others. While studying art at the Boston Museum School of Fine Art, she met her future husband Peter Whyte in 1927. They married in 1930, settling in Peter's hometown of Banff. In 1931 they built their log-studio home along the Bow River.

Catherine quickly came to adore the mountains, the couple dedicating much of their time to traveling and painting the wilderness. Although she fostered the art community that included such notables as Carl Rungius and the Group of Seven and selflessly promoted her husband's painting, she did not consider her own paintings to be of true merit.

As philanthropists, the Whytes developed an interest in preserving Rocky Mountain heritage, establishing a foundation in 1958.

After Peter's death in 1966, Catherine immersed herself in the cultural community, travel, skiing and conservation. In 1968 their Wa-Che-Yo-Cha-Pa Foundation building opened, which would later become the Whyte Museum of the Canadian Rockies.

Catherine received the Order of Canada in 1978 and died in 1979 at the age of 72. Catherine and Peter Whyte's legacy in Banff and the Canadian Rockies lives on in their paintings and life's work.

Banff Park Museum National Historic Site, 91 Banff Avenue (at Central Park downtown). The oldest (1903) natural history museum in Western Canada displays an extensive collection of animal, bird, insect and geological specimens. Children's Discovery Room and Reading Room. Guided tours available. Open mid-May to September 30, 10 am to 6 pm and October 1 to mid-May, 1 to 5 pm. Adult $4, senior $3.50, youth $3, family/group $10. Cash or traveler's checks only.

Buffalo Nations Museum (formerly known as the Luxton Museum of the Plains Indians), ☎ 403-762-2388, 1 Birch Avenue. (Follow Banff Avenue over the Bow River, then turn right on Birch Avenue.) Discover the heritage of the Indians of the Northern Plains and the Canadian Rockies. Artifacts and taxidermy displays that celebrate the culture of Native peoples. Open every day May through October from 10 am to

6 pm and 1 to 5 pm in winter. Adult $8, student/senior $6, child (six-12 years) $2.50, family $16.50.

Park Administration Building, 101 Mountain Avenue. (To reach the parking area, follow Banff Avenue over the Bow River, turn left at the traffic lights that are in front of the Administration Building, then turn right on Mountain Avenue.) Three free attractions located in and around the building are:

> **Canada Place** – A fun interactive exhibit that features Canada's land, people, history, culture and accomplishments. Great for kids. Open 10 am to 6 pm every day from mid-May to mid-October.

> **Siksika Nation Interpretive Center** – Have you ever been inside a tipi? Learn about the culture of the Siksika (Blackfoot) Nation and their historical connection with Banff National Park from Native interpreters. Open from July to mid-September with traditional dancing on Tuesdays at noon.

> **Cascade Gardens** – A peaceful respite from busy downtown. Gazebos, bridges, flagstone paths and waterfalls weave between prolific tiers of flowerbeds. This internationally known garden was designed and built in the 1930s as a relief project during the Depression. The reflecting pool in front of the Administration Building sits in line with Banff Avenue and Cascade Mountain – one of Banff's most recognized postcard views. Between 40,000 and 43,000 plants of about 50 varieties bloom in this garden paradise from June to September.

Cave and Basin National Historic Site, ☎ 403-762-1556, 311 Cave Avenue. (Follow Banff Avenue over the Bow River, turn right at the traffic lights in front of the Parks Canada Administration Building onto Cave Avenue and follow it to the end.) A year after the Hot Springs Reserve was established – the beginning of Canada's national park system – two bathhouses were constructed. In the years following, the facilities were expanded and upgraded, closed, re-opened and renovated. Today, you can visit the cave that started it all, as well as the open-air basin (look for the Banff Springs snail, a species at risk) and the replica bathhouse and exhibits (bathing is no longer permitted). Take time to walk along the self-guided .4-km (.2-mile) **Discovery Boardwalk Trail** above the bathing pavilion to see the cave vent and the .5-km (.3-mile) **Marsh Boardwalk Trail** where the spring water flows and creates an oasis for plant and animal life – including tropical fish! Explore the longer 2.7-km (1.7-mile) **Marsh Loop** and the 7.4-km (4.6-mile) **Sundance Trail**, also popular cross-country ski trails.

Open mid-May to September 30, 9 am to 6 pm, October 1 to mid-May, Monday to Friday 11 am to 4 pm and weekends 9:30 am to 5 pm. Adult $4, senior $3.50, youth $3, family/group $10. Cash and travelers checks only. Wheelchair-accessible. Guided tours are available.

Banff Upper Hot Springs, ☎ 403-762-1515, Mountain Avenue. (Follow Banff Avenue over the Bow River, turn left at the traffic lights in front of the Parks Canada Administration Building, then turn right on Mountain Avenue and follow it 3.3 km or two miles to the parking lot.) The soaking pool is outdoors at the base of Sulphur Mountain, with a view of the Bow Valley and Mount Rundle. The temperature averages about 40°C (104°F). It can get extremely crowded; the least busy times are mid-morning and early afternoon. Changing rooms have showers and hair dryers as well as locker rentals (it is not recommended to leave valuables in your locker). Patio, terrace, café, and gift shop.

Mid-May to mid-September 9 am to 11 pm, mid-September to mid-May 10 am to 10 pm Sunday to Thursday, 10 am to 11 pm Friday and Saturday. Adult $7.50, child/senior $6.50, family (two adults, two children) $23, extra child $3.50. Wheelchair-accessible.

 How about a massage? **Pleiades Massage**, ☎ 403-760-2500, at the Upper Hot Springs offers massage, shiatsu, reflexology, reiki and body treatment sessions. Prices start at $50 for 30 minutes. Open year-round; appointments recommended.

Around the World in Six Days

People from around the world come to see Banff's natural wonders and attractions, such as the Upper Hot Springs. While soaking in the pool, I met a Korean couple holidaying with their six-year-old daughter. With their limited broken English and my non-existent Korean, they were able to convey that this was their first visit to Canada and that they were traveling from Vancouver to Toronto in a rented car – in six days! This seemed crazy to me, and I kept repeating "six days?" They kept nodding and explained that in Korea, most working people are only permitted six days vacation per year. They were flying back to Korea as soon as they reached Toronto.

I suggested that if they return to Canada they might spend the entire six days in one location such as Banff. I think the idea sounded ludicrous to these happy international travelers who shed a new light on making the most out of a vacation.

Banff Gondola

Drive: Five minutes from Banff townsite, next to the Upper Hot Springs Pool on Mountain Avenue.

Watchable wildlife: Eagles, bighorn sheep, Columbian and golden-mantled ground squirrels.

Glide up to the top of Sulphur Mountain (2,281 m or 7,483 feet) in only eight minutes. Overlook Banff townsite and the Bow Valley, including Bow Falls, Lake Minnewanka and the Banff Springs Hotel. Interpretive displays help you find the names of the surrounding mountains – Cascade Mountain, Mount Norquay and the Sundance Range. Walk along the boardwalk and to the historic meteorological station.

Open year-round (except during annual maintenance in January and Christmas day), including restaurant and snack bar; dining room from May to late October. Adult $23.50, child (six-15 years) $11.75.

If you'd rather get a workout, a 5.6-km (3½-mile) trail climbs from the Upper Hot Springs Pool to the ridge top of Sulphur Mountain – the gondola ride down is free. (The gondola trail climbs beneath the gondola line, very closely at times. If you're going to hike this route, try doing it before the first gondola of the day.) ☎ 403-762-2523, www.banffgondola.com.

NORMAN SANSON

Completed in 1903, the meteorological observatory building that sits atop Sanson Peak was named in honor of Norman B. Sanson, curator of the Banff Park Museum from 1896 to 1942 and Park Meteorologist who tended to the recording equipment for nearly 30 years, hiking from Banff townsite to the top of Sulphur Mountain more than 1,000 times.

Sulphur Mountain Cosmic Ray Station

The Cosmic Ray Station National Historic Site is close to the summit of Sulphur Mountain, linked by a path from the upper terminal of the Banff Gondola.

The Cosmic Ray Station consisted of a laboratory building that was completed in 1957. It came about as a result of Canada's contribution to the International Geophysical Year of 1957-58, when there were 99 cosmic ray monitoring stations worldwide, nine of them in Canada. (Cosmic rays are energy charged particles that flow into our solar system from far away in the galaxy and are deflected by magnetic fields.) The lofty altitude made the Sulphur Mountain laboratory the most significant of the Canadian monitoring stations.

Research continued until 1978 and the building was removed in 1981. When the station was operational, access was by specialized vehicle on a road built up the side of the mountain. Visible from the Trans Canada Highway, the road is now closed. However, you can hike the 8 km (five miles) up Cosmic Ray Road, along a scenic southwest-facing slope. The trailhead is at the Cave and Basin parking lot.

The Banff Center

The Banff Center, ☎ 800-422-2633 or 403-762-6100, www.banffcenter.ca. Box Office, ☎ 800-413-8368 or 403-762-6301, open September to May, Monday to Saturday 12 to 5 pm and June to August, Monday to Saturday 10 am to 5 pm.

The Center's 43½-acre property is on the side of Tunnel Mountain, a 10-minute walk or five-minute drive from downtown. (Off Banff Avenue, take Buffalo Street or Wolf Street/St. Julien Road.)

The Banff Center is Canada's only post-secondary learning facility dedicated to the arts, leadership development and mountain culture. In July and August the Center features numerous performances and exhibitions by resident and visiting artists. The **Arts Festival** includes readings, lectures, music, opera, theater, dance, Aboriginal arts, new media, visual arts and art walks. Over the fall and winter the Center presents special events, exhibitions and openings as well as an extensive concert series.

You can find out what's on at the Center by visiting their website or by picking up festival brochures available all around Banff. Many of the exhibitions, presentations, readings, receptions and concerts are free or by donation.

Pick up a copy of the Center's *Self-Guided Tour & Information* brochure for a one-hour walking tour around 17 of the Center's buildings. A number of biking, hiking, walking and cross-country ski trails are accessible from the Center.

The dining room (offering breakfast, lunch, dinner), pub and café are open to the public. The Sally Borden Building houses a deli and fitness and recreation facility including a swimming pool, steam room, gymnasium, whirlpool, exercise and weight room, climbing wall and squash courts. Public swim sessions vary, so call ahead.

Banff National Park

The Banff Crag & Canyon

Banff's weekly community newspaper has been around since 1900 – almost as long as the town itself. Established by pioneer entrepreneur Norman Luxton, who – among many business ventures – also opened the Luxton Museum of the Plains Indians. The *Crag & Canyon* was Banff's only consistent weekly newspaper and today it is still published weekly and available free of charge all around Banff. Pick up a copy to find out the latest happenings in Banff and the area. www.banffcragandcanyon.com

---

■ Shopping

You can shop 'til you drop in Banff with its wide range of shops and specialty boutiques. Banff's main street, **Banff Avenue**, is lined with shops from Elk Street to Buffalo Street at the Bow River Bridge. There are various small shopping malls extending from Banff Avenue, such as historic **Harmony Lane**. Venture off Banff Avenue onto **Wolf**, **Bear**, **Caribou** and **Buffalo Streets** to discover more shops and mini-malls.

Of course, you'll find the usual assortment of tourist-oriented gift items and souvenirs, but you'll also find a good selection of quality merchandise and intriguing items, including sports gear and clothing, native arts and crafts, gourmet foods, artwork, jewelry and books.

In the summer, most shops are open seven days per week into the evening, with reduced hours in the off-season. Even if you're only window-shopping or people-watching, strolling around the downtown core is an enjoyable way to spend an afternoon. Many of the shopkeepers are local residents, some of whom are related to Banff's pioneer residents, so take the time to strike up a conversation – you never know what you might discover. Some unique and popular shops in Banff include:

The Banff Book & Art Den, 94 Banff Avenue. The best selection of books in the Canadian Rockies since 1965. If you're looking for books relating to the Rockies, you'll find them here. Gift items, CD's and greeting cards as well. Friendly and helpful staff.

Banff Indian Trading Post, 101 Cave Avenue. From downtown, cross the Bow River Bridge and turn right on Cave Avenue to reach this amazing shop with its incredible variety of genuine Indian artifacts. This store is worth visiting just for a look-see. Norman Luxton, a Banff pioneer businessman, owned the original building, which was where the CIBC bank is now, and floated across the river in 1903 to its present location. See www.banffindiantradingpost.com for mail order.

Silver City Mercantile, 201 Banff Avenue. I had loads of fun browsing this funky shop that carries a huge selection of jewelry, beads, glassware, blown glass and pottery.

Spirit of Banff, 225 Banff Avenue. If you like real maple syrup, browse this shop for a huge selection of Canadian maple products and sample some, including cookies, tea, candies and my favorite, maple butter... mmm! They carry another popular Canadian gourmet food – smoked salmon, vacuum packed and ready for shipping. There's also a selection of chocolates, souvenir items and fleece clothing. Overseas visitors can visit the adjoining duty free shop.

Made in Canada - Pure Maple Syrup

It's not made in the Rockies, but pure Canadian maple syrup from the province of Quebec is an authentic Canadian treat. Made from the sap of the sugar maple (the sugar maple leaf is on the Canadian flag) and the grey maple, it contains various minerals and vitamins. Not only is maple syrup used traditionally on foods such as pancakes, waffles, and french toast, it's an excellent flavoring for hot milk, in hot or cold cereals, in milkshakes and eggnog, in coffee or tea, in yoghurt and in fruit salads. To make maple lemonade, mix equal amounts of fresh-squeezed lemon juice with maple syrup, add water to taste and serve over ice. Simply delicious.

Whyte Museum of the Canadian Rockies Gift Shop, 111 Bear Street. The gift shop at the Whyte Museum carries a good selection of unique handmade Canadian jewelry (I couldn't resist), books, artwork, art cards and gift items. Very nice and helpful staff. They also have a gift shop on the corner of Banff Avenue and Buffalo Street.

Harmon's Photographs, Harmony Lane Mall at 111 Banff Avenue. Visit this photo gallery shop to view the historic prints of Byron Harmon, Banff's pioneer photographer. The prints are handmade by Carole Harmon, granddaughter of the photographer. Limited edition 16 x 20-inch prints, as well as more affordable open-edition smaller sizes, all matted. The collection of original negatives is in The Whyte Museum.

Byron Harmon

The fledgling tourist town of Banff was without a photographer or photographic studio in 1903, when 27-year-old Byron Harmon arrived from the US for a visit. His career as a portrait photographer held little interest compared to the lure of the mountains so he decided to make Banff his home and begin attaining his lofty goal of photographing every peak in the Canadian Rockies.

In 1906 he opened a photographic shop on Banff Avenue, across from today's Harmony Lane. By this time he was able to offer the largest collection of Canadian Rockies images ever. He became a charter member and official photographer of the Alpine Club of Canada. On club trips he was able to develop his portfolio as well as his skills as a mountaineer.

In 1924, Harmon and writer Lewis R. Freeman undertook, in Freeman's words, "What was probably the roughest continuous pack-train journey made in the Rockies since the time of the pioneers." The 70-day, 500-mile Columbia Icefield expedition, in which Harmon took 400 glass plate still photographs as well as movie film, completed his original program for photographing the Rockies. The journey is described in Freeman's book *On the Roof of the Rockies, The Great Columbia Icefield of the Canadian Rockies*. Freeman dedicated the book to Harmon "who, through his photographs, has given the Canadian Rockies to the world."

■ Where to Eat

 You'll find the best selection and variety of eating establishments in the Canadian Rockies in Banff townsite. Eating out in Banff is an adventure in itself, the difficulty is in choosing where.

DINING PRICE CHART	
Price per person in Canadian $ for an entrée, not including beverage, tax or tip.	
$	Under $10
$$	$10-$25
$$$	Over $25

There are a number of dining guides available at various businesses or from the Visitor Information Center, the best (and most unbiased) of which is *Taxi Mike's Dining Guide*! This simple brochure gives honest opinions on where to eat and drink ("the best of" in a number of categories) and is updated seasonally, so you won't be confused with outdated information.

Banff has two grocery stores, **Keller Foods** on Bear Street (free coffee while you shop) and **Safeway** (with a pharmacy) on the corner of Banff Avenue and Elk Street.

Following are some casual dining restaurants in Banff that won't leave you disappointed (all are very busy, especially during the summer):

Melissa's, ☎ 403-762-5511, 218 Lynx Street, $$. A local favorite for over 25 years. Family dining in a heritage rustic log building. Choices galore with fabulous breakfasts (best eggs benedict in town) served until 4:30 pm; gourmet burgers, deep dish pizza, soups, salads and sandwiches for lunch; steaks, seafood, and ribs for dinner. Upstairs bar (happy hour from 4-7 pm) and summer patio. Children's menu.

Wild Bill's, ☎ 403-762-0333, 201 Banff Avenue, $$. Named after the famous Bill Peyto, this Western-themed saloon and restaurant is on the second story of a downtown building. Flanked by outdoor patios overlooking Banff Avenue, patrons can dance to live music from country to top-40 bands. Extensive Western/Tex-Mex fare with lots of appetizers, steaks, burgers, ribs, chicken, soups, and salads. No minors.

Coyotes Deli & Grill, ☎ 403-762-3963, 206 Caribou Street, $$. This cozy little establishment serves unique Southwestern cuisine with a Mediterranean influence in a casual open-kitchen design. Try the "Mountain Man" breakfast with fresh-squeezed juice or choose from soups, salads, frittatas, deli sandwiches or corn-crusted pizza and calzone for lunch. Dinner entrées include fresh pasta, market-fresh seafood and innovative dishes such as corn tortilla crusted beef tenderloin with chile-dusted onion rings and a porcini chipotle sauce. Reasonably priced wine complements the menu. Reservations recommended.

Giorgio's Trattoria, ☎ 403-762-0661, 219 Banff Avenue, $$. Giorgio's features fresh Italian dinners at affordable prices in a stylish setting. Specialties include fresh pasta dishes and pizza baked in the wood-burning oven, as well as seafood and meat – try the Osso Buco Milan-style. Reservations for eight or more only.

Typhoon, ☎ 403-762-2000, 211 Caribou Street, $$. For the best curry in Banff as well as other Thai, Indian and Asian samplings, try what has been described as "one of the hottest new Asian restaurants in Canada." Every appetizer and main course on the menu sounds exotic and makes my mouth water. The décor is chic, the artwork a feast for the eyes. Open for lunch and dinner. Reservations recommended.

Barpa Bill's Souvlaki, ☎ 403-762-0377, 223 Bear Street, $. This is one of those great little family-operated hole-in-the-wall places. Barpa Bill's serves delicious Greek specialties from an open kitchen behind tile counters with bar stools. A staff of two takes orders, cooks and keeps the steady stream of customers happy. I was quite content watching customers come and go while I enjoyed my chicken souvlaki (kebob) with homemade fries. The only thing missing: a glass of crisp Greek wine. Sorry, no washrooms, no liquor license. Open from 11 am to 9 pm daily with free delivery on minimum $8 orders.

East Express, ☎ 403-760-3988, 202 Caribou Street, $. Tasty Japanese fast food, prepared fresh and hot. Teppan, tempura, udon, ramen, donburi, curry, soups, salad and vegetarian fare. Order your favorite take-out dishes and enjoy at one of Banff's myriad scenic locations.

Sunfood Café, ☎ 403-760-3933, 215 Banff Avenue, $ to $$. A large selection of creative vegetarian breakfasts, lunches and dinners. Soups, salads, sandwiches and wraps, omelettes, pasta, stir-fry, curry, tofu and decadent desserts. A few tempting entrées include Tortilla Espanola, a flat potato omelette made with free-range eggs, onions and red peppers, sautéed in olive oil and served with fresh tomato and zucchini salad; Mushroom Stroganoff, a mix of shiitake, portobello, oyster and white mushrooms tossed in a rich and creamy paprika and red wine sauce, served on fresh pasta. Even if you're not vegetarian, you'll enjoy this fresh and healthy food.

Evelyn's Coffee Bar, $. Sit and enjoy a specialty coffee and watch the crowds stroll by. Soups, salads, burritos, pizza and an assortment of muffins, cookies, scones, pies and pastries to satisfy your sweet tooth, all reasonably priced. Two locations on Banff Avenue and one in the Wolf & Bear Street Mall.

THE BEST ICE CREAM IN THE ROCKIES

As much as you'll see Rocky Mountain tourists sightseeing everywhere during the busy summer months, you'll also see them all about the towns enjoying ice cream cones. Tucked in the back corner of Harmony Lane Mall at 111 Banff Avenue, **Chocolates by Bernard Callebaut** is a chain store I make exception for. Sumptuous soft-serve semi-sweet chocolate or white chocolate cones are available only in the summer at a few select locations across Canada and the US. This crème de la crème of ice cream is so good I've detoured off the Trans Canada just to get my favorite chocolate-vanilla twist cone. You can also stock up on a variety of top-quality Belgian chocolate, from bulk baking chocolate (great energy boost for hiking) to award-winning chocolates for any occasion, or in my case, no occasion at all – a chocoholic's paradise.

■ Where to Stay

Finding affordable accommodation during the summer in Banff is a challenge. The average daily rate during the peak season in most hotels, inns and lodges for a standard room is about $200. Select private accommodations are an excellent alternative; although many are equally pricey, most offer a unique charm you won't find elsewhere.

HOTEL PRICE CHART

Reflects the price of an average room for two in Canadian $, May-Sept. Rates lower rest of year (except Christmas and New Year's).

$	Under $50
$$	$50-$100
$$$	$101-$150
$$$$	$151-$250
$$$$$	Over $250

The Banff-Lake Louise Tourism Bureau (see *Information Sources*) produces an ***Accommodation Guide*** brochure that lists hotels, motels, inns and lodges in Banff, Lake Louise and surrounding areas. Available at the Visitor Information Center. (See the Lake Louise section for accommodations in that area.)

Downtown

Homestead Inn, ☎ 800-661-1021 or 403-762-4471, 217 Lynx Street, www.homesteadinnbanff.com, $$$. Located across from the Banff Park Lodge (see below) and beside Melissa's Restaurant (see *Where to Eat* section). Basic affordable rooms with television.

Banff Park Lodge Resort Hotel & Conference Center, ☎ 800-661-9266 or 403-762-4433, 222 Lynx Street, www.banffparklodge.com, $$$$$. The only full-service resort hotel located downtown. Superior rooms, deluxe Jacuzzi rooms and suites. Spacious rooms include television, coffee maker, and balcony or patio. Indoor parking, indoor salt-water pool, steam room, Jacuzzi, two restaurants, lounge, coin-operated and valet laundry, Internet access in lobby and shopping arcade.

The Rundlestone Lodge, ☎ 800-661-8630 or 403-762-2201, 537 Banff Avenue, www.rundlestone.com, $$$$ to $$$$$. Over 15 styles of rooms from sleeping rooms to loft suites or two-bedroom apartments. Special features such as kitchens, Jacuzzi tubs, and wood-burning fireplaces are available. Lodge amenities include health club with lap pool and whirlpool, sun deck, guest laundry, ski and bike lock-up, and video games arcade.

Near Banff Townsite

Elkhorn Lodge, ☎ 877-818-8488 or 403-762-2299, 124 Spray Avenue, http://elkhornbanff.ca, $$$$. A small privately owned and operated rustic lodge at the south end of the townsite, near the Banff Springs Hotel. Sleeping rooms or

Banff Avenue

Banff Hoodoos

Canoeing on the Bow River, Banff

Chateau Lake Louise

suites with kitchens and wood-burning or gas fireplaces. Television and outside sitting area.

Douglas Fir Resort & Chalets, ☎ 800-661-9267 or 403-762-5591, 525 Tunnel Mountain Road, www.douglasfir.com, $$$$ to $$$$$. Located along scenic Tunnel Mountain Road, this busy resort caters to families. Studios, lofts, one-bedroom units or rustic one- , two- or three-bedroom chalets all include kitchen and wood-burning fireplace; specialty suites available. Indoor waterpark with waterslides, indoor pool, Jacuzzis, saunas, steamroom and kiddy pool. Other guest facilities include barbecues, indoor parking, laundry, liquor store, convenience store, televisions, free daily coffee, fitness room, racquetball, squash and tennis courts, outdoor playground, skating rink, video arcade and e-mail kiosk.

Hidden Ridge Resort, ☎ 800-661-1372 or 403-762-3544, 901 Coyote Drive, www.bestofbanff.com, $$$$ to $$$$$. Located off Tunnel Mountain Road behind the Banff Alpine Center Hostel. Standard, deluxe, Jacuzzi and premier condos and chalets. Hot-tub, barbecue pits and complimentary downtown shuttle.

BANFF SPRINGS HOTEL

"The Castle in the Rockies" was advertised in 1888 as "The Finest Hotel on the North American Continent." Indeed, today's visitor cannot help but be impressed by this magnificent landmark.

The hotel was constructed under the watchful eye of the Canadian Pacific Railway's Vice-President and General Manager, Sir William Cornelius Van Horne, whose prominent statue at the entrance to the hotel indicates where he wanted the hotel built. In fact, when Van Horne visited the construction site he was aghast to find the building being constructed backwards, with grand views afforded the kitchen, not the guest rooms! He corrected the matter in short order and the largest hotel in the world opened in June of 1888.

The hotel was an immediate success and wealthy late Victorian era tourists and adventurers flocked to the Rockies. In 1903 Brewster began operating its "Tally-Ho" carriage service, transporting guests between the hotel and Banff Station and on sightseeing excursions.

In the 1920s and 1930s the hotel was a seasonal "home-away-from-home" for privileged guests, some of whom arrived for a three- to four-month stay. Guests enjoyed luxury, exquisite service and a room with a view along with such pastimes as afternoon tea in the Conservatory, relaxing in the Writing Room, soaking in the outdoor pool with its water piped down from Sulphur Mountain, dining in the Alberta Dining Room and dancing in the Cascade Ballroom.

Business slowed to a trickle during the Great Depression and except for the summer months, the hotel was closed during the Second World War. Over its history, the hotel has been overhauled, expanded and reconstructed a number of times.

Today, the hotel employs 1,300 staff in the summer and between 700 and 900 in the winter. There are 16 eating establishments on the premises that serve between 6,000 and 7,000 meals per day and 771 rooms are available with a capacity of 2,000 guests. The Presidential Suite, consisting of nine rooms, is occupied every night in the summer, at a cost of $7,000 per night.

Free historical tours run throughout the summer. Tour guides provide fascinating information and tales about the hotel – well worth the time spent. Call ahead for tour times or ask at the concierge desk. ☎ 403-762-2211, www.fairmont.com/banffsprings.

Rental Cabins & Apartments

 The Banff-Lake Louise Tourism Bureau produces a *Bed & Breakfast Guide* brochure that lists over 40 licensed bed & breakfasts in Banff. Available at the Visitor Information Center.

The following are all within easy walking distance of downtown:

Two Twenty Beaver Street Suites and Cabins, ☎ 403-762-5077, 218-220 Beaver Street. Hosts: Diane & Kathie. $$ to $$$$. The James Thomson House and Tourist Cabins were built in the 1920s and 1930s when homeowners in Banff were building backyard accommodations in the rush to meet the onslaught of tourists. These quaint historical accommodations in the heart of downtown Banff behind the Visitor Information Center offer a choice of one- or two-bedroom cabins with kitchenettes. Television, outside sitting area and off-street parking. Weekly rates available.

Blue Mountain Lodge, ☎ 403-762-5134, 137 Muskrat Street, www.bluemtnlodge.com. Hosts: Hugh & Irene Simpson. $$$ to $$$$. These hosts make guests feel at home in their 1908 heritage home minutes from downtown. Single or double rooms and the Trapper's Cabin (sleeps five). Large common area with full kitchen, Internet kiosk, television, off-street parking, pet-friendly room. Complimentary coffee, tea, hot chocolate and fresh-baked cookies daily. Deluxe buffet continental breakfast included.

Country Cabin, ☎ 403-762-3591, 419 Beaver Street, countrycabin@telusplanet.net. Hosts: Bunny & Kerry Julius. $$$. Cozy private log cabin in quiet neighbourhood, not in the country but minutes to downtown. Newly renovated with Jacuzzi tub, TV/VCR, off-street parking. Continental breakfast included. Children welcome.

Tarry-A-While, ☎ 403-762-0462, 117 Grizzly Street, www.tarry.ca, $$ to $$$$. This is the former home of one of the Rockies' most notable women explorers, Mary Schäffer (see *Jasper* chapter). The heritage house is operated in support of the Whyte Museum. Three well-appointed guest rooms accommodate two adults each (one will accommodate an extra person), all with handmade pine furniture and private bathrooms; great room, sitting room, dining room, and sunroom. Breakfast with fresh baking, complimentary beverages, television, reading material, free admission to the Whyte Museum and Museum Shop discount, off-street parking, bike/ski storage, and winter and Christmas ski packages. Beautiful historic accommodations in the heart of Banff. Unfortunately, no children under 16 permitted.

Camping

 Parks Canada operates nine campgrounds (13 including multiple section campgrounds) in Banff National Park with a total of 2,468 sites available during peak season.

CAMPING/HOSTELS	
Rates in Canadian $, not including taxes.	
$	Under $13
$$	$13-$22
$$$	$23-$30
$$$$	Over $30

Tunnel Mountain, including the Trailer Court, Village 1 and Village 2, as well as Lake Louise Trailer Court and tent site now accept reservations. See www.pccamping.ca for the Parks Canada Campground Reservation Service, or call ☎ 877-737-3783, international calls ☎ 905-426-4648.

Fully serviced sites are available only at Tunnel Mountain Trailer Court. Year-round camping includes Tunnel Mountain

Village 2 near Banff townsite, Lake Louise Trailer Court in Lake Louise village and Mosquito Creek along the Icefields Parkway.

 See the Lake Louise section for campgrounds along the Icefields Parkway in Banff National Park, along the Bow Valley Parkway and in the village of Lake Louise.

Campsites in Banff Townsite
Tunnel Mountain

On Tunnel Mountain Road 2.4 km (1½ miles) from Banff town center; disabled access; showers, sani-dump. Reservations accepted. This is the largest campground in North America and the third-largest in the world!

- Village 1 Campground has 618 unserviced sites, $$; interpretive programs; open May 3 to October 4.
- Village 2 Campground has 188 electrical serviced sites, $$$; open year-round.
- The Trailer Court Campground has 321 sites with full hook-ups, $$$; interpretive programs; open May 3 to October 4.

Two Jack

Located 12 km (7.4 miles) from Banff townsite on the Minnewanka Loop.

- The Main Campground has 380 unserviced sites, $$; disabled access; kitchen shelters; open May 21 to September 7.
- The Lakeside Campground has 74 unserviced sites, $$; disabled access; showers; open May 21 to September 20.

Kootenay National Park

If campgrounds at Banff and Lake Louise are full or if you're just tired of the crowds, consider the more peaceful and natural setting at Marble Canyon Campground in Kootenay National Park. With a driving time of only 30 minutes to either Lake Louise or Banff, it's a convenient base for day-trips in Banff Park. See the *Kootenay National Park* chapter *Where to Stay* section for details.

Banff National Park

Backcountry Camping

 Be sure to get a copy of Banff Park's *Backcountry Visitor's Guide* from the Visitor Information Center. The brochure explains basic information about planning your trip, safety issues, trail descriptions for two- , three- , four- and five-day or more trips and a map.

There are 50 backcountry campsites in Banff Park. If you are planning on camping overnight in Banff's wilderness campgrounds, you must purchase a wilderness pass, $9 per person per night or $63 for an annual permit. You can reserve your camping up to three months in advance, ☎ 403-762-1550 or Banff.Trails@pc.gc.ca. A $12 non-refundable reservation fee applies and/or a modification fee for changes. Wilderness Pass fees, excluding reservation and modification fees, are refundable until 10 am of your date of departure.

Reservations are advisable for busy trails during the peak hiking months of July and August. If your pass is mailed or faxed to you, contact a Park Information Center prior to your departure for current trail conditions, closures and other important information.

Hosteling

Reservations, ☎ 866-762-4122 or 403-670-7580 or centralres.sa@hihostels.ca. (See the *Lake Louise* section for hostels along the Icefields Parkway in Banff National Park, along the Bow Valley Parkway and in the village of Lake Louise.)

Banff Alpine Center

Located on Coyote Drive off Tunnel Mountain Road minutes from downtown Banff. 216 beds; members $$$, non-members $$$$, weekly rates available in low season; family rooms; check-in 24 hours. Consists of two buildings, with cheaper rates in the older building (shared bathrooms) and slightly higher rates in the newer Marybelle building (en suite bathrooms). Amenities include a restaurant, pub and game room. Rated "Top 10" in a network of 5,000 hostels worldwide. Very busy hostel, yet very friendly staff that took the time to show me around. Various activities and packages available, including whitewater rafting. Linen provided; no sleeping bags permitted.

■ Adventures

Sports & Camping Equipment Rentals

 **Snow Tips/Bactrax**, ☎ 403-762-8177, 225 Bear Street, www.snowtips-bactrax.com. Demo ski packages $35/day, high performance ski packages $30/day, recreation ski packages $16/day, junior snowboard packages $20/day; three-, five-, and seven-day rental discounts. Town bikes $8/hour or $30/day, trail bikes $10/hour or $36/day. Also available for rent: child and junior bikes, baby backpacks, hiking poles, binoculars, tents, sleeping bags, etc. Road bike tours $20/hour from one to three hours.

The Ski Stop, ☎ 403-762-5333 at the Fairmont Banff Springs Hotel or ☎ 403-760-1650 at 203 Bear Street, www.theskistop.com. All of the latest skis, snowboards and bicycles available for rent with a free rental equipment pick-up service. Town bikes $7/hour or $25/day, mountain bikes $8/hour or $28/day, full suspension $10/hour or $35/day; any bike $129.95 for five consecutive days. Bike tours $20/hour, including the guide, with maximum charge $80.

Glacier Shop, ☎ 760-5130, 317 Banff Avenue (Cascade Plaza). Competitive rates on the latest ski equipment.

Bow River Canoe Rentals, Bow River at Bow Avenue & Wolf Street. From the dock along Bow Avenue, an easy 20- to 30-minute paddle up the Bow River to Vermilion Lakes. Open daily May to September. $16 per hour, $40 per day.

Guided Tours

Discover Banff Tours, ☎ 877-565-9372 or 403-760-5007, 215 Banff Avenue (Sundance Mall), www.banfftours.com. Small personalized summer and winter tours that include hotel pick-up and drop-off, refreshments and use of binoculars.

Banff National Park

◆ **Discover Banff** – three hours. Highlights include Bow Falls, Banff Springs Hotel, Surprise Corner, Hoodoos & Bow Valley Viewpoint, Lake Minnewanka and Cave & Basin National Historic Site. Adult $49, child (six-12 years) $25.

◆ **Discover Lake Louise & Moraine Lake** – four hours. Highlights include Bow Valley Parkway, Castle Mountain, Lake Louise, Chateau Lake Louise and Moraine Lake. Adult $59, child $30; combine this tour with the morning Discover Banff tour and lunch is included.

◆ **Classic Hikes** – seven hours. A full-day tour that includes four-six hours of hiking time. Call to find out weekly destinations or make a trail request. Adult $69, includes packed lunch.

◆ **Discover Grizzly Bears** – 10 hours. Observe an orphaned grizzly bear in a natural bear habitat refuge. Also includes Lake Louise, Takakkaw Falls (Yoho), Kicking Horse Canyon and gondola ride up Kicking Horse Mountain. Mountain-top gourmet lunch at Canada's highest restaurant. Adult $119, child $79. (Also departs from Lake Louise.)

◆ **Evening Wildlife Safari** – two hours. Travel through a variety of landscapes giving the best chance to observe animals in their natural environment. Wildlife seen on over 95% of the tours. Adult $39, child $20.

Brewster Transportation and Tours, ☎ 800-760-6934 or 403-760-6934, 100 Gopher Street, www.brewster.ca. Guided motorcoach tours from Banff and Lake Louise, May to October:

◆ **Columbia Icefield** – 9½ hours round-trip. Adult $106, child $53; add optional Ice Explorer ride (SnoCoach) – adult $33.95, child $17. (See the *Icefields Parkway* chapter for detailed information about the Columbia Icefield.)

◆ **Mountain Lakes & Waterfalls** – 9½ hours round-trip. Banff to Lake Louise and Yoho National Park; highlights include Bow Valley Parkway,

Johnston Canyon, Moraine Lake, Victoria Glacier, Spiral Tunnels, Takakkaw Falls, Emerald Lake and the Natural Rock Bridge. Adult $72, child $36.

White Mountain Adventures, ☎ 800-408-0005 or 403-678-4099, www.whitemountainadventures.com.

◆ **Johnston Canyon Icewalk** – four hours round-trip. Interpretive guided walk through the bottom of frozen Johnston Canyon and over suspended catwalks. Leads past frozen waterfalls and through a tunnel – a unique winter experience. Includes a hot chocolate break, ice cleat use and hotel pick up. $270 for one to six people; family rates also available.

◆ **Sunshine Meadows Hikes** – Sunshine Meadows is west of Banff at the Sunshine Village Ski Resort. White Mountain Adventures operates the shuttle bus service up a six-km (3.7-mile) restricted-access road that begins at the Sunshine Village parking lot and ends at the village, providing access to some of the best sub-alpine and alpine walking and hiking in Banff. (The gondola operates only during the ski season.) You can explore the network of trails on your own – from easy, short strolls recommended for anyone in reasonable physical condition (also suitable for children) to challenging full-day hikes and backpacking routes. Or join a full-day guided hike. **Sunshine Vistas** is a 12-km (5½-mile) easy, guided day-hike that winds past waterfalls and lakes. Offered daily at $25 per person plus shuttle fare (bring lunch and wear suitable clothing).

The shuttle bus is $21 adult, $11 child (three-12) from Sunshine Village parking lot, or $41 adult, $21 child from Banff. Departs Banff at 9 am and Sunshine parking lot every hour, beginning at 9:30 am (8:30 am July 1-September 1), returning to Banff at 2 and 5 pm, or to the Sunshine parking lot every hour on the hour until 5 pm.

The Sunshine Village parking lot is eight km (five miles) west of Banff on the Trans Canada Highway and a further eight km to the parking lot. (You are permitted to hike the access road to reach the meadows.) I highly recommend a visit to Sunshine Meadows.

Wildflower Paradise

If you love wildflowers – or awesome scenic hiking – you shouldn't miss a visit to Sunshine Meadows in mid-summer. This unique 15-km (nine-mile) stretch along the continental divide covering more than 40 sq km (15 sq miles) is a combination of subalpine and alpine meadowland. The incredible variety of wildflowers and plants – more than 340 species, some of which are rare in the Rockies – thrive under harsh growing conditions and a short growing season.

Access to Sunshine Meadows (Sunshine Village Ski Area) is eight km (five miles) west of Banff on the Trans Canada Highway and a further nine km (5.6 miles) on the Sunshine Road to the Bourgeau Parking Lot at the gondola base station (the gondola only operates during the ski season). For a fee you can ride the shuttle bus from the parking lot on the limited access road to the meadows or you can hike 6.5 km (four miles) on the steep access road.

Once at the meadows, you have myriad hiking and backpacking choices. The Egypt Lakes area is the most popular backpacking destination in Banff Park, with a backcountry campground available at Egypt Lake. More information is available in Parks Canada's Backcountry Visitors' Guide Banff National Park.

Horseback Riding

Holiday on Horseback (Warner Guiding and Outfitting), ☎ 800-661-8352 or 762-4551, 132 Banff Avenue (The Trail Rider Store), www.horseback.com. Trail rides, downtown carriage rides, wilderness cookouts, day rides, two- to six-day backcountry lodge rides, wilderness tenting trips, winter sleigh rides, special interpretive rides each year and private rides available. From mid-May to November.

Departures from Fairmont Banff Springs Corral:

◆ **Spray River Ride** (one hour) – departs on the hour 9 am to 5 pm daily, $39.

◆ **Sulphur Mountain/Spray River Ride** (three hours) – departs at 9 am and 2 pm daily, $95.

Departures from Martin Stables (at the end of Sundance Road off Cave Avenue):

◆ **Bow River Ride** (one hour) – departures 9 am to 6 pm daily, $34.

◆ **Sundance Loop Ride** (two hours) – departs at 10 am, 12 pm, 2 pm and 4 pm daily, $62.

◆ **Bow Valley Loop Ride** (three hours) – departs 9 am and 1 pm daily, $84.

◆ **Covered Wagon Cookout** (three hours) – departs 11 am, $78. Menu: barbecue steak, salads, cowboy baked beans, rolls, dessert, and drinks.

◆ **Explorer Day Ride** (seven hours) – departs 9:30 am, $162. This is their most popular trail ride. Ride through the wilderness to panoramic views of the Spray River Valley from Sulphur Mountain and round-trip via the base of Mount Rundle. Western barbecue lunch along the Spray River.

Whitewater Rafting

 Whitewater outfitters in the area run the Bow, Kicking Horse, Kananaskis, Kootenay and Spillimacheen Rivers with the **Kicking Horse River** the most popular run (approximately 1½ hours drive from Banff). With the exception of Bow River trips that originate in Banff, transportation from Banff, Lake Louise or Canmore to put-in areas is available for the following trips. (See also *Whitewater Rafting* sections in Yoho National Park and Kootenay National Park chapters for additional options on the Kicking Horse River.)

Rocky Mountain Raft Tours, ☎ 403-762-3632, tickets at Wolf & Bow Avenue, Banff Springs Hotel, or at the Bow Falls launch.

◆ **Bow River Float** – One-hour gentle scenic tours from the bottom of Bow Falls, along Tunnel Mountain, under the hoodoos, to the end-point near Mount Rundle. Departures 9 am, 11 am, 1 pm and 3 pm. Adult $28, child $14.

Canadian Rockies Rafting Company, ☎ 877-226-7625 or 403-678-6535, www.rafting.ca. This company offers a choice of four trips – from mild to wild – on four different rivers. If whitewater doesn't provide enough excitement, they also offer body surfing on any of their trips and cliff jumping where available. Transportation included. Banff departures from the Visitor Information Center. Reservations required.

◆ **Twilight Eco Float on the Bow River** – Opportunities to view beaver, elk, and osprey on a leisurely float with close up views of the Three Sisters Mountain and some of the tallest peaks in the front ranges. Short nature stop included. Departs Banff at 6 pm. Round-trip three hours with two hours on the river. Adult $42, senior $36, student/youth (nine to 16 years) $30, child (three to eight years) $20.

◆ **Family Whitewater on the Kananaskis River** – A half-day run along the front ranges with grade 2 to 3 rapids. A good introduction to whitewater. Departs Banff 8 am and 1 pm. (Canmore departures also available.) Round-trip 4½ hours with two hours on the river. Adult $59, student/youth (five to 15 years) $53.

◆ **Whitewater Excitement on the Bow River-Horseshoe Canyon** – The Bow River Horseshoe Canyon has spectacular scenery, big waves and grade 3 to 4 whitewater. Excellent opportunities to view large birds. Optional cliff jump. Departs Banff at 8 am and 1 pm. (Canmore departures also available.) Round-trip 4½ hours with two hours on the river. Adult $62, student/youth (10 to 15 years) $56.

◆ **Maximum Whitewater on the Kicking Horse River** – Big waves, long rapids (Class 3 and 4) and spectacular scenery on the challenging Kicking Horse. Includes lunch in Lake Louise on the return trip. Departs Banff 8 am. (Lake Louise and Field departures also available.) Round-trip eight hours with 2½ to three hours on the river. Adult $99, student/youth (12 to 15 years) $89 – participants must be over 40 kg (90 pounds).

◆ **Wild Water Adventures**, ☎ 888-647-6444 or 403-522-2211, www.wildwater.com. Smoothwater or whitewater trips on the Kicking Horse River and a two-day trip on the Spillimacheen River. All trips depart from the river base day lodge two km (1.2 miles) west of the Yoho National Park entry booth on the Trans Canada Highway (between Field and Golden) and include snacks and beverages or lunch. Transportation from Lake Louise also available.

◆ **Whitewater Exciter** – The most popular trip is an action-packed half-day adventure with 14 rapids (Class 2 to 4). Morning and afternoon departures daily. Round-trip three hours with 1½ hours on the river. $72 from river base, $80 from Lake Louise. Participants must be minimum 12 years and 40 kg (90 pounds).

◆ **Gentle River Journey** – For the mildly adventurous with Class 1 to 3 rapids. Morning departure only. Round-trip three hours with 1½ hours on the river. Adult $64, youth (eight to 14 years) $52 from river base; $72/$59 from Lake Louise. Minimum age eight years.

◆ **Classic Adventurer** – Journey through Yoho National Park on the gentler upper section of the Kicking Horse along with plenty of rapids (Class 1 to 4). Barbecue lunch at the river base included. Daily morning departures. Round-trip five hours with 2½ to three hours on the river. Adult $99 from river base or $115 from Banff or Lake Louise. Participants must be minimum 12 years and 40 kg (90 pounds).

◆ **Two-Day River Escape** – Spillimacheen and Kicking Horse float with Class 1 to 4+ rapids. Includes meals and overnight camping. Departures select weekends from late June to mid-August. $399.

Banff National Park

Wet 'n' Wild Adventures, ☎ 800-668-9119 or 250-244-6546 (Golden), www.wetnwild.bc.ca.

◆ Full-day Kicking Horse whitewater run with daily departures. Includes transportation from Golden and riverside barbecue lunch, $92; $15 extra for shuttle bus from Banff or Lake Louise. Good trip for newcomers; minimum 12 years of age and 90 lbs. Morning introduction, Half-Day, Double Excitement and other trips available.

Lake Boating & Fishing

Alpine Anglers, ☎ 403-762-8223, www.alpine-anglers.com. Fly fishing guides and instruction for catch-and-release fishing. Rates include all equipment, transportation to and from hotels, snacks and/or lunch.

◆ **Upper Bow River** – Known as one of the premier fly fishing rivers in the world with healthy populations of large brown and rainbow trout as well as cutthroat, bull and brook trout. Spectacular scenery and wildlife viewing opportunities including bald eagles, osprey and waterfowl. Full day (eight hours of fishing) of drift and wade fishing $440, half-day (five hours of fishing) $375.

◆ **Lower Bow River** – Home to a mix of rainbow and brown trout with an average size of 40 cm (16 inches) or larger. Full day (10 hours of fishing) $500. Overnight camping trips can also be arranged.

◆ **Walk-and-wade trips** – Offered on some of Alberta's premier smaller mountain streams where bull and cutthroat trout abound. Lots of solitude with 15-20 minutes of easy hiking. Full day $450.

Banff Fishing Unlimited, ☎ 403-762-4936, www.banff-fishing.com. Offering fly fishing, spin casting and trophy lake trout fishing on the Upper Bow River and Lake Minnewanka. Walk-and-wade trips offered year-round. Ice fishing from December to April with heated huts to cook your catch. Private guided trips include licensed professional guides, transportation from lodgings, all fishing gear, foul weather gear and expert instruction. "Many well kept secrets revealed."

◆ **Lake Minnewanka** – From the end of May to September, 4½- or 6½-hour private charters in covered comfortable seven-m (23½-foot) and six-m (19½-foot) covered cruisers. Lake trout to 22 kg (50 lbs) and Rockies up to 2.2 kg (five lbs). "A catch is a virtual guarantee – 99% success." A 4½-hour charter for one or two anglers $320; each additional angler $60, children six-15 years and non fishers $35 (max. six people/boat).

◆ **Bow River** – From April through October, day float and wade trips in drift boats. Fly fishing or spin casting for brown trout to 4½ kg (10 lbs) and Rockies to 2.2 kg (five lbs) – 40 km (25 miles) of catch and release waters. Trips depart from Canmore. Seven to eight hours on the water for one angler, $395; each additional angler $60 (max. three people/boat).

Lake Minnewanka Boat Tours, ☎ 403-762-3473, www.minnewankaboattours.com. The only lake in Banff National Park where power boats are permitted. A fishing paradise with abundant lake trout and Rocky Mountain whitefish. Rentals or guided charter fishing trips. Eight hp engine on 4.8-m (16-foot) boat with safety equipment and fuel. $32 first hour, $12 each additional hour, $92 per day.

 If you are planning to do any hiking, backpacking or biking on Banff Park's trails, be sure to stop by or call the Visitor Information Center for the latest trail information, safety reports and advice. Three very useful brochures are: *Day Hikes in Banff National Park – 61 day hikes around Banff, the Bow Valley Parkway, Lake Louise and the Icefields Parkway* (provides a map and trailhead locations, but does not give detailed trail descriptions); *Backcountry Visitor's Guide*; and *Mountain Biking and Cycling Guide*.

Mountain Biking & Bicycle Touring

 With more than 190 km (118 miles) of mountain bike trails as well as many road riding opportunities, Banff Park is ideally suited for travel by bicycle. Parks Canada produces the *Mountain Biking and Cycling Guide* for Banff National Park, available free of charge at the Visitor Information Center. In it you will find general information on biking, details on 17 Banff and 10 Lake Louise area trail and road rides as well as a map. Guided mountain biking is not permitted on trails in Banff National Park.

Banff townsite trails are popular with various users and are open to cyclists (except for Tunnel Mountain Trail, Sulphur Mountain Trail, Sundance Canyon Loop, the Cave and Basin boardwalks and marked sections of the Bow River and Bow Falls trails).

The **Sundance Trail** is an easy 3.7-km (2.3-mile) paved trail from Cave and Basin National Historic Site. Suitable for children, the paved trail winds along the Bow River and climbs gently to the Sundance Canyon picnic area.

Popular Banff road rides include Mount Norquay Road (7½ km or 4.6 miles one way, difficult), **Lake Minnewanka Road** (24-km or 15-mile loop, moderate), **Tunnel Mountain Drive** (15-km or nine-mile loop, moderate), **Golf Course Drive** (15-km or nine-mile loop, easy) and **Vermilion Lakes Drive** (5.7 km or 3½ miles one way, easy).

Drives, Sights, Activities & Hikes

Bow Falls

 Banff townsite is blessed to have the picturesque Bow River flowing through town. The walk along the river's banks can begin anywhere om the 2.1-km (1.3-mile) mostly paved wheelchair-accessible route, but a good starting point is the canoe docks at Wolf Street and Bow Avenue.

Follow Bow Avenue across the Bow River Bridge, take your first left on Glen Avenue, then left on Bow Falls Drive to a parking area and viewpoint over the 10-m (33-foot) falls. The Spray River enters the Bow River downstream from the falls.

Climbing Mount Rundle

 Are you a strong hiker interested in climbing Banff's classic front range mountain? Mount Rundle is the prominent wedge-shaped peak south of the townsite. Most of the climb is steep and strenuous – seven to eight hours average round-trip time to the 2,949-m (9,675-foot) summit. Stop by the Visitor Information Center and pick up the free brochure, *A Climber's Guide to Mount Rundle*. It provides a detailed route description, directions on getting to the start of the climb (near the Spray River bridge on the road to the Bow Falls viewpoint) as well as tips, recommendations and gear lists. And did you know Rundle formation rock was used in building the Banff Springs Hotel?

Tunnel Mountain

Drive: 10 km (6.2 mile) loop.

Originally surveyed as the site for a railway tunnel, the plan was changed for a more economical route but the name remained. Tunnel Mountain Drive (don't confuse Tunnel Mountain Drive with Tunnel Mountain Road) offers many points-of-interest and views near the townsite. Parking is rather limited along this busy route so drive cautiously and slow down near crowded sites.

 Tunnel Mountain Drive is closed from about mid-October to the end of May.

Follow Buffalo Street from the corner of Banff Avenue, just before the Bow River Bridge. The first viewpoint is at **Surprise Corner**, where there is a small parking lot on the right side of the road. From here there is an overlook of the Bow River and Bow Falls (a steep unmarked trail leads to the river) and the imposing Banff Springs Hotel – one of Banff's many recognizable postcard views. Above the parking lot you can climb to an observation deck.

The road continues past the Banff Center and crosses the upper trailhead to the top of Tunnel Mountain, a short steep 1½-km (.9-mile) hike. Hardly considered a mountain at only 1,692 m (5,551 feet), Tunnel Mountain is one of Banff's most popular hikes, with panoramic views of the townsite and Bow Valley.

Turn right when you reach the intersection of Tunnel Mountain Drive and Tunnel Mountain Road (at Douglas Fir Resort). The road skirts the edge of Tunnel Mountain Campground, across from which is a parking area for the popular **Hoodoos Trail**, a paved .5-km (.3-mile) wheelchair-accessible path leading to viewpoints above the formations and the Bow Flats. These odd-looking limestone rock pillars have been eroded by weather for thousands of years and continue to be sculpted into remarkable forms. Unmarked trails lead to the base of some of the hoodoos. (Hoodoo formations can also be seen along the Trans Canada Highway between Banff and Canmore.)

Tunnel Mountain Road intersects Banff Avenue .5 km (.3 miles) south of the Trans Canada Highway interchange. Turn left to return to the townsite or right to reach the Trans Canada Highway.

 Did You Know? The Stoney Indians called Tunnel Mountain "Sleeping Buffalo Mountain" because of its resemblance to the animal at rest. Try to picture a sleeping buffalo as you approach it from the east on the Trans Canada Highway.

Vermilion Lakes

Drive: 4.8 km (three miles) one way.

Watchable wildlife: Many species of birds including ospreys and bald eagles (at the first lake), American dippers and red-winged blackbirds; waterfowl including mallards, Canada geese and tundra swans (spring and fall); beavers and muskrats (at the second lake); mountain sheep, coyotes, wolves, elk.

Fed by warm and cold springs, the Vermilion Lakes are a scenic marsh area that is one of the best birdwatching locations in the Rocky Mountain Parks. The **Vermilion Lakes Road** branches from the Mount Norquay Road, 200 m (650 feet) from the Trans Canada interchange and skirts the shorelines of the three lakes. Each lake has pullouts and viewing areas with a parking area and washrooms at the third lake.

Archaeologists have discovered that early Albertans stopped at the Vermilion Lakes nearly 11,000 years ago. They have found the remains of campsites older than 9,500 years with mountain sheep bones and knives.

The **Fenland Trail** is a flat 2.1-km (1.3-mile) interpretive loop on the edge of the first Vermilion Lake. The forested path runs beside Echo and Forty Mile Creeks with a peaceful picnic area. The trail is closed during elk-calving season in late spring/early summer.

Mount Norquay

Drive: 5.8 km (3.6 miles) one way.

Watchable wildlife: Columbian ground squirrels, bighorn sheep.

From Banff townsite, follow the signs to the Trans Canada Highway interchange and cross the overpass. The road switchbacks steadily, with a number of good viewpoints along the way, the best of which is the last and highest one at km 5 (mile 3). From this vantage point at 1,675 m (5,495 feet), you overlook the Bow Valley, with Mount Rundle dominating the scene. The road ends at the Mount Norquay ski area less than one km farther along.

CLIMBING CASCADE MOUNTAIN

Cascade Mountain is the awesome peak you see as you look northeast up Banff Avenue, the highest peak in the Banff vicinity. Most of the climb is steep and strenuous – nine hours average round-trip time to the 2,998-m (9,836-foot) summit. Stop by the Visitor Information Center and pick up the free brochure, *A Climber's Guide to Cascade Mountain*. It provides a detailed route description, directions on getting to the start of the climb (Mt. Norquay Ski Area) as well as tips, recommendations and gear lists.

Lake Minnewanka Road

Drive: 15½-km (9.6-mile) loop.

Watchable wildlife: Mountain sheep, deer, elk, bears, golden eagles.

This loop drive from the Trans Canada Highway interchange is not long but it is chock-full of recreational and historic sites, so bring a picnic lunch and plan to spend a full day exploring by vehicle or by bicycle.

Note that the west side of the Minnewanka loop is closed annually from about mid-November to mid-April in order to help restore natural travel routes for wildlife along the base of Cascade Mountain. Access to Johnson Lake, Two Jack Lake and Lake Minnewanka is maintained via the eastern portion of the loop road.

The tour starts at the foot of Cascade Mountain. In just over a km is the Johnson Lake Road Junction, from where you can travel in either direction to complete the loop. Turn right at this junction if you are staying at Two Jack Campground or if you want to visit Johnson Lake, a preferred site for swimmers, sunbathers and picnickers. The **Johnson Lake Trail** is an easy 2.4-km (1½-mile) flat circuit of the lakeshore.

The **Two Jack Lake Picnic Area**, a few km farther along, is another pleasant stop for a rest or picnic.

Be sure to stop at the **Palliser Viewpoint**, in less than one km. This is one of the main viewing areas for the spring and fall golden eagle migrations, when thousands of these birds travel between wintering grounds in Colorado and Wyoming and summer nesting territory in Alaska and Siberia. The road follows the crest of the Lake Minnewanka dam to the parking area for visitors to the lake.

"Water of the Spirits" as the Stoney Indians named it, was always one of the largest and deepest lakes in the the Rockies, but human intervention has deepened, lengthened and altered it to today's dammed and regulated dimensions of 24 km (15 miles) long and 142 m (466 feet) deep, the longest and second-deepest lake in the mountain parks and the largest body of water in Banff National Park.

Archaeologists have recorded occupation sites along Minnewanka's shoreline spanning 10,000 years. Only resident fish and scuba divers explore the resort of Minnewanka Landing, which is now submerged.

The only lake in Banff Park where motorized boats are permitted is well known for record-size trout. **Lake Minnewanka Boat Tours** rents motorized boats and offers guided charter fishing trips (see *Lake Boating & Fishing* section). From mid-May to early October you can cruise to Devil's Gap (1½ hours round-trip) in glass enclosed tour boats. Adult $37, child (five to 11 years) $18, with departures at 10:30 am, 12:30 pm, 3 and 5 pm and 7 pm until early September. Transportation to the lake is available from most hotels or from **Brewster Transportation and Tours**, ☎ 403-762-6767.

Beyond the concession stand and picnic area is the 1.4-km (.8-mile) wheelchair-accessible **Stewart Canyon Trail** that meanders along the north shore of the lake. Hikers or bikers may wish to continue along the trail for another 6.4 km (four miles) to **Aylmer Pass Junction** and backcountry campground, **Aylmer Lookout** or beyond to the eastern end of the lake.

Continuing the drive, two km farther along is the **Upper Bankhead Picnic Area** and the trailhead for the 3.9-km (2.4-mile) **C Level Cirque Trail** (elevation gain 455 m or 1,492 feet). Along the short climb the trail passes two remnant buildings of the Bankhead coal operation, where the highest coal seams were worked on the eastern slope of Cascade Mountain. Just past the buildings at km 1.3 (mile .8) is a panoramic viewpoint of Lake Minnewanka from a coal tailing pile. The remainder of the hike climbs through forest that opens up to views just before reaching the cirque.

If you need to use washroom facilities, do so at the Upper Bankhead picnic area as there are no facilities at the next stop, Lower Bankhead, a half-km farther along the road.

The CPR (Canadian Pacific Railway) opened the Bankhead Mine in 1903 to help fuel its Prairies-Pacific route. The town flourished and at its peak in 1911, 450 men processed 500,000 tons of coal. Bankhead was home to 900 people, mostly immigrants from Poland, Italy, Russia, Germany, Ireland, Wales and China. Bankhead became bigger than Banff and the comfortable homes even had indoor plumbing! Sadly, the Chinese immigrants were not treated as equals and were forced to live separate from the Europeans in a shantytown behind the slack heaps. A testament to their presence, the rhubarb plants they grew in their gardens grows wild at Bankhead today.

Although there is still plenty of coal in Cascade Mountain, by 1922 production was down and the market glutted with cheap coal. The miners went on strike and the mine was closed. The government ordered the entire town removed, with most of the homes moved to Calgary, Banff or Canmore.

The transformer building escaped removal or destruction and today houses excellent displays at the **Lower Bankhead Self-Guided Trail**, a fascinating 1.1-km (.7-mile) interpretive trail through the remains of Lower Bankhead.

Bow Valley Parkway

The Bow Valley Parkway (Highway 1A) boasts many picnic areas, interpretive pullouts, trailheads, wildlife viewing opportunities and tourist attractions and services.

Midway between Lake Louise and Banff is **Castle Junction**. Here the parkway links up with the Trans Canada Highway and the Banff-Windermere Highway 93 South, also known as the Banff-Radium Highway or the Kootenay Parkway. The classic shape of **Castle Mountain** (2,766 m or 9,074 feet) sets it apart from other mountains. Part of the main ranges, its flat layers of rock are several km thick. The **Castle Cliffs Viewpoint** is on the north side of the highway, one km west of the junction.

Johnston Canyon

Thirty-three km (20 miles) southeast of Lake Louise is Johnston Canyon, a very high-volume tourist attraction. Like Maligne Canyon near Jasper, it is a steep, narrow limestone canyon that has been formed by the relentless action of water and sediment over thousands of years. More enticing and much less crowded are the **Ink Pots**, a series of seven spring-fed pools three km (1.8 miles) farther along a trail from the Upper Falls.

● Johnston Canyon Lower & Upper Falls & Ink Pots

Hike: 1.1 km (.7 miles) to the Lower Falls, 2.7 km (1.7 miles) to the Upper Falls or 5.8 km (3.6 miles) to the Ink Pots (11.6 km or 7.2 miles round-trip).

Elevation gain: 215 m (705 feet) to the Ink Pots.

From the parking lot on the northeast side of the highway (across the creek from the resort), take the bridge over Johnston Creek and follow the paved path. You'll walk over steel catwalks en route to the Lower Falls (15 m or 49 feet high), which you can view from the trail or through a cave. The Upper Falls (30 m or 98 feet high) can be viewed from below or above. The crowds thin considerably beyond the Upper Falls, where a wide dirt path (an old access road) ascends steeply through forest to the Ink Pots, a pretty spot to relax before returning to the parking lot.

Cory Pass – Mount Edith Circuit

Hike: 13 km (eight mile) circuit.

Elevation gain: 915 m (3,000 feet).

I love this hike. I love it because it's a challenging workout and, with in-your-face views of rock pinnacles such as Mount Louis, the average hiker can feel like a mountaineer.

Half a km before the Bow Valley Parkway exit west of Banff townsite, take the Fireside Picnic Area access road one km to the picnic area.

Cross the bridge over the creek and follow the trail through forest to a junction at km 1.1 (mile .7). Go left toward Cory Pass – you'll return the other way from Edith Pass. Here you begin your workout with a heart-pounding climb to a grassy knoll overlooking the Bow Valley. Take a rest and a drink of water – the grunt continues before you crest a narrow for-ested ridge. The trail follows a ridgeline and then climbs grad-ually across the open slope of Mount Edith. Cory Pass is at km 5.8 (mile 3.6), with Mount Louis north across Gargoyle Valley.

 *Day Hikes in Banff National Park* brochure warns that this is one of the most difficult hikes in Banff National Park, "suitable for strong hikers with good route finding skills." If you are unfit, choose a differ-ent hike. If you are afraid of steep slopes or loose rock, choose a different hike. But if you are up to the challenge, bring plenty of water – especially on hot sunny days – and avoid hik-ing alone. The circuit is open by mid-July, af-ter the snow and ice have melted.

To descend the north side of the pass, follow along to the right beneath Mount Edith's cliffs across steep talus into the Gar-goyle Valley. The trail through an open rockslide becomes somewhat vague – watch for the scree slope leading up to the right. Near the top, the trail branches to the left off the scree, into the forest.

Follow the trail into Edith Pass, a gradual forested descent, then alongside a stream and back to the Cory Pass junction. And give yourself a pat on the back.

 Fireside Picnic Area: If you're not up to the Cory Pass-Mount Edith hike, the Fireside Picnic Area is a great out-of-the-way spot for a picnic. You can combine it with a shorter hike to the Cory Knoll viewpoint or simple enjoy the picnic area. On a hot day, the creekside location makes it ideal and, conversely, on a dreary day you can take advantage of the stone fireplace. You don't need a fire permit to use it.

Winter Adventures

Covered under a blanket of snow, Banff National Park sparkles with life during the winter months. State-of-the-art facilities, consistent snowfalls and one of North America's longest ski seasons – mid-November to late May – have earned the area's three ski resorts – Mount Norquay, Lake Louise and Sunshine Village – world-class reputations and awards.

There are many winter activities if skiing or snowboarding aren't on your list – guided scenic motorcoach tours, horse-drawn sleigh rides, Johnston Canyon icewalks, ice-fishing, snowshoeing, skating, tobogganing, and more. Along with special winter and Christmas events and festivities, you might be surprised at how much there is to do during the winter months in Banff.

Alpine Skiing

Banff's three superb alpine skiing and snowboarding areas leave nothing to be desired except more time to experience them fully.

If you're prepared to venture a little farther, two additional ski areas are within easy driving distance:

◆ **Nakiska** combines gentle beginner terrain with fast downhills on Olympic quality runs, only 83 km (51 miles) from Banff, www.skinakiska.com (see *Kananaskis Country* chapter).

◆ **Kicking Horse Mountain Resort** has been ranked the best powder in North America, with over 2,750 acres of terrain, 1½ hours west of Banff, www.kickinghorseresort.com (see Yoho National Park chapter).

Ask at the front desk of your hotel for discounted lift tickets or purchase a tri-area lift pass (three-day minimum) which includes transfers between hotels and ski areas, lift ticket valid at all three Banff area hills and one free night pass at Norquay on Friday nights. Three- to 15-day passes available. Three-day pass (three of four days) $187.53 adults. Shuttle bus to the ski areas is available from most hotels in Banff and Lake Louise. ☎ 403-762-4561, www.sblls.com.

Banff National Park

Mount Norquay Ski Area, ☎ 403-762-4421 or 24-hr snowphone 403-760-7704, www.banffnorquay.com. A 10-minute drive from Banff with 31 runs (20% easy, 36% more difficult, 28% advanced, 16% expert) serviced by five lifts, including three quad chairlifts. Snowmaking 90% of skiing terrain. Skiing by the hour (two to five hours), night skiing and snowboard park. Cascade Lodge features a deli, cafeteria and pub. Daycare, ski/snowboard school, group/private lessons. Lift tickets, adult $52, student (13-17) $40, child (six-12) $17, senior $40.

Sunshine Village, ☎ 877-542-2633 or 403-760-5280 or 24-hr snowphone 403-760-7669, www.skibanff.com. Located eight km (five miles) west of Banff on the Trans Canada Highway, Sunshine Village ski area straddles the continental divide and is spread across three mountains in both Alberta and British Columbia. Sunshine boasts the world's fastest gondola and six quad chairlifts as well as over nine m (30 feet) of powder annually. **Goat's Eye Mountain**, **Lookout Mountain** and **Mt. Standish** all offer easy to expert terrain. **Delirium Dive** is a special extreme ski and riding area that attracts experts from around the world.

Ski and snowboard rentals, retail store, ski school, daycare, snow host tours and day lodge featuring a deli, cafeteria and restaurant. **Sunshine Inn** is Banff's only "ski-in, ski-out" hotel with ski packages available (☎ 877-542-2633). Lift tickets adult $64.95, youth $49.53, child $24.30, senior $53.27.

Nordic Skiing

 There are over 80 km (50 miles) of cross-country trails within a short drive of Banff townsite. Ask for the brochure called *Cross-Country Skiing Banff Area* for details on 11 easy and moderate trails.

From the Fairmont Banff Springs Hotel, you'll find groomed and track-set ski trails along the 12½-km (7.7-mile) **Spray River Loop**, with a picnic spot beside the river at the halfway point. The **Cascade Trail** is a 14-km (8.7-mile) one-way easy groomed trail from the Lake Minnewanka parking lot that follows a section of an old fire road; offers pleasant skiing, good views and a fun downhill run on the return. For an easy ungroomed beginner trail, try the five-km (three-mile) **Boom Lake Trail**, seven km (4.3 miles) west of Castle Junction on Highway 93.

Outdoor Ice Skating

Take to the ice outdoors in Banff by the canoe docks on the Bow River.

■ Wildlife

Wildlife population estimates in Banff National Park: 55-80 grizzly bears; 50-60 black bears; 3,200 elk (summer), 1,600 (winter); 50-80 moose; 2,000-2,600 bighorn sheep; 800-900 mountain goats; 850-950 mule deer; 300-350 white-tailed deer; 50-60 wolves; 150-250 coyotes.

Elk may often be seen around the Banff townsite, at the Fairmont Banff Springs Golf Course, along Tunnel Mountain Drive and near Vermilion Lakes. Bighorn sheep are commonly seen throughout the park, including the Mt. Norquay Road and Lake Minnewanka Road. At the Vermilion Lakes area beavers and muskrat are common and you might even spot a coyote or wolves. The Bow Valley Parkway is well known for wildlife viewing opportunities such as elk, deer, coyote and bighorn sheep.

There are 256 bird species in the park. The best birding areas are the Vermilion Lakes, Cave and Basin marsh and Johnson Lake.

■ Scenic Must-See's

Suggestions for the first-time summer visitor on a four-day schedule. If you don't have your own vehicle, rent a car in town or choose a tour with one of the local tour operators.

♦ **Day 1** – Learn about the history and culture of Banff National Park and the Canadian Rockies at the **Banff Park Museum** and the **Whyte Museum of the Canadian Rockies** (they're across the street from each other). Take the **Tunnel Mountain Drive** and stop at all of the points of interest along the route, including a short hike up **Tunnel Mountain** for panoramic views over the townsite and the Bow Valley.

◆ **Day 2** – Start out early and drive the **Bow Valley Parkway** to **Lake Louise**. Enjoy at least one day in the Lake Louise area visiting **Moraine Lake** and Lake Louise. Hike the **Plain of Six Glaciers Trail** along **Lake Louise** with a visit to both teahouses, of course.

◆ **Day 3** – Spend a day driving and stopping at points of interest along **Lake Minnewanka Drive**. Stroll Banff's downtown district for some late evening shopping after dinner in one of Banff's many exceptional restaurants.

◆ **Day 4** – Start your day with a soak at the **Upper Hot Springs**, then visit the **Cave & Basin National Historic Site** and tour the **Banff Springs Hotel**. You don't need to be an expert canoeist to paddle up the **Bow River** to the **Vermilion Lakes**. Rent a canoe at the docks at the corner of Bow Avenue and Wolf Street for a peaceful sunset paddle. Take in a concert or cultural event at the **Banff Center**.

■ To Do List

Next time I visit Banff National Park I would like to...

Backpack the Sunshine-Citadel Pass-Assiniboine Trail. This 58.7-km (36-mile) route makes for a four-day trip, although I would allow an extra day or two to explore the Lake Magog area in Mount Assiniboine Provincial Park (see below). The trail starts at the Sunshine Village ski area base village by either walking up the six-km (3.7-mile) restricted-access road or arranging for a ride via the privately run shuttle (my preference). The trail via Citadel Pass and Valley of the Rocks is considered the most scenic approach to Mount Assiniboine. The trip exits at Mount Shark in Kananaskis Country.

It's necessary to purchase a wilderness pass and book backcountry campgrounds in advance, including separate BC Parks campground reservations for Mount Assiniboine Provincial Park.

More information: Consult Parks Canada's *Backcountry Visitors' Guide to Banff National Park*. For this trip, detailed trail descriptions and a topographic map are a must.

Mount Assiniboine Provincial Park

British Columbia's Mount Assiniboine Provincial Park is a 386-sq-km (149-sq-mile) area that is roughly triangular in shape and is bound on the east by Banff National Park, on the west by Kootenay National Park and by BC forestland to the south. It was included in the Rocky Mountain Parks World Heritage Site in 1990. Access is by backpacking, skiing or helicopter only. The main attraction of the park is "the Matterhorn of the Rockies," 3,618-m (11,870-foot) pyramid-shaped Mount Assiniboine.

At the base of Mount Assiniboine beneath the mountain's north face are **Lake Magog** and the **Lake Magog Campground**, the destination of most hikers and a base from which to explore the area. There are also five alpine cabin shelters operated by BC Parks, as well as the privately operated Mount Assiniboine Lodge.

Information on Mount Assiniboine Provincial Park is available from **BC Parks**, www.env.gov.bc.ca/bcparks. For information on camping in the campground, contact the **Ministry of Water, Land and Air Protection, Kootenay Region Office**, ☎ 250-489-8540. For information on camping in the shelters or staying in the lodge, contact **Mount Assiniboine Lodge**, ☎ 403-678-2883 or info@assiniboinelodge.com.

■ Useful Information

Fire, Police, Ambulance: ☎ 911.

Hospital: 301 Lynx Street, ☎ 403-762-2222.

Royal Canadian Mounted Police: ☎ 403-762-2226.

Park Warden Office: ☎ 403-762-1470; 24-hour emergency, ☎ 403-762-4506.

Post Office: Corner of Buffalo and Bear Streets, Monday to Friday, 8:30 am to 5 pm, Saturday 9 am to 5 pm, closed Sundays and holidays.

Currency Exchange Custom House: 211 Banff Avenue.

Public Library: Corner of Bear and Buffalo Streets. Monday to Thursday 10 am to 8 pm, Friday 10 am to 6 pm, Saturday 11 am to 6 pm, Sunday 1 to 5 pm (closed Sundays Victoria Day through Labour day and holidays). Public Internet access.

Laundromats:

◆ Cascade Coin Laundry in the Cascade Plaza;

◆ Chalet Coin Laundry (Douglas Fir Resort) on Tunnel Mountain Road.

Liquor store: Liquor World, 202 Wolf Street.

Camera shop: Image Wizard, 101 Banff Avenue.

Trail conditions: ☎ 403-760-1305.

Road conditions: ☎ 403-762-1450.

Winter avalanche conditions: ☎ 403-762-1460.

Weather forecast: ☎ 403-762-2088.

Banff Park Radio: FM 101.1.

Lake Louise

Anyone who has seen photos of the Canadian Rockies has likely seen Lake Louise. The Rockies' famous turquoise glacial lake has been avidly photographed for more than a century. Viewed from the

grandiose **Chateau Lake Louise**, **Mount Victoria** and the **Victoria Glacier** loom at the opposite end of the lake.

The Chateau sits on glacial moraine that created a natural dam and formed the lake thousands of years ago. Although relatively small, two km (1.2 miles) long and a half-km (.3 miles) wide, 70 m (230 feet) deep at its maximum, it is one of the deeper lakes in the Rockies. Glacial melt keeps the lake at a frigid temperature (an average of about 8°Celsius or 46°F at the surface in midsummer) during the ice-free period of mid-June to late November. The lake is not always so captivatingly iridescent; in the absence of mid-summer runoff shortly after thaw around June and before freeze-up around November, the color is much darker.

Don't confuse the Village of Lake Louise with the actual lake. The village and its environs are referred to as Lake Louise but the lake itself, along with the Chateau Lake Louise, is located four km (2½ miles) southwest of the village.

■ History

Canadian Pacific Railway (CPR) outfitter Tom Wilson was packing supplies for the railway survey during the summer of 1882. When Wilson heard the sounds of distant thunder from his camp, Stoney Indians told him the sounds came from avalanches on a snowy mountain above "the Lake of Little Fishes." The following day, a Stoney named Edwin Hunter led Wilson through the forest to the lake, where he was probably the first white man to gaze upon the beauty of what was later named Lake Louise, for Princess Louise Caroline Alberta, Queen Victoria's fourth daughter, the wife of the Governor General of Canada in 1884. The province of Alberta is also named in her honor.

Wilson eventually cut a trail to the lake and in 1890 the CPR built a small log chalet, which subsequently burned. The Chateau was originally called "Chalet Lake Louise" until 1925, when it was re-christened Chateau Lake Louise, with the opening of the new center block. Over the years the Chateau evolved as new structures were built and various wings added until 1988, with the current capacity of 1,100 guests.

Lake Louise became the focal point of activity during the 1890s as mountaineers flocked to climb the peaks surrounding the lake. Travel to the area was by train to Laggan Station (later renamed Lake Louise Station), then by carriage on a crude road to the Chateau. Before the road was improved, a tramway was constructed to shuttle guests from the station.

TOM WILSON

At the age of 16, Thomas Edmonds Wilson left his home in Ontario in search of adventure. Life as a police constable with the North-West Mounted Police proved to be more interesting than farming back at home, but it did not squelch his wanderlust. After a short stint as a police constable, he was hired as a packer for the Canadian Pacific Railway. It was a decision that shaped the remainder of his life.

Wilson signed-on to accompany Major A.B. Rogers, the stalwart CPR engineer in charge of finding a route across the mountains. Although the relationship between the two was often stormy, they forged a life-long friendship and the position provided valuable experience in horse packing and route-finding.

Among other firsts, Wilson is credited with discovering Lake Louise and Emerald Lake and he made one of the earliest crossings of Kicking Horse Pass. He was present in November of 1885 for the driving of the last railway spike at Craigellachie, marking the end of an era for both the CPR and Wilson's life.

After an unsuccessful attempt at prospecting, Wilson launched his career as an outfitter and guide. The town of Banff was booming and knowledgeable guides to lead sightseers, hunters and fishing parties were in high demand. Wilson was permitted to advertise his services as "Guide to the CPR." Along with this work, he also began assisting with survey work for the Dominion Topographic Survey, taking part in several first ascents.

Over the years, Wilson's business grew and he hired a number of guides to assist on trips, including Bill Peyto and Jimmy Simpson, who both forged legendary careers of their own. By the late 1800s, the length and type of trips increased from week-long hunting, fishing and sightseeing excursions to major mountaineering, exploring and hunting expeditions that lasted up to two months. Wilson became Banff's pre-eminent guide and outfitter.

After his departure from the trail in 1904, Wilson helped found the Alpine Club of Canada in 1906, extolling the virtues of the Canadian mountains while condemning the English and wealthy Canadians for touring the Alps and mountains of other countries.

Wilson's unsuccessful attempt to obtain title to his Kootenay Plains ranch precipitated his decision to leave Banff for British Columbia. But after seven years the mountains called him back and from 1927 until his death in 1933 he entertained guests at the Banff Springs Hotel with his many colorful stories of trail life.

Lake Louise

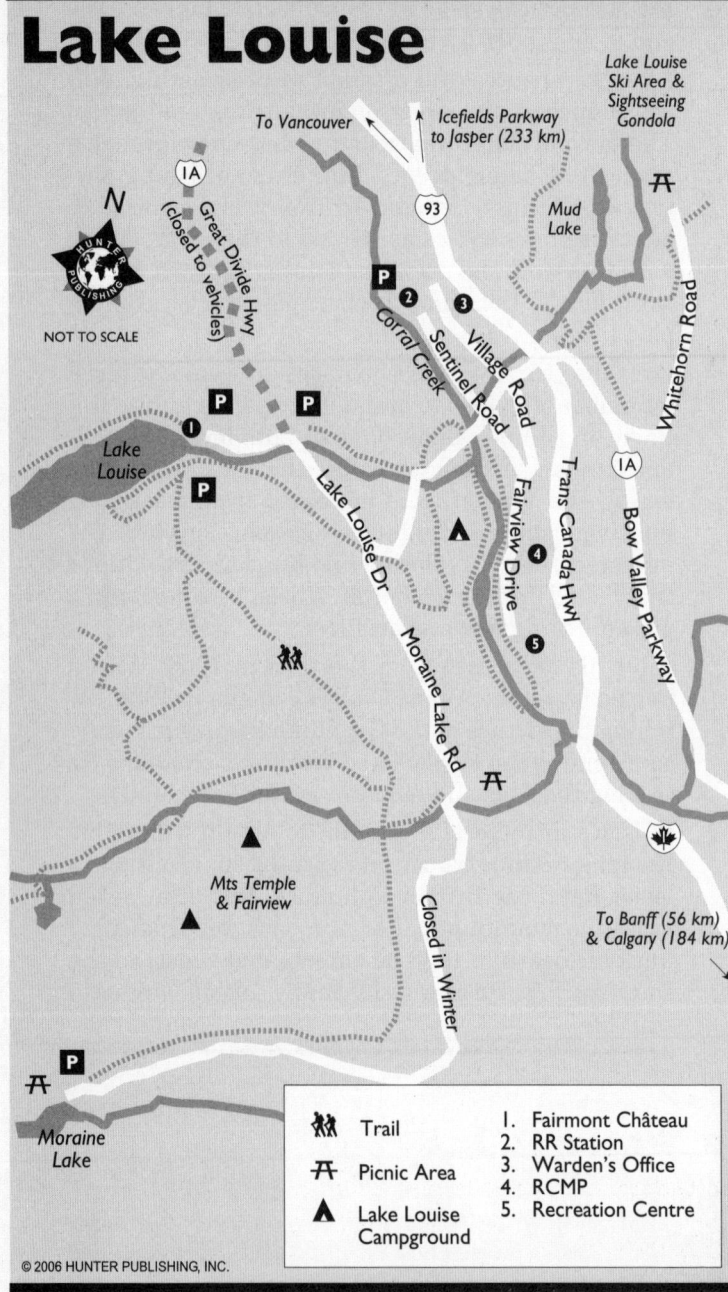

Lake Louise

To Vancouver

Icefields Parkway to Jasper (233 km)

Lake Louise Ski Area & Sightseeing Gondola

N HUNTER PUBLISHING
NOT TO SCALE

1A

93

Mud Lake

Great Divide Hwy (closed to vehicles)

Corral Creek

Sentinel Road

Village Road

Whitehorn Road

Lake Louise

Lake Louise Dr

Fairview Drive

Trans Canada Hwy

1A

Bow Valley Parkway

Moraine Lake Rd

Mts Temple & Fairview

Closed in Winter

To Banff (56 km) & Calgary (184 km)

Moraine Lake

	Trail		1. Fairmont Château
	Picnic Area		2. RR Station
	Lake Louise Campground		3. Warden's Office
			4. RCMP
			5. Recreation Centre

■ The Village

The population of the Village of Lake Louise is 1,500, including 700 Chateau Lake Louise staff. Each day during the peak summer months Lake Louise sees some 20,000 visitors. The Village of Lake Louise is the highest permanent settlement in Canada at 1,536 m (5,039 feet).

The village has limited services, the hub of which is Samson Mall shopping plaza located at the main crossroads. Samson Mall houses gift shops, the ubiquitous sweet /ice-cream shop, a liquor store, a sports store, a camera shop, postal services, a café, a bakery, a grocery store and public washrooms. The liquor store aside, prices are generally higher than in Banff, so, if you're camping and preparing your own food, stock up before traveling to Lake Louise. There are two service stations in the village; both stock convenience items.

Lake Louise Visitor Information Center, ☎ 403-522-3833, located at the entrance of Samson Mall off Village Road, e-mail ll.info@pc.gc.ca. The largest, most elaborate visitor center in the mountain parks features numerous exhibits. Operating hours are 9 am to 7 pm throughout the summer with reduced hours in the off-season (9 am to 4 or 5 pm). The Friends of Banff National Park operate a retail outlet in the center where you can purchase books, maps and souvenirs.

Distances from Lake Louise Village

Jasper	230 km (143 miles)
Banff	58 km (36 miles)
Field (Yoho)	27 km (17 miles)
Lake Louise	four km (2½ miles)
Moraine Lake	14 km (nine miles)

■ Where to Eat

Many of the restaurants in the Lake Louise area are at the hotels and lodges, some of which offer two or more choices. The Banff-Lake Louise Tourism Bureau produces an information flyer (available at the Visitor Information Center) that lists most of the restaurants in Lake Louise, but it gives a rather glowing description of each establishment. You can select from a large number of fine dining restaurants, many with grand views, and

DINING PRICE CHART	
Price per person in Canadian $ for an entrée, not including beverage, tax or tip.	
$	Under $10
$$	$10-$25
$$$	Over $25

from typical Canadian cuisine such as prime rib, salmon and lamb; a limited selection of international cuisine; deli food; bakery items. There are cafés, a few lounges and pubs. Prices tend to be on the high side and portions on the small side.

 Where not to eat: I'm not sure why there was a line-up at the Mountain Restaurant on Village Road (beside the Esso service station) because my lunch partner and I both agreed that we had not made a good choice – enough said.

Bill Peyto's Café, Lake Louise Alpine Center Hostel, ☎ 403-521-8421, $$. Don't expect the prices to be cheap because this café is at a hostel but it is one of the less pricey places to eat in Lake Louise. Burgers, pasta, steak, stir-fry, in a very casual, busy atmosphere with rustic décor. Open for breakfast, lunch and dinner; outdoor patio.

Laggan's Bakery & Café, Samson Mall, $ to $$. A very busy bakery with lines out the door at times. Fresh pastries, bread, sandwiches and specialty coffees. Eat-in or take-out.

Lake Louise Station, Sentinel Road, ☎ 403-522-2600, $$ to $$$. Enjoy contemporary Canadian cuisine in the oldest building in Lake Louise – the restored 1909 heritage railway station. Alberta beef, game, seafood, vegetarian meals and burgers served for lunch or dinner. Fine dining in restored vintage railway cars; open for dinner daily during the summer as well as for afternoon tea. Private dining rooms available. Garden patio and gift shop.

Fairmont Chateau Lake Louise, ☎ 403-522-1818, $$$. Dining at the Fairmont Chateau Lake Louise is amazing, but with so many offerings it's difficult to choose from their gastronomic line-up. There's the contemporary dinner menu and extensive wine list in the elegant **Fairview Dining Room** (reservations required), or classic Swiss dining and rustic décor at **Walliser Stube** (reservations recommended). **Poppy Brasserie** is open for breakfast, lunch and dinner and features international specialties. There's the ever-popular brunch buffet featuring a lavish selection of hot and cold specialties in the European-styled ballroom of the **Victoria Room**, with its table-to-ceiling windows overlooking the lake. If none of the above satisfies your needs, the **Chateau Deli** is open 24-hours-a-day for early breakfasts to late-night snacks and everything in between. including gourmet backpacker lunches to go ($$). The **Lakeview Lounge** and **Glacier Saloon** serve an extensive selection of beverages as well as snacks, pub-style food and desserts. Afternoon tea, exclusively blended, is served daily from noon to 4 pm in the Lakeview Lounge.

■ Where to Stay

 There are a limited number of hotels, lodges and inns in the Lake Louise area and, unfortunately, all are priced at the high end of the scale. Private guesthouses are not available. The **Lake Louise Alpine Center** is the only hostel in the village and the atmosphere is more like a resort than a hostel, as are the prices. My preferred accommodation here is the campground in the village.

HOTEL PRICE CHART	
Reflects the price of an average room for two in Canadian \$, May-Sept. Rates lower rest of year (except Christmas and New Year's).	
\$	Under \$50
\$\$	\$50-\$100
\$\$\$	\$101-\$150
\$\$\$\$	\$151-\$250
\$\$\$\$\$	Over \$250

Lake Louise

Available at the Visitor Information Center, the Banff-Lake Louise Tourism Bureau (see *Information Sources*) produces an *Accommodation Guide* brochure that lists the hotels, motels, inns and lodges in Banff, Lake Louise and surrounding areas.

Hotels/Inns/Lodges

Lake Louise Inn, ☎ 800-661-9237 or 403-522-3791, 210 Village Road, www.lakelouiseinn.com, $$$$ to $$$$$. A modern resort with rooms from economy to superior as well as executive rooms, family lodges and superior loft rooms, all with kitchens and wood/gas fireplaces. Indoor pool, whirlpool, steam room; café, lounge, dining room; laundry facilities; Internet access ($1 for 10 minutes); gift shop. Discounts for seniors and AAA/CAA members.

Moraine Lake Lodge, ☎ 877-522-2777 or 403-522-3733 or 403-760-2380 (winter), located at Moraine Lake (15 minutes from the village), www.morainelake.com, $$$$$. Open June through September. Luxury accommodation in the spectacular surroundings of the Valley of the Ten Peaks. All rooms and cabins offer great views, with private balconies. Feather duvets, (no TVs or phones), complimentary canoe rentals, guided hikes, afternoon tea, and naturalist presentations. Dining room, café, outdoor patio, library, gift shop, Internet service.

The Fairmont Chateau Lake Louise, ☎ 800-257-7544 or 403-522-3511, 111 Lake Louise Drive, www.fairmont.com/lakelouise, $$$$$. Indulge in a little luxury in one of 487 guest rooms and suites with views of the Chateau grounds or Lake Louise. Choose from alpine-décor Fairmont rooms; 19th-century décor deluxe rooms; junior or one-bedroom suites with fireplaces, canopy beds and whirlpool baths. Or, if you need a little more space and a touch more luxury, try one of the four Belvedere penthouse suites. They have spiral staircases to a roofed private balcony with towering views, en suite bath and secluded bedroom. And just when you decide money really can buy happiness, the 780-sq-foot Royal Suite awaits those who are satisfied with nothing but the best.

Bed and breakfast, celebration, discovery, ski and wellness packages available. The "Canadian Rockies Experience Summer Package" includes one night accommodation, three meals, a guided seasonal activity, a one-hour spa treatment and a hotel heritage tour. Prices start from $556 per person per day, based on double occupancy in a Fairmont Room. The "Chateau Experience Package" includes one night accommodation, breakfast, dinner and afternoon tea service, a guided seasonal activity, and a 30-minute spa treatment. Rates start from $312 in winter and $452 in summer.

The Health Club offers an indoor heated pool, whirlpool, steam room and fitness center. The Escape Spa has a full line of body and hair care services.

General services include babysitting, laundry services, ski storage, and high-speed Internet access in many rooms, as well as wireless in many locations throughout the hotel. Wheelchair-accessible; small pets permitted.

If your sightseeing schedule permits some down time and you care for a little shopping, you don't have to wander far from the hotel as there are over 20 shops and specialty boutiques to browse, including leather or Muskox fibre garments, souvenirs, Christmas decorations, sports clothing and gear, books, gourmet food products, jewelry, a photo lab and more.

Baker Creek Chalets, ☎ 403-522-3761, 10 minutes from Lake Louise on the Bow Valley Parkway, www.bakercreek.com, $$$$ to $$$$$. One-bedroom, Jacuzzi or deluxe loft suites, loft or two-bedroom chalets and deluxe trapper's cabin – all with kitchens or kitchenettes, wood or gas fireplaces and deck. Tasteful rustic décor in a beautiful setting. Family-operated. Fine dining at **Baker Creek Bistro**.

Camping

Three campgrounds are located along the Icefields Parkway near Lake Louise in Banff National Park, as well as three along the Bow Valley Parkway. All are more peaceful than the Lake Louise campground, which is the only one in the village of Lake Louise. It's listed as two separate campgrounds in some brochures and publications as it has a tenting section and a trailer section.

Lake Louise Trailer and Tent accepts reservations. Consult www.pc-camping.ca for the Parks Canada Campground Reservation Service, or call ☎ 877-737-3783, international calls ☎ 905-426-4648.

Overflow sites are open only when other campgrounds in the area are full. Along the Icefields Parkway between Saskatchewan Crossing and Waterfowl Lakes Campground is **Silverhorn Creek Campground** (51.7 km or 32 miles north of Lake

CAMPING/HOSTELS	
Rates in Canadian $, not including taxes.	
$	Under $13
$$	$13-$22
$$$	$23-$30
$$$$	Over $30

Louise). It's used as an overflow campground for the north end of Banff Park and it's unusually scenic for an overflow. When the Lake Louise Campground is full (usually throughout the summer), there is an overflow five km (three miles) east along the Trans Canada Highway toward Banff. It's not a nice place in the least (plan to arrive late and depart early), but it's convenient when the main campground is full.

Campsites in Lake Louise & Vicinity

Rampart Creek. $$, 50 primitive sites. 88 km (55 miles) north along Icefields Parkway. Disabled access; kitchen shelters, firewood and fire pits, food storage. Season: June 26-Sept 6.

Waterfowl Lakes. $$, 116 unserviced sites. 57 km (35 miles) north along Icefields Parkway. Disabled access; kitchen shelters, firewood and fire pits, food storage, sani-dump; trailhead to Cirque and Chephren Lakes. Season: June 18-Sept 19.

Mosquito Creek. $$, 32 primitive sites. 24 km (15 miles) north on Icefields Parkway. Disabled access; kitchen shelter, firewood and fire pits. Season: Year-round.

Lake Louise. Tent sites $$, trailer sites with power $$$, 189 trailer/210 tent sites. Fairview Drive (past Samson Mall, across the railway tracks, left on Fairview Drive at the four-way stop). Disabled access; showers, kitchen shelters; firewood and fire pits; food storage; interpretive programs; nice setting along the Bow River (the tenting section is protected by an electric fence to help keep bears out). Season: Trailer section open year-round (tents and soft-sided trailers are not permitted April/May and Oct/Nov), tent section open May 21 to Oct 1. Reservations accepted.

Protection Mountain. $$, 89 unserviced sites. 48 km (30 miles) from Banff or 17 km (10½ miles) from Lake Louise on the Bow Valley Parkway. Disabled access; kitchen shelters, firewood and fire pits, kitchen shelters, food storage. Season: June 25 to Sept 6.

Castle Mountain. $$, 43 unserviced sites. 34 km (21 miles) from Banff or 28 km (17 miles) from Lake Louise on the Bow Valley Parkway. Kitchen shelters. Season: May 28 to Sept 7.

Johnston Canyon. $$, 132 unserviced sites. 25 km (15½ miles) from Banff on the Bow Valley Parkway. Disabled access; showers, sani-dump. Season: June 4 to September 20.

Hosteling

Two hostels are located along the Icefields Parkway and one along the Bow Valley Parkway near Lake Louise in Banff National Park. The **Lake Louise Alpine Center** is conveniently located in the village. Linen is provided at all of the hostels; no sleeping bags are permitted. Reservations: centralres.sa@hihostels.ca, ☎ 866-762-4122 or 403-670-7580.

HOSTELS IN LAKE LOUISE & VICINITY

Rampart Creek Wilderness Hostel
Members $$, non-members $$$, 24 beds.
95 km (59 miles) north of Lake Louise and 34 km (20 miles) south of the Columbia Icefield Center.
Check-in 5 to 11 pm. Some closure dates apply.
World-class rock and ice climbing nearby.

Mosquito Creek Wilderness Hostel
Members $$, non-members $$$, 32 beds, family rooms.
27 km (17 miles) north of Lake Louise.
Check-in 5 to 11 pm. Some closure dates apply.
Peaceful setting close to hiking and ski trails; sauna.

Lake Louise Alpine Center
Members and non-members $$$$, 150 beds, family rooms.
Village Road in Lake Louise.
Check-in 3 pm.
Consists of two buildings and includes many amenities such as a restaurant with a patio, sauna and

Lake Louise

more. This is a very busy hostel that is more like a resort than a hostel and, unfortunately, the staff were not particularly helpful during my visit.

Castle Mountain Wilderness Hostel
Members $$, non-members $$$, 28 beds.
At Castle Junction along the Bow Valley Parkway.
Check-in 8 am to10 am and 5 pm to 10 pm.
This hostel has a rather particular caretaker, so don't forget to remove your shoes!

■ Adventures

Sports & Camping Equipment Rentals

Wilson Mountain Sports, ☎ 403-522-3636, Samson Mall. Full line of bicycle rentals from high-performance mountain bikes, $20/hour or $49/day, to touring bikes with panniers, $15/hour or $39/day, and kids' equipment; servicing also available. Fishing rods, climbing and mountaineering equipment as well as camping equipment available for rent.

Canoe Rentals

Chateau Lake Louise Boathouse, ☎ 403-522-3511, rents canoes at $32/hour; the **boathouse at Moraine Lake**, ☎ 403-522-3733, does the same at $30/hour.

Horseback Riding

Timberline Tours, ☎ 888-858-3388 or 403-522-3743, behind Deer Lodge (on Lake Louise Drive just before the Chateau parking), www.timberlinetours.ca. Paul Peyto has been guiding and outfitting in Banff Park for over 30 years. If the name sounds familiar, his great uncle was the legendary Bill Peyto, one of the first guides, outfitters and park wardens in Banff Park.

Trail rides from Lake Louise lakehead:

◆ 1½ hours $55.

◆ Lake Agnes Teahouse three hours $75.

◆ Plain of Six Glaciers 4½ hours $90.

◆ All-day rides on the Highline Trail, Paradise Valley, Baker Lake or Skoki Lodge $130.

◆ Overnight pack trips three to 10 days, from $330 to $1,450 per person. Rides are limited to 12 people, but most are smaller groups.

Mountain Biking

The Bow River Loop is an easy 7.1-km (4.4-mile) loop, ideal for families. Starting at the Lake Louise Campground or the Bow River Bridge opposite the Station Restaurant (historic train station), the riverside trail travels both sides of the Bow River with interpretive signs along the way. The **Great Divide Bike Path** is a 10½-km (6½-mile) one-way paved historic route (old Highway 1A) no longer open to vehicles. Starting at the parking lot at the 3.6 km (2.2 mile) mark of Lake Louise Drive, the ride along the road is easy with little elevation gain. Interpretive displays and a picnic shelter mark the Great Divide at 7½ km (4.6 miles). The road continues to the Trans Canada Highway in Yoho.

Hikes, Drives, Sights & Activities

Lake Louise Sightseeing Gondola and Interpretive Center, ☎ 403-522-3555, www.skilouise.com/summer. Located five minutes from the Trans Canada Highway junction at the Lake Louise ski area. Open May 15 to September 30.

Gondola visits begin with a brief presentation about the area. The 14-minute ride in an open chair lift or enclosed gondola car travels to an elevation of 2,088 m (6,850 feet) on Mount Whitehorn. Magnificent panoramas of Lake Louise, glacier-topped Mount Temple and Mount Victoria, natural springs and wildflowers. The area is a grizzly bear habitat so you might spot them grazing in the alpine meadows.

The Wildlife Interpretation Center features information and exhibits as well as complimentary theater presentations.

Forty-five minute guided walks, $5 per person and two-hour guided hikes, $7 per person, are on a first-come, first-served basis. Unescorted hiking is restricted to areas on the upper

Lake Louise

mountain only and it is strongly recommended to hike in groups of six or more (due to the possible presence of bears).

The Lodge of the Ten Peaks is open year-round for breakfast or lunch in the restaurant or cafeteria.

Adult $21, senior/student $19, child (six-12 years) $9.95. Add $2 for the breakfast buffet. Complimentary shuttle service from Lake Louise village and hotels.

Lake Louise

To reach the lake, from the Trans Canada Highway junction follow Lake Louise Drive straight through the village for four km (2½ miles) until you reach the public parking areas (lower and upper) for the Chateau.

The lake is the major tourist attraction in the area. The parking lot and Chateau grounds are very congested during the summer months so, if you want to avoid the crowds, go early in the morning or late in the afternoon.

◆ Canoe rentals are available from the boathouse.

Lake Louise Lakeshore

Walk: 3.8 km (2.4 miles) round-trip.

Watchable wildlife: Humans of all shapes, sizes, and nationalities.

This is the most popular short walk at Lake Louise. To avoid the hordes, go in the early morning or evening. Otherwise, be prepared to share the trail with a lot of people. The trail starts at the busy Chateau along the north shore of the lake and skirts the west (right) side of the lake. Wheelchair-accessible.

Lake Agnes

Hike: 6.8 km (4.2 miles) round-trip.

Elevation gain: 385 m (1,263 feet).

Watchable wildlife: Hoary marmots and pikas in the rockslides above Lake Agnes; chipmunks, red squirrels, Columbian ground squirrels and golden-mantled ground squirrels near the teahouse.

Follow the lakeshore trail just beyond the Chateau where a trail branches uphill to the right and reaches picturesque **Mirror Lake** at km 2.6 (mile 1.6). The trail diverges to the right up a steep ascent or to the left up a series of switchbacks;

you may want to take the route on the right to ascend and descend the other way. The **Lake Agnes Teahouse** serves beverages, pastries and light meals. If you want to venture farther, trails lead to Big and Little Beehives, as well as the Plain of the Six Glaciers trail (see below).

One of the earliest trails in the Lake Louise area, **Lake Agnes Trail** is named in honor of Lady Susan Agnes Macdonald, wife of Canada's first Prime Minister, Sir John A. Macdonald, who trekked to the lake in 1890.

Plain of Six Glaciers

Hike: 13.2 km (8.2 miles) round-trip or 14.6 km (nine miles) round-trip via Lake Agnes.

Elevation gain: 380 m (1,246 feet).

Watchable wildlife: Hoary marmots, pikas, mountain goats.

Don't miss this popular hike that leads to the back of Lake Louise and the foot of Mounts Victoria and Lefroy, with spectacular views of the Victoria Glacier and Lake Louise. Six glaciers are visible from the forefield or plain of lower Victoria Glacier.

After following the Lakeshore Trail, stay left as you leave the Chateau crowds behind. The trail climbs across avalanche slopes, glacial moraines and switchbacks before you reach a rest area (and outhouses) beside the teahouse, km 5½ (mile 3.4). Here you can sit back on one of the benches and take in the view. A sign identifies the peaks. Set back in the trees, perched on a meadow, the teahouse awaits hikers.

Beside the rest area, cross the bridge over the creek as the trail branches toward Victoria Glacier for 1.3 km (.8 miles) along the crest of a lateral moraine and on a steep talus slope. From this excellent vantage point you can see Abbot Pass Hut – a National Historic Site and the highest permanent housing structure in Canada – between Mount Victoria (3,464 m/11,365 feet) and Mount Lefroy (3,441 m/11,290 feet). The Alberta/British Columbia border runs through the middle of the hut! CPR Swiss guides constructed the hut in 1922 and today the Alpine Club of Canada operates it. The lake and Chateau, clearly visible in the distance to the northeast, complete the grand view.

Lake Louise

My preference is to return to the Chateau via **Lake Agnes**. Watch for the trail signs and turn left 1.4 km (.8 miles) from the teahouse on the highline route toward Lake Agnes and Mirror Lake. You'll come upon eye-popping views of Lake Louise and the Bow Valley.

Plain of Six Glaciers Teahouse

Built in 1927 by Swiss guides as a half-way resting point to Abbot Hut, the teahouse continues to provide a welcome respite for thousands of tourists who visit the area each year. Joy Kimball and her daughter Susanne Smith have operated the teahouse for over 40 years. Supplies are flown in by helicopter at the beginning of each season and brought by packhorse throughout the summer. There is no electricity, and water is from an underground spring. Bread and sweets are baked fresh each day using propane stoves.

Beverages, soup, sandwiches and goodies such as scones, chocolate cake and apple pie are carefully hoisted in the dumbwaiter to the second floor balcony. A simple slice of fresh bread with honey and a cup of tea never tasted better anywhere else.

TRAGEDY NEAR LAKE LOUISE

In the summer of 1896, members of the Appalachian Mountain Club made an attempt to reach the summit of the yet unclimbed Mt. Lefroy (3,423 m or 11,230 feet). Young attorney and alpinist Phillip Abbot fell to his death near the summit of the mountain, the first known mountaineering fatality in the Canadian Rockies and in the history of North American climbing. Abbot Pass and Abbot Hut commemorate Abbot and his untimely death.

Recommended Reading: *The Guiding Spirit* by Andrew J. Kauffman and William L. Putnam, Footprint Publishing, 1986, Revelstoke, BC.

THE SOUND OF THUNDER

After touring and hiking alone in the Rockies for over a week, the prospect of meeting up with my dear friend Brian in Lake Louise was uplifting. We had impulsively planned to rendezvous only a few days earlier and seeing a familiar face among the crowds is always comforting.

Greetings out of the way, we departed the busy parking lot of Samson Mall for the busier parking lot of the Chateau Lake Louise. It took at least a half-hour before we found parking spaces and made our way to the hotel grounds after 2 pm. It seemed as if half the world had congregated at Lake Louise on this particular day. Carefully manoeuvring our way through the crowds along the lakeshore, the congestion finally thinned and then dwindled to a trickle of only a few people along the Plain of Six Glaciers trail.

Conversing non-stop, we stopped often to soak up the views and concur that meeting up in the Rockies was a great idea. By the time we reached the teahouse most of the other hikers had made their way back down the trail. I can certainly appreciate the foresight of the Swiss guides who built the teahouse – undeniably civilized. Refreshments gratefully gobbled-up, we left the comfort of our perches on the balcony of the teahouse and carefully made our way along the lateral moraine towards awesome Victoria Glacier. A loud thundering sound broke the silence. "Is that thunder?" Brian quizzed. "That's not thunder, those are avalanches," I replied, although we didn't see any movement on the slopes ahead. We scrambled up the talus slope and brought out the binoculars. Returning along the moraine ridge we heard the roars from behind, even louder this time and rather eerie. As we arrived at the teahouse junction I heard another roar and quickly turned around to see an avalanche of snow tumbling in the distance. "Look!" I exclaimed as I aimed my camera toward the avalanche. Click, click, click "I got it!" I exclaimed as we stared at the snow settling in the distance.

Thrilled to have captured an avalanche on film, we began our descent via Lake Agnes. The in-your-face views of Lake Louise are jaw-dropping. Dusk was quickly approaching as we arrived at peaceful Lake Agnes, not another soul to bee seen. As I skirted the teahouse a young employee glared at me from inside, "I'm sick of tourists, we're closed, go home," I read in her mind. As we continued our descent and approached lovely little Mirror Lake, two lovers along the shore abruptly stopped kissing, surprised to see yet two more straggling hikers – no need to read their minds. We arrived back at the lake by dusk, the lights of the Chateau beginning to glow and only a handful of tourists out for an early evening stroll. "I'm really glad I decided to meet you here," Brian said. I smiled.

Panther Falls

Moraine Lake

Herbert Lake, Banff

Above: Iceline Trail, Yoho (© Lenard Sanders)
Below: Stanley Glacier Cirque, Kootenay

Fairview Lookout

Hike: Two km (1.2 miles) round-trip.

From near the Lake Louise Boathouse on the east (left) side of the lake, follow the **Saddleback Trail**, and then right onto the Fairview Lookout Trail to climb to the viewpoint.

Saddleback/Fairview Mountain

Hike: 10.6 km (6.6 miles) round-trip.

Elevation gain: 600 m (1,968 feet) to Saddleback plus 414 m (1,358 feet) to Fairview.

The Saddle is a meadow pass between Fairview and Saddleback Mountains. The trail to Saddleback and Fairview is steep but solid and often crowded; well worth it for a bird's eye perspective of Lake Louise and a panorama of the Bow and Paradise Valleys.

From near the boathouse, keep straight on the **Saddleback Trail** as it climbs through forest and avalanche paths before it switchbacks through larch trees to the subalpine meadows and the Saddle at km 3.7 (mile 2.3).

For the **Fairview Trail**, follow the signs that continue into the pass, then direct you to the right and then switchback to the summit of Fairview Mountain.

Stay on the signed trails and return the way you came – some hikers have become lost in this area. Late September is one of the nicest times to hike this trail, when the alpine larch needles turn golden.

Moraine Lake

Hard to imagine there could be another lake near Lake Louise that rivals her exceptional scenic beauty. Moraine Lake and the Valley of the Ten Peaks may not be as well publicized as Lake Louise, but it is quintessential Rocky Mountain postcard scenery at its best.

Set within the forbidding backdrop of the Wenkchemna (a Stoney Indian word meaning 10) Peaks, the lake was created by a rockslide from the Tower of Babel at the northeast end of the lake. Moraine Lake is much smaller than Lake Louise and relatively shallow; as such, the water levels fluctuate seasonally. To the north, **Mount Temple** (3,544 m or 11,627 feet) covers 15 sq km (six sq miles), one of the largest mountains in the Rockies and the third-highest in Banff National Park.

To reach Moraine Lake from the village, follow Lake Louise Drive three km (1.8 miles) to the Moraine Lake Road, which branches south (left) for 12½ km (7.7 miles) to the busy parking area at the north end of the lake.

With excellent hiking trails and a lodge, the Moraine Lake area is very busy during the summer. Canoe rentals are available at the boathouse. The road is not plowed in winter.

 Did You Know? The Valley of the Ten Peaks is featured on the verso of some Canadian $20 bills.

Moraine Lakeshore

Walk: 2.4 km (1½ miles) round-trip.

Watchable wildlife: Ground squirrels, chipmunks.

Continue past the lodge along the flat lakeside trail that terminates at the lake's inlet at the southwest end.

Larch Valley - Sentinel Pass

Hike: 2.8 km (1.7 miles) to Larch Valley or 5.8 km (3.6 miles) to Sentinel Pass.

Elevation gain: 724 m (2,375 feet).

This hike is most popular in late September, when autumn turns the Larch Valley into a golden landscape. During the summer the wildflower meadows also attract many hikers. Along with a captivating vista over the Ten Peaks, it is a not-to-be-missed adventure.

Walk along the lakeshore past the lodge where the trail branches to the right at the trail sign. The trail climbs through a forest and follows a series of switchbacks. The trail branches right at km 2.4 (mile 1½) and climbs to the open meadows of Larch Valley. At 3,235 m (10,613 feet), **Mount Fay** is the most striking of the Ten Peaks.

Continuing to Sentinel Pass, the trail passes between the tiny **Minnestimma Lakes** (meaning "sleeping water"). Straight ahead is the summit of **Sentinel Pass** (2,611 m or 8,566 feet) between Pinnacle Mountain on the left and Mount Temple on the right. The steep trail leading to the pass – one of the highest trail-accessible passes in Banff Park – switchbacks on open talus slopes before the crest. Unusual rock formations or spires, the tallest of which is called **Grand Sentinel**, give the pass its name.

To avoid disappointment, be sure to contact the Lake Louise Visitor Information Center before you plan to hike the Moraine Lake area trails. Restricted access applies when grizzly bears are using the area each year. By law hikers must travel in tight groups of six or more during restricted access.

Winter Adventures

Alpine Skiing

Lake Louise, ☎ 800-258-7669 or 403-522-3555 or 24-hr snowphone 403-762-4766, www.skilouise.com. The Rockies' biggest ski area offers more than 4,200 acres of skiing over four mountain faces with 11 lifts, including four high-speed chairs. There's a well-planned mix of runs for all abilities, with beginners able to use every chair as each has an easy run down.

Four day-lodges with a variety of food services, ski shop/rentals, daycare, ski school, free guided tours twice daily and free shuttles from Lake Louise hotels.

Lift tickets: adult $69, student $50, child $20, senior $56.

Nordic Skiing

Ask for the brochure *Cross-Country Skiing in the Lake Louise Area* for a list of easy, moderate and difficult trails. **The Great_Divide** is an easy 7½-km (4.6-mile) one-way double trackset trail that ends at the Great Divide exhibit and picnic area on the Banff-Yoho National Park boundary.

Outdoor Ice Skating

Lake Louise at the Chateau Lake Louise is the perfect setting for ice skating.

■ Useful Information

Fire, Police, Ambulance, Wardens, Search & Rescue: ☎ 911.

Royal Canadian Mounted Police: ☎ 403-522-3811.

Medical Center: Across from the Visitor Information Center, ☎ 403-522-2184.

Park Warden Office: ☎ 403-762-4506 (Banff).

Post Office: The Depot, Samson Mall.

Laundromat: Use the coin-operated facilities at Lake Louise Inn, 210 Village Road.

Information Sources

www.pc.gc.ca/banff

Parks Canada website with extensive information about the park, including fees, visitor information, natural wonders, activities, and public safety, with trail reports, road conditions, and avalanche reports. Banff National Park, PO Box 900, Banff, Alberta, T1L 1K2, ☎ 403-762-1550.

www.banfflakelouise.com

Visitor information site for Banff and Lake Louise by the Banff Lake Louise Tourism Bureau, ☎ 403-762-8421.

www.discoverbanff.com

Canadian Rockies tourism and travel guide.

www.banffnationalpark.com

A locally produced travel planner for the Canadian Rockies.

www.banffalberta.ca

Banff travel guide including accommodations, tours and activities, shopping, transportation and restaurants. Central reservations as well.

Kananaskis Country

Adjacent to Banff National Park, Kananaskis Country encompasses over 4,000 sq kilometres (1,600 sq miles) of provincial parks and recreation areas on the eastern slopes of the Canadian Rockies and the foothills southwest of Calgary. Not a national park, Kananaskis Country is a multi-use recreation area that supports many activities. If you are an avid outdoor enthusiast or if you simply enjoy stunning scenery and wildlife viewing, "K-Country," as it's

known locally, has a huge variety of accessible quality outdoor activities, as well as a wide array of tourist services.

On the northern fringes of Kananaskis is the town of **Canmore**, the hub of K-Country and a rapidly growing tourist center that has been described as North America's mountain adventure capital. Stretching along the Bow Valley and sandwiched between the Rocky Mountains of Banff National Park and the Three Sisters Mountain, it's easy to see why mountain-dwellers have flocked to Canmore – over 14,000 people call Canmore home. Canmore hosts many festivals and events throughout the summer, has excellent walking trails and boasts one of the best winter sports facilities in all of Canada.

K-Country includes **Canmore Nordic Center Provincial Park**, **Spray Valley Provincial Park**, **Bow Valley Provincial Park** and **Bow Valley Wildland Provincial Parks**, **Evan-Thomas Provincial Recreation Area** (Kananaskis Village) and the most popular and scenic park, **Peter Lougheed Provincial Park**.

Other parks and areas in K-Country (not covered in this book) include Sheep River Provincial Park, Bluerock Wildland Provincial Park, Elbow-Sheep Wildland Provincial Park, Don Getty Wildland Provincial Park, as well as Sibbald, Elbow Valley, Sheep River, Highwood and Cataract Creek areas.

Kananaskis Country

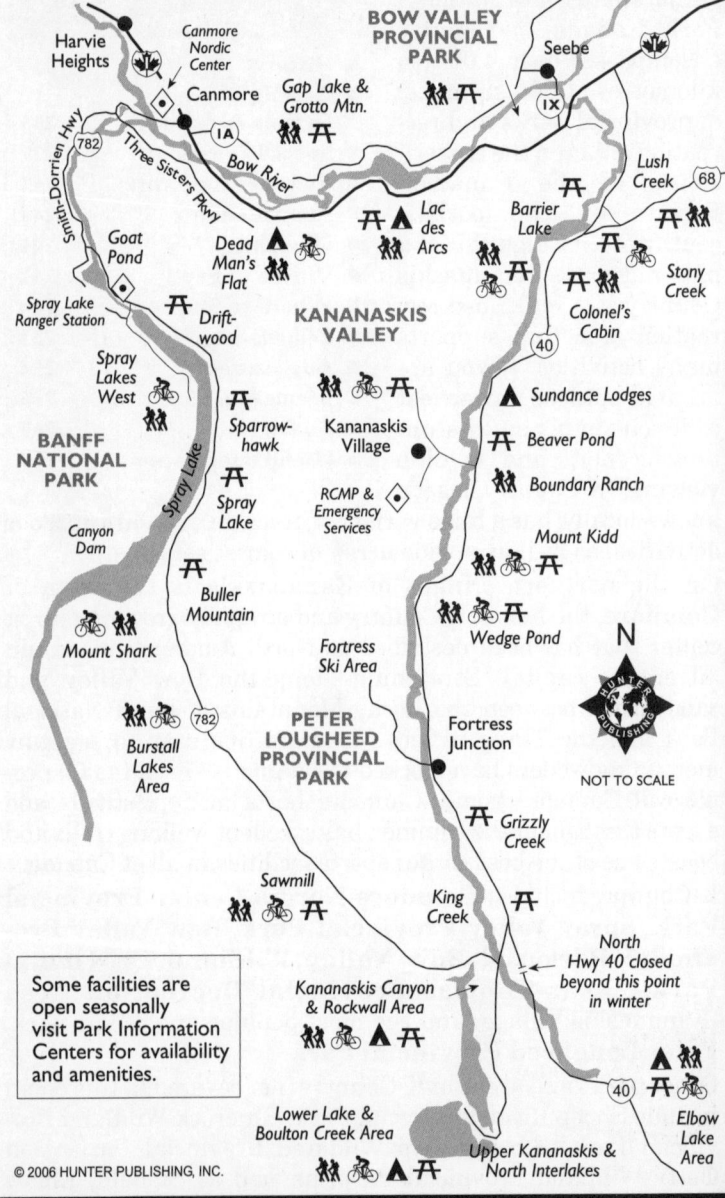

Harvie Heights

Canmore Nordic Center

Canmore

Smith-Dorrien Hwy

782

Three Sisters Pkwy

1A

Bow River

BOW VALLEY PROVINCIAL PARK

Seebe

IX

Gap Lake & Grotto Mtn.

Lush Creek

68

Barrier Lake

Lac des Arcs

Dead Man's Flat

Goat Pond

Spray Lake Ranger Station

Drift-wood

KANANASKIS VALLEY

Colonel's Cabin

40

Stony Creek

Spray Lakes West

Sparrow-hawk

Kananaskis Village

Sundance Lodges

Beaver Pond

Boundary Ranch

BANFF NATIONAL PARK

Spray Lake

Spray Lake

RCMP & Emergency Services

Mount Kidd

Canyon Dam

Buller Mountain

Wedge Pond

Mount Shark

Fortress Ski Area

PETER LOUGHEED PROVINCIAL PARK

Fortress Junction

N

HUNTER PUBLISHING

NOT TO SCALE

782

Burstall Lakes Area

Grizzly Creek

Sawmill

King Creek

North
Hwy 40 closed beyond this point in winter

Kananaskis Canyon & Rockwall Area

40

Elbow Lake Area

Some facilities are open seasonally visit Park Information Centers for availability and amenities.

Lower Lake & Boulton Creek Area

Upper Kananaskis & North Interlakes

The lack of congestion compared to the national parks, combined with numerous campgrounds, myriad activities, including hiking and backpacking, biking, boating, whitewater rafting, kayaking, fishing, horseback riding, Nordic and alpine skiing, snowboarding, snowshoeing and interpretive programs, makes for an incredible all-season destination.

■ History

Native peoples used the Bow Valley as a travel route between the Rocky Mountains and the Prairies for 11,000 years. Captain John Palliser led a British scientific expedition through the area in the mid-1800s and he named a river and two mountain passes after a Native named "Kin-e-ah-kis."

In 1883, the settlement of Canmore was recognized as an important divisional point for the Canadian Pacific Railroad. Later, the discovery of an abundance of coal provided employment until 1979, when the last mine closed. Canmore did not go the way of Bankhead in Banff or other deserted mining communities. Since mining has ceased, tourism has become the town's principal industry.

Canmore and Kananaskis Country gained world recognition in 1988 as co-host with Calgary of the Winter Olympic Games. Both the alpine and Nordic events were held within Kananaskis; Kananaskis Village and The Canmore Nordic Center remain a legacy. This attention, combined with a development boom, has put Canmore and Kananaskis Country on the vacation destination map.

■ Getting There & Getting Around

By Road

Canmore is a 15-minute drive east of Banff and an hour's drive west of Calgary on the Trans Canada Highway 1.

Kananaskis Trail (Highway 40) traverses Kananaskis Country north from the Trans Canada Highway, 30 km (18.6 miles) east of Canmore, to the south for 110 km

Kananaskis Country

(68 miles); the highway is closed from just south of the Kananaskis Lakes Trail Road in Peter Lougheed Provincial Park to Highwood House Junction from December 1st to mid-June. **Kananaskis Lakes Trail** branches from Kananaskis Trail in the center of Peter Lougheed Provincial Park and provides access to Upper and Lower Kananaskis Lakes.

 Don't be confused by streets or highways in Alberta that are referred to as "Trail"; some are major thoroughfares.

It is possible to make a round-trip loop from Canmore (145 km or 90 miles) via Kananaskis Village and the Smith-Dorrien/Spray Trail (Highway 742), which provides access to the Smith-Dorrien Pass region in K-Country's northwest corner. The **Smith-Dorrien/Spray Trail** is a 64-km (38-mile) gravel road with some rough sections; it follows Spray Lake for 20 km (12 miles) and descends to Canmore over Whiteman's Pass.

Distances from Canmore

Banff. . . . . 25 km (15 miles)
Calgary. 108 km (67 miles)
Kananaskis Village . . . . 54 km (33 miles)
Canmore Nordic Centre Prov Park 4 km (2½ miles

Bus Service

 **Greyhound**, ☎ 403-678-4465 or 800-661-8747 for fare and schedule information, 801 8th Street, www.greyhound.ca. Frequent bus service from/to Calgary and Banff.

Rocky Mountain Sky Shuttle, ☎ 888-762-8754, www.rockymountainskyshuttle.com. Transportation between the Calgary International Airport and Banff, Lake Louise and Canmore in summer (May to November) and Banff, Lake Louise, Canmore, Sunshine Village, Panorama and Fernie in winter (December to April). Door-to-door service; reservations strongly recommended.

Brewster Transport, ☎ 403-762-6767. Brewster Airporter daily bus service year-round.

Canmore Airport Express, ☎ 403-609-1395.

The Mountain Connector, ☎ 888-786-3641, www.mountainconnector.com. Transportation between Canmore, Banff, Lake Louise, and Jasper in winter from December to April. Transfers to and from Calgary are also available.

Car Rentals

Budget, ☎ 403-609-3360, 1 Silvertip Trail.

Hertz, ☎ 403-678-1630, Radisson Hotel, 511 Bow Valley Trail.

Car rentals are also available at the Calgary International Airport.

Taxis

VIP Taxi, ☎ 403-678-8897.

By Air

Calgary International Airport, ☎ 403-735-1200.

By Rail

There is no passenger train service in Canmore.

■ Special Events

Many events and festivals take place in the Canmore area throughout the year – art exhibits, children's activities, concerts, sporting activities, races, and more. Check with **Tourism Canmore** (☎ 403-678-1295, www.tourismcanmore.com) for an up-to-date list of each year's special events.

February

Canmore Winterfest has indoor and outdoor events galore. Festival highlights include the Rocky Mountain Ski Marathon, a two-day event on the trails of the Canmore Nordic

Kananaskis Country

Center, concerts, sled dog races, art exhibitions, hockey games, curling, skating, dances, food, music and more.

The **Kananaskis Ski Marathon** is held at Peter Lougheed Provincial Park. A cross-country ski race has 400+ competitors.

March

The **Arc'teryx Canmore International Ice Climbing Festival**. Experience ice climbing on the 60-foot man-made ice wall in the middle of town or watch competitors test their skill. Clinics, gear exhibitions and social evening. www.canmoreiceclimbingfestival.com.

May

The **Canmore Children's Festival** is great fun for all ages, with a community picnic, games, crafts, storytelling, magic, puppets, theatre, juggling and more.

June

Canmore Quilt Festival and Sale features the work of local quilters.

Annual ArtSPeak showcases local and visiting visual, literary and performing artists; street performers, concerts, art walks and art talks, artisan's fair, film screenings and more. www.mountainartsfoundation.com.

Race the Rockies 18 Hour Challenge – Three person teams and solo competitors paddle, orienteer, mountain bike and trek a 100-km (62-mile) course through the Rocky mountains. www.racetherockies.com.

July

Canada Day holds July 1st festivities that include a parade and fireworks; pancake breakfast at Centennial Park, music, kids' games, and family fun at the Canmore Nordic Center.

Canmore Miner's Day commemorates the history of Canmore's coal mines. Special events throughout the day.

Parks Day celebrations in Kananaskis' Provincial Parks include demonstrations and displays, refreshments and more.

24 Hours of Adrenalin Mountain Bike Race is an annual round-the-clock mountain bike race. www.24hoursof-adrenalin.com.

August

Canmore Folk Music Festival is a Canmore tradition and Alberta's longest-running folk music festival, held each Heritage Day Long Weekend (first weekend in August). Entertainers from around the world perform throughout the weekend. Pancake breakfast, children's entertainers and activities, workshops, food booths, arts and crafts, extensive family area. www.canmorefolkfestival.com.

Canmore Challenge Trail – annual race with international participants in six- or 12-km trail races; kids have a one-km trail romp. www.mountainrunning.com.

September

Canmore Highland Games, Labour Day weekend each year. Get into the Celtic spirit with hundreds of participants; Highland dance, bagpiping, drumming and sporting competitions. Pancake breakfast, beer garden, demonstrations, ethnic music and food, entertainment and Celtic merchandise.

CAUSE Canadian Rocky Mountain Half Marathon held annually at the Canmore Nordic Center. Join more than 1,000 racers for the eight-km or half-marathon on one of the most scenic courses in Canada. Benefit for relief and development work in under-assisted countries. www.cause.ca.

October

Festival of the Eagles is a celebration of the annual Golden Eagle migration through the Canadian Rockies. Interpreters and telescopes available, along with a guided hike and guest speaker presentation.

Light Up Canmore Christmas Celebration – Celebrate the beginning of the Christmas season at this downtown light-up ceremony. Choirs, horse-drawn wagon rides, refreshments and shopping promotions.

December

Canmore's New Year's Eve Celebration – Ring in the new year downtown with a bonfire, skating, music, food, entertainment and fireworks.

Kananaskis Country

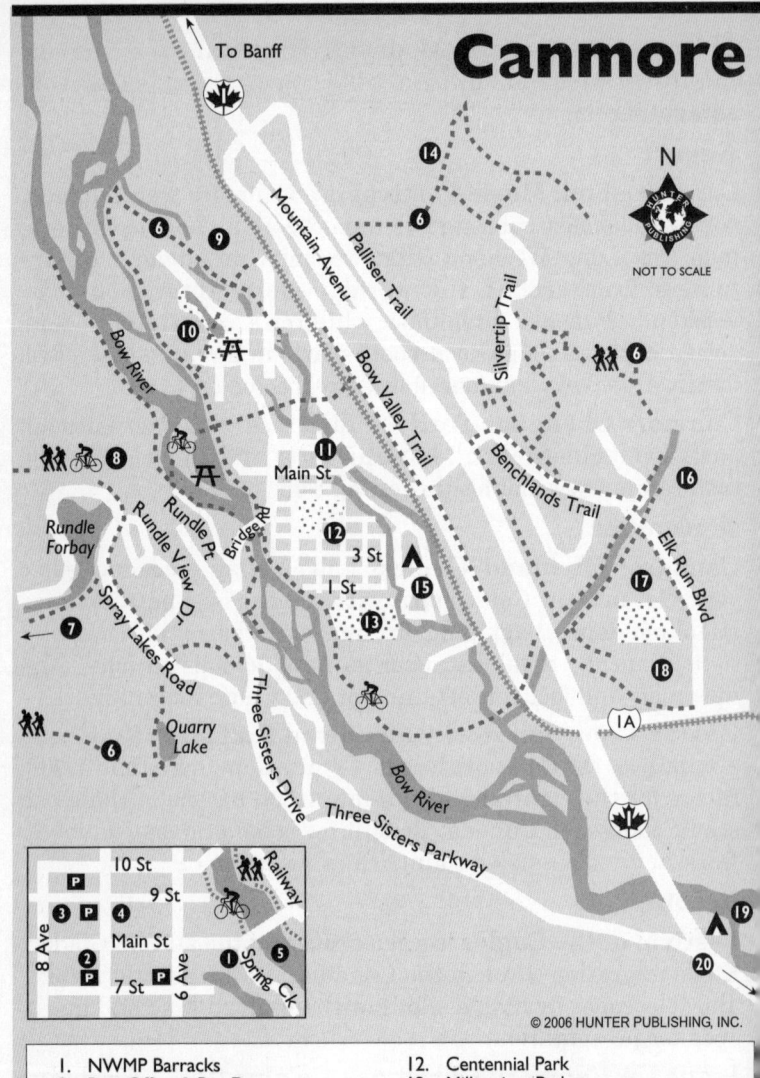

Canmore

N

NOT TO SCALE

To Banff

Mountain Avenu

Palliser Trail

Bow Valley Trail

Silvertip Trail

Benchlands Trail

Bow River

Rundle Forbay

Rundle Pt

Bridge Rd

Rundle View Dr

Spray Lakes Road

Main St

3 St

1 St

Elk Run Blvd

Quarry Lake

Three Sisters Drive

Bow River

Three Sisters Parkway

1A

10 St

9 St

Main St

7 St

8 Ave

6 Ave

Railway

Spring Ck

© 2006 HUNTER PUBLISHING, INC.

1. NWMP Barracks
2. Post Office & Bus Depot
3. Library & Art Center
4. Centennial Museum
5. Policeman's Creek
6. Hiking & Biking Trails
7. To Kananaskis Country (Smith-Dorrien Highway)
8. Canmore Nordic Centre
9. Canmore Golf & Curling Club
10. Lions Park
11. Town Center (see detail inset)
12. Centennial Park
13. Millennium Park
14. Golf Course at Silver-Tip
15. Restway Trailer Park, Cabins & Campgrounds
15. Cougar Creek
17. Elk Run Park
18. RCMP Headquarters
19. Bow River Campground
20. To Dead Man's Flats, Lac des Arcs, Seebe, Calgary

■ Canmore Townsite

The major artery in town is the **Bow Valley Trail**, which runs east-west, parallel to and between the Trans Canada Highway and the railway tracks. Many accommodations, restaurants and other tourist services are located along here. The easiest way to reach the town center (south of Bow Valley Trail) is from Railway Avenue off Bow Valley Trail, which leads to 8th Street, also called Main Street.

 Pick up a **free town map** at the Visitor Information Center for details on the **Canmore Historic Walking Tour** as well as the extensive nature trail system that is open to walkers and cyclists. **Tourism Canmore Information Center** (and offices) ☎ 403-678-1295, 907 7th Avenue, www.tourismcanmore.com. Operating Hours: Victoria Day (May) to Labour Day (September), 9 am to 8 pm; Labour Day to October, 9 am to 6 pm; November to Victoria Day, 9 am to 5 pm.

■ Attractions

 **Canmore Centennial Museum and Geoscience Center**, ☎ 403-678-2462, Civic Center downtown. Canmore and three other Alberta communities designated 2003/2004 as "Year of the Coal Miner," celebrating 100 years of coal mining heritage. Learn about Canmore's coal mining past with mining, railway and geology displays. Open Monday to Friday, 9 am to 5 pm and weekends 12 pm to 4 pm. Admission is by donation.

■ Shopping

 You won't find any malls or big box stores in Canmore – that's partly why shopping there is so enjoyable. With a growing population and vibrant tourist trade, downtown Canmore shops offer an eclectic selection of merchandise as well

Kananaskis Country

as personalized service. Sports stores carry the latest gear and equipment, specialty shops sell items such as hand-crafted soap and bath products; gift emporiums, clothing boutiques and galleries are all competitively priced.

Two worthwhile shopping stops:

The Settler's Cabin Gift Shop, 829 8th Street. Located in a heritage building, this shop sells quality gift items, antiques, ladies' sweaters and clothing, quilts and limited edition prints by Canadian folk artist Linda Evans.

The Second Story, 713 Main Street, www.canrockbooks.com. I found an excellent selection of used and half-price new books on the Rocky Mountains at this bookstore. Be sure to allow plenty of time to browse. Topographic maps are also available.

■ Where to Eat

If it's variety you're looking for, Canmore is reputed to have more restaurants per capita than anywhere else in North America!

And if you've spent the day working up an appetite in Kananaskis Country, the two resort hotels in the Village offer plenty of choice without having to venture far.

Canmore has several grocery stores, including **Safeway** (with a pharmacy and liquor store), on Railway Avenue and 9th Street, **Sobey's**, on Railway Avenue at the entrance to downtown, and **Marra's Grocery**, on Main Street downtown.

For those not into cooking, some favorite restaurants in Canmore include:

French Quarter Café, ☎ 403-678-3612, 102 Boulder Crescent, $$. Oddly, some of the best restaurants are located in industrial parks. It's worth going out of your way to dine at the French Quarter Café, located in the Elk Run Industrial Park on the eastern outskirts of Canmore. Enjoy New Orleans-style Cajun and Creole specialties using the freshest ingredi-

DINING PRICE CHART	
Price per person in Canadian $ for an entrée, not including beverage, tax or tip.	
$	Under $10
$$	$10-$25
$$$	Over $25

ents and seasonings in a friendly, intimate atmosphere. Start your day with the Eggs Canal, poached eggs on beef tenderloin with wild mushroom sauce, served with Cajun potatoes. Try the catfish and chips or a crawfish omelette for lunch. Dinner entrées include crawfish, catfish, shrimp Creole, jambalaya, lamb, steak, chicken and pasta. Chef Michael Raso entertains from the open kitchen. Live jazz nights and cooking classes. Open Monday through Saturday for breakfast, lunch and dinner, closed Sundays and holidays. Reservations recommended.

Murrieta's Westcoast Grill, ☎ 403-609-9500, 737 Main Street, $$ to $$$. Casual dining in a comfortable yet elegant atmosphere with fabulous views from the second-floor location downtown. Succulent dishes include pasta, steak, lamb, pheasant, paella, bouillabaisse and seafood at its best. Enjoy the lounge, which offers over 25 wines by the glass, 30 single malts and classic martinis accompanied by live jazz on Friday and Saturday evenings. Reservations recommended.

The Grizzly Paw Brewing Company, ☎ 403-678-9983, 622 Main Street, $ to $$. How about a pint of "Grump Bear Honey Wheat" or "Rutting Elk Red"? The Grizzly Paw pub and restaurant offers six selections of beer – brewed on-site in small batches without additives or preservatives. All of the beers are available for sale in individual six-packs. The restaurant is famous for its halibut fish and chips and Brewers Pasta – marinated Cajun chicken with sun-dried tomatoes, spinach and parmesan, tossed in a creamy tomato sauce and served over fettuccini. They also have the best "grizzly wings" (chicken wings) – seven flavors – in town. The extensive menu, with appetizers, soups, salads, sandwiches, pasta, pizza, seafood, vegetarian choices, chicken and more, changes every spring and fall. Open for lunch and dinner and until 2 am when busy; children welcome until 10 pm.

Bolo Ranchhouse, ☎ 403-678-5211, Main Street & 8th Avenue, $ to $$. This casual restaurant and pub, centrally located downtown in a log house, is a popular local gathering place. It's especially appealing on a sunny day when you can enjoy the fabulous mountain views on the huge sundeck. Pub-style food includes burgers, steaks, pizza and sandwiches; tasty for breakfast, lunch or dinner.

Rocky Mountain Bagel Co., ☎ 403-678-9978, 830 8th Street (at Main), $. A casual downtown café offering fresh bagel sandwiches, desserts, specialty coffees and teas. Enjoy the comfortable indoor seating or sit outside and people watch. Fast, cheap and good.

A few other locals' favorites:

Zona's Late Night Bistro, ☎ 403-609-2000, 710 9th Street, $$. Featuring tapas, curry dishes and original creations in a hip and fun atmosphere.

Patrinos Steak House and Pub, ☎ 403-678-4060, 1602 Bow Valley Trail, $$. Family restaurant with great lunches, excellent prime rib and Sunday brunch in a casual atmosphere with beautiful views and good prices.

Rose & Crown Restaurant and Pub, ☎ 403-678-5168, 749 Railway Avenue, $$. Tasty pub fare – excellent fish and chips, cheap drinks and a huge outdoor patio.

 Pick up a free copy of *Taxi Mike's Dining Guide* for more tips on where to eat and drink in Canmore.

■ Where to Stay

 Canmore offers a wide range of accommodations in the townsite. If you prefer to stay at Kananaskis Village, hotel accommodations are available at two luxury resorts and guest ranches. In Canmore, the following have rooms with mountain views.

Downtown

The Georgetown Inn, ☎ 800-657-5955 or 403-678-3439, 1101 Bow Valley Trail, www.georgetowninn.ab.ca, $$$ to $$$$. The Georgetown Inn is a family-operated 20-room inn that oozes unique charm and a friendly atmosphere. Very tastefully decorated with antiques throughout and beautifully appointed guest rooms, each with its own character. Each room features modern conveniences such as television, clock radio, hair dryer, coffee maker and kettle, plus down duvets. Extras in some rooms such as jetted tubs in the bedroom, robes, fireplaces, kitchenettes, comfortable armchairs, sitting areas and vaulted ceilings. Discounts for longer stays; breakfast included; outside garden sitting area.

Westridge Country Inn, ☎ 800-268-0935 or 403-678-5221, 1719 Bow Valley Trail, www.westridge-countryinn.com, $$$$. Rooms have fireplaces and balconies; superior rooms have Jacuzzis. Spacious log cabins also available. European-style breakfast in the rustic fireside room included. Sauna and ski room. Seniors discount; family-operated.

HOTEL PRICE CHART	
Reflects the price of an average room for two in Canadian $, May-Sept. Rates lower rest of year (except Christmas and New Year's).	
$	Under $50
$$	$50-$100
$$$	$101-$150
$$$$	$151-$250
$$$$$	Over $250

The Drake Inn, ☎ 800-461-8730 or 403-678-5131, 808 Railway Avenue, www.drakeinn.com, $$ to $$$. Spacious rooms at reasonable rates. Creekside rooms or suites available. Pets allowed, $10/night. The Drake pub and restaurant is a local favorite for live entertainment, pub fare, lunch specials and one of the best patios in town.

Bow Valley Motel, ☎ 800-665-8189 or 403-678-5085, 610 8th Street, www.bowvalleymotel.com, $$$. Basic affordable accommodations in the center of town. In-room coffee and tea, refrigerators, cable TV and telephone, some units with kitchens. Outdoor hot tub, coin-operated laundry.

Bed & Breakfast

The Canmore-Bow Valley Bed and Breakfast Association produces a *Bed & Breakfast Accommodation Guide* that lists over 40 licensed B&Bs in Canmore and area. The brochure is available from the Visitor Information Center or from the association – PO Box 8005, Canmore, Alberta, T1W 2T8.

The following are all within walking distance of downtown:

A Room With A View, ☎ 866-678-6624 or 403-678-6624, 711 Larch Place, www.aroomwithaview.ab.ca, $$ to $$$$. Mountain chalet with large windows, fireplace, bar, hot tub, and sauna. Self-contained family suite and honeymoon suite. Access to library and TV/VCR. Gourmet breakfast.

Canadian Artisans, ☎ 403-678-4138, 1016 9th Avenue, www.canadianartisans.ca, $$$. Located on a quiet forested trail, two-minute walk to downtown or river. Unique handcrafted honeymoon suite with full-length windows, fireplace and double steam shower.

Riverview & Main, ☎ 403-678-9777, 918 8th (Main) Street, www.riverviewandmain.com, $$ to $$$. Three bright sunny rooms to choose from, private great room with fireplace, TV and breakfast nook. Complimentary beverages and full breakfast.

Quilter's Inn, ☎ 403-678-6785, 702 2nd Street, www.quiltersinn.com, $$. These affordable, clean and quiet accommodations are inspirational and unique – a quilter's dream.

Guest Ranches & Lodges

Executive Resort, ☎ 888-591-7501 or 403-591-7500, www.executivehotels.net/kananaskis, $$$$. At Kananaskis Village (Evan-Thomas Provincial Recreation Area) this resort offers spacious, attractively decorated suites, executive suites, loft suites with fireplaces or deluxe rooms. Amenities include a restaurant and pub; golf packages available.

Delta Lodge, ☎ 866-432-4322 or 403-591-7711, www.delta-lodgeatkananaskis.ca, $$$$ to $$$$$. At Kananaskis Village, this large full-service resort offers superior accommodations with premier rooms, deluxe family rooms and loft rooms. The "Signature Club" is an extension of the lodge that provides upgraded amenities in an adult-oriented environment. Many packages available, including bed & breakfast, ski, golf, romance, girl power, stress escape, discovery, heritage, Christmas and family long weekends. They have a spa, game room and five dining venues.

Brewster's Kananaskis Guest Ranch, ☎ 800-691-5085 or 403-673-3737, www.brewsteradventures.com, $$$$. Located on the Bow River 30 minutes east of Banff – follow the Trans Canada Highway then north on Highway 1X. Open June through September. This is the site of the original 1923 Brewster family homestead, now a ranch house with dining room and cocktail lounge. Western barbecues, horseback riding and overnight pack trips, rafting on the Bow and Kananaskis Rivers, golf, hiking, Voyageur canoe trips and guest ranch activities. Choose from one- or two-bedroom cabins or one-bedroom chalets with antique furnishings and natural cedar interiors. Breakfast and dinner included in room rates.

Mt. Engadine Lodge, ☎ 403-678-4080, www.mountengadine.com, $$$$$. A quiet retreat at the base of Mount Engadine on the Mt. Shark access road from the Smith-Dorrien/Spray Road in Spray Valley Provincial Park. The main lodge has single or double rooms and one room for four with shared bathrooms. Lodge suites with private bathrooms, lounge area, gas fireplace and balcony. Three private cabins for two or four people. All rooms are tastefully decorated and include down comforters; no telephones or television. Designed for enjoying the wilderness, the lodge provides beautiful views – moose, heron, beaver, deer and elk are often seen in the meadows. There is a hot tub and sauna. They offer ski trails for all levels and abilities, snowshoeing, hiking, mountain biking, canoeing, kayaking and fishing. Rates include a set menu of two-course buffet breakfast, lunch, afternoon tea and a gourmet dinner served in the dining room of the main lodge. Two-night minimum booking.

Rafter Six Ranch Resort, ☎ 888-267-2624 or 403-673-3622, www.raftersix.com, $$$$ to $$$$$. Located in Bow Valley Provincial Park, 20 minutes east of Canmore off the Trans Canada Highway, four km (2½ miles) west of Highway 40, then south on Ranch Road from Highway 1X. Open May through December with 18 guest rooms in the large log lodge, cabins and chalets as well as wilderness camping for self-contained units. Bed and Breakfast, "Runaway Package" (includes breakfast and dinner) and "Ranch Package" (includes three meals and two hours horseback riding daily) are available. Amenities include an outdoor heated pool and indoor hot tub, picnic areas, restaurant, saloon, dance hall and museum. Pets not permitted.

Horseback riding is available year-round, with one-hour trail rides $34 per person, two-hour trail rides $59 per person, as well as half- , full-day and overnight rides, for all levels of riders. "Adventure Ride" for experienced riders, is 1½ hours, $59 per person. Sunset supper rides and pony rides also available.

This historic ranch on the Kananaskis River, where the Kananaskis Valley and the Bow Valley meet, has been the location for a number of movies since the 1940's, when Walt Disney visited, including *River of No Return*, starring Marilyn Monroe.

Camping

 There are three campgrounds in Canmore, all within walking distance of downtown. If you prefer not to stay in town, a short drive leads to Kananaskis Country, with many roadside wilderness campgrounds that are more secluded and offer a more authentic camping experience.

Campgrounds in Canmore

Canmore Wapiti Tents Campground, ☎ 403-609-0771, Ray McBride Street (next to Visitor Information Center), $ to $$. Over 60 tent sites, open May 21 to September 6. Kitchen shelter and showers; weekly rates. This small tenting-only campground is inexpensive, but it's beside the noisy Trans Canada Highway.

Rundle Mountain Campground, ☎ 403-678-2131, Bow Valley Trail, $$$. A small family operated campground with sites close together, open year-round. Weekly and monthly rates available. Full hook-ups, fire pits and firewood, showers, coin laundry; pets welcome.

Restwell Trailer Park, ☎ 403-678-5111, 3rd Avenue, www.restwelltrailerpark.com, $$$ to $$$$. A large pricey campground, open year-round with weekly rates available. Full hook-ups, sani-dump, fire pits and firewood, showers, coin laundry; wheelchair-accessible. Tents not permitted. Fully equipped modern cabins also available.

Campgrounds in Bow Valley Provincial Park

Roadside wilderness campgrounds in Bow Valley Provincial Park are seasonal; operating dates are approximate. Most campgrounds are first-come, first-served; some are self-register while others have on-site managers; $$ to $$$ with hook-ups.

 For more information or to make reservations (where accepted and beginning April 1 each year) call ☎ 403-673-2163, www.bowvalley-campgrounds.com.

Bow River. Located only two km (1.2 miles) east of Canmore along the Trans Canada Highway. Open May to September; 32 sites located along the Bow River. Pit toilets, picnic shelter. Nearby activities include fishing in the Bow River and hiking.

Lac Des Arcs. Take the Lac Des Arcs exit along the Trans Canada Highway, 19 km (12 miles) east of Canmore. Open May to September; 28 secluded sites. Pit toilets, picnic shelter. Nearby activities include canoeing, lake fishing and hiking.

Three Sisters. Access is from Dead Man's Flats exit along the Trans Canada Highway, 10 km (six miles) east of Canmore. Open mid-April to October; 36 sites. Pit toilets, picnic shelter. Nearby activities include fishing and hiking.

Willow Rock. 28 km (17 miles) east of Canmore along the Trans Canada Highway. Open April to October; 124 sites. Power, coin showers, coin laundry, flush toilets, fire pits and firewood, picnic shelter, sani-dump. Nearby activities include hiking and biking and guided horseback trail rides.

Bow Valley. 27 km (16.8 miles) east of Canmore on the Trans Canada Highway. Open May to mid-October; 169 sites. Store, power and water, coin showers, flush toilets, sani-dump, interpretive programs, playground, fire pits and firewood, horse-

CAMPING/HOSTELS	
Rates in Canadian $, not including taxes.	
$	Under $13
$$	$13-$22
$$$	$23-$30
$$$$	Over $30

Kananaskis Country

shoes; reservations accepted. Nearby activities include river fishing, hiking, biking and guided horseback trail rides.

Campgrounds in Evan-Thomas Provincial Recreation Area (Kananaskis Valley)

These two campgrounds are privately owned and operated; call or e-mail for reservations.

Sundance Lodges Tipis & RV Park, ☎ 403-591-7122, www.sundancelodges.com, $$. 22 km (13.7 miles) south of the Trans Canada Highway along Highway 40. Open end of May to September; 30 sites. Showers, flush toilets, coin laundry, equipment rentals, volleyball and badminton courts, fire pits and firewood, snack bar and gift shop, Internet access; pets permitted.

This campground offers a unique family camping experience that I highly recommend. In addition to camping, guests can stay in authentic tipis or trappers' tents in secluded campsites, both reasonably priced. (Bring your own bedding or you can rent bedding and camping equipment.)

Nearby activities include hiking, mountain biking, fishing and guided horseback trail rides.

Mount Kidd RV Park, ☎ 403-591-7700, www.mount-kiddrv.com, $$$ to $$$$. 28 km (17.4 miles) south of the Trans Canada Highway along Highway 40. Open year-round; 229 sites. Showers, flush toilets, coin laundry, full hook-ups including cable, indoor whirlpool, sauna, wading pool, tennis and volleyball court, horseshoe pits, playground, fire pits and firewood, snack bar and gift shop.

Nearby activities include hiking, mountain biking, golfing and guided horseback trail rides.

MOUNT KIDD

One of the most stunning mountains in the Kananaskis Valley, 2,958-m (9,705-foot) Mount Kidd is a Main Range mountain that dominates the landscape if you're traveling south beyond Kananaskis Village on Highway 40.

Campgrounds in Peter Lougheed & Spray Valley Parks

 The roadside wilderness campgrounds in Peter Lougheed Provincial Park are near the Kananaskis Lakes and are accessed via the Kananaskis Lakes Trail.

These campgrounds are seasonal and operating dates are approximate. Most campgrounds are first-come, first-served and have on-site managers; $$.

For more information or to make reservations (where accepted) call ☎ 403-591-7226, www.kananaskiscountry-campgrounds.com.

Canyon. Open mid-June to early September; 52 treed and alpine meadow sites. Pit toilets, sani-dump, fire pits and firewood, playground, interpretive trail, boat launch. Nearby activities include biking and hiking trails, boating and fishing.

Elkwood. Open mid-May to early September; 130 spacious well-treed sites. Coin showers, flush toilets, fire pits and firewood, playground, interpretive trails, amphitheater presentations. Nearby activities include biking and hiking trails.

Boulton Creek. Open May to mid-October; 118 sites. Coin showers, flush toilets, sani-sump, fire pits and firewood, interpretive trails, amphitheater presentations, store and restaurant; reservations accepted. Nearby activities include biking and hiking trails and fishing.

Lower Lake. Open mid-May to mid-October; 104 spacious well treed sites. Pit toilets, fire pits and firewood, playground, hand boat launch. Nearby activities include biking and hiking trails and boating and fishing.

Mt. Sarrail. Open end of June to early September; 44 walk-in tent sites in heavily treed and alpine meadow settings. Pit toilets, fire pits and firewood, bear bins. Nearby activities include biking and hiking trails and fishing. Located between the Upper and Lower Kananaskis Lakes, a short walk from most trailheads and fishing holes.

Interlakes. Open mid-May to mid-October; 48 spacious well-treed and lakeside sites. Pit toilets, fire pits and fire-

Kananaskis Country

wood, hand boat launch. Nearby activities include biking and hiking trails and boating and fishing.

Campgrounds in Spray Valley Provincial Park

Eau Claire. North of Peter Lougheed Provincial Park off Highway 40. Open end of May to mid-September; 51 spacious sites, some along the Kananaskis River. Pit toilets, fire pits and firewood, playground, interpretive trail. Nearby activities include biking and hiking trails and fishing.

Spray Lake West. Located 20 minutes south of Canmore on gravel Smith-Dorrien Highway (Highway 742). Open mid-May to snow; 50 primitive sites on the west side of Spray Lakes with spectacular views. Pit toilets, fire pits and firewood, hand boat launch. Nearby activities include biking and hiking trails and boating and fishing (abundant lake trout and cutthroat).

Backcountry Camping

Backcountry camping permits are required at all designated backcountry campgrounds in Kananaskis Country. Permits cost $3.21 per person per night, plus a non-refundable charge of $6.42 per party per trip. Persons under 16 years of age are not required to pay the fee but require a permit. Permits may be purchased in person at the Barrier Lake or Peter Lougheed Provincial Park Visitor Information Centers. It's advisable to phone ahead and be sure you can obtain a campsite. To purchase a permit by phone, call ☎ 403-678-3136 or in Alberta toll free by first dialing ☎ 310-0000.

There are two backcountry campgrounds with a total of 29 sites in Bow Valley Park, three campgrounds with a total of 48 sites in Spray Valley Provincial Park (access from Highway 40 side), and six campgrounds with a total of 83 sites in Peter Lougheed Provincial Park. There are also backcountry campgrounds located in Sibbald, Elbow River Valley and Sheep River Valley. Closure dates apply at some campgrounds. Random camping without a permit is NOT allowed in Provincial Parks or Provincial Recreation Areas.

Hosteling

Canmore. On Indian Flats Road off Highway 1A east of Canmore; 46 beds; members $$, non-members $$$; check-in

24 hours. Made up of two buildings, each with a fully equipped kitchen, living room, fireplace, deck and barbecue, sauna in main building; one family room available. Great view, quiet atmosphere and friendly staff. Operated by the Alpine Club of Canada. Reservations ☎ 403-678-3200, ext. 1, or info@alpineclubofcanada.ca.

Kananaskis Wilderness Hostel (Ribbon Creek). 25 km (15½ miles) south on Highway 40 near Kananaskis Village; 47 beds; members $$, non-members $$$. Family rooms; check-in 5-11 pm; some closure dates apply. Close to over 60 mountain biking, hiking and cross-country ski trails. Linen provided, no sleeping bags permitted. Reservations ☎ 866-762-4122 or 403-670-7580, centralres.sa@hihostels.ca.

■ Wildlife

Elk can often be seen in Canmore townsite; other large animals that call Kananaskis home include white tail deer, mule deer, moose, big horn sheep, mountain goats, black bears, grizzly bears, cougars, lynx, bobcats, wolverines, coyote, and wolves.

COYOTE MARKS ITS SPOT

We sat in our vehicle at the Highwood Meadows parking area, waiting and hoping for the low clouds to clear enough to hike Ptarmigan Cirque. As we stared out the window, sipping our hot chocolate and contemplating the weather, a coyote appeared in the meadow directly in front of us. Unconcerned with our presence, it kicked at a spot on the ground with its hind legs, barking and yelping. Although their sight and hearing are acute, canids (wolves, foxes and coyotes) rely heavily on their sense of smell for hunting prey and "reading" scented areas marked with the urine of other animals. We watched and photographed for about five minutes before it continued on its way.

■ Adventures

 If you are planning to do any hiking, backpacking, biking or skiing on Kananaskis Country trails, be sure to stop by or call one of the Visitor Information Centers for the latest trail information and safety reports. The **Canmore Visitor Information Center** provides free printed information on easy walks and hikes, day-hikes and scrambles and challenging hikes in Canmore and Kananaskis.

 Very useful trail brochures can be purchased for a minimal cost ($1.25 each) at the Visitor Information Centers. *Summer Trails* and *X-Country Trails* brochures for the various parks in Kananaskis Country detail day-hikes, trails for mountain bikers, hikers and cross-country skiers, backcountry campgrounds and facilities, and provide valuable information as well as a map.

Sports & Camping Equipment Rentals

Gear Up Mountain Sport and Rentals, ☎ 403-678-1636, 1302 Bow Valley Trail (across from hospital), www.gearupsport.com. Mountain bikes $20-$40 per day with hourly rates available. Kayaks $40 per day, canoes $50 per day. Mountaineering and climbing equipment, camping gear, skis and snowboards, skates and snowshoes.

Couloir Ski and Bike, ☎ 403-678-0088, 712 Bow Valley Trail. Performance skis, demo skis, ski and snowboard service.

Trail Sports, ☎ 403-678-6764, at the Canmore Nordic Center. Everything you need for cross-country skiing and mountain biking, including rentals and instruction.

Guided Tours

Back of Beyond Adventure Co, ☎ 800-732-7251 or 403-678-6606, www.backofbeyond.ca. Professionally guided hiking, backpacking, snowshoeing and backcountry skiing throughout the Canadian Rockies. Award winning family adventures; lodge based treks, mountain hut treks, unique birding tours, and custom trips for all ages and abilities.

Picture Perfect Adventures, ☎ 403-678-1703, www.pictureperfectadventures.com. Half-day guided hiking adventures on wilderness mountain trails for all ages and abilities from May to October. Morning and afternoon departures, packed lunch included.

- ◆ **Cougar Canyon** – Spectacular scenery as you venture up the canyon, $55.

- ◆ **Grotto Canyon** – This canyon is known for its petroglyphs and spectacular views, $55.

- ◆ **Chinaman's Peak** – Breathtaking views from the top, $60.

- ◆ **Grassi Lakes Romance Package** – Incredible views at sunset, waterfalls and two tranquil lakes, $85, includes champagne.

- ◆ **Canmore Walking Tours** – Two hours around Canmore, $15.

White Mountain Adventures, ☎ 800-408-0005 or 403-678-4099, 107 Boulder Crescent, www.whitemountain-adventures.com. An outdoor guiding company offering daily summer hikes and walks; wildlife and nature sightseeing tours; multi-day hiking and backpacking trips; snowshoeing, icewalks and cross-country skiing trips from mid-December to mid-April.

- ◆ **Premier Guide Service** – Guides fluent in English, French, German and Japanese. Half-day hikes/walks, nature tours $270, full-day $390 (transportation available at additional cost).

- ◆ **Grotto Canyon Icewalk** – Walk along the bottom of an ice-covered canyon floor and see two dramatic frozen waterfalls. Suitable for children over eight. Transportation, guide, ice cleats, hiking poles and trail snacks included. One to six people, $270.

Canmore Caverns, ☎ 877-317-1178 or 403-678-8819, 1009 Larch Place, www.canadianrockies.net/wildcavetours.

◆ A 10-minute drive from Canmore, **Rat's Nest Cave** in Grotto Mountain is a wild undeveloped cave. Exploring the cave is only permitted by booking a tour with Canmore Caverns. Tours begin with a 30-minute hike to the cave entrance with expert guides that take you on a natural history tour through twisting passages and chambers of stalactites and stalagmites, animal bones and fossils. All caving equipment supplied; caving is physically challenging but no experience is necessary. Minimum age nine years. Tours operate year-round with the cave temperature a constant 5°C (41°F).

◆ **Adventure Tour** – Six hours. Climb and traverse large and narrow passages, rappel an 18-m (60-foot) drop, $115.

◆ **Explorer Tour** – Four hours. Similar to above but with no rappel, $89.

Yamnuska Climbing & Hiking Adventures, ☎ 866-678-4164 or 403-678-4164, 50 Lincoln Park, www.yamnuska.com. Mountain school and guide service offers year-round rock climbing, mountaineering, hiking, backpacking, ice climbing and ski touring programs for all ages and experience levels. Half-day, full-day and multi-day trips from $70 per person.

Snowy Owl Sled Dog Tours, ☎ 888-311-6874 or 403-678-4369, 602 Bow Valley Trail (across from the Radisson Hotel), www.snowyowltours.com. Experience spectacular winter wilderness scenery from one of the most unusual modes of winter transport, along with hands-on interaction with over 150 friendly huskies. Two-hour, four-hour, full-day, moonlight and overnight winter dog-sledding trips from November to April. Transportation from hotels in Canmore (and Banff/Lake Louise) is available.

◆ **Powder Hound Express** – Two hours. Adult $110, child eight and under $75.

◆ **Legend of the Snow Moon** – Two-hour evening program. Adult $160.

Inside Out Experience, ☎ 877-999-7238 or 403-949-3305, www.insideoutexperience.com. Whitewater rafting, mountain biking, hiking, horseback riding and ski tours. Half-day, full-day, multi-day and combination tours available.

♦ **The Whitewater Rafting Experience** – Half-day thrilling introduction to whitewater rafting on the Kananaskis or Elbow Rivers, suitable for families. $59 per person.

♦ **Riding and Rafting Experience** – Half-day mountain bike ride and half-day rafting, includes lunch. $126 per person.

♦ **Saddle & Paddle Experience** – Half-day horseback ride and half-day rafting, includes lunch. $136 per person.

Horseback Riding

 **Boundary Ranch**, ☎ 877-591-7177 or 403-591-7171, www.boundaryranch.com. Five minutes south of Kananaskis Village on Highway 40. Restaurant and lounge open seasonally for lunch and dinner. Hourly, half-day and full-day trail rides in the backcountry surrounding the ranch with an opportunity to spot deer, moose and elk. Pack trips from overnight to six days also available.

♦ **Ridge Ride** – Two hours. A good introduction to trail riding, $52.50.

♦ **Adventure Ride** – Full-day with a trail lunch provided, $121.50.

♦ **Surf & Saddle** – Seven hours. Wear your jeans and bring your bathing suit for a full-day of adventure. Scenic two-hour Ridge Ride, barbecue steak lunch, then some whitewater rafting on the Kananaskis River. $126.

Cross Zee Ranch, ☎ 403-678-4171, www.canadianrockies.net/crosszeeranch. Located off Palliser Trail (which parallels the Trans Canada Highway) on the northeast boundary of Canmore. Trail rides in the Bow Valley benchlands with small groups as well as pony rides for children five and under.

♦ **Ranger Ridge or Bone Gully** – One hour. $30.84.

♦ **Great Aspens or Fuzzy Forest** – Two hours. $50.47.

Whitewater Rafting

Whitewater rafting in the Canmore area is on the Bow and Kananaskis Rivers from May to September.

Canadian Rockies Rafting Company, ☎ 877-226-7625 or 403-678-6535, www.rafting.ca. Transportation and beverages included; reservations required.

◆ **Family Whitewater on the Kananaskis River** – A half-day run along the front ranges with class 2-3 rapids. A good introduction to whitewater. Departs 8:30 am and 1:30 pm with two hours on the river. Adult $59, student/youth (five to 15 years) $56.

◆ **Whitewater Excitement on the Bow River Horseshoe Canyon** – The Bow River Horseshoe Canyon has spectacular scenery, big waves and class 3-4 whitewater. Excellent opportunities to view large birds. Optional cliff jump. Departs Canmore at 8:30 am and 1:30 pm with two hours on the river. Adult $65, student/youth (10 to 15 years) $59.

Canmore Rafting Center, ☎ 888-312-7238 or 403-678-4919, corner of Lincoln Park & Bow Valley Trail, www.canmoreraftingcenter.com. Transportation and beverages included.

◆ **Bow River** – A mild 1½-hour float trip suitable for everyone. Departures 10 am, 2 and 6 pm, $45.

◆ **Kananaskis River** – Introduction to whitewater rafting with novice class 1-3 rapids for first-timers and families (children five+ years welcome). Three-hour round-trip, departures 10 am and 1:30 pm, $69.

◆ **Horseshoe Canyon** – Whitewater thrills on the lower Bow River with intermediate class 2-4 rapids. Some size restrictions (children 12+ welcome) with moderate fitness and swimming ability required. Three-hour round trip, departures 9:30 am and 12:30 pm. $79.

Rainbow Riders Adventure Tours, ☎ 877-717-7238 or 403-678-7238, 20 minutes east of Canmore at Highway 1 &

1X (Rafter Six Ranch), www.rainbowriders.com. Daily departures at 10 am, 2 and 6 pm. Full-day rafting trips also available.

◆ **Introductory** – Class 1-3 rapids on the Kananaskis River for ages six+, $59.

◆ **Thrilling** – Class 2-4 rapids in Horseshoe Canyon on the Bow River for ages 12+ and 90 lbs+, $69.

◆ **Scenic** – Float trips on the Bow and Kananaskis Rivers suitable for everyone, $39.

Lake Boating & Fishing

 The Upper and Lower Kananaskis Lakes and Spray Lake provide excellent fishing in Kananaskis. Numerous lakes and ponds are stocked annually.

If you are planning to do any unguided fishing, be sure to check the *Alberta Guide to Sportfishing Regulations* and be sure you have a valid provincial fishing license before you go. Licenses and copies of regulations are available at local sports stores.

Wapiti Sports & Outfitters, ☎ 403-678-5550, 1506 Railway Avenue, www.wapitisports.com. Full-service retail fishing store and year-round guided fishing trips. Stop in for free advice and local secrets. Guided trips include float trips on the Upper Bow – home to brown trout, bull trout, brook trout, cutthroat and Rocky Mountain whitefish; year-round Bow River Walk & Wade; lake fishing trips for brown trout, rainbow trout, lake trout, cutthroat trout, brook trout and bull trout; and ice fishing from December to April on the Spray Lakes for one- to three- lb lake trout or a chance of hooking up to a 20-lb fish.

Banff Fishing Unlimited, ☎ 403-762-4936, www.banff-fishing.com. See *Banff* chapter for Bow River tours departing Canmore, pages 191-195.

Mountain Biking

 The popular **Canmore Nordic Center trail system** offers 65 km (40 miles) of family biking or more serious mountain bike trails. Biking lessons and tours as well as bike rentals are available at the Center.

Many of the Canmore and Kananaskis Country hiking trails are open to bikers. Two popular and easy trails include **Watridge Lake Mountain Biking and Hiking Trail**, a 4½-km (three-mile) trail beginning from the Mt. Shark access road off the Smith-Dorrien/Spray Lakes Road, 38½ km (24 miles) south of Canmore. (Note that the short .8 km trail from Watridge Lake to Karst Spring is hiking only.)

Goat Creek Trail is an 18-km (11-mile) downhill trail, from eight km (five miles) southwest of Canmore via Spray Lakes Road. It follows Goat Creek and the Spray River along old fire roads all the way to the Fairmont Banff Springs Hotel (for shuttle service, contact **Giddy Goat Adventures**, ☎ 866-464-4339 or 403-609-9992).

Drives, Sights, Activities & Hikes

Kananaskis Country Provincial Parks

 The landscape is a mosaic of mountains, rivers, lakes, open meadows and forests. You can explore boundless trails on foot, mountain bike, on horseback or skis. Try fishing in the Bow and Kananaskis Rivers or in one of the stocked lakes. Take a scenic drive, enjoy a picnic at one of the myriad picnic sites and relax in the local accommodations and facilities that cater to tourists. Stop in at one of the Visitor Information Centers for the latest trail information and suggestions for additional recreational opportunities.

Canmore Nordic Center Provincial Park, ☎ 403-678-2400 (toll free in Alberta 310-0000), Canmore.NordicCenter@gov.ab.ca. Only four km (2½ miles) from Canmore town center, off the Spray Lakes Road. Surrounded by panoramic views, there is an exhilarating "Olympian" trail system with a variety of terrain for bikers and skiers of all skill levels. Roller blading or roller skiing on three km (1.8 miles) of paved trails and an 18-hole disc golf course are also here. You'll find world-class competitive mountain biking and skiing events, day lodge (showers, lockers and change rooms), mountain bike and ski shop, café, boutique, biking lessons and tours, ski school, and rentals. Day lodge open from 9 am to 5:30 pm, seven days a week.

Grassi Lakes

Walk: 3.8 km (2.3 miles) round-trip.

Elevation gain: 250 m (820 feet).

Climb through the forest to two beautiful aquamarine lakes. Highlights include a waterfall, caves, wildflowers and spectacular views of Canmore and surroundings. Interpretive signs and benches are set along the route.

Follow the Spray Lakes Road about 1½ km (.9 miles) past the Nordic Center to just after the end of the pavement. Turn left to the parking lot.

Bow Valley Provincial Park

Barrier Lake Visitor Information Center, ☎ 403-673-3985 (toll free in Alberta 310-0000), BarrierVisitor.InfoCenter@gov.ab.ca. On the west side of Highway 40, seven km (4.3 miles) south of the Trans Canada Highway exit.

Contact the Barrier Lake Visitor Information Center for specific information about Bow Valley Wildland, Bow Valley Provincial Parks and Evan Thomas Provincial Recreation Area. Operating Hours: End of June to early September, Monday to Thursday 9 am to 5 pm, Friday, Saturday & Sunday 9 am to 6 pm; fall/winter/spring, daily 9 am to 4 pm.

Only 26 km (16 miles) east of Canmore, tiny Bow Valley Provincial Park is a gateway to the Rockies. Walk a few of the park's six interpretive trails such as Many Springs.

Many SpringsWalk: 1.6-km (1-mile) interpretive loop. An easy walk through montane forest and meadows to water fed by springs that bubble up through the lakebed and remain above freezing year-round. This trail is renowned for wildflowers including yellow lady's slipper orchids.

From Highway 1X follow the park road to Middle Lake, turn left and park at Many Springs parking lot.

IT'S FREE!

Hour-long original musical theater shows at one of four amphitheater locations in Kananaskis Country campgrounds – Bow Valley, Elkwood, Boulton Creek and Mt. Kidd – begin at 8 pm throughout the

Kananaskis Country

summer. Programs are free but children under 12 years must be accompanied by an adult.

Join a park interpreter for a weekend guided walk to learn about Kananaskis Country, from bird watching to animal tracks. The guides are knowledgeable and engaging.

For more information, ask at Visitor Information Centers or look for posters with times and locations at campgrounds.

Evan-Thomas Provincial Recreation Area

Also known as the Kananaskis Valley, this recreation area branching west of Highway 40 and sandwiched between Bow Valley Wildland Provincial Park and Spray Valley Provincial Park, comprises **Nakiska Resort** downhill ski and snowboard area, world-class **Kananaskis Country Golf Course**, **Boundary Ranch**, campgrounds, extensive day trails for mountain bikers, hikers and backpackers as well as **Kananaskis Village**. Developed for the 1988 Winter Olympics, Kananaskis Village is not a village per se, rather a complex that consists of two high-end hotels, restaurants, shops and recreational facilities.

Peter Lougheed Provincial Park

Peter Lougheed Provincial Park is one of Alberta's most scenic protected areas. The park offers several hundred miles of hiking, mountain biking, cross-country skiing and paved biking trails, as well as some of the finest wilderness hiking and camping experiences in the Canadian Rockies.

Peter Lougheed Provincial Park Visitor Information Center, ☎ 403-591-6322 (toll free in Alberta 310-0000), plh.visitorinfocenter@gov.ab.ca. Located 3½ km (2 miles) south of the Highway 40 junction on Kananaskis Lakes Trail (54 km or 33½ miles south of the Trans Canada Highway).

Contact the Peter Lougheed Provincial Park Visitor Information Center for specific information about this park and Spray Valley Provincial Park. Operating Hours: End of June to early September, Monday to Friday 9 am to 5 pm, Saturday & Sunday 9 am to 6 pm; mid-December to end of March, Monday to Friday 9:30 am to 4 pm, Saturday & Sunday 9 am to 4:30 pm. In the off-season (spring and fall) the operating hours are usually 9:30 am to 4 pm.

Friends of Kananaskis Country

A non-profit organization "dedicated to promoting the appreciation, enjoyment and understanding of Kananaskis Country while preserving its ecological integrity." Friends of K-Country support trails, interpretive programs, environmental education, the development of Visitor Center displays and contribute to heritage appreciation and outdoor recreation. Junior Naturalist summer programs are offered each year for children. You can help support the Friends' valuable programs and efforts by purchasing items such as guidebooks, maps and quality souvenirs from their retail shops at the Visitor Information Centers in Peter Lougheed Provincial Park and Barrier Lake. Each year the Friends of K-Country produce a beautiful wildlife/scenic poster series that makes an excellent souvenir – check them out at the retail shops. ☎ 403-678-5593, www.kananaskis.org.

Ptarmigan Cirque

Hike: Six km (3.7 miles) round-trip.
Elevation gain: 210 m (689 feet).
Watchable wildlife: Mountain sheep, ptarmigan.

This hike starts at Highwood Pass, the highest drivable pass in Canada (2,206 m or 7,238 feet), and thus is one of the shortest routes to the alpine region in the mountain parks. Park on the west side of the road at the Highwood Meadows parking area, just south of the summit on Highway 40.

Follow the Meadows Nature Trail. At km .4 the trail splits; stay right and cross to the east side of the highway. It's a steady steep climb through forest but well worth the effort, especially during the early summer when the area is filled with wildflowers. Stay left at the 1.1 km junction to loop through the meadows of the cirque. When the trail reaches a steep rocky terminal moraine, it turns right, crosses a stream and descends along the southeast side of the meadows. Before re-entering the forest there is a viewpoint for the waterfalls.

Spray Valley Provincial Park

The **Smith-Dorrien/Spray Trail** links Kananaskis Lakes and Canmore and provides access to the many summer and winter recreational opportunities in Spray Valley Provincial Park. Popular summer activities include backcountry camping, hiking and fishing. In winter the park offers ice fishing, cross-country skiing and dogsledding.

Karst Spring

Hike: Nine km (5.6 miles) round-trip.

Elevation gain: 200 m (656 feet).

A good family hike leading to Karst Spring. The first 3.6 km (2.2 miles) are open to cyclists. From Canmore, drive 39 km (24 miles) south on the Smith-Dorrien/Spray Trail. Turn right on the Mount Shark access road traveling five km (three miles) to the trailhead at the Mount Shark parking lot. Follow the signs to Watridge Lake.

Mount Assiniboine

Rising 3,618 m (11,870 feet), Mount Assiniboine is visible on the western side of the Smith-Dorrien/Spray Trail, shortly after passing the Mount Shark road. Mount Assiniboine Provincial Park lies entirely within British Columbia but popular hiking and skiing trails also run through Banff National Park (see that chapter) and Kananaskis Country.

Named after the Stoney Indians of the Assiniboine nation, on clear days it is a powerful sight to behold.

Winter Adventures

 Canmore and Kananaskis Country have become world-renowned all-season destinations that offer fantastic winter activities. The area is an alpine and Nordic skiers' paradise that attracts Olympic-calibre athletes. Many special events are held throughout the season such as the annual Canmore Winter Festival and ski marathons at the Canmore Nordic Center and Peter Lougheed Provincial Park.

Alpine Skiing

 **Nakiska Resort**, ☎ 403-591-7777 or central reservations 800-258-7669, www.skinakiska.com. Located 56 km (35 miles) from Canmore, east on the Trans Canada Highway then south on Highway 40. Site of the 1988 Winter Olympic Games. 750 acres plus 35 gladed (cleared wooded) acres, two quads, one triple lift, one double lift, one T-Bar and one Magic Carpet, servicing 28 trails from early December to mid-April. Gentle beginner terrain with over 40 acres of long easy runs as well as fast downhills. Snow school, rentals, childcare, bus transportation from Banff and Canmore. Lift tickets: Adult $54, senior $44, youth (13-17) $39, child (six-12) $15.

Nordic Skiing

 With several hundred km of groomed and natural trails to choose from in Canmore and Kananaskis, this is one of Canada's best areas for cross-country skiing.

Built as part of the 1988 Winter Olympic Games, the **Canmore Nordic Center** offers over 60 km (37 miles) of groomed and trackset trails designed for all levels of skiers, with most trails suitable for intermediate and advanced skiers. Competitions and training camps, some illuminated night skiing trails (until 9 pm), ski school and ski rentals. Winter trail fees: adult $7.50, junior (12-17) $6, senior (55+) $6, child (six-11) $4.50.

In Peter Lougheed Provincial Park there are over 75 km (46 miles) of groomed cross-country ski trails in the Kananaskis Lakes area, of which most are easy or intermediate, from .6

km to 10 km in length. On the Smith-Dorrien/Spray Lakes Trail the **Smith-Dorrien Trail System** offers a skier set (ungroomed) backcountry trail system and the **Mount Shark Cross-Country Ski Trail System** offers mainly intermediate skiing. The **Ribbon Creek Cross-Country Ski Trails** in Evan-Thomas Recreation Area offer 60 km (37 miles) of groomed trails.

Outdoor Ice Skating

With stunning mountain views, **10th Street Pond** in Canmore is 1½ blocks off Main Street at 7th Avenue; lit for evening skating.

At Kananaskis Village, from Highway 40, 24 km (15 miles) south of the Trans Canada Highway, there is a small skating pond/hockey rink.

■ Scenic Must-See's

Suggestions for the first-time summer visitor on a four-day schedule.

♦ **Day 1** – Spend a day wandering about downtown Canmore. Browse the shops and visit the **Canmore Centennial Museum and Geoscience Center**. Take a nature walk on one of the nearby trails and enjoy a meal at one of the many restaurants.

♦ **Day 2** – Saddle up at one of the local ranches that offer **horseback rides** or book a **whitewater rafting** tour on the Kananaskis or Bow Rivers – do both if you're up to it. Want to try something different? Caving in **Rat's Nest Cave** in Grotto Mountain with Canmore Caverns is a fun and unique experience.

♦ **Day 3** – Drive through Kananaskis Country, stopping for recreational opportunities such as interpretive walks. Bring a packed lunch, spend the night in one of the parks or resorts or, better yet, how about spending a night in an authentic tipi?

♦ **Day 4** – Spend a day **hiking** one or more of the trails in K-Country such as **Ptarmigan Cirque** and **Grassi Lakes**.

■ To Do List

Next time I visit Kananaskis Country I would like to...

Spend more time hiking the trails in **Peter Lougheed Provincial Park**. **Mount Indefatigable** is a five-km (three-mile) steep round-trip hike (elevation gain 482 m or 1,581 feet) that reaches spectacular viewpoints overlooking the Kananaskis Lakes. **Rawson Lake** is a moderate half-day trek (7.8-km or 4.8-mile round-trip) to a small lake in a cirque. The **Upper Kananaskis Lake circuit** is a 16.2-km (10-mile) trip with panoramas of the lake and mountains.

■ Useful Information

i   **Fire, Police, Ambulance**: ☎ 911.

Hospital: 100 Hospital Place, Canmore, ☎ 403-678-5536.

Royal Canadian Mounted Police: ☎ 403-678-5516 in Canmore; ☎ 403-591-7707 in Kananaskis.

Kananaskis Emergency Services Center: ☎ 403-591-7755.

Post Office: 801 Main Street, Canmore.

Weather Report: ☎ 403-762-2088.

Laundromat: Bow Valley Wash N' Dry, 610 Main Street, Canmore.

Liquor store: Safeway, 1200 Railway Avenue, Canmore.

Internet: High Country Office Services, 12 - 801 Main Street, Canmore.

Information Sources

Explore Kananaskis Country – A free magazine guide to the activities and facilities in Kananaskis Country published once a year by the Friends of Kananaskis Country, ☎ 403-678-5500 ext. 288 or explore@kananaskis.org.

www.cd.gov.ab.ca/parks/kananaskis

Government of Alberta site with links to trails and avalanche reports, general park information, recreational opportunities and more.

Kananaskis Country

www.tourismcanmore.com

Places to stay, things to do, services, history and other interesting information. Tourism Canmore, PO Box 8608, Canmore, Alberta ☎ 866-CANMORE.

www.canmorealberta.com

Vacation travel guide and business directory.

www.kananaskisvalley.com

Kananaskis Valley of Adventure – Winter and summer adventures, accommodations, heritage, business directory, maps and photo gallery.

www.kananaskis.com

Canmore and Kananaskis Country – About the area, accommodations, activities and business services.

Yoho National Park

Yoho is a Cree Indian word meaning astonishment or wonder and that's exactly what this national park offers visitors – a unique rugged landscape that will take your breath away. It is a park of rock walls – 28 mountain peaks over 3,000 m (9,800 feet) high; a park of waterfalls, one of the highest in Canada among them; and a park of glacial lakes, including two of the most famous and beautiful in the Rockies.

The park protects 1,310 sq kilometres (507 sq miles) on the western slopes of the Rocky Mountains in British Columbia. It borders Banff National Park to the east and Kootenay National Park to the south. Although it is the smallest of the four contiguous national parks, it has the heaviest concentration of high impact scenery. The most popular attractions are **Takakkaw Falls**, **Emerald Lake** and the **Spiral Tunnels** viewpoint. The most unusual attraction is the renowned **Burgess Shale**, one of the most significant fossil beds in the world, preserving rare fossils 515 million years old.

Yoho's excellent trail system boasts over 400 km (250 miles) of hiking trails, most of which are day-hikes concentrated in three areas – the Yoho Valley, Emerald Lake and the limited access Lake O'Hara region.

Many Canadian Rockies tourists who visit Banff and Jasper National Parks bypass lesser-known Yoho National Park. Many of my personal friends and acquaintances have spent time in Jasper and Banff on numerous occasions yet have never made the short trek across the Kicking Horse Pass from Lake Louise to Yoho, a fact I find astonishing. But be forewarned if you decide to go: Yoho is a magical place that casts a spell on all who take the time to discover it, a spell that leaves you in a state of astonishment and forever tries to lure you back.

■ History

 Yoho National Park's origins begin with the construction of the Canadian Pacific Railway (CPR). In 1867, the British Parliament passed the British North America Act, creating the Dominion of Canada. Prime Minister John A. Macdonald's "national policy" dictated that the Dominion would be linked east to west by a railway, ensuring the admission of British Columbia into the Canadian confederation.

The mountain section of the railway was the most difficult and costly. By 1883 the track reached the crest of Kicking Horse Pass. Although the Palliser expedition of 1858 had advised that the pass leading to the valley of the Kicking Horse River was the least hospitable, for political reasons it was the CPR's chosen route. Before it could be completed, construction costs threatened to ruin the CPR financially and to take down the government. But, despite looming disaster, Macdonald's "national dream" was completed, with the "last spike" on November 7th, 1885. The impossible had been achieved.

To save the expense of hauling heavy dining cars over steep grades, CPR general manager William Cornelius Van Horne built dining rooms so that passengers could eat before proceeding up the line. In 1886, the dining room at Field was expanded to include overnight accommodations and thus the CPR's first luxury hotel, Mount Stephen House (no longer in existence), was built. The railway brought tourists, adventurers, scientists and artists from around the world to explore Yoho's mountain scenery and it soon became an "alpine playground" for the wealthy.

In 1886, Yoho National Park was established, Canada's second national park. It began as a 16-sq-km (10-sq-mile) area at the base of Mount Stephen and the boundaries were changed four times before the present ones were finalized in 1930.

Yoho National Park

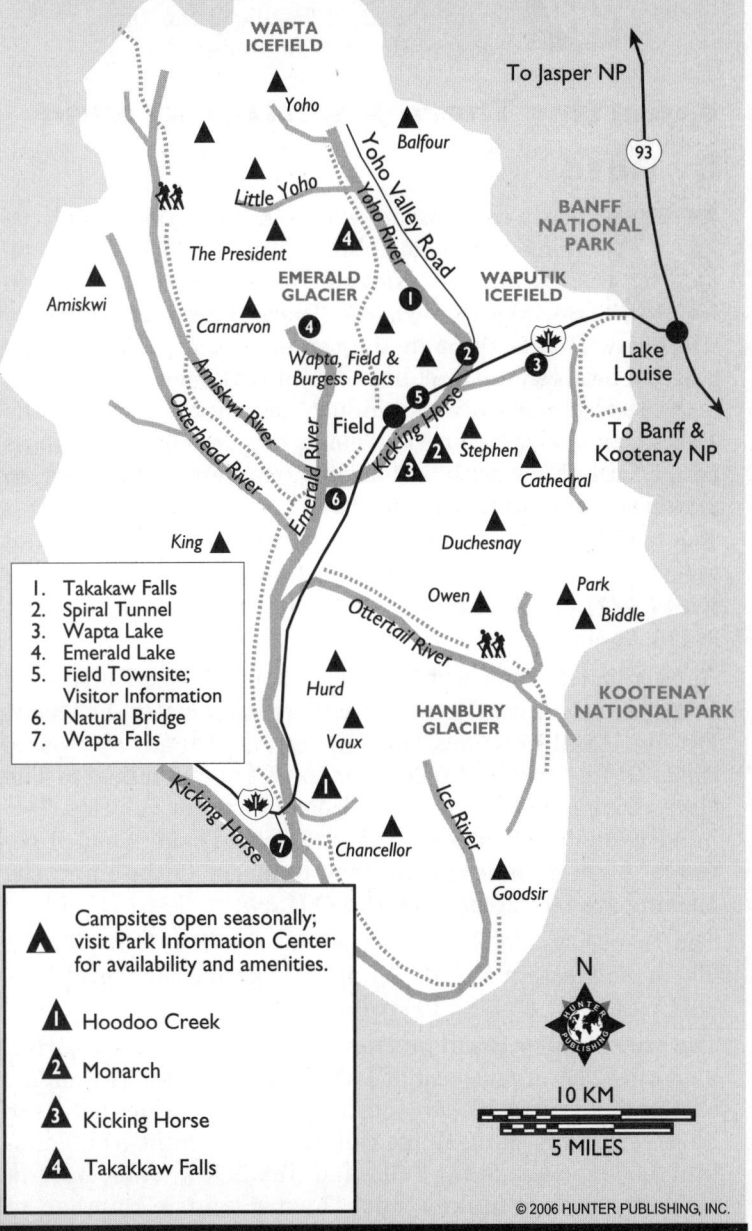

WAPTA
ICEFIELD

To Jasper NP

93

Yoho

Balfour

Little Yoho

Yoho Valley Road

Yoho River

BANFF
NATIONAL
PARK

The President

4

WAPUTIK
ICEFIELD

Amiskwi

EMERALD
GLACIER

1

Carnarvon

4

Wapta, Field &
Burgess Peaks

2

3

Lake
Louise

Amiskwi River

Field

5

Kicking Horse

To Banff &
Kootenay NP

Otterhead River

Emerald River

Stephen

2

3

Cathedral

6

Duchesnay

King

Owen

Park

Biddle

1. Takakaw Falls
2. Spiral Tunnel
3. Wapta Lake
4. Emerald Lake
5. Field Townsite;
   Visitor Information
6. Natural Bridge
7. Wapta Falls

Ottertail River

KOOTENAY
NATIONAL PARK

Hurd

HANBURY
GLACIER

Vaux

1

Ice River

Kicking Horse

7

Chancellor

Goodsir

Campsites open seasonally;
visit Park Information Center
for availability and amenities.

1 Hoodoo Creek

2 Monarch

3 Kicking Horse

4 Takakkaw Falls

N

10 KM

5 MILES

Don't Forget: Yoho National Park is on Mountain Time, one hour ahead of Pacific Time (and most of British Columbia).

■ Getting There & Getting Around

By Road

If you're going anywhere in Yoho, you'll likely be going either downhill or uphill. Along with the CPR and the Kicking Horse River (a Canadian Heritage River), the **Trans Canada Highway** (Highway 1) cuts through the center of the park. In some places – between the west boundary and Golden in particular – the road is narrow and winding. During the summer, the Trans Canada highway is extremely busy, not only with tourist traffic, but also with fast-moving commercial transport, so slow down and drive defensively.

The boundary between Banff National Park in Alberta and Yoho National Park in British Columbia is at the crest of **Kicking Horse Pass**, approximately 10 km (six miles) west of Lake Louise.

Approximately 2.7 km (1.7 miles) west of Kicking Horse Pass is the junction with Highway 1A, more aptly called the **Great Divide Road** junction. This old section of roadway crosses the CPR line and backtracks for three km (1.8 miles) to The Great Divide, but it is no longer open to motor vehicles. Two hundred meters (656 feet) from the Great Divide Road Junction a .8-km (.5-mile) gravel road branches to the right, the parking area for access to **Lake O'Hara**.

The Trans Canada Highway descends the **"Big Hill,"** almost 300 m (984 feet) in six km (3.7 miles), passing the Spiral Tunnels Viewpoint and the townsite of Field.

The **Yoho Valley Road** junction is at the base of the Big Hill, 22.3 km (13.8 miles) west of Lake Louise, 3.7 km (2.3 miles) east of Field. This 13-km (eight-mile) road provides access to Monarch and Kicking Horse campgrounds, Cathedral Mountain Lodge, Takakkaw Falls and Takakkaw Falls walk-in campground, Whiskey Jack hostel and a number of trailheads. The road is steep and narrow with tight switch-backs (at km seven/mile 4.3). Trailers and large recreational vehicles can be parked in the parking area across from Monarch Campground. The road is open from late June to early October, or as snow conditions permit.

Approximately 2½ km (1½ miles) west of the Field townsite exit is the **Emerald Lake Road** Junction, an eight-km (five-mile) road leading to the Natural Bridge (km 1.4/mile .9) and Emerald Lake.

Beyond the west boundary of Yoho National Park, 28 km (17.4 miles) from Field, the Trans Canada Highway follows the Kicking Horse River for 27 km (17 miles) to the full-service town of **Golden** and the junction with the Columbia River.

Distances from Field

Calgary.	210 km (130 miles)
Lake Louise	27 km (17 miles)
Golden	55 km (34 miles)

THE GREAT DIVIDE

You can bike or walk the three km (1.8 miles) to the Great Divide on the original Great Divide Road through Kicking Horse Pass. You'll find interpretive displays and commemorative cairns at this view-point along the provincial boundary and the Continental Divide. Here, Divide Creek branches: all water east of this point flows into the Atlantic Ocean and water to the west flows to the Pacific Ocean.

Bus Service

Greyhound, ☎ 250-344-2917 in Golden or 800-661-8747 for fare and schedule information, www.greyhound.ca. Daily bus service to Golden and to Lake Louise. There is no bus depot in the park but there is a flag stop along the Trans Canada Highway at the Field intersection, near the Visitor Information Center.

By Rail

There is no longer passenger train service in the park.

■ Special Events

Golden's **Spring to Life Celebration** welcomes the arrival of spring with a variety of community events held in May, www.springtolife.ca.

Canada Day is on July 1st; festivities include a parade.

Canada's Parks Day celebrations are held the second or third Saturday in July. Ask at the Visitor Information Centers about local planned activities.

■ Field Townsite

In the shadow of Mt. Stephen and Mt. Dennis, the tiny community of Field dates from the construction of the CPR in 1884 and is named for Cyrus W. Field, promoter of the first trans-Atlantic communications cable, who visited that same year. Originally occupying both sides of the Kicking Horse River, many of the homes on the north side of the river were damaged or destroyed by an avalanche off Mt. Burgess in 1909.

With a population of about 300, Field is still a divisional point for the CPR and it serves as an administrative post for Parks Canada. Tourist amenities in the village include a lodge and restaurant/pub, café and general store, post office, gas station, a pond beach with a playground and picnic area next to the Visitor Information Center and numerous guesthouses.

MOUNT STEPHEN

If you're wondering about the mountain that dominates the Kicking Horse Valley, it's 3,199-m (10,495-foot) Mt. Stephen. Situated very close to the highway, it looms almost two vertical km (1.2 miles) above the valley floor, standing guard over the village of Field. Composed of limestone, quartzite and shale formations, it was near mid-height on the mountain that railway workers discovered fossils in 1886, known today as the famous **Mt. Stephen Fossil Beds**. At the turn of the 20th century, this was the most popular mountain for climbing in the Canadian Rockies. It also supplied lead, iron and ore during the First World War. It is named for George Stephen, first president of the CPR.

The Visitor Information Center, ☎ 250-343-6783, yoho.info@pc.gc.ca. Located along the Trans Canada Highway at Field, the Center offers Parks Canada and Travel Alberta information services, a Friends of Yoho gift shop as well as natural history and Burgess Shale fossil displays.

If you are planning a visit to Yoho, you can contact the center and ask them to mail you the current *Trip Planning Guide* to help you make the most of your visit.

Operating Hours: End of June to early September 9 am to 7 pm; early to mid-September 9 am to 5 pm; mid-September to end of April 9 am to 4 pm; May to end of June 9 am to 5 pm.

FRIENDS OF YOHO NATIONAL PARK

A non-profit charitable society that works with Yoho National Park to promote understanding and enjoyment of the park, the Friends of Yoho offer summer weekend courses, outdoor summer programs for children as well as historic walking tours of the village of Field. Programs change from year to year; contact them for a list of upcoming offerings. The Friends operate a retail shop at the Field Visitor Information Center with a selection of books, trail guides, maps and gift items. A mail order list of trail guides, reference books and topographic maps is available. ☎ 250-343-6393, www.friendsofyoho.ca.

■ Shopping

Visitors come to Yoho for the scenery, not the shopping. But shopaholics who need a fix can find all sorts of great "stuff" at **The Friends Of Yoho Shop** in the Visitor Information Center, **The Velvet Antler Pottery Studio** across from

Field

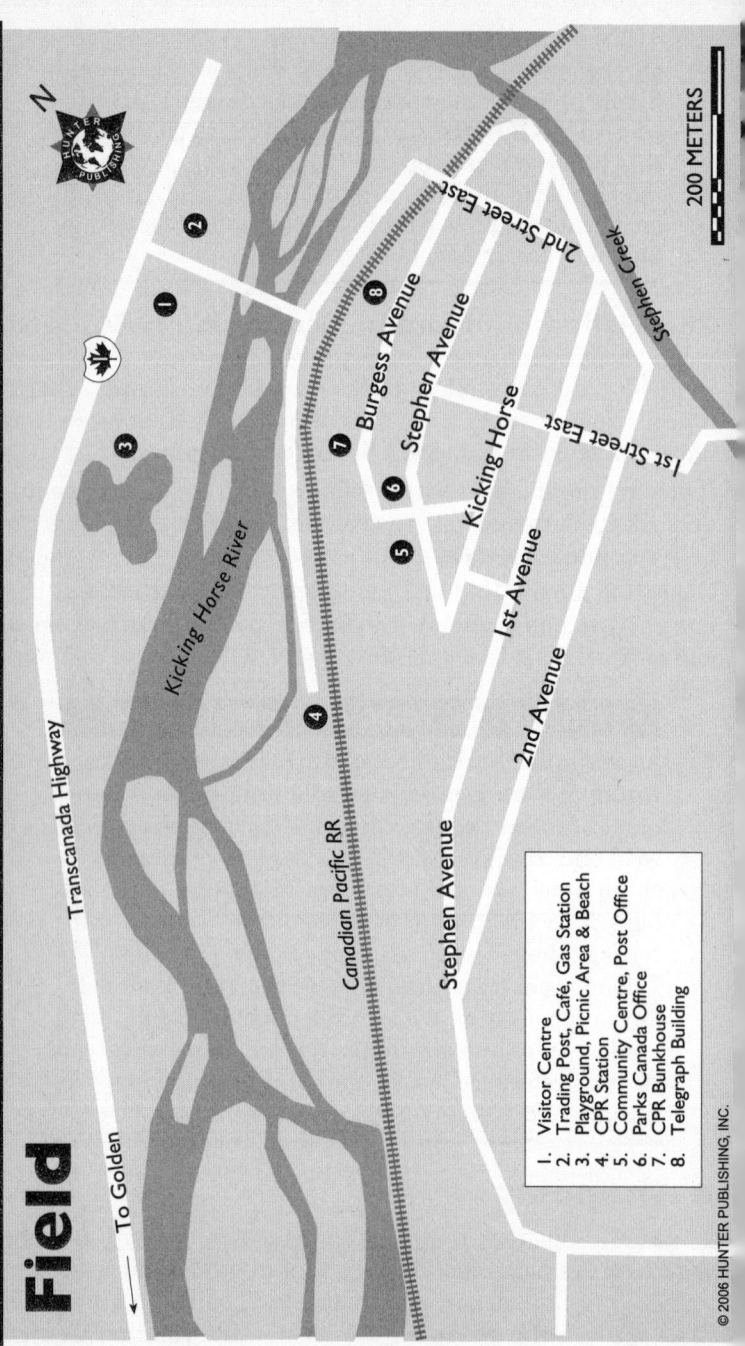

N

To Golden

Transcanada Highway

Kicking Horse River

Canadian Pacific RR

Stephen Creek

2nd Street East

1st Street East

Burgess Avenue

Stephen Avenue

Kicking Horse

1st Avenue

2nd Avenue

Stephen Avenue

1. Visitor Centre
2. Trading Post, Café, Gas Station
3. Playground, Picnic Area & Beach
4. CPR Station
5. Community Centre, Post Office
6. Parks Canada Office
7. CPR Bunkhouse
8. Telegraph Building

200 METERS

Above: Emerald Lake, Yoho National Park (© *Lenard Sanders*)
Below: Lake O'Hara, Yoho

Above: Takakkaw Falls (© Lenard Sanders)

Above: *Bighorn sheep, KootenayNational Park* (© Lenard Sanders)
Below: *Flowers on Lineham Ridge,*
Waterton Lakes National Park (© Lenard Sanders)

Bighorn sheep in Waterton Townsite

the Community Center and **Emerald Sports and Gifts** at Emerald Lake.

Emerald Sports and Gifts at Emerald Lake. Open all year except mid-October to mid-December, this gift shop with friendly and helpful staff is packed full of interesting items, from walking sticks to decorative throws, packaged gourmet foods to polished rocks. Even my son Oliver enjoyed browsing and surprised me with a box of delicious maple tea that we enjoyed back at our campground. Open 9 am to 7 pm during the summer months and in winter, 10 am to 4 pm weekends, 12 pm to 4 pm weekdays.

■ Where to Eat

There are two restaurants in the village of Field, both of which offer good food and are extremely busy throughout the summer.

If you're camping, stock up on food beforehand or make

DINING PRICE CHART	
Price per person in Canadian $ for an entrée, not including beverage, tax or tip.	
$	Under $10
$$	$10-$25
$$$	Over $25

the 55-km (34-mile) trek to Golden. **Truffle Pigs Café & General Store**, Cathedral Mountain Lodge, carries a limited selection of groceries. ☎ 250-343-6462, $$. Open daily 8 am to 9 pm, serving breakfast, lunch and dinner; deli and bakery. This has been rated among the best places to eat in Canada. Their dinner menu includes spinach maple pecan salad, gourmet buffalo burgers and prawn pesto pasta. Kids menu available.

Roundhouse Pub & Grill, ☎ 250-343-6303, at Kicking Horse Lodge (across from Truffle Pigs Café), $$. Open daily noon to 10 pm. Serving burgers, tasty vegetarian panini, specialty pizzas, salads, soups, and *poutine* (French fries and cheese curd smothered in gravy). Kids menu available.

There is a restaurant and dining room at **Emerald Lake Lodge**, ☎ 250-343-6321.

The 40-seat dining room (with a deck overlooking Kicking Horse River) at **Cathedral Mountain Lodge**,

☎ 250-343-6442, has been rated among the best nationally in *Where to Eat in Canada*, offering regional specialties such as salmon and Alberta beef. Continental breakfast served 7 to 10 am, candlelit dinner from 6 to 9 pm, $$$.

Lunch and afternoon tea are available for non-guests in the dining room at **Lake O'Hara Lodge** (reservations required), ☎ 250-343-6418.

■ Where to Stay

For me, over $100 per night for accommodation seems high, so in Yoho I camp or stay at the hostel. The average daily rate for a standard room during the peak season in Yoho lodges is about $168 and $116 in guesthouses (private accommodations). If money is not a consideration, there are three luxury lodges, but you will need to book well in advance. A complete

HOTEL PRICE CHART	
Reflects the price of an average room for two in Canadian $, May-Sept. Rates lower rest of year (except Christmas and New Year's).	
$	Under $50
$$	$50-$100
$$$	$101-$150
$$$$	$151-$250
$$$$$	Over $250

list of accommodations in Yoho is available at the Visitor Information Center. You can also find accommodations listed at the Burgess-shale website, www.burgess-shale.bc.ca/field/accommodations.htm.

Kicking Horse Lodge, ☎ 800-659-4944 or 250-343-6303, www.kickinghorselodge.net, $$$ to $$$$. Other than guesthouses, this is the only accommodation located in the village. A nice facility with 14 comfortable rooms, some with kitchenettes. Cable TV; laundry; dining room and lounge; small pets welcome.

West Louise Lodge, ☎ 888-682-2212 or 250-343-6311, $$$ to $$$$. I wasn't impressed with this lodge, which is sorely in need of renovation. The facility features an indoor pool, sauna, satellite TV, cafeteria-style breakfast and lunch, dining room and lounge. Rates include breakfast. Located 14 km

(8.7 miles) west of Lake Louise along the Trans Canada Highway, across from Wapta Lake.

Cathedral Mountain Lodge, ☎ 250-343-6442, www.cathedralmountain.com, $$$$$. Open June through September, luxuriously appointed log cabins with views (some with lofts) along the Kicking Horse River on Yoho Valley Road. Log cabins feature wood-burning or gas fireplaces, pine beds with down duvets, sitting areas furnished with antiques, soaker bathtubs and private decks. In keeping with the "retreat" theme, no televisions or telephones. Continental breakfast included. Multi-night packages, including meals and services, are available.

Emerald Lake Lodge, ☎ 800-663-6336 or 250-343-6321, www.crmr.com, $$$$ to $$$$$. Situated on a private 13-acre peninsula overlooking Emerald Lake. The restored main lodge was built in 1902 by the CPR and houses a dining room, lounge, bar and games room. The Clubhouse features an outdoor hot tub, sauna and exercise equipment. The guest rooms, in chalet-style buildings, have fireplaces, sitting areas and private balconies; executive rooms are available in studio or one-bedroom suites. Also available, the exclusive "Point Cabin." **Cilantro on the Lake**, a restaurant serving Southwestern cuisine, is open during the summer months. Daily ski shuttle to Lake Louise in winter. This is a rather exclusive facility with an atmosphere to match.

Lake O'Hara Lodge, ☎ 250-343-6418, www.lakeohara.com, $$$$$. For a luxurious getaway, the lodge at beautiful and secluded Lake O'Hara is open from mid-June to early October. There are no fax machines, televisions, radios or e-mail access (a public phone is nearby). Lodge rooms with shared or private bathrooms, lakeshore cabins, and guide cabins are available. All meals, afternoon tea, round-trip bus fare on the access road, all taxes and gratuities are included in the daily rate. Meals are served at a single sitting with a set menu. Minimum stay is two nights. Contact the lodge well in advance for reservations as priority is given to returning guests and, at the time of writing, reservations were being made two years in advance. Although this is an exclusive lodge, the atmosphere when I visited was warm and welcoming.

Meals for non-guests are by reservation with limited availability, $$$.

Beaverfoot Lodge, ☎ 888-830-6060 or 250-344-7144, www.rockies.net/~beaverft. Located 40 km (25 miles) southwest of Field on the Beaverfoot Road (one km west of the Yoho Park west gate, then 13 km along a gravel road).

This "down-home" rustic lodge is family-owned and -operated in a spectacular wilderness valley adjacent to Yoho National Park. The two-story log lodge contains 11 rooms and shared bathroom facility upstairs and on the main floor a central fireplace in the lounge.

Activities include trail riding, hiking, canoeing on nearby lakes or on the Beaverfoot River below the lodge, fishing, birding (over 110 species have been recorded in the area), horseshoes and hayrides – or just plain relaxing.

Canadian meals are served ranch-style in the dining room. Rates include breakfast or breakfast and dinner – adult $$, child $. All-inclusive (room, all meals and activities) – adult $$$, child (six-12 years) $$, (three-five years) $. All-inclusive weekly rates also available. Book at least two months in advance for the summer season.

See also *Camping* and *Horseback Riding* sections for more information about Beaverfoot Lodge.

Rental Cottages & Apartments

Although prices seem high ($$$ to $$$$), guesthouses in Field are well-suited to groups who are willing to share accommodations in the two-bedroom apartments or suites, which sleep up to six. Guests have full autonomy, including facilities for cooking. Prices may be negotiable, especially if you're staying more than one night and during the shoulder season. Many accept credit cards.

The guesthouse list changes frequently so phone or e-mail the Visitor Information Center for an up-to-date list of the approximately 18 guesthouses in Field. ☎ 250-343-6783, yoho.info@pc.gc.ca.

Camping

Campsites in Yoho Park can be hard to come by during peak season. All Yoho National Park campgrounds (at the time of writing) take no reservations and are on a first-come, first-served basis only; a res-

CAMPING/HOSTELS	
Rates in Canadian \$, not including taxes.	
\$	Under \$13
\$\$	\$13-\$22
\$\$\$	\$23-\$30
\$\$\$\$	Over \$30

ervation system is planned for the near future. With only 273 sites in four Parks Canada campgrounds, you had better arrive early to secure a site. **Kicking Horse**, the only campground with showers in Yoho Park, fills up by early afternoon. We stay at nearby **Monarch** when Kicking Horse is full. Monarch is somewhat noisy as it's situated along the busy Trans Canada Highway and it can get dusty in the summer, but it is cheaper and we were told we could use the showers at Kicking Horse. There are no serviced sites in Yoho campgrounds; all have disabled access. There is a day-use area that serves as an overflow campground next to **Hoodoo Creek** campground. Sani-dump stations are at Hoodoo Creek campground and on the Yoho Valley Road. Camping is also available in nearby Golden.

Monarch campground has some unserviced winter sites but most winter campers visiting Yoho stay at Lake Louise, where there are more amenities.

Campsites in Yoho

Kicking Horse. \$\$; 86 unserviced sites. Near the start of Yoho Valley Road. Showers, kitchen shelters, playground, interpretive programs. Season: Mid-May to mid-October.

Monarch. \$\$; 36 unserviced and eight walk-in sites. Along the Trans Canada Highway near the start of Yoho Valley Road. Kitchen shelter; some noise from the Trans Canada Highway; campfires not permitted. Season: Early June to early September.

Hoodoo Creek. $$; 105 unserviced sites. 22½ km (14 miles) west of Field along the Trans Canada Highway. Sani-dump. Season: June through September.

Takakkaw Falls. $$; 35 walk-in (tenting) sites. Next to Takakkaw Falls on Yoho Valley Road. Food storage; kitchen shelter. Season: End of June to end of September.

A Walk in the Past

During the construction of the CPR, 12,000 men came to work in the Rockies during the summer of 1884. Kicking Horse work camp was located where the Kicking Horse Campground is today. The old bake oven still sits in the trees. A Walk in the Past is a four-km (2½-mile) round-trip, self-guiding trail that begins at the trailer circle in the campground, crosses the Yoho Valley Road and terminates at an abandoned narrow-gauge locomotive used to build the Spiral Tunnels.

Camping Near Yoho National Park

Beaverfoot Lodge, ☎ 888-830-6060 or 250-344-7144, www.rockies.net/~beaverft. 40 km (25 miles) southwest of Field on the Beaverfoot Road (one km west of the Yoho Park west gate, then 13 km along a gravel road).

Campsites are in a large field with some clumps of trees. No hook-ups; showers, sauna, fire pits and firewood included, $5 per person.

The Beaverfoot Lodge features a **covered wagon campground**. From mid-May to early September you can sleep in an actual covered wagon like the ones you see in Western movies. Twenty stationary wagons each sleep two people and are circled around a central campfire (bathroom and shower facilities are nearby). Nestled among trees with a mountain backdrop, this is a real Western experience. Bed & breakfast: Adult $30, child (six-12 years) $15, (two-five years) $6. Bedding available on request only.

See also *Where to Stay* section for information about Beaverfoot Lodge and its amenities.

Backcountry Camping

Be sure to get a copy of the *Yoho National Park Backcountry Guide* from the Visitor Information Center. The brochure explains basic information about planning your trip, safety issues and trail descriptions for short walks, half-day hikes, and full-day hikes, as well as a map.

Park staff at the Visitor Center can help you plan your backcountry trip. If you are planning an overnight trip, you must purchase a wilderness pass ($9 per night, $63 per season), available from Parks Canada Visitor Information Centers. Campers can stay a maximum of four nights at one campground or site; one tent allowed per site. Contact a Visitor Information Center prior to your departure for current trail conditions, closures and other important information. Campfires are not allowed in Yoho's backcountry.

Backcountry campgrounds are located at **McArthur Creek**, **Yoho Lake**, **Laughing Falls**, **Twin Falls** and **Little Yoho**. A percentage of campsites can be reserved three months in advance of your first day of stay. A $12 non-refundable fee applies. Contact the Field Visitor Information Center.

Campgrounds at **Takakkaw Falls** (see above) and **Lake O'Hara** (see *Lake O'Hara* section) become backcountry campgrounds during the winter months; a wilderness pass is required.

The Alpine Club of Canada operates cabins at Lake O'Hara (Elizabeth Parker Hut), Abbott Pass (Abbott Pass Hut), Little Yoho Valley (Stanley Mitchell Hut), and on the southwest corner of Mt. Daly (Scot Duncan Hut). Contact the ACC for information and reservations through www.alpineclub-ofcanada.ca.

Random camping is permitted in Amiskwi, Otterhead, and Ice River Valleys. Camps must be set up at least three km (1.8 miles) from the highway, 100 m (320 feet) from water and 50 m (160 feet) from the trail. There is a three-day maximum stay for one spot. A wilderness pass is required.

Hosteling

Yoho National Park Whiskey Jack, ☎ 866-762-4122 for reservations or 403-670-7580 or centralres.sa@hihostels.ca. 13 km (eight miles) along Yoho Valley Road (from the Trans-Canada Highway). 27 beds; members & non-members $$$; check-in 5 to 11 pm. Closed October to mid-June. This is a small, tidy hostel in an incredible setting, across from Takakkaw Falls and on the doorstep of fabulous hiking.

■ Wildlife

Roadside locations for viewing moose, elk, bears and coyote include the braided creek bed of **Bath Creek**, along the Trans Canada Highway approach to Kicking Horse Pass (this is actually in Banff National Park, east of the Yoho border). Watch for elk and coyote along the **Trans Canada Highway**, as well as moose and coyote along **Emerald Lake Road**. The **Ottertail Viewpoint** at the confluence of the Ottertail and Kicking Horse rivers, 11.6 km (7.2 miles) west of Field, is a good location to spot moose, coyote and perhaps an elusive wolf. Bird checklists are available at the Visitor Center.

■ Adventures

If you are planning to do any hiking, backpacking or biking on Yoho Park's trails, be sure to stop by or call the Visitor Information Center for the latest trail information and safety reports.

Tour Operators

Two fossil bed sites exist in Yoho National Park – sites that have been hailed as "the world's most significant fossil discovery." Railway workers discovered the Mt. Stephen trilobite beds in 1886 and Charles Walcott of the Smithsonian Institution discovered the **Burgess Shale** or **Walcott Quarry** on the ridge connecting Wapta Mountain and Mt. Field in 1909. The fossils date from the Cambrian period, 505 million years ago. Interpretation of the findings has changed many scientists' views of evolution.

Access to the Mt. Stephen fossil beds and the Burgess Shale is restricted; you may not visit the fossil sites on your own. The Burgess Shale Geoscience Foundation, a not-for-profit society, offers a program of educational hikes during the summer (July to mid-September) to both protected fossil sites in this UNESCO Rocky Mountain Parks World Heritage Site. These are two of the most unusual tours available in the Rocky Mountain Parks – I highly recommend them.

The Burgess Shale Geoscience Foundation, ☎ 800-343-3006 or 250-343-6006, www.burgess-shale.bc.ca. Reservations are required and may be made after February 15th by calling one of the above numbers Monday to Friday between 10 am and 3:30 pm or via e-mail at info@burgess-shale.bc.ca.

Payment is by Visa or MasterCard only, no refunds, $20 fee for changes to reservations. Participants meet at the Yoho Brothers' Trading Post at the Field and Trans Canada Highway intersection. For the Walcott hike, participants drive to the Takakkaw Falls trailhead. If you are not able to secure a reservation, you can go to the meeting place with cash and hope for some no-shows.

Participants must be physically fit and wear appropriate hiking boots and clothing. Bring lunch, snacks, and water in a daypack along with suitable additional clothing and gear appropriate for a strenuous day-hike. Scheduled hikes may be cancelled due to extreme weather.

Why is it that kids love trilobites? Tri-lobites are fascinating little animals that lived in shallow seas during the Cambrian period for some 350  million years. They evolved into many bizarre forms and their fossils are very easily recognizable. The Mt. Stephen hike is recommended for children as the fossils are relatively large and the hike is shorter than the hike to the Walcott Quarry.

Mt. Stephen Fossil Beds

Guided hike: 6 km (3.6 miles) round-trip.
Elevation gain: 780 m (2,560 feet).
Difficulty: Moderate – short but steep.
Duration: Six hours.
Departs: 10 am, Saturday/Sunday.
Returns: 4:30 pm approximately.
Cost: $48.15 adult, $37.45 student, $16.05 child under 12.

Burgess Shale (Walcott Quarry)

Guided hike: 20 km (12 miles) round-trip.
Elevation gain: 760 m (2,500 feet).
Difficulty: moderate.
Duration: 10 hours.
Departs: 8 am, Friday/Saturday/Sunday/Monday.
Returns: 6:30 pm.
Cost: $69.55 adult, $37.45 student, $26.75 child under 12.

Horseback Riding

 **Beaverfoot Lodge,** ☎ 888-830-6060 or 250-344-7144, www.rockies.net/~beaverft. 40 km (25 miles) southwest of Field on the Beaverfoot Road (one km west of the Yoho Park west gate, then 13 km (eight miles) along a gravel road).

Trail rides from 30-minute afternoon excursions to three-day pack trips with 19 trails totaling 160 km to choose from, including high alpine meadows, breathtaking glacial fields, quiet trails through the woods by the Beaverfoot River and a spectacular viewpoint facing Wapta Falls. (Trails are all outside the park with some along the border.) Horses available for beginners or experienced riders.

First hour $25, 1½ hours $32, two hours $40, three hours $55, day ride with lunch $85, alpine ride with lunch $110.

Whitewater Rafting

 All trips start outside the park, just beyond the west park boundary. See *Whitewater Rafting* in the *Banff National Park* and *Kootenay National Park* chapters for additional options on the Kicking Horse River, one of Canada's top whitewater rivers.

Yoho National Park

Alpine Rafting, ☎ 888-599-5299, www.alpinerafting.com. Kicking Horse River runs through Yoho National Park to Golden. Departures times are on Mountain Standard Time.

◆ **Introduction to Whitewater** – Class 2 and small Class 3 rapids; recommended for families. Departs daily at 9 am. $60 adult, $30 child 12 and under. Includes a riverside BBQ lunch.

◆ **Kicking Horse Challenge** – This company's most popular trip, an action-packed, adrenaline-filled day. Class 2 and 3 rapids in the morning and in the afternoon Class 3 and 4 rapids through the Middle Canyon and through the relentless rapids of the legendary Lower Canyon, one of North America's most intense whitewater canyons. Departs daily at 9 am. $150 including a riverside BBQ lunch. Minimum age 16 years.

◆ **Ultimate Whitewater** – Combines Class 3 and 4 rapids of the Middle Canyon with the whitewater of the Lower Canyon. Departs daily at 11:30 am. $105. Minimum age 16 years and prior rafting experience recommended.

Lake Boating & Fishing

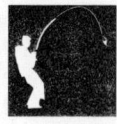

Some sections of the Kicking Horse River are navigable by canoe and kayak. Powerboats are not permitted on waters in Yoho National Park. Fishing is permitted in the Kicking Horse River year-round from the confluence of the Kicking Horse and Yoho rivers to the west park boundary below Wapta Falls. Check the current regulations for opening and closing dates of mountain lakes and catch limits.

Mountain Biking

Eight former fire roads, from three km to 21.3 km (1.8 miles-13.2 miles) one-way, have been converted to trails in Yoho National Park. These are the only trails in the park where mountain biking is permitted. A popular ride is to Lake Louise via the **Great**

Divide route, 10½ km (6½ miles), or via the **Ross Lake** trail, 8.3 km (5.1 miles).

Drives, Sights, Activities & Hikes

Trans Canada Highway

The Spiral Tunnels

When the Canadian Pacific Railroad was completed in 1885, the tracks down the "Big Hill," from the Wapta Lake to Field, reached a grade of 4½% in some sections, the steepest in North America and one of the toughest sections of railway building on the entire line. A temporary exception to the original agreement between the CPR and the government that the grade of the line not exceed 2.2% had been made; otherwise, it would have required expensive tunneling and a long delay in the linking of the Dominion. The first train to attempt the Big Hill was a runaway that killed three workers. Trains traveling uphill were fraught with delays and the Big Hill became a costly bottleneck.

The CPR was not able to fulfill its obligation until 25 years later, after many attempted solutions to the challenges faced along the Big Hill, many accidents and several deaths. In 1909, after almost two years of construction by a thousand men, 1½ million pounds of explosive and a cost of $1.5 million, two ingenious spiral tunnels constructed half-way down the hill reduced the grade to the required 2.2 percent. Not only did construction of the spiral tunnels help alleviate the danger of runaway trains, but before the spiral tunnels the line required four engines to haul 14 cars uphill; after the spiral tunnels were completed, two engines could haul 18 cars at five times the speed.

The upper spiral tunnel cuts through Cathedral Mountain (see *Yoho Valley* section) while the lower spiral tunnel in Mount Ogden, one km (.6 miles) long, is visible from a viewpoint along the Trans Canada Highway. If you happen to see a long train passing through the tunnel, you may see the engine emerge from one portal before the last car has disappeared into the other. (Freight trains don't run on a regular schedule, so consider yourself fortunate if you see one here.)

This point-of-interest is extremely popular and very busy during the summer months. Use caution when pulling in and out of the parking area.

Leanchoil Hoodoos

Hike: 3.2 km (two miles) round-trip.

Elevation gain: 455 m (1,492 feet).

Watchable wildlife: Mountain goats.

They take some effort to reach, but these hoodoos are much more impressive than the ones visible along Tunnel Mountain Road in Banff (most of them still have cap rocks and thus are well preserved). In fact, they're the most impressive I've seen throughout British Columbia and Alberta and well worth a visit.

The trail is accessed via Hoodoo Creek campground, 22½ km (14 miles) west of Field along the Trans Canada Highway. At the campground entrance, a road branches right to a parking area and a trail circles around to the rear of the campground and the trailhead. I find it easier to park near the campground entrance and walk through the campground (past section F) to the trailhead.

Cross the bridge over the creek and begin the steep ascent. The trail splits near the hoodoos; go above them for the most impressive views, but be very careful, especially if it's wet and slippery as there are no guardrails and it's a very long drop. Then go down to Hoodoo Creek for another perspective; on a nice day it's a good picnic spot.

The name Leanchoil is of Scottish origin and is pronounced, "lee-ann-coil."

Wapta Falls

Walk: 4.8 km round-trip (three miles).

Elevation gain: 45 m (150 feet).

Every waterfall is unique. While Takakkaw is celebrated for its height, Wapta is special because of its breadth. This virtually level 4.6-km (2.8-mile) round-trip walk is excellent for families. In my son's words "Make sure you put this hike in your book, Mum, it's the best!"

The Wapta Falls access road is 25 km (15½ miles) west of Field along the Trans Canada Highway, just past Hoodoo

Creek campground, where the highway curves. If you're coming from the east, there is no left turn lane so you must continue three km (1.8 miles) to the west entrance of the park and turn around. Follow Wapta Falls access road 1.8 km (1.1 miles) to the trailhead parking area.

The walk follows an old access road for one km (.6 miles), then along a trail through forest before reaching an upper viewpoint at km 1.9 (mile 1.2). But the most fun is if you walk down to the riverside. It was here that my son Oliver taught me the fine art of rock skipping. At low water, you can continue upstream for better vantage points. The view of the falls is partially obscured by a ridge of erosion-resistant rock. The Kicking Horse River plunges 30 m (100 feet) – Yoho's largest waterfall by volume. The mountain backdrop is the Chancellor Range. If you go early in the morning or late in the afternoon you might have the place to yourself. Once again, use extreme caution around swift-moving water and remember that the ground around waterfalls is wet and slippery from the mist.

The Kicking Horse

Dr. James Hector explored the Kicking Horse Pass for the Palliser Expedition in 1858. It was near Wapta Falls that an incident occurred on that expedition that led to the naming of the Kicking Horse River and Pass. After rescuing a fallen packhorse from a stream, Hector was kicked in the chest by his own horse, knocking him unconscious. His guides thought he was dead and began to bury him until they saw his eyes flicker. Despite his injury and the group's near state of starvation, Hector and his guides proceeded over the pass.

Yoho Valley

Two viewpoints are worth stopping at along the first section of the Yoho Valley Road:

Upper Spiral Tunnel Viewpoint

At km 2.1 (mile 1.3) you can look across the valley to the Upper Spiral Tunnel in Cathedral Mountain.

Meeting of the Waters Viewpoint

Km 2½ (mile 1.6) is the confluence of the Kicking Horse and Yoho Rivers. Although both rivers are glacially fed, the Yoho River is milky in color due to glacial silt, while the Kicking Horse appears clear due to a series of upstream lakes on its tributaries in which the glacial silt has settled out.

Takakkaw Falls

The highlight for many visitors to Yoho is at the end of the Yoho Valley Road. Takakkaw is a Cree word for magnificent, the name given the falls by CPR general manager William Cornelius Van Horne. The falls are fed by the meltwaters of Daly Glacier, part of the Waputik Icefield. They drop 380 m (1,248 feet) over a sheer wall of limestone to the valley floor. There is some argument as to how waterfalls should be measured in order to rank their height, thus you may read that Takakkaw Falls is anywhere from the highest to the fourth-highest in Canada. Nevertheless, Takakkaw Falls is most impressive and certainly one of the highest in Canada.

Amenities at the site include picnic tables, viewing platforms and wheelchair-accessible paved paths. You can walk near the base of the falls and feel the cool spray. Try photographing the falls from different vantage points; in the summer, the best light is from late morning to early evening.

Iceline hike: 6.4 km (four miles) to Iceline summit.

Elevation gain: 690 m (2,265 feet).

With relatively quick access to the open avalanche slopes of the President Range and dazzling postcard scenery across the valley, this is one of Yoho's most scenic and popular hikes.

Whiskey Jack Hostel is located off the Yoho Valley Road, .7 km (.4 miles) before reaching Takakkaw Falls parking area. The trailhead to the Iceline begins at the hostel parking lot. If you are not staying at the hostel, park at the falls parking area and hike the connector trail back to the trailhead. A number of trails connect from the Iceline, giving numerous hiking options.

From the hostel parking lot, the trail climbs steeply and ascends switchbacks through forest. Keep right; after emerging from the trees you traverse the moraines of the **Emerald Glacier**, sitting high on your left. On your right, across the valley, is **Takakkaw Falls** and **Daly Glacier**. Rock-hop over two (or three, depending on how far you decide to continue) lake outlet streams of rockbound lakes, the first of which you pass at km 4.6. From the 5.7-km (3½-mile) junction, stay left and proceed to the summit on the crest of a moraine at km 6.4 (mile 4); this is where many people turn around and return the same way.

If you are prepared for an overnight, the trail continues to the Little Yoho Valley. You can also return via the Lake Celeste trail; this route branches downhill from the 5.7-km (3½-mile) junction and terminates at the Takakkaw Falls parking area, a total of 17 km (10½ miles) for the circuit.

On hot sunny days, the high elevation and open slopes increase your exposure to the sun. Be sure to take precautions against sunburn and sunstroke: use sunscreen, wear a hat and drink plenty of water.

FIRE & ICE

August 12: Unexpectedly arriving after dark in Yoho National Park, we cautiously drove northeast up the Yoho Valley Road to Whiskey Jack Hostel, planning to hike the Iceline Trail the following day. After settling in, we discovered that we would be treated to an amazing astronomical event: on August 12th, the 2004 Perseid meteor shower peaked! From the hostel parking lot, with Takakkaw Falls cascading nearby, we watched in wonder as the skies opened up. Hundreds of meteors streaked across the northeast sky. "There's another one, and another one," we repeatedly exclaimed over the course of a few hours before we were too exhausted to keep our eyes open any longer. What timing and what an incredible vantage point!

Our late night necessitated a late start on the Iceline Trail; fortunately it was mere steps to the trailhead. Clear skies had permitted a fabulous view of the meteors, but with the sun beating harshly down upon us, we stopped often for water breaks. If you're packing a water filter, there's no shortage of sources along this trail. It was a challenge not getting our feet soaked, balancing on the rocks as we crossed the fast moving streams. Oliver needed some prodding to continue the steep ascent, but once we reached the avalanche slopes the gargantuan rock slabs captured his interest. The trail climbed relentlessly, but my curiosity and the continually improving views enticed me past the summit to an ice-filled tarn. The Iceline begged to be further discovered, but it was time to head back. Returning the way we came, we were grateful for the shade once we re-entered the forest.

Back at the hostel, we packed our gear and drove back down the valley in search of more adventure. It would be difficult to match the events of the past 16 hours, but then again, "this is Yoho," I thought, "anything is possible."

Emerald Lake Road
The Natural Bridge

En route to Emerald Lake is the natural bridge over the Kicking Horse River at km 1.4 (mile .8). The river has eroded a channel through a ridge of limestone and the full force of the river now runs through it. As with many natural features in the Canadian Rockies, this sight will one day disappear, as the river will eventually erode the limestone to the point of collapse.

Do not attempt to cross the natural rock bridge – it is very slippery and dangerous! You can cross the river over the "unnatural" wooden bridge built by Parks Canada. Use extreme caution near swift-moving water.

Emerald Lake

Seems that CPR packer Tom Wilson's discovery of Lake Louise in 1882 wasn't a big enough feather in his cap. Even though it was quite by accident – the tracks of his stray horses led him there – Wilson went on to discover Emerald Lake later that summer. And, like Lake Louise, after the CPR's construction of cabins on the lakeshore, this beautiful glacially fed lake became a major tourist attraction. To the north are the glacier-clad peaks of the President Range, from which silt-laden waters drain into the lake, resulting in its blue-green color. To the south is Mount Burgess, at one time featured on the verso of the Canadian 10-dollar bill.

The 5.2-km (3.2-mile) Emerald Lake self-guided nature trail is a popular circuit around the lake. The first 2½ km (1½ miles) are wheelchair-accessible (on the west or dry side of the lake). Note the lush forest on the east side (wet side) of the lake. It's more typical of BC's interior forests than that of the Canadian Rockies. A cool microclimate is a result of the low elevation of the lake and the high surrounding mountains that trap storms, resulting in heavy rainfall and snowfall. Instead of the typical pines and spruce, you'll find western red cedar, western hemlock and lush vegetation.

Several **hiking trails** begin at Emerald Lake including **Emerald Basin**, **Emerald Triangle (Yoho Pass-Burgess Pass)** and **Hamilton Falls/Lake**. During the summer, Emerald Lake is not the place to be if you're looking for solitude, unless you hike away from the lakeshore.

Canoe rentals are available from mid-May to mid-October at **Emerald Sports and Gifts**, ☎ 250-343-6000 ($22 per hour).

TAKING THE PLUNGE

It's a sweltering summer day at Emerald Lake and the place is packed. The parking lot is jammed – one tour bus leaves, two more arrive. I'm hot, sticky and cranky from sitting in a sweltering van and the thought of joining the masses is making me even crankier. We make our way through the parking lot and begin walking along the west lakeshore where we come upon a small beach. But I can't quite figure it out. Only one family among hundreds of tourists intent on experiencing this beautiful setting appears to be having fun. They're sunbathing on the beach and swimming in the emerald-colored water. "Let's get our bathing suits," I suggest, as we do an about face and return to the van. In record time we're splashing about in the glacial lake. The water is intoxicatingly refreshing. Across the lake, people are milling about on the lodge dock, but no one is in the water. I swim the short distance to the dock where a young girl stares at me enviously. "Can I go in?" she pleads to her parents. "No, we have to go back to the car and keep going," they say. "That's too bad," I say to her, "the water's really nice." I want to ask her parents to postpone their itinerary so she can swim too. Beyond doubt, Emerald Lake is worthy of admiration, but to be truly appreciated, immerse yourself in its cool blue-green water and watch your cares float away.

Swimming in glacial lakes during the hottest days of summer is a treat that few enjoy, but remaining in the water for too long can be dangerous due to the risk of hypothermia. If you decide to take the plunge, remain close to shore and, as always, closely supervise children.

Lake O'Hara

The Lake O'Hara area has been popular ever since its discovery in 1887 by surveyor J.J. McArthur. An Irishman, Lieutenant-Colonel Robert O'Hara, was most likely the first tourist here after hearing about it from McArthur. He then became a frequent visitor. You'll want to brush up on your Stoney

Indian vocabulary if you go, as many of the names in the area are from the Stoney language.

Quite simply, the Lake O'Hara region is one of the most beautiful in the Canadian Rockies. Located across the continental divide, the mountains that tower above the lake – Mounts Lefroy and Victoria – are the same that give Lake Louise its magnificent setting. From Lake O'Hara, a heavily concentrated network of well-maintained trails leads hikers within a matter of minutes or hours past a dozen pristine lakes, rugged mountains and alpine meadows, not to mention its unique plants and wide variety of wildlife.

The abundance of extraordinary **day-hikes** in the region includes the challenging **Alpine Circuit**. The 12-km (7.4-mile) alpine route traverses the Lake O'Hara basin allowing grand views of the region's best scenery; it is *the* premier hike in the area, but hikers must be comfortable with route finding, heights and traversing exposed terrain. Another favorite route is to stunning **Lake McArthur**; cradled by mountains and a glacier, it is the largest, deepest and bluest lake in the region.

That's the good news. The bad news is that you'll be facing some fierce competition if you want to visit the area. The Lake O'Hara region is considered sensitive to human use. In order to protect the fragile meadows and wildlife, a quota limits the number of visitors using the public bus service. To put it in perspective, 1% of the 700,000 people that visit Yoho National Park each summer – that's 7,000 people – will be able to visit Lake O'Hara. The area is heavily managed and there are many rules and regulations. If you are planning a visit, keep your expectations reasonable and be flexible with scheduling. That said, I suggest three days in the area, though four is ideal. If you can't make a reservation, hike in for just a day and get a taste of all that the area offers.

The bus service from the parking lot to the campground (along an 11-km/6.8-mile access road) and the 30-site backcountry campground operates from about mid-June to the beginning of October (call for exact dates). Reservations are accepted a maximum of three months in advance of the day you hope to be at Lake O'Hara. When you reserve a campground you are also reserving seats on the bus for the people in your party. You may stay a maximum of three nights in the campground and book a maximum of two sites (maximum one tent and four people per site, with site selection made upon arrival). For day use, the maximum number of bus seats you can reserve is six. Reservation fees are $12 and campground fees are in accordance with wilderness pass fees, $9/person/night. Bus fees are adult $15, child under 16 years $7.50 and children under five years ride free. Payment for reservations is by credit card: MasterCard, Visa or American Express. Inbound, the bus departs the Lake O'Hara access road parking lot at 8:30 and 10:30 am and 3:30 and 5:30 pm. Outbound, the bus departs Le Relais day-use shelter at 9:30 and 11:30 am and 2:30, 4:30 and 6:30 pm. Each camper is restricted to one large or two small pieces of luggage; coolers, musical instruments, radios and lawn chairs are not permitted. Dogs are not permitted on the bus.

Cancellations are received by an answering machine at ☎ 250-343-6344. The $12 reservation fee is non-refundable. All fees are forfeited if cancellations are not received at least four days prior to the first reserved date or if no cancellation notice is received.

You have the following options for transportation and camping at Lake O'Hara:

- ◆ **Advance Reservations** – May be made by phone or in person at the Field Visitor Information Center. You may reserve a maximum of three months in advance of the day you hope to be at Lake O'Hara. You can call Lake O'Hara reservations, from about mid-March to the beginning of October, ☎ 250-343-6433, from 8 am to 12 pm and 1 to 4 pm. Exact dates for opening and closing vary. This option is highly recommended due to the popularity of the area.

- ◆ **24-Hour Reservations** – These may be made by telephone only. Parks Canada reserves six day-use bus seats and three to five campsites for 24-hour bookings. These reservations can be made by calling the above reservations phone number the day before you wish to visit the area only. Each individual may reserve either two day-use seats or one campsite for one night. These places fill up quickly.

♦ **Stand-By** – If there are any cancellations or "no-shows," seats are available on a first-come, first-served basis on the 8:30 am and 10:30 am buses. You should arrive at least a half-hour early and speak to the attendant at the Lake O'Hara parking lot. Seats are not given out until immediately prior to departure. Payment is cash only. No-shows are unlikely.

♦ **Hike** – More good news, or bad news, depending on how you look at it. There are no restrictions on the number of people who wish to hike in on the 11-km (6.6-mile) access road for day use, but bicycles are not permitted. (You should not attempt to hike in on the old Cataract Brook Trail as it's no longer maintained and the bridge over Cataract Brook has been removed.) If you hike in, you are guaranteed a bus ride out if you arrive on time and pay the $10 fee. You can catch the bus from Le Relais day-use shelter at 2:30, 4:30 or 6:30 pm.

The Parks Canada campground offers well-spaced tent pads, lockup boxes for valuables (bring a medium-sized padlock), cook shelters, picnic tables, food storage, fire-pits, firewood and well water. It's a compact campground so don't expect a quiet hideaway. Le Relais day-use shelter, across from the warden cabin, is operated by the Lake O'Hara Trails Club and offers visitor information, including trail conditions, pamphlets, maps, guidebooks and light refreshments.

Other accommodations include the **Elizabeth Parker Hut**, a cabin operated by the Alpine Club of Canada. Reservations are handled on a lottery basis; you do not need to be a member of the ACC to request dates, but, if you win the lottery you are required to purchase a membership. Visit the ACC website, www.alpineclubofcanada.ca, for detailed information.

If you're not into camping, there's **Lake O'Hara Lodge** (see *Where to Stay* section), but you'll have to plan a little in advance – try two years. Meals and afternoon tea are available for non-guests but reservations are required; call ahead for availability, ☎ 250-343-6418.

For more information, ask for the *Parks Canada / Lake O'Hara Trails Club Lake O'Hara Backcountry Map* brochure at the Visitor Information Center. It has valuable trail information, including limited-access and bear-encounter routes. If you plan to hike extensively in the area or are interested in the fascinating history of Lake O'Hara, purchase a copy of two inexpensive little books: Don Beers' *Lake O'Hara Trails*, a detailed guide to 26 short walks, half-day trips, long hikes and challenging alpine routes; and *History of Lake O'Hara* by Lillian Gest, an accomplished alpinist with a lifelong passion for the area.

YOHO FRIENDS

When I'm on the road working, I find it almost impossible to plan in advance, as I simply don't know where I'll be from one day to the next. (Okay, I admit it, I'm no good at planning in general and, when I do, I have a terrible time keeping appointments – just ask my hairdresser.) However, there are certain drawbacks, such as my visit to Lake O'Hara. I was a little put off at the prospect of figuring out how I was going to get there. The first option was out since it included the words "reservations required." Option number two, limited 24-hour advance bookings, wasn't an option and I didn't want to wait around on stand-by. There was but one choice remaining, hike in the 11 km on the access road and take the last bus out.

It was my good fortune to be blessed with beautiful weather. I was making good time hiking solo along the old fire road, although I was a bit disheartened when the bus drove past, leaving me in its dust. Feeling a little sorry for myself I plodded on, all the while thinking I was the only one without a bus reservation. (Wasn't that my New Year's resolution – plan ahead and be on time more often?) Stopping to refresh myself in a rushing creek, I looked up startled to see three other hikers who looked even more disenchanted than myself.

"Oh hi, are you guys heading to Lake O'Hara?" I quizzed (dumb question). "Yeah," they all said dejectedly, then one of them explained, "my friend works up at the lodge and he was supposed to get us on the bus but the driver didn't know anything about it." "Too bad," I said, "it's a fair way to hike but at least it's a gorgeous day." They all agreed but my words didn't seem to lift their spirits. I introduced myself and they did the same. Evan, Phil and Adam from New York City were driving across the USA and up through Alberta and British Columbia to experience some of the Canadian Rockies during their summer off from university studies. Feeling upbeat at the prospect of company, I asked if they wanted to hike together and they readily agreed.

We walked and talked with a little more of a skip to our step. "Are you going just for the day?" Adam asked. "Well, actually, yes," I admitted sheepishly. "I couldn't make a reservation so I'll take the last bus out." I explained that I was researching and writing a guidebook, which usually elicits the proverbial question "how do you get that kind of a job?"

Nearing Lake O'Hara, I suggested we veer off the road to the left for a more scenic approach along the forested trail that follows the shore of Lower O'Hara Lake. It was time for lunch when we finally arrived at our destination. Gawking in awe at Lake O'Hara and its picture-perfect surroundings, we found comfortable spots to sit among the lakeshore boulders. I leaned back against my pack, closed my eyes and breathed deep. We were all silent.

Evan was voted cook and offered to share their macaroni and cheese. After lunch we snapped some photographs and bid farewell. I was ready to tackle a hike, carefully calculating the time so as not to be late for the last departing bus and they were going to search for their friend. "If you can't spend the night I might see you on the bus," I said, waving goodbye.

"Good luck with your book," they offered, and we were off.

I chose Opabin Plateau for a short hike, a 5.9-km (3.7-mile) circuit that climbs atop a hanging valley high above Lake O'Hara. Opabin means "rocky" in Stoney language. I climbed the talus slope to the plateau and, along with a number of hoary marmots and pika, admired Mary Lake, named for pioneer adventurer Mary Schäffer.

When it was time to catch the bus, there was no sign of Evan, Phil or Adam. I'm sure their friend was happy to finally see them, just as I had been happy to meet them. The best travel adventures are people adventures. My visit to Lake O'Hara would be memorable not only because of the special place that it is, but more importantly because I met three fellow travelers with whom I shared an afternoon, travelers that I will always remember as my "Yoho friends."

Winter Adventures

Cross-country **ski and snowshoe rentals** are available from **Emerald Sports and Gifts**, ☎ 250-343-6000, at Emerald Lake.

Alpine Skiing

See the *Banff* chapter for information on skiing the Rockies' biggest ski area, Lake Louise.

Kicking Horse Mountain Resort, ☎ 866-754-5425 or 250-439-5424, www.kickinghorseresort.com. This resort has been ranked as having the best powder in North America, with over 2,750 acres of terrain and the highest vertical in the Canadian Rockies, 1,260 m (4,133 feet). Located 14 km (8.7 miles) off the Trans Canada Highway overlooking Golden, it's less than an hour's drive west of Field.

There are 106 runs (20% beginner, 20% intermediate, 45% advanced, 15% expert) serviced by an express gondola, three chairlifts and one surface lift. Lift tickets: adult $59, youth (13-18) $49, child (seven-12) $27, senior $49.

They have a Day Lodge, Eagle's Eye Restaurant, Snow School and a Rental Shop. Snow Hosts provide complimentary guided tours of the mountain.

Nordic Skiing

Cross-country skiing is a unique way to enjoy Yoho National Park, which offers an extensive cross-country ski trail system for every level of ability. Over 40 km (25 miles) of trails are track set regularly. If you are planning an overnight trip you must have a wilderness pass. The brochure *Cross Country Skiing and Ski Touring in Yoho National Park*, available at the Visitor Information Center, rates a number of trails as easy or moderate with a few extended trips where strong skiing ability and more experience in assessing hazards are required.

Easy trails: Suitable for inexperienced skiers, trails are flat and may have short, wide downhill runs. Try the 8.2-km (5.1-mile) round-trip **Wapta Falls Trail** and the 5.2-km (3.2-mile) **Emerald Lake Circuit**.

Moderate trails: Longer trails requiring more stamina, or trails with downhill stretches that require some ability to turn and make quick stops. Skiers must be able to recognize avalanche zones. Moderate ability trails include the 26-km (16-mile) round-trip **Yoho Valley Road to Takakkaw Falls**, which is track set to the base of the switchbacks (km 7 or mile 4.3) and the 23.4-km (14½-mile) round-trip **Lake O'Hara Fire Road**.

Outdoor Ice Skating

There is an outdoor rink in the village of Field and an area cleared at Emerald Lake. If there is a good freeze in the fall, then all the ponds, sloughs and lakes can be used for skating. Individuals are responsible for making an assessment of ice thickness for themselves. Some areas, outflow sections in particular, maintain open water all year so skaters must use extreme caution and be vigilant about their own safety.

■ Scenic Must-See's

Suggestions for the first-time summer visitor on a four-day schedule.

◆ **Day 1** – Take a scenic drive up the Yoho Valley Road and start the day with a hike along the **Iceline Trail** for eye-popping scenery. I highly recommend it. Afterwards, enjoy a leisurely visit to **Takakkaw Falls**, near the trailhead.

◆ **Day 2** – Visit the amazing **Spiral Tunnels Viewpoint** – if you're lucky, you might get to see a train going through the tunnels. Farther down the Trans Canada Highway, do the short hikes to **Wapta Falls** and the **Leanchoil Hoodoos**. Don't forget a packed lunch. For a different perspective on Wapta Falls, take a trail ride from Beaverfoot Lodge to the viewpoint facing the falls.

◆ **Day 3** – Drive up to **Emerald Lake**, stopping at the natural bridge en route. You can hike around the lake or try one of the more challenging trails such as the **Emerald Triangle**. If it's a hot day be sure to bring a bathing suit and go for a paddle and maybe even a swim. And don't forget the sunscreen!

◆ **Day 4** – Book a tour well in advance to hike to either the **Burgess Shale** or the **Mt. Stephen Fossil Beds**. You won't be disappointed in this World Heritage Site. If hiking has got you weary, there is a Burgess Shale display at the Visitor Information Center.

■ To Do List

Next time I visit Yoho National Park I would like to...

Hike, hike and hike some more! There's never enough time to experience all the incredible trails in the Canadian Rockies' Parks.

Ottertail Fire Road to Goodsir Pass. This challenging route combines a 30-km (18.6-mile) bicycle ride plus a 21.4-km (13.3-mile) round-trip hike. The destination: Goodsir Pass, a vast alpine meadow beneath the twin peaks of the Goodsirs, the highest mountains in Yoho (3,562 m/11,686 feet). Because the pass is not easy to reach, it's quite likely one can achieve some solitude, not often synonymous with the Rocky Mountain Parks during the summer. Anyone not up to completing the route in one day can make arrangements with the Field Visitor Information Center to stay at the McArthur Creek backcountry campground, at the end of the Ottertail Trail (15 km/9.3 miles), which is as far as bicycles are permitted. The trailhead is off the Trans Canada Highway, 8.4 km (5.2 miles) west of Field.

Lake O'Hara. I would like to spend three days hiking in the Lake O'Hara region. If I can't secure a reservation during the summer season when the bus is operating, October is an alternative as it's much less busy. However, I would have to hike in the 11 km (6.8 miles) and obtain a wilderness pass to stay in the campground. Additionally, there's about a 50/50 chance that October would be snow free – a formidable concern due to avalanches and other hazards.

■ Useful Information

i

Fire, Police, Ambulance: 911.

Park Warden Office: ☎ 250-343-6142; 24-hour emergency, ☎ 403-762-4506.

ATM & liquor store: Truffle Pigs Café and General Store, downtown Field.

Internet access: No access available in Field; go to Golden or Lake Louise.

Weather forecast: ☎ 403-762-2088.

Road conditions: ☎ 403-762-1450.

Golden Visitor Information Center: ☎ 250-344-7125 or 800-622-4653.

Information Sources

www.pc.gc.ca/yoho

Parks Canada website with extensive information about the park, including fees, visitor information, natural wonders, activities, and public safety such as trail reports, road conditions, and avalanche reports. Yoho National Park, Box 99, Field, BC, V0A 1G0, ☎ 250-343-6783.

www.alpineclubofcanada.ca
The Alpine Club of Canada, Box 8040, Canmore, AB, T1W
2T8, ☎ 403-678-3200

Kootenay National Park

Kootenay National Park protects 1,406 sq km (543 sq miles) of Rocky Mountain wilderness in the southeastern corner of British Columbia. The park is bordered on the northwest by Yoho National Park, on the northeast by Banff National Park and on the east Mount Assiniboine Provincial Park; the Continental Divide forms the border between Kootenay and Banff Parks. The 94-km (58-mile) **Kootenay Parkway** (Highway

93 South) cuts through the center of the park – paralleling the Vermilion and Kootenay rivers for most of its length – from Castle Junction at the Trans Canada Highway in Banff National Park to the village of Radium Hot Springs in the Columbia Valley.

This is a park diverse in its landscape, ecology and climate. You'll find glacier-clad peaks as well as grasslands where cactus grows. A number of short self-guided interpretive trails throughout the park are designed to provide the visitor with an appreciation of Kootenay's diversity. There are also many points of interest, picnic sites and more than 250 km (155 miles) of hiking trails that await discovery. The park's most popular attractions are the **Radium Hot Springs** pools, located at the base of Sinclair Canyon's sheer rock wall just inside the park's west gate, and the unique, not-to-be-missed **Paint Pots**.

The **Columbia Valley** (also know as the Windermere Valley) is on the western slope or warmer side of the Rockies – where summers are noticeably hotter – and separates the Rocky Mountains from the **Purcell Mountains**. The resort town of Radium Hot Springs, immediately outside the park's west gate, is the gateway to the Columbia Valley and the Purcell Mountains. The village of Radium Hot Springs has abundant accommodations and restaurants as well as bighorn sheep that migrate into town and the surrounding area in the fall, winter and spring.

If you're a birder, you'll want to experience the **"Wings Over the Rockies Bird Festival"** in May, celebrating the annual return of thousands of birds to some of the most extensive wetlands in North America.

About 1.2 million people visit Kootenay National Park each year. Driving and sightseeing along the parkway can easily be accomplished in a day but only provides a glimpse of the park's sheer natural beauty. If experiencing wilderness tranquility is high on your list of priorities, Kootenay Park offers a less crowded alternative to the better-known Rocky Mountain Parks.

Don't Forget: Kootenay National Park is on Mountain Time, one hour ahead of Pacific Time (and most of British Columbia).

■ History

According to archaeological evidence, the Ktunaxa and other aboriginal peoples hunted and traveled in the area as much as 10,000 years ago. They used the hot springs for centuries before the first recorded visit in 1841, when the governor of the Hudson's Bay Company, Sir George Simpson, enjoyed its soothing properties. An Englishman named Roland Stuart purchased the springs in 1890 and owned them until 1922, when they were expropriated for inclusion in the park. The park was established in 1920 as part of an agreement between provincial and federal governments to build the Banff-Windermere Highway. Completed in 1922, it is the first motor road across the Canadian Rockies.

Forest Fires - Beauty & the Beast

As you tour the Rocky Mountain National Parks, you'll see signs of past forest fires. Nowhere is this more evident than Kootenay National Park. Kootenay Park's most active fire season in living memory was 2003, when much of the northern part of the park was ablaze. Nearly 400 firefighters fought to protect park facilities and prevent the fires from spreading into the Bow Valley. The fires were all started by lightning – as are most of the fires in the park. The largest burned 12.6% of the park, including bridges and railings along the Marble Canyon trail and portions of the Marble Canyon campground.

Forest fires may seem like an ecological disaster, but fire is part of the natural cycle. It renews the forest, opening up dense growth and turning it into natural fertilizer, creating better forage for large and small creatures. Preventing forest fires breaks the natural cycle and causes a build-up of dead wood, which may lead to uncontrollable wildfires. Controlled burning helps maintain a healthy mixture of young, middle-aged and old forests, reducing the risk of wildfires.

What initially may seem unsightly eventually grows into a beautiful landscape. Growth is now emerging from the 2003 burned forests. Fireweed, a tall showy plant with pink flowers, is usually the first wildflower to emerge after burns and the contrast with blackened trees is stunning. From the Fireweed Trail you can see how the Vermilion Pass burn of 1968 has produced a healthy lodgepole pine forest.

If you decide to walk through a previously burned area, use extreme caution. Burned trees are unstable, especially during high winds.

Kootenay National Park

■ Getting There & Getting Around

By Road

 **Highway 93**, the **Banff-Windermere Highway** (also known as the Banff-Radium Highway or the Kootenay Parkway), is a 94-km (58-mile) scenic drive that runs north-south through the center of Kootenay National Park. This is the only road through the park.

The town of Banff is 33 km (20 miles) east of Kootenay Park's north entrance, the village of Lake Louise, 28 km (17 miles) west. The village of Radium Hot Springs is at the junction of Highways 93 and 95, just outside the park's west (southwest) gate.

Many visitors to Kootenay Park travel via Lake Louise, Banff or Calgary. Traveling from Golden along Highway 95, the one-hour scenic drive runs alongside the Columbia River Wetlands and is especially stunning during autumn. Coming from southeastern British Columbia, the drive takes you past a diverse landscape of mountains and valleys and along Columbia and Windermere Lakes.

Distances from Radium Hot Springs

Calgary	264 km (164 miles)
Banff	135 km (84 miles)
Golden	103 km (64 miles)
Invermere	16 km (10 miles)
Windermere	24 km (15 miles)
Fairmont	44 km (27 miles)

Bus Service

 **Greyhound**, ☎ 250-347-9726 or 800-661-8747 for fare and schedule information, www.greyhound.ca. Daily bus service to/from Calgary, Banff, Golden, Vancouver and Cranbrook; bus stop at the Esso service station in Radium Hot Springs village center, 7507 Main Street west.

Car Rentals

MicRidge Auto Rentals, ☎ 250-342-9700 or 866-312-9700 (Invermere).

Taxis

Invermere Valley Taxi, ☎ 250-342-2222.

By Air

South of Radium Hot Springs, the **Fairmont Airport** is adjacent to the Fairmont Hot Springs Resort. The 2,000-m (6,200-foot) runway serves private and charter aircraft.

■ Special Events

For more information about special events that take place throughout the Columbia Valley, contact the **Radium Chamber of Commerce**, ☎ 250-347-9331, or the **Columbia Valley Chamber of Commerce**, ☎ 250-342-2844.

Wings Over the Rockies Bird Festival is an annual event held in early May. This weeklong festival that draws up to 3,500 participants celebrates the annual return of summer birds to the Columbia River headwaters. Almost 200 km (125 miles) of Columbia River wetlands – one of the longest continuous wetlands in North America – provide habitat for over 265 bird species. Creative, educational, cultural and entertaining events include field trips, hikes, horseback rides, Voyageur canoe trips, art exhibits, workshops and presentations. For more information call ☎ 888-933-3311 or visit www.adventurevalley.com/wings.

Canada Day, July 1st, festivities and fireworks.

Canada's Parks Day celebrations, held the second or third Saturday in July.

Valley Appreciation Day is held in July with many activities including a free pancake breakfast, children's festival, local entertainment and demonstrations throughout the day.

Sounds Over the Rockies is a free country/folk outdoor family concert at the Radium Stadium on the BC Day long weekend in July/August.

Columbia Valley Classic Car Show & Shine, is hosted annually in Radium in September.

Radium
Hot Springs

To Golden

To Banff
& Calgary

1

2

Kootenay Pk Dr

95

Sinclair Creek

Sinclair Ck Rd

3

KOOTENAY
NATIONAL
PARK

N

HUNTER
PUBLISHING

93

7

Madsen Rd

Forsters Lodge Road

Jackson

Columbia

Stanley

6

93

95

4

Columbia River

5

To Invermere

1. Sinclair Canyon
2. Radium Hot Springs Pools
3. Park gate (1.3 km from 93/95 junction)
4. Springs Golf Course
5. Resort Golf Course
6. Kootenay Park Administration
7. Redstreak Campground

NOT TO SCALE
© 2006 HUNTER PUBLISHING, INC.

■ Village of Radium Hot Springs

Just outside the park's west (southwest) boundary – and not bound by strict National Park regulations – Radium Hot Springs, population 705, is a resort town that boasts a wide array of commercial services with many types of accommodations and restaurants.

INVERMERE – SMALL-TOWN CHARM

The mountain resort town of Invermere (only 16 km/ 10 miles south of Radium Hot Springs), population 3,000, is considered the economic hub of the Columbia Valley. It sits on the northwest shore of popular Lake Windermere, and summer visitors enjoy its sandy beaches, swimming, boating and fishing; ice-fishing, cross-country skiing and skating are winter pleasures. History buffs will enjoy the Windermere Valley Museum and the town's historical walk. Artists have flocked to the area, helping create a vibrant atmosphere. The Pynelogs Cultural Center sells the work of local artists and offers art classes. Invermere offers myriad visitor services, with unique shops and restaurants as well as recreational opportunities, making it a fun side-trip from Kootenay National Park.

Kootenay National Park Visitor Information Center, ☎ 250-347-9505 (mid-May to mid-October), kootenay.reception@pc.gc.ca.

Radium Hot Springs Chamber of Commerce Visitor Information Center, ☎ 800-347-9704 or 250-347-9331, info@radiumhotspringschamber.ca.

On the corner of Main Street East and Redstreak Campground Road in the village of Radium Hot Springs, the Center offers seasonal (summer and fall) Parks Canada information services and year-round Chamber of Commerce information services, as well as a Friends of Kootenay National Park gift shop. Operating hours fluctuate during the off-season so you may want to call ahead to confirm. Operating Hours: May to

Kootenay National Park

early September, 9 am to 7 pm; early September to October, 9 am to 5 pm; October to May, closed Sundays and Mondays, 9 am to 5 pm.

There is a privately operated **Visitor Information Center** at the **Kootenay Park Lodge General Store**, located along Highway 93 at Vermilion Crossing, 42 km (26 miles) south of the Trans Canada Highway Junction. Open mid-May to mid-October, the Center houses informative interpretive displays (no telephone).

Friends of Kootenay National Park

Friends of Kootenay National Park Association is a non-profit organization that "promotes awareness and appreciation of the cultural and natural history of Kootenay National Park and its surrounding ecosystem." The Friends operate a gift shop inside the Radium Visitor Center. Summer activities include special presentations, historical and heritage walks, Parks Day/Visitor Appreciation Day events, hiking tours and the Junior Naturalist Program at Redstreak Campground and Invermere. ☎ 250-347-6525, www.friendsofkootenay.bc.ca.

■ Attractions

Radium Hot Springs Pools, ☎ 250-347-9485, along Highway 93 at the base of Sinclair Canyon, three km (1.8 miles) east of the village of Radium Hot Springs or one km inside Kootenay National Park's west gate. Of the three Canadian Rockies hot springs, Radium is my favorite. The two open-air pools nestled among the rock cliffs of Sinclair Canyon are less busy and more spacious than the others. With four sources of hot water emerging from the canyon of Sinclair Creek beneath the pools, the water is 44°C (114°F) and is chlorinated and cooled to a comfortable 39°C (103°F) in the hot pool. Kids love the cool pool – at 29°C (84°F) and from one to three metres (three to 10 feet) deep, it's great for diving, swimming laps and splashing about.

Radium Hot Springs is named because of small traces of radon in the water. Although the amount of radioactivity is harmless, it's interesting to note that these springs are the most radioactive of any hot springs in Canada and among the most radioactive in North America.

The springs are open year-round (except Christmas Day), daily 9 am to 11 pm from early May to mid-October and from mid-October to early May, Sunday through Thursday 12 pm to 9 pm, Friday and Saturday 12 pm to 10 pm. Single admission is $6.50 adult, $5.50 child or senior; family rates available. If you are only stopping in the park to use the hot springs, a park user fee is included in the admission price.

Visitors can enjoy the poolside café, the picnic areas and nature trails around the springs complex and watch for bighorn sheep that make Sinclair Canyon home.

Pleiades Massage and Spa at the Radium Hot Springs Pool is eastern BC's largest day spa. Certified therapists offer aromatherapy, facials, massage, Shiatsu, reflexology, hot stone and Reiki treatments. Appointments are recommended, ☎ 250-347-2100.

Fairmont Hot Springs, ☎ 800-663-4979 or 250-345-6311, at Fairmont Hot Springs Resort (see *Where to Stay* section), is 44 km (27 miles) south of the village of Radium Hot Springs along Highway 93/95, then two km (1.2 miles) east to the parking lot

Nestled at the base of the Rockies, Fairmont's developed hot springs complex includes a large public outdoor pool with three sections: a hot soaking pool kept at about 39°C (102°F) and a swimming pool kept at 30°C (86°F) with a semi-detached diving pool at one end. The pools are open year-round from 8 am to 10 pm daily. Rates are $6.78 adult, $6.31 youth (13-17 years) and senior (65+ years), $4.91 child (four-12 years). Day- and five-day passes are available.

My two favorite reasons to visit Fairmont are the historic bathhouses, as well as the natural pools under the waterfall. You can reach them by a short drive from Kootenay National Park; they are always open and are free of charge. The **Historical Baths**, formerly called the Indian Baths, are on a tufa knoll on the left, just before entering the pool parking lot.

(Tufa is porous calcium carbonate deposited by many hot springs, often forming extensive layers.) There are three little bathhouses, with water piped into small cement bathtubs in the houses, each at a different temperature from cool to hot.

My other favorite spot is behind the public pools. If you've never been to an undeveloped spring, you're in for a wonderful surprise. Walk across the bridge into the RV Park and follow the trail along the creek down the canyon to the **waterfall and natural pools** formed by overflow from the main pools above. The springs coat the rocks with tufa and colorful algae, adding visual appeal to the "natural" setting. Although this warm water flows from the pools, here you can better imagine what a welcome diversion soaking in natural springs was for early Aboriginal people and explorers in the Rockies.

SUNSET AT FAIRMONT

After spending a delightful leisurely afternoon soaking in the natural pools at Fairmont, it was time to hit the road so we could find a campground, make dinner and settle in for the evening. But when we walked back to our van and discovered the keys missing, our spirits sank. How could this be? After much discussion we came to the conclusion that the keys must have fallen out of bathing suit pockets while we were splashing about. We had no choice but to walk back to the pools and begin a search. None of the few remaining people still soaking had found keys, so we began to look everywhere. The pools are fairly shallow but there are a number of them. Late afternoon turned to early evening and I was getting tired but, despite my gloomy outlook, 11-year-old Oliver seemed to be enjoying our predicament. When I offered him a reward for finding the keys, he became more determined than ever. "They're probably under the waterfall," he suggested, as he repeatedly dove under the churning water. Just when I was ready to give up, Oliver surfaced with keys in hand. We congratulated him on his perseverance and diving skill and he was quick to remind me that a reward was due.

After changing into dry clothes we pulled out of the parking lot and immediately realized that we had more cause to celebrate before leaving Fairmont. The hot springs are set on a bench on the east side of the valley, high above the Columbia River. A spectacular sunset draped the distant mountains in radiance as we drove away and Oliver asked, "Can we come back tomorrow?"

■ Shopping

 If you've got a hankering to lighten the load on your pocketbook or give your credit card a workout, the town of **Invermere**, 10 minutes south of Radium Hot Springs, is the place to do it. With a thriving artistic community, Invermere offers an eclectic selection of galleries, working studios and shops. You can spend a leisurely day browsing about the art galleries, pottery studios, a glass blowing studio as well as antique shops, outdoor equipment and clothing stores, giftware boutiques and more. Many shops operate seasonally, so call ahead for current operating hours. You won't want to miss:

The Artym Gallery, 934 7th Avenue, Invermere, ☎ 250-342-7566, www.artymgallery.com. Original paintings, sculpture, glass and raku by over 50 Canadian artists. Demonstrations held throughout the summer. Shipping worldwide. Open 10 am to 5:30 pm Monday to Saturday, 12 pm to 4 pm Sunday.

The Blue Rooster Pottery, 402 12th Avenue, Invermere, ☎ 250-342-0526, www.blueroosterpottery.ca. A working pottery studio featuring handcrafted functional ware using the Maiolica technique of decorating. Open May through early September, Tuesday to Saturday 11 am to 5 pm.

Bavin Glassworks, across from the Invermere Airport, ☎ 250-342-6816, www.bavinglass.com. One-of-a-kind handblown glass creations. Weekly demonstrations from March to October with the public always welcome to watch the glassblowers at work. Items packaged for travel. Open mid-February to December.

■ Where to Eat

Kootenay Park Lodge, ☎ 403-762-9196, along Highway 93 at Vermilion Crossing, 42 km (26 miles) south of the Trans Canada Highway Junction, $ to $$. The lodge's dining room offers fresh home-style food for breakfast, lunch or dinner at very reasonable prices in comfortable rustic surroundings. Open mid-May through September.

DINING PRICE CHART	
Price per person in Canadian $ for an entrée, not including beverage, tax or tip.	
$	Under $10
$$	$10-$25
$$$	Over $25

The Village of Radium Hot Springs and the Columbia Valley have a huge array of dining choices. There are many Austrian- and European-style establishments that offer casual fine dining, family-style restaurants, pubs, bakeries, ice-cream shops and cozy specialty coffee shops.

Groceries are available at **Mountainside Market** on Main Street in Radium Hot Springs and at **AG Valley Foods** on 7th Avenue in Invermere.

Locals recommend the following:

Helna's Stube, ☎ 250-347-0047, 7547 Main Street West, $$ to $$$. "Stube" is a German word meaning a warm cozy place – a fitting moniker for this restaurant known for its authentic Austrian cuisine, including scrumptious desserts. Soups, salads, house specialties, venison, lamb, beef, chicken and turkey, steaks, seafood and vegetarian dishes. Open for dinner only from 5 to 10 pm. Closed in January and on Tuesdays and Wednesdays from fall through spring. Reservations recommended during the summer.

Horsethief Creek Pub & Eatery, ☎ 250-347-6400, Main Street East, $$. A casual, friendly pub featuring a Western/Canadian menu with over 90 items, including appetizers, soups, burgers, pasta, salads, sandwiches, steak, chicken, ribs, seafood, and dessert. Meals are tastefully prepared and portions are generous. Open for breakfast, lunch and dinner (kitchen open late), with air conditioning and a patio.

Portabella, ☎ 250-342-0606, 13th Street off Main in downtown Invermere, $$ to $$$. Casual, relaxed fine dining in a Mediterranean atmosphere. Gourmet ethnic cuisine featuring soups, salads and steaks. Open for dinner 5 pm to 10 pm, with patio dining available. Reservations recommended. Open year-round, closed Mondays.

Quality Bakery, ☎ 888-681-9977 or 250-342-9913, downtown Invermere – the place with the pretzel on top. It's not often you come across a bakery where you can watch the baker work while you enjoy a specialty coffee and Swiss pastry. With a huge selection of high-quality healthy baked goods, using organic flour and no artificial additives or preservatives, this is a mandatory stop when I visit the Columbia Valley. They offer breads, including wood-fired oven specialty loaves, pastries, cakes, pies, cookies and a selection of imported products. Best-selling homemade chocolate bars include almond cranberry, kick ass café and rum raisin. See www.healthybread.com for information including mail order.

■ Where to Stay

Resorts, Hotels & Motels

Kootenay Park Lodge, ☎ 403-762-9196 or 403-283-7482, www.kootenayparklodge.com, $$ to $$$. This lodge gets my vote for authentic heritage-style Canadian Rockies cabin accommodations at a reasonable price. Set along Highway 93 at Vermilion Crossing in the heart of Kootenay National Park (42 km or 26 miles south of the Trans Canada Highway Junction), it is the only accommodation available in the heart of the park, other than camping. Opened by the Canadian Pacific Railway in 1923 (known as Vermilion River Camp), the rustic main lodge is most welcoming, with a fireplace, big comfy couch and a library. Also in the main lodge, the acclaimed dining room (see *Where to Eat* section) serves home-style meals. Accommodations are in 10 cabins (book well in advance), some with fireplace, kitchen, hotplate or microwave, and some with separate bedrooms. All cabins have bar-sized refrigerators and coffee makers. Pets welcome. Open mid-May through September. The adjacent General

Store sells snacks, souvenirs and gift items, also providing laundry facilities and a Tourism Information Center.

I highly recommend Kootenay Park Lodge as an ideal place to stay while you explore the park, or to just curl up with a good book in front of the fireplace.

The Matterhorn of the Rockies

 Approximately 2½ km (1½ miles) south of Vermilion Crossing is a pullout on the east side of the highway. This is the only area along the parkway where, on a clear day, if you look to the southeast, you can see the tip of Mount Assiniboine – the sixth-highest peak in the Canadian Rockies.

Nipika Mountain Resort, ☎ 877-647-4525 or 250-342-6516, www.nipika.com, $$$$ to $$$$$. This eco-lodge is 14 km (8.7 miles) down Settlers Road, 32 km (20 miles) from Radium Hot Springs, bordering Kootenay National Park and the Kootenay River. Accommodations include rooms for groups of up to 13 guests in the main lodge, with shared bathrooms, a great room, fireplace, full kitchen and dining area (catering is available to groups but there is no restaurant). Cabins that sleep from two to eight are well appointed, with fully equipped kitchen, fireplace, deck and barbecue. Guests are encouraged to enjoy the over 50 km (31 miles) of maintained hiking or cross-country ski trails on their own or for a fee you can participate in programs and activities that include cross-country ski lessons, snowshoe tours, kayak and canoe tours, guided day-hikes and whitewater

HOTEL PRICE CHART	
Reflects the price of an average room for two in Canadian $, May-Sept. Rates lower rest of year (except Christmas and New Year's).	
$	Under $50
$$	$50-$100
$$$	$101-$150
$$$$	$151-$250
$$$$$	Over $250

rafting. (Hikes visit the provincial parks of Height of the Rockies and Mt. Assiniboine.) They have a hot tub, sauna, swimming/skating pond and bicycle and ski rentals. For the equine types, horse boarding is available. One cabin is wheelchair-accessible. Pets welcome. Minimum two-night stay.

Radium Hot Springs Lodge, ☎ 888-222-9341 or 250-347-9341, www.radiumhotspringslodge.com, $$$ to $$$$. Overlooking the Radium Hot Springs pools on the fringe of Kootenay National Park, this lodge is more aptly described as a hotel/motel. Very clean and quiet pool-view or valley-view rooms, as well as executive suites. They also have a hot tub, sauna and games room.

 One of the first things you'll notice about the village of Radium Hot Springs and the Columbia Valley is that the area offers a huge array of accommodations. You'll find B&Bs, condo rentals, resorts, hotels, motels and more motels. More than 30 motels/hotels provide nearly 1,000 rooms in the village of Radium Hot Springs alone. (Be wary of accommodations located along noisy Highway 93/95.)

The **Radium Hot Springs Chamber of Commerce** website provides a list of places to stay in the area, www.radiumhotsprings.com, and the **Visitor Information Center** provides a list of the same.

Chalet Europe, ☎ 888-428-9998 or 250-347-9305, www.chaleteurope.com, $$ to $$$. (Not only does the Chalet Europe website provide information about the facility, it also provides helpful information about the area.) High above the village of Radium Hot Springs, overlooking the valley, this quiet hotel offers excellent views, with telescopes in their corner rooms to enjoy the panoramas. It's a family-operated business. The owner went out of her way to show me around and provide details of the area. Helping plan your vacation in the region is one of the many "extras" offered here, including fresh-baked muffins. There is an exercise room, games room, hot tub, sauna, laundry facilities, barbecue area. Rooms include a fireplace, kitchenette and Internet data port, as well as private balconies. Wheelchair-accessible suites and pet-friendly suites. Hiking trails are nearby, with a three-km (1.8-mile) hike to the hot springs pools. Rates include continental breakfast; special rates for extended stays, wellness spa packages, ski and stay specials and more.

Radium Resort, ☎ 800-667-6444 or 250-347-9311, www.radiumresort.com, $$$ to $$$$. A golfer's paradise featuring two courses, a golf academy and practice facilities, with course-side hotel accommodations. Dining room and lounge, health and fitness center, indoor pool, hot tubs and sauna, racquetball, squash and tennis courts. Golf and accommodation packages available.

Fairmont Hot Springs Resort, ☎ 800-663-4979 or 250-345-6311, www.fairmonthotsprings.com, $$$$ to $$$$$. This is a large and popular hot springs resort. Located 44 km (27 miles) south of the village of Radium Hot Springs along Highway 95, then two km (1.2 miles) east to the parking lot. Aside from the hot spring pools, including a private hot soaking pool for hotel guests, there are three golf courses, tennis courts, a family alpine ski area and cross-country ski trails, a spa facility, two boutiques and award-winning dining. Scheduled recreation activities for adults and children include hiking, yoga, entertainment shows, mini-golf, arts and crafts, lawn games, pool playtime and more. Pool-view or mountain-view rooms, with kitchenettes, lofts, suites or cottages available. Hotel guests enjoy free unlimited access to the hot springs pools. Romance, spa, golf and multi-day packages are available. Wheelchair-accessible.

Camping

There are four campgrounds in the park that provide a total of over 400 sites. All campgrounds include a wheelchair-accessible washroom. All sites are available on a first-come, first-served basis. Redstreak Campground now accepts reservations – see www.pccamping.ca for the **Parks Canada Campground Reservation Service**, or call ☎ 877-737-3783, international ☎ 905-426-4648.

Campsites in Kootenay National Park

Marble Canyon. Set 17 km (10½ miles) south of the Trans Canada Highway Junction or 86.7 km (53.8 miles) north of Radium Hot Springs; 61 unserviced sites; $$. Kitchen shelters, with stoves, fire pits and firewood, food storage, sani-dump. Close to the Vermilion River and the self-guided interpretive trail along Marble Canyon. This uncrowded (almost deserted when I was camping in mid-summer) campground is a great base for exploring Kootenay Park as well as Banff and Lake Louise. Open from the end of June to early September.

Dolly Varden (Winter). Located 36 km (22 miles) north of the village of Radium Hot Springs near Dolly Varden Creek; seven unserviced sites for winter camping only; $$. Drive-through sites and kitchen shelters. Open from mid-September to mid-May.

McLeod Meadows. This one is 27 km (17 miles) north of Radium Hot Springs along the Kootenay River; 98 well-treed and spacious unserviced sites; $$. Campground hosts, kitchen shelters, fire pits and firewood, food storage, sani-dump. This scenic campground is typically quiet and rarely full. A 2.6-km (1.6-mile) trail leads to Dog Lake. Open from the end of May to mid-September.

Redstreak. Set 2½ km (1½ miles) above the village of Radium Hot Springs (turn next to the Visitor Information Center); 242 sites, with 50 full hook-ups and 38 electrical serviced sites; $$ to $$$. Showers, kitchen shelters, food storage, fire pits and firewood, sani-dump, playgrounds, interpretive programs. A 1.8-km (1.1-mile) trail leads to the village and a 2.7-km (1.7-mile) trail goes to the hot spring pools. This is the largest, busiest and only serviced campground in the park. Open early May to mid-October.

Campgrounds in the Columbia Valley

The **Radium Hot Springs Chamber of Commerce** website provides a list of campgrounds and RV parks in the area, www.radiumhotsprings.com, as does the **Visitor Information Center**.

Dry Gulch Provincial Campground. 4½ km (2.8 miles) south of Radium Hot Springs off Highway 93/95; 26 shaded and typically quiet, basic vehicle/tent sites; $$. Facilities include washrooms, fire pits and firewood, water and some wheelchair-accessible sites. Often used as an overflow campground for Kootenay National Park. First-come, first-served –

CAMPING/HOSTELS	
Rates in Canadian $, not including taxes.	
$	Under $13
$$	$13-$22
$$$	$23-$30
$$$$	Over $30

reservations not accepted. Open May through October.

The Canyon RV Resort on Sinclair Creek, ☎ 250-347-9564, www.canyonrv.com, $$$ to $$$$. On Sinclair Creek Road in Radium Hot Springs. Full-service deluxe RV pads and grassy tent sites; washrooms, with showers, laundry facilities, fire pits and firewood, sani-dump, playgrounds; pets permitted. Reservations taken from March 1st for the coming season; book well in advance, especially for long weekends.

Fairmont Hot Springs Resort, ☎ 800-663-4979 or 250-345-6311, www.fairmonthotsprings.com, $$$ to $$$$. Located 44 km (27 miles) south of the village of Radium Hot Springs along Highway 95, then two km (1.2 miles) east to the parking lot. This large recreation vehicle park offers paved full-service sites but little in the way of privacy or an authentic camping experience. Washrooms with showers, laundry facilities, sani-dump, central fire pit, covered pavilion and playground. Pets permitted; tents not permitted. (See also *Attractions* and *Where to Stay* sections.)

Backcountry Camping

 Be sure to get a copy of the *Kootenay National Park Backcountry Guide* from the Visitor Information Center. The brochure explains basic information about planning your trip; safety issues; trail descriptions for short hikes, day-hikes, multi-day hikes; and a map.

Park staff at the Visitor Center can help you plan your backcountry trip. If you are planning an overnight trip, you

Above: Blakiston Falls, Waterton Lakes (© Lenard Sanders)

Mule deer, Waterton Lakes National Park (© Lenard Sanders)

Above: Crypt Lake Tunnel, Waterton Lakes

Prince of Wales Hotel, Upper Waterton Lake (© Lenard Sanders)

must purchase a wilderness pass ($9 per night, $63 per season), available from Parks Canada Visitor Information Centers. Contact a Visitor Information Center prior to your departure for current trail conditions, closures and other important information. Campfires are allowed only at campsites where fireboxes are provided.

Backcountry campgrounds are located at **Kaufmann Lake**, **Helmet/Ochre Junction**, **Helmet Falls**, **Tumbling Creek**, **Numa Creek**, **Floe Lake** and **Verdant Creek**. Some campsites can be reserved three months in advance of your first day of stay. A $12 non-refundable fee applies. Call ☎ 250-347-9505 June to September and ☎ 250-403-522-1264 September to May.

The Alpine Club of Canada operated the Fay Hut, which was near the northern park boundary, but it was destroyed by the 2003 fire. The ACC plans to rebuild the hut. Contact the ACC for information, www.alpineclubofcanada.ca.

FLORA IN KOOTENAY NATIONAL PARK

Canada's Rocky Mountain Parks are ablaze with a mosaic of wildflowers in mid-summer. Did you know that there are 22 species of orchids in Kootenay National Park? Early summer is the best time to enjoy them. Bring along your field guide and look in damp areas for varieties such as white bog, pink calypso and the less common mountain lady's slippers. Look and smell, but remember not to disturb or pick them. In the arid habitat of the southern Rocky Mountain Trench from Radium south is the prickly pear cactus, with its showy yellowy pink flowers. Look for it just inside the southwest boundary of the park.

Kootenay National Park

Hosteling

Radium Hot Springs International Hostel (Misty River Lodge), ☎ 250-347-9912, www.radiumhostel.bc.ca. On the boundary between Kootenay National Park and the village of Radium Hot Springs on Highway 93 (near the park gate), this is an independent hostel but the owners offer discounts with "Hosteling International" cards, "Pacific Hostels" coupons or "ISIC" (student) cards. Dorm beds $$; private and family rooms also available. Kitchen facilities, bicycle storage and rental, canoe rental; lounge area with reference books, large deck with barbecue and great views.

■ Wildlife

 Elk, moose, bighorn sheep and bears often feed alongside Highway 93. Mountain goats can sometimes be seen at a mineral lick at Mount Wardle along the parkway, 48 km (30 miles) north of Radium (one km north of the Hector Gorge Viewpoint). In the fall, winter and spring, bighorn sheep can be found in village of Radium Hot Springs – the bighorn sheep capital of BC.

There are many excellent birding locations in Kootenay National Park and the Columbia River Valley. The valley's lakes, ponds, marshes, grasslands, forest and alpine tundra provide habitats to over 265 bird species, including trumpeter swans, gulls, bitterns, herons, hawks, bald eagles, loons, terns and over 100 songbird species. The **Wings Over the Rockies** website, www.adventurevalley.com/wings (see also *Special Events* section), provides useful information for birders.

■ Adventures

 If you are planning to do any hiking, backpacking or biking on Kootenay Park's trails, be sure to stop by or call the Visitor Information Center for the latest trail information and safety reports and pick up a copy of the *Kootenay National Park Backcountry Guide*.

Kootenay National Park offers 200 km (124 miles) of hiking trails. The **Columbia Valley** is a popular destination for hikers. In the village of Radium Hot Springs there are easy walking trails from the Visitor Information Center to **Redstreak Campground** and to the hot springs pools as well as the **Juniper Trail** along **Sinclair Canyon**. The Radium Hot Springs Chamber of Commerce and Visitor Information Center can provide information on easy, moderate and difficult day and backpacking hikes throughout the valley.

Tour Operators

Columbia River Outfitters, ☎ 250-342-7397, Invermere, www.adventurevalley.com/cro. Canoe and kayak rentals as well as self-guided tours along Lake Windermere and the Columbia River Wetlands from mid-May to October. Frequently sighted bird species include eagles, ospreys and blue herons, not to mention beavers, otters and turtles. Self-guided half-day (three hours), $65 canoe, $45 kayak, $75 double kayak; shuttle service included. Canoe and single kayak rentals $38 half-day, $48 full day; double kayak $55 half-day, $70 full day.

White Mountain Adventures, ☎ 800-408-0005 or 403-678-4099, www.whitemountainadventures.com.

◆ **Premier Guide Service** – Don't want to head out on the trails alone? Hire an experienced and knowledgeable guide/interpreter, available daily throughout the year. Half-day $270, full day $390 (transportation available at additional cost).

◆ **Rockwall Highline** – Eight days hiking along Kootenay Park's famous high route. $1,100 per person.

Horseback Riding

 **Diamond B Outfitting Adventures on Horseback**, ☎ 250-342-5128, at Fairmont Hot Springs Resort. Trail rides through the Stanford Range in the Rocky Mountains; one hour $30 or two-hour rides, $55. Three-hour cookout ride includes a one-hour trail ride and a horse-drawn wagon ride, $50; one-hour wagon ride cookout, $35. Open from Easter to Canadian Thanksgiving.

Whitewater Rafting

Kootenay River Runners, ☎ 800-599-4399 or 250-347-9210, office one km west of the Kootenay National Park west gate, www.rafting-therockies.com. Challenging whitewater and family rafting or Voyageur canoe trips on the Kicking Horse, Kootenay and Columbia Rivers as well as Toby Creek. Transportation is available to the Kicking Horse River from Radium Hot Springs ($15).

◆ **Kicking Horse Upper River** – Some of the best whitewater in the Canadian Rockies. Trip starts at base camp near the border of Yoho National Park, with a 20-km (12-mile) ride down the river. Children must be minimum 12 years and weigh a minimum of 40 kg (90 lbs). Departures at 9:30 am and 12 pm daily, $88 or $95 with barbecue.

◆ **Kicking Horse Upper and Lower** – As above, but stay aboard for the extra excitement of the Lower Canyon, with Class 4 rapids. $140 with barbecue.

◆ **Kootenay River** – Experience Class 2 and 3 rapids on this family-oriented trip down the more spirited stretches of the Kootenay. Includes a morning snack and a riverside buffet lunch. Full-day trip departs 9 am daily, returns by 5 pm, $90 adult, $74 children 14 years and under. Half-day trip includes brunch and returns by 1:30 pm, $64 adult, $49 child.

◆ **Toby Creek** – The Toby Creek trip is based out of Panorama Mountain Village (see *Skiing* section) in the Purcell Mountains. Two hours on this Class 1 to 3 river is suitable for first-time rafters with a minimum age of eight years. $49 adult, $39 child.

◆ **Voyageur Canoe Float Trips** – Paddle along the scenic Columbia River wetlands in a 10-m (34-foot) Voyageur Canoe while enjoying stories of the historic fur traders. Allow 2½ hours, $49 adult, $35 child.

Boating & Fishing

 Kootenay National Park is not a renowned location for anglers, although good things come to all those with a little patience. Non-motorized watercraft are permitted on all lakes and rivers in the park. The Kootenay and Vermilion Rivers are considered to be the only easily accessible waters but are suitable for experienced paddlers only. Ask at the Visitor Information Center for suitable put-in and take-out points.

The Columbia Valley offers a wide range of fishing opportunities, with rainbow trout the dominant fish species; talk to anglers at local sporting goods stores for the best advice.

The Columbia River (between Invermere and Golden) is suitable for novice paddlers, offering beautiful day paddles, with plenty of opportunity to spot birds and wildlife. There are also numerous small lakes that offer serene paddles. Lake Windermere is popular with all types of boaters, in kayaks and canoes, powerboats and sailboats. In attempts to catch trout and ling in winter, ice-fishing huts dot the lake.

Mountain Biking & Bicycle Touring

 Former fire roads have been converted to mountain biking trails in Kootenay National Park. These are the only trails in the park where mountain biking is permitted. Ask for information and a map at the Visitor Information Center as well as information about popular mountain bike routes outside the park.

The "Golden Triangle" is a 310-km (193-mile) loop encompassing Radium Hot Springs, Golden and Lake Louise that requires a minimum of three days to cycle. This bicycle tour passes through Kootenay, Yoho and Banff National Parks in the valleys of the Columbia, Kicking Horse, Bow and Kootenay rivers and crosses the Great Divide twice. You can begin at any point on the triangle or from the town of Banff, but it is an extra 30 km (19 miles) each way from Banff townsite to Castle Junction on the Bow Valley Parkway. You can travel either clockwise or counter-clockwise; the two passes, Kicking Horse and Vermilion, are at about the same elevation but require a climb of more than 500 m (1,640 feet)

from the BC side, so take your pick as to which one you want to coast along and which one you will climb. The easiest section, albeit with narrow shoulders, is the 105-km (65-mile) stretch along the Columbia River between Radium and Golden. About two-thirds of the highways have wide paved shoulders. Be prepared for some long hills and fast-moving traffic, especially along the Trans Canada Highway between Golden and Field. There are a number of lodging and camping opportunities along the route. The only store to purchase food and supplies in Kootenay Park is at Vermilion Crossing. The Golden Triangle is one of Canada's premier road cycling tours. For more information on this incredible bicycle route, see www.canadatrails.ca/biking/bc/goldentriangle.html.

Drives, Sights, Activities & Hikes

The following are listed traveling north to south:

Continental Divide, Vermilion Pass & the Fireweed Trail

 Ten kilometres (six miles) from the Trans Canada Highway at an elevation of 1,651 m (5,415 feet) is Vermilion Pass, the dividing line between Pacific and Atlantic watersheds and between Banff and Kootenay National Parks. The Fireweed Trail is a 15-minute (.8-km/.5-mile) wheelchair-accessible interpretive loop through a portion of the Vermilion Pass burn of 1968. This interpretive trail provides an excellent example of the ecological importance of forest fires.

 Don't confuse Vermilion Pass with Vermilion Crossing, which is 30.7 km or 19 miles farther south along the parkway.

Stanley Glacier

Hike: 11.2 km (6.9 miles) round-trip.

Elevation gain: 484 m (1,587 feet).

Watchable wildlife: Hoary marmots, pikas, ptarmigans, moose.

This is considered the nicest day-hike in the park and is also a suitable early summer or rainy day hike. The trailhead parking area is on the southeast side of the highway, approximately 3.2 km (two miles) south of Vermilion Pass.

The fires of 1968 and 2003 showed no mercy along this trail, but the hike through the wildflower-filled blackened forest – a photographic gem – reaches only mid-way to Stanley Glacier, at the head of a rockbound hanging valley.

Cross the Vermilion River Bridge and switchback along the trail up through the burn. At km 2.4 (mile 1½) the trail crosses a bridge and enters the valley. Follow Stanley Creek upstream and ascend a rocky slope into the heart of the valley. Here you can view the entire boulder-strewn basin including Stanley Glacier and the many waterfalls cascading down Stanley Peak. Most impressive are the massive limestone cliffs that make one feel rather insignificant in the scheme of things. Continue to ascend the talus, following a faint trail and cairns to a plateau at the head of the valley for outstanding views back down the U-shaped glacial valley below.

Marble Canyon

The Marble Canyon Trail is a .8-km one-way (.5-mile) interpretive trail that criss-crosses the narrow limestone and dolomite gorge of Marble Canyon, ending at the waterfall of Tokumm Creek. Use extreme caution in the canyon – deaths have occurred here!

The parking lot is 17.2 km (10.7 miles) south of the Trans Canada Highway or .2 km south of the Marble Canyon Campground.

Paint Pots

Be sure not to miss this unique interpretive trail, 19.7 km (12.2 miles) south of the Trans Canada Highway. An easy one-km (.6-mile) walk from the parking lot leads to three pots or ochre beds (cold mineral springs), that are rich in iron oxide, staining the earth a beautiful deep ochre color. Using fire, Aboriginal people converted the liquid ochre into red oxide pigments. At the turn of the century the ochre was dug by hand, sacked and hauled by horse-drawn wagons to the Canadian Pacific Railway, where it was shipped to Calgary for use as a pigment base for paint. Mineral claims still existed in the area when Kootenay National Park was conceived in 1916.

Kootenay National Park

Just beyond the suspension bridge over the Vermilion River, a 2.7-km (1.7-mile) trail on the right leads to Marble Canyon. The trail is wheelchair-accessible to the ochre beds only but continues as an extensive network of trails and backcountry campgrounds.

Sinclair Canyon

Sinclair Canyon is a dramatic exit or entrance – depending on which way you are traveling – to Kootenay National Park. Just inside the park's west gate, it is the only highway tunnel in the Canadian Rockies. The limestone and dolomite cliffs of the Redwall Fault have been stained by iron oxides in the mineral waters, which are the source of the water at Radium Hot Springs pools. (The iron oxide originated when the frag-mented and reconsolidated rock, known as breccia, was formed by intense tectonic activity.)

You can stop at the roadside parking area (pool overflow park-ing) and follow nature trails along the side of the canyon, including a .3-km trail along Sinclair Creek to the hot springs main parking area and entrance. On a hot day this shaded trail is particularly satisfying.

PICNICKING ALONG THE PARKWAY

Planning a picnic along the parkway? (Say that fast three times!) You won't be disappointed as there are many sites to choose from. A few good picnic areas along the Kootenay Parkway include:

- **Numa Creek** – 24½ km (15.2 miles) from the Trans Canada Highway, 79½ km (49½ miles) from Radium. Beside the Vermilion River, with the Numa Falls a short walk from the parking lot.

- **Vermilion Crossing** – 42 km (26 miles) from the Trans Canada Highway, 62 km (38½ miles) from Radium. Picnic tables, a playground, a store and Visitor Information Center make this a good spot for families to stop (if you forgot your picnic, try the restaurant in Kootenay Park Lodge). Across the highway is another picnic area, com-plete with shelter and wood stove.

- **McLeod Meadows** – 77½ km (48 miles) from the Trans Canada Highway, 26½ km (16½ miles) from Radium. This picnic area is separated from McLeod Meadows Campground by an open meadow. In the summer you'll probably have Columbian ground squirrels for company. A shelter with a wood stove makes this is a good rainy day spot.

- **Olive Lake** – 92 km (57 miles) from the Trans Canada Highway, 12 km (7½ miles) from Radium. At the summit of Sinclair Pass (1,486 m/4,875 feet), a short trail leads to a pretty emerald-green lake nestled in the forest. Archaeological evidence indicates that Olive Lake was a camping spot for Aboriginal peoples 11,000 years ago. Displays, fish-viewing deck and wheelchair accessibility along the .5 km round-trip trail and boardwalk.

A Golfer's Mecca: Of the many links throughout the Canadian Rockies, the Columbia Valley is known for its concentration of golf courses for every skill level. A total of 14 courses – all with gorgeous mountain backdrops and within minutes of each other – typically operate from mid-March to November. Where else in March can you take in some skiing in the morning and follow it with a round of afternoon golf?

Winter Adventures

Skiing

Panorama Mountain Village, ☎ 800-663-2929 or 250-342-6941, www.skipanorama.com. Nestled on the Purcell Mountains 18 km (11 miles) west of Invermere and framed by the Canadian Rockies, Panorama Mountain Village is a four-season resort that offers myriad activities, foremost of which is skiing. With 1,220 vertical m (4,000 feet) – the most in the Canadian Rockies region – along with 3,000 acres of patrolled skiing and snowboarding terrain, Panorama is one of the premier resorts in British Columbia. More than 100 runs are broken down into 15% beginner, 55% intermediate and 30% expert, serviced by 10 lifts, including new quad chairs. The hill has hosted World Cup Downhill racing and is a training facility for national teams from around the world. Lift rates: $59 adult, $54 teen or senior, $27 junior, $12 child (six or under). Multi-day tickets are available.

The **Beckie Scott Nordic Center** features more than 30 km (18 miles) of groomed trails, along with a clubhouse and equipment rentals.

Summer activities at the village include an 18-hole golf course, mountain biking, horseback riding, whitewater rafting, hiking, and a water park.

Panorama Mountain Village has accommodations for 1,500 people, six year-round dining facilities (12 in winter), a general store and liquor store, childcare, equipment rentals and repair, a world-class ski school, a spa, "slope-side hot pools" and more.

Fairmont Ski Hill (see also *Attractions* and *Where to Stay* sections). Four km (2½ miles) beyond the Hot Springs Resort, this hill provides family skiing and snowboarding, as well as cross-country ski trails. Two lifts service 14 runs (60% intermediate) on 304 m (1,000 feet) of vertical. A cafeteria, lounge, ski school and equipment rentals are offered and you can ski out to the hotel.

■ Scenic Must-See's

Suggestions for the first-time summer visitor on a four-day schedule.

◆ **Day 1** – Hiking into the **Stanley Glacier Cirque** and visiting the historic **Paint Pots** are classic Kootenay Park recreational activities that will not disappoint.

◆ **Day 2** – Take at least one full day to travel at a leisurely pace along the parkway. Enjoy the various viewpoints and stops of interest. Bring a picnic lunch to enjoy at one of the many scenic picnic areas.

◆ **Day 3** – Visit Kootenay's most popular attraction, the **pools at Radium Hot Springs**. If you're fortunate, you might spot bighorn sheep on the cliffs of Sinclair Canyon while you're soaking. Explore the artsy resort town of **Invermere**.

◆ **Day 4** – A **Voyageur canoe float trip** along the Columbia River wetlands is an ideal way to spend a sunny morning or rent a kayak or canoe for a self-guided paddle. After lunch visit the historic baths and natural pools at **Fairmont**.

■ To Do List

Next time I visit Kootenay National Park I would like to . . .

Backpack to The Rockwall. The Rockwall is Kootenay Park's most renowned hiking area and one of the finest backcountry destinations in the Canadian Rockies. One of the most prominent features of the Vermilion Range, glimpses of the 50-km-long (31-mile) massive limestone wall are visible to the west from Highway 93 between Vermilion Crossing and the Paint Pots. But seeing The Rockwell up close is worth the grunt. The trail passes through meadows and larch forests, high alpine passes, beneath hanging glaciers and along lakes and waterfalls, including **Helmet Falls** (350 m/1,148 feet), Kootenay's highest waterfall.

A number of valleys lead to The Rockwall with well-maintained trails providing access on the long approaches. The **Floe Lake trailhead**, 22½ km (14 miles) south of Vermilion Pass, is the most popular point of departure for backpackers as well as day-hikers. (The Floe Lake section of the trail was affected by the 2003 fires.) Floe Lake, 10½ km (6½ miles), elevation gain 732 m (2,400 feet), is a beautiful spot to camp the first night but it's very busy in the summer; reservations are strongly recommended to be sure of getting a campsite. Backcountry campgrounds are also at Numa Creek, Tumbling Creek, Helmet Falls and Helmet/Ochre Junction. The 55-km (34-mile) hike terminates at the Paint Pots trailhead.

Kootenay National Park

This is a strenuous three- to five-day journey suitable for fit hikers only.

 You must purchase a wilderness pass to camp in the backcountry. More information is available in Parks Canada's *Kootenay National Park Backcountry Guide*. For this trip, detailed trail descriptions and a topographic map are a must.

For those not prepared to camp in the backcountry, the challenging **day-hike to Floe Lake** is one of the most popular backcountry destinations in the park. Named for the icebergs that float in its turquoise-colored water, the glacier that feeds it clings to a limestone wall in the cirque. The best time to visit is in mid-summer when the wildflowers are in full bloom or in fall when the larches turn golden.

■ Useful Information

 **Ambulance, Fire, Police**: 911.

Ambulance: ☎ 250-342-2055.

Fire: ☎ 250-347-6590.

Royal Canadian Mounted Police: ☎ 250-342-9292.

Hospital (Invermere): ☎ 250-342-9201.

Forest Fire Reports: ☎ 800-663-5555 or *5555 on cell phones.

Park Warden Office: ☎ 250-347-9361; 24-hour emergency, ☎ 403-762-4506.

Laundromat: On the corner of the Highway 93/95 intersection.

Liquor store: At Main Street west or at the Horsethief Pub.

Internet access: At the Visitor Information Center in Radium.

Post Office: Radium Boulevard off Main Street.

Weather forecast: ☎ 403-762-2088.

Road conditions: ☎ 403-762-1450 or 800-748-7275.

Information Sources

www.parkscanada.gc.ca/kootenay

Parks Canada website with information about the park, including fees, visitor information, natural wonders, activities, and public safety. Trail reports, road conditions, and avalanche reports. Kootenay National Park, PO Box 220, Radium Hot Springs, BC, V0A 1M0, ☎ 250-347-9615.

www.radiumhotsprings.com

Information about the village, hot springs, activities, events, accommodations, things to do, dining, shopping and services. Radium Hot Springs Chamber of Commerce, PO Box 225, Radium Hot Springs, BC, V0A 1M0, ☎ 250-347-9331.

Kootenay National Park

Waterton Lakes National Park

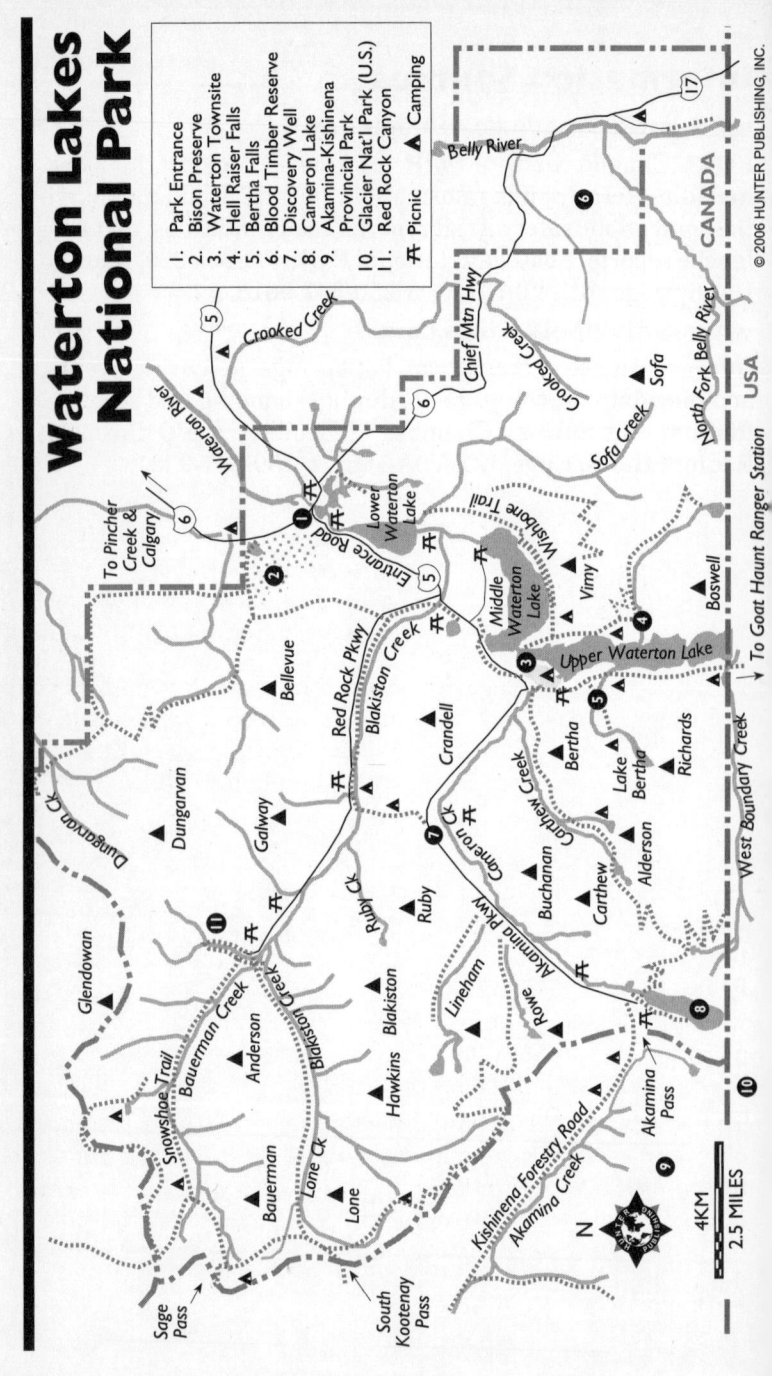

1. Park Entrance
2. Bison Preserve
3. Waterton Townsite
4. Hell Raiser Falls
5. Bertha Falls
6. Blood Timber Reserve
7. Discovery Well
8. Cameron Lake
9. Akamina-Kishinena Provincial Park
10. Glacier Nat'l Park (U.S.)
11. Red Rock Canyon
 ⊼ Picnic   ▲ Camping

© 2006 HUNTER PUBLISHING, INC.

Waterton Lakes National Park

Waterton Lakes National Park is a place "where the mountains meet the prairie," a unique juxtaposition of prairie flatlands and some of the most ancient mountains in the Canadian Rockies. Protecting 525 sq km (203 sq miles) in the southwest corner of Alberta, the park is bordered by British Columbia on the west, Montana to the south and to the north and east by forest and private

lands. A World Heritage Site, Waterton Lakes National Park and Montana's Glacier National Park are designated as the Waterton-Glacier International Peace Park, a symbol of peace and goodwill between Canada and the United States and a partnership of shared resources.

The smallest and least-known Canadian Rockies National Park is by far the most diverse, with high mountains, prairie grasslands, deep canyons, forest belts, lakes and rivers. More than half of Alberta's plant species, some very rare, can be found in the 45 different habitat types, with grasslands, wetlands, lakes, forests and alpine areas. Waterton is home to a great variety of wildlife, with some of the best wildlife viewing opportunities in the Mountain Parks.

The Waterton Lakes Chain consists of over 100 km (62 miles) of rivers, streams, wetlands and about 80 lakes and ponds, including Upper, Middle and Lower Waterton Lakes. The international boundary runs across the Upper Waterton Lake – the deepest lake in the Canadian Rockies – about halfway down its length.

Waterton's diversity extends to its recreational opportunities, with 200 km (124 miles) of trails that lead to spectacular scenery as well as its namesake chain of lakes. There are many accommodation choices within the townsite that range from camping along Upper Waterton Lake to the stately Prince of Wales Hotel. The park is open year-round, though most of the 400,000 people that visit each year do so during the peak season in July and August.

Waterton's Wonder

For a number of years photographs of Waterton's most recognized landmark, **The Prince of Wales Hotel**, high on a bluff above Upper Waterton Lake, piqued my interest. When I finally made the pilgrimage to southwest Alberta I was immediately taken by Waterton's unique landscape – the contrast between prairie flatlands and mountains is a treat for the eyes. The Prince of Wales sits harmoniously with the landscape, a photographer's paradise. Although the park is generally busy throughout the summer, the atmosphere remains unhurried, an ideal place for shedding life's everyday cares and rediscovering a sense of self. According to an early brochure on the park, "Here nerves that have been tightened for years slowly relax." I couldn't agree more.

Roads lead *to* Waterton, not *through* it. Because Waterton is relatively isolated from main travel routes, it has remained less known to tourists. Southern Albertans, however, have visited this holiday paradise for years and many of its cottages have been in families for two or three generations.

Don't wait years to take the road less traveled – get on the road that leads to the wonder of Waterton and leave your cares behind.

■ History

Aboriginal hunting and gathering began along Waterton's lakes and over its mountain passes 12,000 years ago. Some 200 archaeological sites, such as campsites, burials, bison kills and fishing stations, have been identified in the park. The tribes of the Blackfoot nation dominated the western plains for generations. To them, the Rockies were known as the "Backbone of the World." Their life revolved around the buffalo hunt, but they also hunted elk, antelope and deer. The Blackfoot way of life began to change dramatically in

Crowfoot, Chief of the Blackfoot Nation, 1887

the 1860s when prospectors discovered gold in Montana. The last buffalo herds disappeared in 1880 and over the years the Blackfoot tribes turned to ranching and farming.

Lt. Thomas Blakiston of the famous Palliser Expedition of 1858 named Waterton Lakes in honor of British pioneering naturalist Charles Waterton (1782-1865). In 1893, Pincher Creek rancher Frederick Godsal first suggested that the Waterton Lakes area be set aside as a national park. In 1895 the federal government designated 140 sq km (54 sq miles) as a Dominion Forest Park and it became Canada's fourth national park. The first European settler in the area was John George "Kootenai" Brown, who became the first "Warden in Charge" in 1911. The present townsite was settled as a result of oil drilling in the park. The fist oil strike occurred in the Cameron Valley in 1902, and today "Original Discovery No. 1," the first oil well in western Canada, is a National Historic Site.

The stately Prince of Wales Hotel opened in 1927. It was the brainchild of James Hill, then president of the American-owned Great Northern Railway, who wanted to attract affluent tourists of the day on the railway and make Glacier and Waterton Lakes National Parks "the playground of the Northwest." The hotel was designated a National Historic Site in 1995.

In 1932, members of Alberta and Montana Rotary Clubs encouraged their governments to establish the world's first international peace park, which they saw as a way to celebrate the friendship and cooperation between two nations along the world's longest undefended boundary. (Since then, over 170 similar cooperative parks have been established in the world.) Both Waterton Lakes National Park and Glacier National Park were designated as Biosphere Reserves, a UNESCO program that fosters awareness of the relationship between humans, the natural environment and resource management. The Waterton-Glacier International Peace Park became a World Heritage Site in 1995.

The Call of the Mountains

Mary Roberts Rinehart (1876-1958) was a popular author of the early 20th century and one of the most famous mystery writers in America. She was commissioned to write introductions for Great Northern Railway brochures. In one she writes, "The call of the mountains is a real call. Throw off the impediments of civilization. Go out to the West and ride the mountain trails. Throw out your chest and breathe – look across green valleys to wild peaks where mountain goats stand impassive on the edge of space. Then the mountains will get you. You will go back. The call is a real call."

■ Getting There & Getting Around

By Road

From Calgary, take Highway 2 south to Fort Macleod, then west on Highway 3 to Pincher Creek, then south on Highway 6.

From Banff, take Highway 1 east, turn south at Highway 40 and take the route over Highwood Pass to Highway 22. Highway 22 connects with Highway 3; continue east on Highway 3 to Pincher Creek and then south on Highway 6.

From British Columbia, travel by way of the Crowsnest Pass on Highway 3 to Pincher Creek and then south on Highway 6.

From Glacier National Park, Montana, take the Chief Mountain International Highway in summer or any time of year go north through Cardston on Montana Highway 89 to Alberta Highway 2, then west on Highway 5.

The main park (entrance) road begins at the intersection of Highway 5 and Highway 6, 8.4 km (5.2 miles) northeast of Waterton Lakes townsite.

Distances from Waterton

Calgary	264 km (164 miles)
Banff	380 km (236 miles)
Pincher Creek	48 km (30 miles)
Cardston	43 km (27 miles)
Fernie, BC	204 km (126 miles)
St. Mary, Montana	69 km (43 miles)

International Ports of Entry

Carway, Alberta and Peigan, Montana are open year-round from 7 am to 11 pm daily. Chief Mountain (Alberta and Montana) is open seasonally May 15 to 31 from 9 am to 6 pm, June 1 to Labour Day from 7 am to 10 pm and after Labour Day to September 30 from 9 am to 6 pm.

People in tour boats and private boats arriving from Waterton Lakes National Park to Goat Haunt (at the southern tip of

Waterton Lakes

Upper Waterton Lake) in Glacier National Park are not required to clear customs and immigration unless they travel beyond the immediate shore area of the Ranger Station.

All hikers crossing the International Boundary from Canada are considered to be applying for admission to the United States and are required to report to Park Rangers at Goat Haunt for inspection. Canadians or Americans who wish to travel into the United States beyond Goat Haunt must clear customs and immigration at the Goat Haunt Ranger Station. There are restrictions on all backcountry travel from the United States into Canada; report to customs at the RCMP in Waterton townsite. Contact **Canada Customs and Revenue Agency** for information, ☎ 403-653-3535.

Bus Service

 **Greyhound**, ☎ 403-627-2716, in Pincher Creek or 800-661-8747 for fare and schedule information, www.greyhound.ca.

Daily bus from Calgary to Pincher Creek. There is no Greyhound bus service to Waterton. (If you are staying at the Aspen Village Inn or the Kilmorey Lodge, they can arrange to pick you up at the bus stop in Pincher Creek.)

Car Rentals

Pincher Creek Ford Ltd., ☎ 403-627-4461, 835 Waterton Avenue, Pincher Creek.

■ Special Events

Waterton Wild Flower-Fest, 10 days of special events held in June to celebrate more than 900 plant species that call Waterton home. www.watertonwildflowers.com.

Canada Day, July 1st, free park entry, pancake breakfast and various activities.

Canada's Parks Day, with celebrations held the second or third Saturday in July. Special activities include guided hikes and evening theater programs.

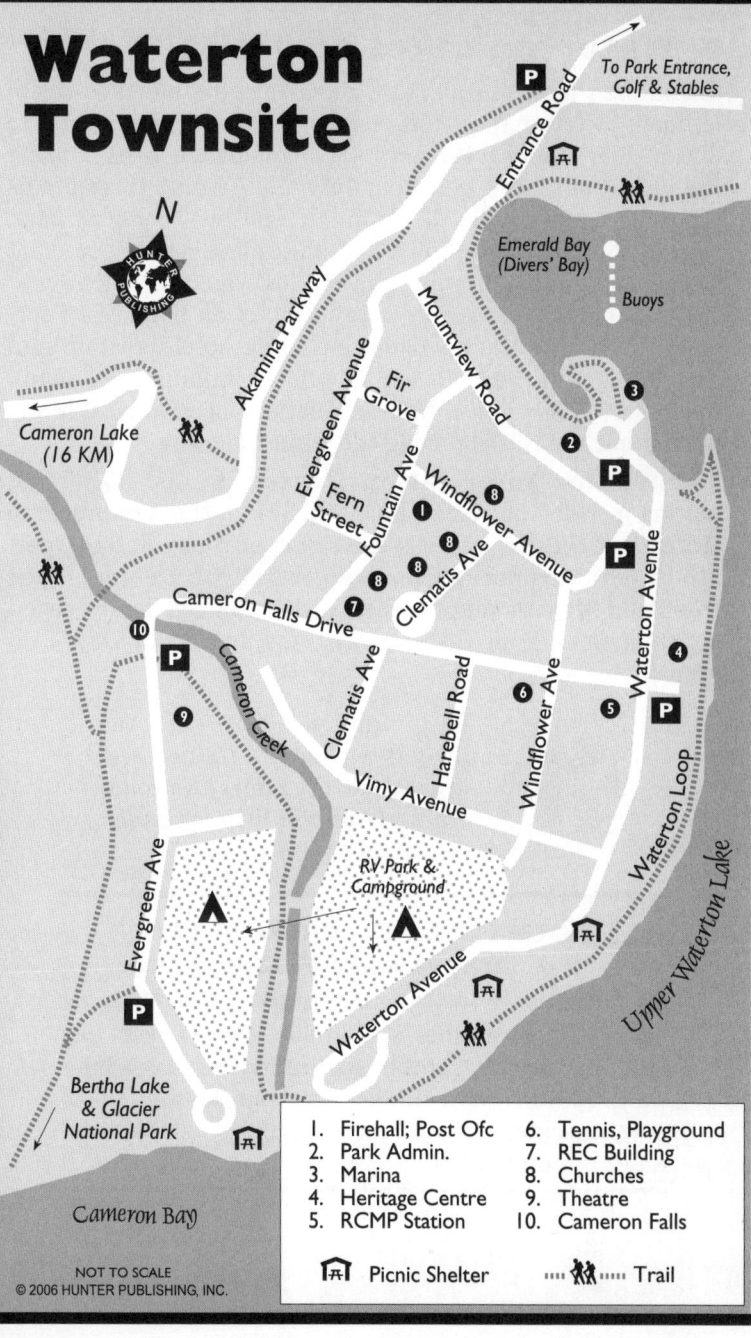

Waterton Townsite

N
HUNTER PUBLISHING

To Park Entrance,
Golf & Stables

Entrance Road

Emerald Bay
(Divers' Bay)

Buoys

Akamina Parkway

Evergreen Avenue

Fir Grove

Mountview Road

Fern Street

Fountain Ave

Windflower Avenue

Cameron Lake
(16 KM)

Clematis Ave

Cameron Falls Drive

Clematis Ave

Harebell Road

Windflower Ave

Waterton Avenue

Waterton Loop

Cameron Creek

Vimy Avenue

Evergreen Ave

RV Park &
Campground

Waterton Avenue

Upper Waterton Lake

Bertha Lake
& Glacier
National Park

Cameron Bay

NOT TO SCALE
© 2006 HUNTER PUBLISHING, INC.

1. Firehall; Post Ofc	6. Tennis, Playground
2. Park Admin.	7. REC Building
3. Marina	8. Churches
4. Heritage Centre	9. Theatre
5. RCMP Station	10. Cameron Falls

🏠 Picnic Shelter   ····🚶···· Trail

■ Waterton Lakes Townsite

Set on the shores of Waterton Lake, Waterton Lakes townsite is home to fewer than 100 people year-round, increasing to 300 residents and cottagers in the summer months. During the height of tourist season in July and August, there are as many as 2,000 people. If it's hustle and bustle you're after, stop in Banff. Waterton is a laid-back place where you don't have to worry about finding parking and you can walk around the townsite at a leisurely pace in about an hour. Most services are within the townsite, including hotels, restaurants and lounges, a gas station, public swimming pool, bank machines, shops and a limited selection of groceries. Many businesses are closed during the winter months.

The Visitor Information Center, ☎ 403-859-5133, waterton.info@pc.gc.ca. Located along the entrance to Waterton townsite (opposite the Prince of Wales Hotel). Operating hours vary year to year but generally the center is open from mid-May to mid-October with extended hours seven days per week from Victoria Day (May) to Labour Day (September).

Pick up a copy of the *Waterton-Glacier Guide* and the *Waterton Lakes National Park of Canada Visitor Guide*.

Waterton Lakes National Park Day/Annual Passes

(Waterton only – subject to change): Adult (17 to 64 years) day $6/annual $30; senior (65 and over) day $4.25/annual $22; youth (six to 16 years) day $3/annual $15; children (under six) free; family (up to seven people, any age, arriving in a single vehicle) day $15/annual $75.

 **It's Free!** Free Parks Canada evening theater programs take place indoors from 8 pm to 9 pm each evening throughout the summer at Crandell and Falls Theatres. Pick up a *Theatre Programs & Guided Hikes* brochure at the Visitor Information Center.

Waterton Natural History Association

The WNHA is a non-profit organization devoted to supporting Waterton Lakes National Park. Through educational programs, displays, publications, special events and other services, the WNHA helps preserve the park's natural and cultural heritage. The association operates The Heritage Center, open mid-May through September, on the main street of town, featuring displays of the park's natural and cultural history, an art gallery, bookstore and gift shop. Natural History Education Programs are taught by internationally recognized experts from mid-June to early August and include programs such as Prairie Wildflowers, Mountain Birds, Brilliant Butterflies, Adventures with Amphibians and Bears of Waterton; one-day courses $75, two-day courses $175. Free entertaining and educational programs are offered Saturday evenings during July and August in the Falls Theatre (near Cameron Falls). Park visitors may become members of the WNHA for a nominal fee; members receive a discount on educational programs and retail purchases. For more information, contact the WNHA ☎ 403-859-2624.

Waterton Lakes

Short Hikes & Strolls
Around Waterton Townsite

 **Townsite Loop** – Takes about an hour, depending on how long you like to linger. Start anywhere in town but be sure to stop at Cameron Falls, the outflow from Cameron Lake.

Prince of Wales Hill Loop – From Emerald Bay, about 45 minutes.

Bear's Hump – Starting at the Visitor Information Center, this very popular short, steep hike (1.4 km/.9 miles one-way, elevation gain 200 m/656 feet) provides access to glorious views of the Waterton valley, townsite, lakes and mountains. Don't miss it, but avoid it on stormy days.

Waterton Recreation Center

Owned and operated by the Waterton Lakes Lodge, which also operates the Waterton Lakes Alpine Hostel (both are located in the same complex). The center is open to the public daily from 10 am to 10 pm and offers a saltwater pool, whirlpool, steam room, dry sauna and gym.

■ Shopping

 Take a stroll around town and browse in Waterton's shops where you'll find fine art, handcrafted jewelry, books, home accessories, fine china, clothing, camping and sports equipment, local and native crafts, souvenirs and gift items.

Waterton Sports & Leisure (Tamarack Village Square), Mount View Road. Outdoor gear and camping supplies, books and maps, hikers' market and camp store, souvenirs and gifts. ATM, currency exchange and hiker shuttle also available (see *Tour Operators* section).

Pat's, Mount View Road. Open Easter to (Canadian) Thanksgiving, 8 am to 11 pm. Confectionary, convenience foods, camping and fishing supplies, souvenirs, and Cuban cigars; ATM available. Pat's rents bicycles (see *Sports Rentals* section).

■ Where to Eat

There are a variety of choices available in Waterton townsite with an emphasis on casual fine dining. Many hotels offer dining such as the award-winning **Lamp Post Dining Room** at Kilmorey Lodge. **New Frank's** is a reasonably priced family restaurant that offers basic Chinese and western food. **Zum's** seems to attract the tourist crowd because of its location but is overpriced ($8 for a basket of fries) and offered poor service when I was there. Small casual cafés that are reasonably priced, such as **Peace Park Pitas**, are springing up in Waterton. There is a very limited selection of groceries so, if you're preparing your own meals, stock up beforehand. And when it comes to ice cream, Waterton rivals any of the Rocky Mountain Parks for its selection of treats.

Lamp Post Dining Room at Kilmorey Lodge, $$ to $$$. Casual fine dining with extensive breakfast, lunch and dinner selections featuring recipes from around the world, adapted to a Western style of cooking. Interesting dinner entrées such as Alexander the Great – grilled chicken breast simmered in brandy mushroom cream sauce and garnished with brandied grapes and Saskatoon berries, or seafood such as Orange Chutney Halibut. They also have Alberta beef, pasta, soups, salads and tempting desserts, along with an extensive wine menu.

Tuscana Ristorante, on Waterton Avenue, $$ to $$$. Lunch menu selections include soup, salads, appetizers, pastas, sandwiches and burgers. Dinner is served from 4:30 pm until 11 pm, with build-your-own pastas, a selection of appetizers, salads, and entrées such as veal, chicken, salmon, beef and a late night tapas menu. Largest patio in town.

DINING PRICE CHART	
Price per person in Canadian $ for an entrée, not including beverage, tax or tip.	
$	Under $10
$$	$10-$25
$$$	Over $25

Pizza of Waterton, on Fountain Avenue, $$. Handcrafted pizza, salads, soups, desserts and more in the licensed dining room, on the patio or take-out. ☎ 859-2660. Open noon to 10 pm.

Coffee Shop, at the Bayshore Inn, $ to $$. Great breakfast specials, lunch for under $10, as well as hiker's lunch to go.

WATERTON WEATHER

Waterton is the second-windiest place in Alberta. The area receives the highest average annual precipitation in the province, with April and June the wettest and cloudiest months. Summer is brief and tends to be cool, with typical highly variable mountain weather. Winters are mild and snowy, with frequent warm spells caused by chinooks, warm winds that make the park one of the warmest areas in Alberta in winter.

■ Where to Stay

If you are planning a trip to Waterton during the peak tourist months of July and August, it's best to book your (roofed) accommodation in advance. Expect to pay a minimum of $120 per night for a hotel room in high season.

Northland Lodge, ☎ 403-859-2353, www.northland-lodgecanada.com, $$$ to

HOTEL PRICE CHART	
Reflects the price of an average room for two in Canadian $, May-Sept. Rates lower rest of year (except Christmas and New Year's).	
$	Under $50
$$	$50-$100
$$$	$101-$150
$$$$	$151-$250
$$$$$	Over $250

$$$$. It's a tradition of Northland Lodge to dry the cotton linens on a line and press them with lavender water. This cozy lodge is snuggled up against the mountainside on Evergreen Avenue near Cameron Falls. Nine unique rooms, spacious balcony, lounge with library and television. Continental breakfast included. Open mid-May to mid-October.

Kilmorey Lodge, ☎ 403-859-2334, www.kilmoreylodge.com, $$$ to $$$$. At the corner of Entrance Road and Mount View Road (as you enter the townsite), this country-style inn was built in the early part of the 20th century on the shores of Waterton Lake and offers 23 guest rooms, each appointed with antique furniture and down comforters and each a little different. Family and deluxe suites have amenities such as king size beds with canopies and sitting areas. All rooms are sans phones and televisions. Two wheelchair-accessible rooms; children under 16 stay free; pets not permitted. Open year-round, with many all-inclusive winter packages available. The **Lamp Post Dining Room** offers gourmet dining in a relaxed atmosphere; the **Ramshead Lounge** has an outdoor lakeside patio. Plus there is the outdoor **Gazebo Café**.

Aspen Village Inn, ☎ 403-859-2255, www.aspenvillageinn. com, $$$ to $$$$$. This is a family-oriented facility that offers deluxe rooms, suites and cottages, some with full kitchens. They offer private balconies, complimentary coffee, whirlpool, picnic area with barbecue and picnic tables and playground. Open year-round. Located on Windflower Avenue.

Waterton Lakes Lodge, ☎ 888-985-6343 or 403-859-2150, www.watertonlakeslodge.com, $$$$ to $$$$$. Eighty guest rooms and suites with fireplaces, jetted tubs and kitchenettes. Free admission to adjacent recreation center (operated by the lodge). **Bighorn Grill** offers casual gourmet dining and **Wolf's Den Lounge** serves contemporary relaxed fare. Retreat packages available. Pets permitted. Open year-round. Located in the center of the townsite between Windflower Avenue and Cameron Falls Drive.

Prince of Wales Hotel, ☎ 403-859-2231, www.prince-ofwaleswaterton.com, $$$$$. This National Historic Site with its steep, sloping gabled roof is an area landmark and is one of the most photographed hotels in the world. The hotel is named for Britain's Prince Edward, and the British tradition is carried throughout. The grand lobby with its huge picture windows give a spectacular view over Upper Waterton Lake. Lakeside, mountainside and value rooms are available but are rather small and in need of some updating. Suites are also available. Hotel facilities include the **Royal Stewart Dining Room** (European and Canadian cuisine, casual attire),

Valerie's Tea Room, the **Windsor Lounge** and a gift shop. Open June to mid-September.

There are no rental accommodations in Waterton Park.

Camping

 Parks Canada operates four campsites in the park. Arrive early if you don't have reservations and want to stay at **Waterton Townsite**, the only campground in the park with showers and wheelchair accessibility. **Crandell Mountain** offers more of an authentic camping experience. The park does not have over-flow camping facilities; if the campgrounds in the park are full, campers are required to look for campgrounds outside the park, of which there are a fair number within a short distance.

All sites are available on a first-come, first-served basis. Waterton Townsite campground now accepts reservations – see www.pccamping.ca for the Parks Canada Campground Reservation Service, or call ☎ 877-737-3783, international ☎ 905-426-4648.

Waterton Townsite. Located at the south end of Waterton townsite. 238 fully serviced and semi-serviced sites; $$ to $$$; wheelchair-accessible; showers; covered shelters; food storage; sani-dump; interpretive programs; mid-April to mid-October. Crowded during the summer with little privacy but some nice sites along the lake; not an authentic camping experience but a convenient location; reservations accepted. Be prepared to share the facilities with bighorn sheep and mule deer that are commonly seen grazing on the grass in the campground.

Crandell. Five km (three miles) from Waterton townsite along the Red Rock Parkway. 129 unserviced sites; $$; covered shelters; food storage; sani-dump; recycling bins; some fire pits and firewood; interpretive programs; mid-May to early

CAMPING/HOSTELS	
Rates in Canadian $, not including taxes.	
$	Under $13
$$	$13-$22
$$$	$23-$30
$$$$	Over $30

September. Forested sites offer some privacy. Crandell Lake is a two-km (1.2-mile) hike. Mule deer and black bears commonly wander through the campground.

Belly River. 26 km (16 miles) from Waterton townsite along the Chief Mountain Highway. 24 primitive sites; $$; covered shelters; food storage; sani-dump; fire pits and firewood; mid-May to mid-September. Forested sites beside the Belly River offer a more secluded camping experience.

Pass Creek Winter Campground. Five km (three miles) from Waterton townsite at Pass Creek picnic site on the entrance road. Eight unserviced sites; no cost; covered shelter with wood stove; end of October to mid-April.

Campgrounds Near Waterton National Park

Crooked Creek. Operated by the Waterton Natural History Association to help support its natural history programs. 5.6 km (3½ miles) east of the park on Highway 5. Full services available. Open mid-May to early September; $ to $$ with weekly and monthly rates available.

Waterton Springs, ☎ 403-859-2247. Three km (1.8 miles) north of the park on Highway 6. Fully serviced and semi-serviced sites with treed tenting as well as pull-through sites; $$ to $$$; showers, laundry facilities, convenience store, covered shelters; outdoor pool, playground, fire pits and firewood, Internet access and arcade room. Reservations accepted.

Backcountry Camping

A wilderness use permit ($9 per person/per night or $63 annually) is mandatory for camping in the backcountry. Permits are available from the Visitor Information Center. For a $12 fee, reservations are available for the nine wilderness campsites in Waterton Park. Reservations may be made 90 days in advance beginning April 1 of each year. From April 1 to mid-May call the warden office, ☎ 403-859-5140, and after mid-May call the Visitor Information Center, ☎ 403-859-5133. Reservations must be paid for at the time of booking by MasterCard or Visa only. Permits must be picked up at the Visitor Information Center no sooner than 24 hours in advance of the start date of the trip.

Waterton Lakes

The wilderness campsites in Waterton Park are at **Bertha Lake**, **Bertha Bay**, **Boundary Bay**, **Alderson Lake**, **Goat Lake**, **Snowshoe**, **Twin Lakes**, **Lone Lake** and **Akamina Pass**.

Hosteling

Waterton Alpine Center. Located on the corner of Cameron Falls and Windflower Avenue. Twenty-one beds, members and non-members $$$$, family rooms; check-in 4 pm. This is a full-facility hostel (operated by Waterton Lake Lodge) located in the same building as The Waterton Spa and Recreation Center. Laundry facilities, Internet access and wheelchair-accessible. Reservations ☎ 888-985-6343 or 403-859-2151 or info@watertonlakeslodge.com.

■ Adventures

Tour Operators

Shoreline Cruises, ☎ 403-859-2362, www.watertoncruise.com, Waterton Marina. Scenic two-hour cruises from Waterton Marina to Goat Haunt, Montana. Large vessels feature indoor and outdoor seating, including the flagship 200-passenger *International*, which has been in service since 1927. The boats make photographic stops to capture the scenery and wildlife. Stopover of 30 minutes at Goat Haunt. (Canadian and US citizens with appropriate identification may hike at Goat Haunt.) Cruises from May to October with sailings at 10 am, 1 and 4 pm from early June to September. $27 adult, $14 youth 13-17 years, $10 child four-12 years.

◆ **Crypt Lake hike water shuttle** service in July and August. Departs Waterton Marina at 9 am and 10 am and Crypt Landing at 4 and 5:30 pm. $14 adult, $7 child four-12 years (dogs permitted).

Canadian Wilderness Tours (White Mountain Adventures), ☎ 800-408-0005 or 403-678-4099, www.whitemountainadventures.com, located in the Aspen Village Inn.

◆ **Half-day hikes** $45 per person; full-day hikes (including Crypt Lake, Rowe Meadows, Carthew-Alderson) $90 per person.

♦ **Evening Wildlife Watching**. Touted as "your best chance to see bears and other wildlife anywhere in the Rockies." $40 adult, $30 child eight-12 years.

♦ **Waterton View Breakfast Walk**. A guided interpretive walk to one of Waterton Lake's best viewpoints for continental breakfast. Every Tuesday and Thursday, $40 adult, $30 child.

Trail of the Great Bear, ☎ 800-215-2395 or 403-859-2663, www.trailofthegreatbear.com, 114 Main Street. This eco-tourism company offers nature and enrichment packages in the Canadian Rockies, including learning programs, special interest group tours, customized self-drive itineraries and guiding services. Waterton activities include Waterton Bears Field Course, Waterton Wildflower Festival and Walking in Waterton escorted group tour. Multi-day packages may come with programs, accommodations, group transportation within Waterton and all meals. Visit their website for detailed information on tours or while in Waterton, stop by their office and gift shop.

Tamarack Outdoor Outfitters, ☎ 403-859-2378, Mount View Road. Daily hiker shuttle services to most of the major trailheads, including the Carthew-Alderson Summit hike (rates vary, one- or two-day advance reservations recommended). This is also an outdoor store, offering a large selection of outdoor gear, with a money exchange and ATM.

Sports Rentals

Cameron Lake Boat Rentals. Open 7:30 am to 7:30 pm daily during the summer. Canoe/rowboat $22 first hour, $17 additional hour; single kayak $20/$17, double $22/$17. Fishing licenses and tackle also available, as well as guided interpretive programs, $40/person. Cash only.

Pat's, ☎ 403-859-2266, Mount View Road. Pat's is well known for its rentals of surreys (two-seater, four-wheeled canopied bicycle), which you'll see all over the townsite ($17 per hour). Mountain bikes ($34/day or $45/day full suspension) and scooters ($70/day). Open Easter to (Canadian) Thanksgiving, 8 am to 11 pm.

Horseback Riding

 **Alpine Stables**, ☎ 403-859-2462, www.alpine-stables.com, is just outside Waterton townsite, across from the golf course road. Open mid-May through September. Beginners and experienced riders can choose from up to 200 km (120 miles) of trails in Waterton, ranging from gentle rolling prairie to steep mountain climbs. Trail rides leave on the hour from 9 am to 5 pm in July and August and from 10 am to 4 pm in May, June and September. Hourly, half-day and full-day rides available (lunch not included). Inquire about bookings for private groups.

◆ **Wildlife Habitat**. A lush trail that meanders through wooded hillsides and includes two creek crossings. Possibility of seeing elk, mule deer and black bears. Two hours, $42.

◆ **Buffalo Paddocks**. A three-hour ride over prairie to the buffalo paddocks. Wildlife viewing may include elk, bears, deer, badgers or coyotes. Three hours, $58.

◆ **Crandell Loop**. Ride through pine and aspen forests to Crandell Lake and around Crandell Mountain. This is the most popular trail ride in Waterton. Five hours, $80.

◆ **Carthew Summit**. A full day takes riders above Cameron Falls, into Alderson Lake and past waterfalls and Carthew Lakes. Climb to the summit ridge for incredible panoramas. Drive back to the stables from Cameron Lake. Eight hours, $119.

Mountain Meadow Trail Rides, ☎ 866-653-2413 or 403-653-2413, www.mountainmeadowtrailrides.com. Located 18 km (11 miles) east of Waterton Park on Highway 5. Historic Nelson Ranch offers wilderness horseback adventures with spectacular scenery. A 1½-hour ride is $30, 2½-hour ride, $47, half-day ride, $70, full-day ride, $110 and cookout ride, $80. Overnight rides to wilderness base camp with cabins and hot tub, $165/person/day.

Adventures on Water

 Boating in Waterton Park is an ideal way to explore the area. The best paddling spot is Cameron Lake; the wind is not as strong as on Waterton Lakes. Canoes, rowboats and kayaks are available for rent at **Cameron Lake Boat Rentals**; powered motors are not permitted.

Motorboats are permitted on Upper and Middle Waterton Lakes. Boat launches are at the marina in the townsite and at the Linnet Lake picnic site on Middle Waterton Lake.

Emerald Bay and Cameron Bay on Upper Waterton Lake are popular scuba diving locations. *Gertrude*, a paddle-wheeler built in the 1900's, lies at a depth of 20 m (65 feet) on the bottom of Emerald Bay. Emerald Bay is the most popular spot for swimming; keep in mind that the lake drops off quickly.

Sailboarders frequent the beach on Upper Waterton Lake along the townsite campground.

Use extreme caution on Waterton Lakes due to frequent high winds, rough water conditions and very cold water.

Fishing is permitted in most waters with an appropriate National Park license – check current regulations.

Whitewater Rafting

Kimball River Sports, ☎ 800-936-6474, www.raft-alberta.ca. Whitewater rafting on the Waterton and St. Mary's Rivers, as well as fishing tours ($175 to $250 per person).

◆ **St. Mary's River**. Two- to three-hour Coal Canyon run. Adult $34, child under 12 $29; four- to six-hour border run, adult $85, child $80.

◆ **Waterton River**. A 25-km (15-mile) run (¾-day), includes lunch. Adult $95, child $80.

Drives, Sights, Activities & Hikes

Maskinonge

 Easy to miss, the shallow waters of Maskinonge Lake lie two km (1.2 miles) south of the park entrance, above the shores of Waterton River. This rich wetland habitat attracts geese, ducks and

other waterfowl, as well as beavers and muskrats, and is teeming with fish. Archaeological evidence indicates that this was one of the main settlement areas for thousands of people starting at least 5,000 years ago. There is an interpretive display on the overlook, with beautiful views.

Waterton Lakes Golf Course

One of the most scenic courses in Canada. Play nine or 18 holes on rolling fairways lined with trees and sand traps. Public tee times are dawn to dusk, seven days a week, May through October. ☎ 403-859-2064.

International Peace Park Hike

 Led by Canadian and American park interpreters, these special hikes are held every Wednesday and Saturday in July and August, starting at 10 am from the Bertha Lake trailhead in Waterton townsite. The 14-km (8.7-mile) moderately difficult hike along Upper Waterton Lake crosses the International Boundary on the way to Goat Haunt in Glacier National Park, which features an International Peace Park Pavilion. The return to Waterton townsite dock by 6:30 pm is via boat (advance reservations recommended), $15 adult, $8 youth 13-17 years, $6 child four-12 years; the hike itself is free. Pre-registration at the Visitor Information Center is required, with reservations accepted for the next scheduled hike only.

Crypt Lake

Hike: 8.7 km (5.4 miles) from Crypt Landing.

Elevation gain: 675 m (2,220 feet).

Watchable wildlife: black bears, mountain goats.

This famous hike has been rated the best hike in Canada. Whether it is or not, it certainly offers an interesting mix of scenic terrain and an "obstacle course" trail unique in the Canadian Rockies.

The trailhead is accessed by a short tour boat ride across Upper Waterton Lake (see *Shoreline Cruises* in *Tour Operators* section). You'll be in a long line of hikers on the initial part of the trail, but don't let that discourage you – the crowd thins as the hike progresses. It is possible to achieve some solitude at Crypt Lake and on the return hike, especially if you book the last return boat.

At km .4 (mile .25) you reach a side-trail to **Hell-Roaring Falls** that reconnects with the main trail at km 3.0 (mile 1.8). You can stay on the main trail and visit these falls on the return trip. The trail climbs and switchbacks through forest with views of Twin Falls, Burnt Rock Falls and Crypt Falls. After crossing a talus slope the obstacles begin: a ladder climbs to a 20-m (65-foot) tunnel that has been blasted through the mountain. It emerges onto a precipice strung with a safety cable. After climbing another .4 km (.25 miles) you reach the entrance to Crypt Lake cirque where the lake's outlet stream plunges over a cliff and forms Crypt Falls.

With its bright green color and 600-m (1,968-foot) surrounding cliffs, Crypt Lake is an idyllic destination. You can also walk around the lake; the far (south) end is on the Canada-US boundary. Be sure to allow enough time to enjoy the lake and for the return hike before catching the return boat. (Average hikers take up to seven hours, not including breaks.)

Butterflying in Waterton

Butterflies have the ability to capture our attention and bring a smile to even the most ill-natured. With their brilliantly patterned wings and spirited flight, they evoke a sense of freedom and serenity. Like birding, butterflying is becoming increasingly popular.

While I was relaxing in the sunshine at Crypt Lake, I was thrilled to see a large number of butterflies feeding on wildflowers along the shore. I was even able to get close enough to photograph one, not a common occurrence.

Butterflies have huge eyes and can distinguish colors that human's can't, so wearing colorful clothing may attract them. But touching a butterfly could harm it, since their wings are covered with thousands of scales that might rub off and affect their ability to fly.

New species of butterflies continue to be discovered. There are more than 17,000 species in the world, 300 in Canada and 90 known from the Canadian Rockies.

If you would like to become familiar with some of the butterflies in Waterton Park, contact the Waterton Natural History Association about their "Brilliant Butterflies" day program.

Happiness is a butterfly, which when pursued is just beyond your grasp, but if you will sit down quietly, may light upon you. – Nathaniel Hawthorne

Akamina Parkway

This 16-km (10-mile) scenic road begins at the entrance road near the townsite and meanders along the Cameron Valley to its terminus at Cameron Lake. There are a number of picnic areas and points of interest, including Western Canada's first producing oil well, a National Historic Site. Cameron Lake, nestled inside a cirque, is ideal for paddling and the short trail along its west shore (1.6 km or 1 mile) is a pleasant walk. Make sure you don't venture to Mount Custer at the southern end of the lake, which is inside Glacier National Park and prime grizzly bear habitat, but do bring binoculars.

The Akamina Parkway provides access to a number of trailheads in Waterton Park, as well as to British Columbia's Akamina-Kishinena Provincial Park.

Wildflowers in Waterton

 Waterton is extraordinarily rich with wildflowers and one, beargrass, is the plant that is most closely identified with the park. It is a common sight in Waterton and it is the only Canadian national park where it grows. A member of the lily family, it thrives in moist meadows and pro-

duces showy white flowering stalks that grow more than three feet tall. Contrary to its name, bears do not eat beargrass, but elk and mountain goats do. If you are a wildflower enthusiast, check out the **Waterton Wildflower Festival**, held each year in June, www.watertonwildflowers.com.

Rowe Lakes - Lineham Ridge

Hike: 6.4 km (four miles) to Upper Rowe Lakes, 8.6 km (5.3 miles) to Lineham Ridge.

Elevation gain: 1,120 m (3,675 feet).

Watchable wildlife: Mule deer, bighorn sheep, Columbian ground squirrels.

Lush wildflower meadows, pretty subalpine lakes and incredible views from the highest trail-accessible point in Waterton Park await hikers on the Rowe Lakes-Lineham Ridge Trail.

From Waterton townsite, follow the Akamina Parkway 10½ km (6½ miles) to the trailhead parking area, on the right side of the road.

The initial part of the trail follows along cascading **Rowe Creek** and its colorful streambed of red argillite, then through a mature forest. A junction at km 3.9 (mile 2.4) branches left to **Lower Rowe Lake**, a small lake set in a rock amphitheater. The trail continues to the Rowe Meadow junction at km 5.2 (mile 3.2), where you'll want to photograph the wildflowers and, if you're lucky, white-tailed deer might make an appearance. After crossing the bridge over a stream at the far end of the meadow, a junction branches left toward Upper Rowe Lakes and ascends the mauve-colored talus slope to Lineham Ridge.

Continuing left, it's a steep grade with switchbacks to the larger of the two Upper Rowe Lakes at km 6.4 (mile 4), where you can drop down to the adjacent smaller lake. From the edge of this hanging valley, you can peer down to Lower Rowe Lake.

Be sure you have enough time and energy to hike the 3.4 km (2.1 miles) from the bridge junction to the crest of Lineham Ridge; otherwise you're missing half the fun. From the ridge,

Waterton Lakes

a vast expanse of mountains surrounds you, with a bird's eye view of your earlier destination, Rowe Lakes. Lineham Lakes are on the opposite side of the ridge. On a sunny day, this is Rocky Mountain paradise.

Red Rock Parkway

Open to vehicles mid-May to mid-October, the turnoff from the entrance road is 3.4 km (2.1 miles) from the townsite. This rolling 15-km (nine-mile) road runs where the mountains and prairie meet in Waterton Park and retraces the trail of people long ago. Meandering through the **Blakiston Valley**, you'll be treated to dramatic views of **Mt. Blakiston**, the park's highest peak (2,910 m or 9,580 feet). The road ends at the remarkably colored rocks and cascading waters of **Red Rock Canyon**. The abundant red argillite comes from oxidized iron; you can learn all about the canyon along the .7-km (.4-mile) interpretive nature trail loop. From the Red Rock Canyon parking area it's about one km (.6 miles) to reach **Blakiston Falls**.

BISON

As you drive the Red Rock Parkway, try to imagine herds of mountain bison that once grazed the alpine grasses. Bison were the chief preoccupation of the nomadic mountain peoples. Hunters trapped them by driving them into corrals or marshy areas or over buffalo jumps. A buffalo jump is visible from a viewpoint 5.2 km (3.2 miles) northwest along Red Rock Canyon Road.

Mountain Biking & Bicycle Touring

Cyclists in Waterton need to be cautious of strong winds and narrow shoulders along the roads. There are four trails in Waterton where mountain biking is permitted (be sure to pick up a copy of the *Waterton Lakes National Park Visitor Guide*):

◆ **Snowshoe** – Beginner. 16.4 km (10.2 miles) round-trip from Red Rock Canyon parking lot. This is an old fire road with spectacular views and some steep sections on an uphill grade to Snowshoe Warden Cabin. (Several creeks must be forded.)

◆ **Akamina Pass** – Moderate. 1½ km (.9 miles) one-way; 14.4 km (8.9 miles) along the Akamina Parkway to the trailhead. This is a short, steep trail that climbs to the Alberta/BC boundary, then continues into Akamina-Kishinena Provincial Park.

◆ **Wishbone** – Moderate. 21 km (13 miles) round-trip plus .5 km (.3 miles) along Chief Mountain Highway from Highway 5 junction. A wide, flat old wagon train road for the first half, with the last half narrow and often overgrown. (You must ford Sofa Creek and are not permitted on the Vimy Trail or to cycle past the Wishbone dock on Middle Waterton Lake.) Trail ends at Wishbone backcountry campsite.

◆ **Crandell Loop** – Advanced. Four km (2½ miles), 20.6 km (12.8 miles) for the entire loop – six km (3.7 miles) along the Akamina Parkway; or six km along the Red Rock Canyon Parkway; or from Waterton townsite a challenging loop around Crandell Mountain.

 Cyclists in Waterton need to be cautious of strong winds and narrow shoulders along roads.

Winter Adventures

 Conditions in winter range from warm wet weather to extreme cold. Driving conditions include poor visibility, icy roads and drifting snow. The entrance road leading to the park is open year-round; the Akamina Parkway is maintained to the Little Prairie picnic site, three km (1.8 miles) from Cameron Lake; the Red Rock Parkway and the Chief Mountain Highway are closed during the winter months. Most facilities are closed during winter.

Ski touring is a popular activity in the park. Trails are not marked or maintained and may be subject to avalanche hazard. Check with a park warden for information regarding

Waterton Lakes

backcountry skiing conditions and avalanche forecasts before touring the backcountry.

There are two designated cross-country ski trails along the upper Akamina Parkway.

- ◆ **Dipper** – Moderate. 6½ km (four miles) round-trip, beginning at the Rowe trailhead.
- ◆ **Cameron** – Easy. Five km (three miles) round-trip, beginning at Little Prairie picnic site.

■ Wildlife

No other Canadian national park protects so much wildlife within such a small area. The variety of vegetation makes it home to a great assortment of animals, including 60 species of mammals, 250 species of birds, 24 species of fish and 10 species of reptiles and amphibians. Waterton and its surrounding region is a crucial north-south Rocky Mountain wildlife corridor. This includes large predators, such as black bears, grizzly bears, cougars, wolves and coyotes. A herd of elk migrates annually between summer mountain habitat in Glacier Park and winter prairie ranges in Waterton. Other ungulates that make Waterton home include mountain goats, bighorn sheep, mule and white-tailed deer. Deer and bighorn sheep are commonly seen wandering about the townsite. At Cameron Lake, moose are often seen feeding along the shores. The international boundary at the south end of the lake is a good area to spot grizzly bears on the avalanche slopes (do not attempt to dock or hike in this grizzly bear habitat).

Late summer and fall offer the best wildlife viewing for larger animals, when they come down from their summer ranges. The best birding time is in late fall when waterfowl migrate through the park. The Maskinonge Lake area (the north end of Lower Waterton Lake), near the park entrance, is particularly rich in bird life.

Bison in Waterton? Bison do not roam freely in the park but there is a bison paddock near the north entrance to the park off Highway 6. This small herd of plains bison is maintained to commemorate the larger herds that once roamed freely in the area. You can view them from your vehicle on a narrow road through the paddock. (Do not leave your vehicle; the road is not suitable for vehicles with trailers.)

■ Scenic Must-See's

Suggestions for the first-time summer visitor on a four-day schedule.

◆ **Day 1** – Get to know Waterton by doing the short hikes and strolls around **Waterton townsite**. Browse Waterton's shops and enjoy a meal at one of the restaurants. Take in a free evening interpretive presentation at the **Falls Theatre**.

◆ **Day 2** – Enjoy a sightseeing drive along the **Akamina Parkway**; start early in the morning to increase your chances of spotting wildlife. Rent a canoe or kayak for a paddle on **Cameron Lake** and enjoy a picnic lunch. Take an afternoon horseback ride.

◆ **Day 3** – Take a hike: try the **Rowe Lakes-Lineham Ridge Trail**; or arrive early at the marina to purchase round-trip tickets for the tour boat ride to Crypt Landing where you can hike to **Crypt Lake**; or sign-up the day before for a guided **International Peace Park Hike**. If hiking isn't your preference, take a scenic boat cruise to **Goat Haunt** in Glacier National Park.

◆ **Day 4** – Drive along the scenic **Red Rock Parkway** to **Red Rock Canyon**. Or combine this drive with previous days' activities and participate in a daylong educational course such as "Waterton Wildflowers." (You must pre-register through the Waterton Natural History Association.)

■ To Do List

Next time I visit Waterton Lakes National Park I would like to hike . . .

Carthew-Alderson Trail. This 20-km (12.4-mile) trail between Cameron Lake and Waterton townsite is touted as the most popular one-way hike in the Canadian Rockies. Highlights include the mauve and red slopes of Mount

Waterton Lakes

Carthew with eye-popping views of Glacier National Park, Carthew Lakes basin and Alderson Lake cirque.

This is a hot, dry climb on sunny days, so packing plenty of water and sunscreen is necessary. Because of its exposure, it's not a good choice when the weather is questionable. The Cameron Express shuttle service is available at **Tamarack Outdoor Outfitters** (see *Tour Operators* section).

■ Useful Information

 **All Emergencies:** ☎ 403-859-2636.

Royal Canadian Mounted Police (May to October): ☎ 403-859-2244. Waterton Avenue and Cameron Falls Drive

Park Warden Office (Monday to Friday): ☎ 403-859-5140.

Hospital: Cardston, ☎ 403-653-4411; Pincher Creek, ☎ 403-627-3333.

Post Office: Windflower and Fountain Avenues.

Internet access: Bayshore Inn Lounge, Waterton Avenue.

Liquor store: Mountain Spirits on Cameron Falls Drive or at the Kilmorey Lodge.

Waterton Visitor Information Center: ☎ 403-859-5133.

Information Sources

www.pc.gc.ca/waterton

Parks Canada website with extensive information about the park, including fees, visitor information, natural wonders, activities, and public safety such as trail reports, road conditions, and avalanche reports. Waterton Lakes National Park, Box 200, Waterton Park, AB, T0K 2M0, ☎ 403-859-5133.

www.watertonchamber.com

Waterton Lakes Chamber of Commerce and Visitors Association, Box 55, Waterton Park, AB, T0K 2M0, ☎ 403-859-5133.

www.watertonpark.com

Waterton Lakes National Park visitors guide, with accommodations, dining, services, travel information, activities and more.

Glossary of Terms

Arthropod: Invertebrate animals having segmented (jointed) bodies and hollow, jointed legs.

Braided River: A river that flows in several dividing and reuniting channels resembling the strands of a braid. Such streams occur where more sediment is brought to any part of a stream than it can remove. The bars of sediment build to a point where the stream is forced to develop an intricate network of interlacing channels.

Cambrian: The first geologic period in the Paleozoic era, 590 to 500 million years ago, marked by a profusion of marine animals, especially trilobites and brachiopods.

Chinook: The warm, dry wind that blows intermittently down the east side of the Rockies during winter and early spring.

Cinquefoil: A plant of the rose family with white, red or yellow flowers and fruit like a dry strawberry.

Cirque: A steep-walled, amphitheater-like recess occurring at high elevations on the side of a mountain, commonly at the head of a glacial valley. It is formed from a mountain glacier's erosive carving.

Ecosystem: A system made up of a community of animals, plants and bacteria and its interrelated physical and chemical environments.

Erratic: A large boulder that has been carried to its resting place by glacial ice. Erratics that have come a great distance can usually be recognized by their difference in composition from the local bedrock.

Escarpment: A steep slope or cliff formed by erosion or by uplift or faulting.

Fossils: Any hardened remains or imprints of plant or animal life from a previous geologic period, preserved in the earth's crust.

Geology: The scientific study of the origin, history, structure and processes of Earth, including the structure and development of its crust, the composition of its interior, individual rock types and fossil forms.

Glacial: Anything produced by a glacier or a glacial period.

Glacial Till: Glacial matter composed of clay, stones, gravel, boulders, etc.

Glaciation: Specifically, the formation, movement and recession of ice sheets, but also referring to the geological processes associated with glacial activity, including erosion and deposition, and the resulting effects of such action on Earth's surface.

Glacier: A large mass of long-lasting ice that forms on land by the recrystallization and compaction of snow and moves slowly downslope or outward in all directions because of its own weight.

Gorge: A deep, narrow pass between steep heights.

Hoodoo: A pillar of stone created when a hard caprock protects soft underlying rock from erosion. The word was originally associated with voodoo culture, and meant "bad luck." Because hoodoos sometimes occur in large numbers in eroded valleys and canyons, to European minds the resulting forest of otherworldly formations seemed sinister and magical.

Karst: Topography, characterized by sinkholes, caves and underground streams formed by the dissolution of rock in water. Most topography of this type develops in regions of limestone.

Kettle: A steep-sided, usually basin- or bowl-shaped depression in glacial drift deposits, often containing a lake and formed by the melting of a large, detached block of ice left behind by a retreating glacier.

Limestone: Rock consisting mainly of calcium carbonate.

Moraine: A mass of rocks, gravel, sand and clay carried and deposited by a glacier along its side, at its lower end or beneath the ice.

Muskeg: A kind of bog or marsh containing thick layers of decaying vegetable matter and usually overrun by mosses.

Nunatak: An isolated knob or peak of land that projects prominently above the surface of a surrounding glacier.

Ochre: An earthy clay colored by iron oxide, usually yellow or reddish brown, used for paint by peoples around the world.

Palaeontology: The study of fossils and ancient life forms.

Petroglyph: A symbol or picture carved into rock.

Pictograph: A picture or symbol painted onto rock using ochre or other pigments and a variety of techniques.

Quartz: A mineral compound of silica and oxygen, most commonly colorless or white, originally formed during crystallization of molten magma and a common constituent of igneous, metamorphic and sedimentary rock.

Quartzite: A hard, unmetamorphosed sandstone, consisting chiefly of quartz grains cemented together by crystalline quartz or a dense conglomerate rock comprised of sand, silt and pebbles compressed and cemented by time and pressure.

Recessional moraines: An end or lateral moraine constructed during a temporary, but significant, pause in the retreat of a glacier.

Riparian: Adjacent to, or living on, the bank of a river, lake or pond.

Rock flour: Fine powder formed when stones embedded in a glacier grind down the underlying bedrock. Suspended in glacial outwash, or meltwater, it can give the water a deep greeny-blue color, which varies depending on the concentration of the particles in the water.

Sandstone: A sedimentary rock composed of rounded to angular fragments of sand, set within a matrix of silt clay, and cemented by calcite, silica or iron oxides. The sand particles most commonly consist of quartz.

Sediment: Matter deposited by wind or water.

Shale: A fine-grained sedimentary rock formed from the consolidation of clay and silt.

Silt: Sediment suspended in stagnant water or carried by moving water that often accumulates on the bottom of rivers, lakes or bays.

Tectonic: Pertaining to, causing or resulting from the structural deformation of Earth's crust.

Topography: A detailed description or drawing of the surface features of a place or region.

Trilobite: A segmented, three-lobed, bottom-dwelling marine arthropod that lived during the Paleozoic era, most abundantly during the Cambrian and Ordovician periods.

Tufa: Porous, spongy calcium carbonate deposited around the outlet of a deep mineral spring.

Ungulate: Having hoofs, or belonging to a group of mammals having hoofs.

(Selected terms from *In Search of Ancient Alberta*. Heartland Associates, Winnipeg, Manitoba: 1998. Reprinted with permission.)

Bibliography/ Recommended Reading

All of the following publications are currently available. The best place to purchase these books is from Friends shops (see individual chapters in this book) located at Visitor Information Centers throughout the parks or through their mail order service; proceeds from sales are used to support various initiatives in the parks.

Beers, Don. *The Wonder of Yoho. Scenes: Tales, Trails.* Calgary, Alberta: Rocky Mountain Books, 1994.

This is an in-depth pictorial hiking guide. The author is especially interested in the historical aspect, which makes for interesting reading.

Cameron, Ward. *Kananaskis: An Altitude SuperGuide*. Canmore, Alberta: Altitude Publishing, 1996.

A colorful and informative guide to Kananaskis Country's many recreational opportunities.

Copeland, Kathy & Craig. *Don't Waste Your Time in the Canadian Rockies: The Opinionated Hiking Guide*. Canmore, Alberta: hikingcamping.com, inc., 2004.

I don't always agree with the authors' ratings, but with so many hiking choices in the Canadian Rockies it's helpful having them rated (premier, outstanding, worthwhile or don't do). Excellent trail descriptions and hiking advice with full color photographs in the fifth edition.

Daffern, Gillean. *Canmore & Kananaskis Country: Short Walks for Inquiring Minds*. Surrey, BC: Rocky Mountain Books, 2003.

This handy trail guide for short walks and hikes in Canmore and Kananaskis is small enough to throw in a pack. Bits of interesting natural and historical information throughout.

Dempsey, Hugh A. *Indians of the Rocky Mountain Parks*. Calgary, Alberta: Fifth House Ltd., 1998.

An overview of how the Kootenay, Shuswap, Stoney and Blackfoot tribes lived; their culture, hunting habits and territory, living structures, wars and truces, legends and the effects of European contact on their lifestyle. Includes historical photographs.

Findlay, Nora. *Jasper, A Backward Glance*. Jasper, Alberta: Friends of Jasper National Park and Jasper-Yellowhead Historical Society, 1992.

Written by a Jasper pioneer to "impart the flavor of life in Jasper in the past," and it does just that. A collection of humorous and interesting columns.

Fraser, Esther. *The Canadian Rockies: Early Travels and Explorations*. Calgary, Alberta: Fifth House, 2002.

Stories and history of the Canadian Rockies from first contact by fur traders to the coming of the transcontinental railroad, with details on various expeditions that conquered the highest peaks.

Gadd, Ben. *Handbook of the Canadian Rockies*. Jasper, Alberta: Corax Press, 1995.

If you have a keen interest in the Canadian Rockies, from the Yukon to Waterton, you should read this "bible" of the Canadian Rockies. With a degree in earth science, the author's geology section is extensive; also included are plants, animals, history and recreation. I appreciate Gadd's sense of humour and uncomplicated writing style. My only complaint: it's heavy to take on hikes. Shameless plug: artist and personal friend Matthew Wheeler did the 333 incredible drawings of mammals, birds and butterflies.

Hahn, Bob. *Kootenay National Park*. Calgary, Alberta: Rocky Mountain Books, 2000.

A naturalist's and recreationist's guide to Kootenay National Park including the surrounding Columbia Valley region. Written by a park interpreter with a flair for humor.

Hart, E.J. *Diamond Hitch*. The early outfitters and guides of Banff and Jasper. Banff, Alberta: Summerthought, 1989.

Describes the colorful lives and times of the "men of the trail" such as Tom Wilson, Bill Peyto, Jimmy Simpson, the Brewster brothers, Fred Stephens and the Otto brothers.

Hart, E.J. *A Hunter of Peace*. Banff, Alberta: Whyte Museum of the Canadian Rockies, 2003.

The life and travels of Mary Schäffer Warren, introduced and edited by E.J. Hart. This edition includes Mary T.S. Schaffer's *Old Indian Trails of the Canadian Rockies* with her heretofore-unpublished account, *1911 Expedition to Maligne Lake*.

Hart, E.J. *Jimmy Simpson, Legend of the Rockies*. Canmore, Alberta: Altitude Publishing, 2002.

An interesting account of Jimmy Simpson, one of the most important guides and outfitters in the Canadian Rockies.

Huck, Barbara and Whiteway, Doug. *In Search of Ancient Alberta*. Winnipeg, Manitoba: Heartland Publications, 1998.

A route-oriented guide to more than 65 outstanding sites in Alberta, from Miette Hot Springs to Waterton Lake. Uses geological, palaeontological and archaeological research to understand the forces that have shaped Alberta. More than 400 color photographs, maps, drawings and precise directions on getting there.

Kauffman, Andrew J. and Putnam, William L. *The Guiding Spirit*. Revelstoke, BC: Footprint Publishing, 1986.

A fascinating account of the golden age of mountaineering in the Canadian Rockies and the life of Edward Feuz Jr., one of the premier Swiss guides hired by the CPR. Based on numerous personal conversations with Feuz.

Kershaw, Linda and MacKinnon, Andy and Pojar, Jim. *Plants of the Rocky Mountains*. Edmonton, Alberta: Lone Pine Publishing, 1998.

A usable and complete field guide. Covers trees, shrubs, berries, wildflowers, ferns, mosses and more with color photographs.

Mussieux, Ron and Nelson, Marilyn. *A Traveler's Guide to Geological Wonders in Alberta*. Edmonton, Alberta: Federation of Alberta Naturalists and Canadian Society of Petroleum Geologists, 2000.

Written by two geologists, this field guide to 110 fascinating sites to explore in Alberta is both compelling and easy to understand. Interesting background information, color photographs and (tiny) maps.

Patton, Brian. *Parkways of the Canadian Rockies: A Road Guide*. Banff, Alberta: Summerthought, 1995.

Although it could use updating, if you are driving or cycling the highways and parkways of the Canadian Rockies, this road guide is invaluable. With kilometer-by-kilometer (and mile-by-mile) roadside descriptions of points of interest, wildlife viewing as well as walks and short hikes in Banff, Jasper, Kootenay and Yoho National Parks. Spiral binding makes it easy to use as you travel.

Patton, Brian. *Tales From the Canadian Rockies*. Toronto, Ontario: McClelland & Stewart Inc., 1993.

A selection of two centuries of writing in the region from the first explorers and travelers to the railway years and the new era.

Patton, Brian and Robinson, Bart. *The Canadian Rockies Trail Guide*. Banff, Alberta: Summerthought Ltd., 2002.

Regularly updated since 1971, a comprehensive trail guide to the national and provincial parks of the Canadian Rockies.

Pole, Graeme. *Canadian Rockies: An Altitude Super-Guide*. Canmore, Alberta: Altitude Publishing, 1997.

Colorful and informative with much geological and historical information.

Smith, Cyndi. *Off the Beaten Track*. Women adventurers and mountaineers in western Canada. Canmore, Alberta: Coyote Books, 1998.

Portraits of fourteen women explorers, writers, artists, mountaineers and trail guides.

Whitaker, John O., Jr. *The Audubon Society Field Guide to North American Mammals*. New York: Alfred a. Knopf, Inc., 1988.

Woodsworth, Glenn. *Hot Springs of Western Canada*. West Vancouver, British Columbia: Gordon Soules Book Publishers, 1999.

A complete guide to Canada's hot springs as well as some in Washington and Alaska. Includes resorts and natural and man-made hot springs pools that can be reached by car, on foot or by boat.

The following publications are out of print. If you have an opportunity to peruse any of these books in a special collection or archive or if you are able to purchase any from antiquarian book dealers, consider yourself fortunate.

Edwards, Ralph. *The Trail to the Charmed Land.* Saskatoon: H.R. Larson Publishing Company, 1950.

Edwards was one of well-known Rockies' outfitter Tom Wilson's regular guides. The book gives insight into trail life in the Rockies during early exploration and describes his trip to explore the Yoho Valley with German Jean Habel.

Freeman, Lewis R. *On the Roof of the Rockies: The Great Columbia Icefield of the Canadian Rockies*. New York: Dodd, Mead and Company, 1925.

Freeman and photographer Byron Harmon make a 10-week pack-train journey to the upper Athabasca Valley. The book includes 62 photographs by the author and Harmon.

Outram, James. *In the Heart of the Canadian Rockies.* London: MacMillan & Co. Ltd., 1906.

A British clergyman, Outram lived in the Canadian Rockies for more than three years in the early 1900s during which he made 28 first ascents, most notably Mount Assiniboine.

Thorington, J. Monroe. *The Glittering Mountains of Canada*. A record of exploration and pioneer ascents in the Canadian Rockies 1914-1924. Philadelphia, PA: John W. Lea, 1925.

Thorington was an American ophthalmologist who became a prominent mountaineer, with 52 first ascents in the Rockies and Selkirks. Thorington dedicated this book to his guides, Edward Feuz, Jr., Conrad Kain and James Simpson.

Index

Index

ADVENTURE GUIDES
from Hunter Publishing

This signature Hunter series targets travelers eager to explore the destination. Extensively researched and offering the very latest information, Adventure Guides are written by knowledgeable, experienced authors. The focus is on outdoor activities – hiking, biking, rock climbing, horseback riding, downhill skiing, parasailing, scuba diving, backpacking, and waterskiing, among others – and these user-friendly books provide all the details you need, including prices. The best local outfitters are listed, along with contact numbers, addresses, e-mail and website information, and recommendations. A comprehensive introductory section provides background on history, geography, climate, culture, when to go, transportation and planning. These very readable guides then take a region-by-region approach, plunging into the very heart of each area and the adventures offered, giving a full range of accommodations, shopping, restaurants for every budget, and festivals. All books have town and regional maps; color photos. Fully indexed.

THE BAHAMAS

3rd Edition, Blair Howard

Fully updated reports for Grand Bahama, Freeport, Eleuthera, Bimini, Andros, the Exumas, Nassau, New Providence Island, plus new sections on San Salvador, Long Island, Cat Island, the Acklins, the Inaguas and the Berry Islands. Mailboat schedules, package vacations and snorkeling trips by Jean-Michel Cousteau.

6 x 9 pbk, 384 pp, $18.99, 1-58843-318-9

BELIZE

5th Edition, Vivien Lougheed

"Down-to-earth advice.... An excellent travel guide." – *Library Journal*

Extensive coverage of the country's political, social and economic history, along with the plant and animal life. Encouraging you to mingle with the locals, Entices you with descriptions of local dishes and festivals. Maps, color photos.

6 x 9 pbk, 400 pp, $18.95, 1-58843-289-0

ANGUILLA, ST. MARTIN, ST. BARTS, ST. KITTS, NEVIS, ANTIGUA, BARBUDA

2nd Edition, Paris Permenter & John Bigley

Far outdistances other guides. Recommended operators for day sails, island-hopping excursions, scuba dives, unique rainforest treks on verdant mountain slopes, and rugged four-wheel-drive trails. Previously called the *Adventure Guide to the Leeward Islands*.

6 x 9 pbk, 288 pp, $17.99, 1-55650-909-X

ARUBA, BONAIRE & CURACAO

Lynne Sullivan

By the author of our top-selling Virgin Islands Adventure Guide, here is the latest and most detailed guide to the three fascinating islands of the Dutch Caribbean. Diving, sailing, hiking, golf and horseback riding are excellent here. Enjoy gourmet cuisine, charming small inns and superb five-star resorts. Duty-free stores and unique island crafts makes the islands a shopper's delight. All of them are fully explored, with details on the history and culture that makes each one so appealing. Color photos.

6 x 9 pbk, 288 pp, $18.99, 1-58843-320-X

BERMUDA

3rd Edition, Blair Howard

Botanical gardens, pink sand beaches, historic houses, 17th-century forts, tennis clubs and a decidedly British air await! Bermuda retains much of its legndary charm even as a major tourist destination. Its golf courses are some of the best in the world, drawing an upscale crowd year-round.

6 x 9 pbk, 240 pp, $18.99, 1-58843-392-7

THE CAYMAN ISLANDS

2nd Edition, Paris Permenter & John Bigley

The only comprehensive guidebook to Grand Cayman, Cayman Brac and Little Cayman. Encyclopedic listings of dive/snorkel operators, along with the best sites. Enjoy nighttime pony rides on a glorious beach, visit the turtle farms, prepare to get wet at staggering blowholes or just laze on a white sand beach. Color photos.

6 x 9 pbk, 320pp, $18.99, 1-55650-915-4

COSTA RICA

5th Edition, Bruce & June Conord

"... most comprehensive... Excellent sections on national parks, flora, fauna & history." – *CompuServe Travel Forum*

Incredible detail on culture, plants, animals, where to stay & eat, as well as practicalities of travel. E-mail and website directory.

6 x 9 pbk, 384 pp, $17.99, 1-58843-502-4

DOMINICAN REPUBLIC

4th Edition, Fe Liza Bencosme & Clark Norton

Virgin beaches, 16th-century Spanish ruins, the Caribbean's highest mountain, exotic wildlife, vast forests. Visit Santa Domingo, revel in Sosúa's European sophistication or explore the Samaná Peninsula's jungle. Color photos.

6 x 9 pbk, 360 pp, $17.99, 1-58843-402-8

DOMINICA & ST. LUCIA

Lynne Sullivan

An in-depth guide to these highly popular English-speaking Caribbean islands by the author of our top-selling Virgin Islands Adventure Guide. Dominica is unique in that it was never farmed over; it remains jungle-covered, mountainous and the only island still occupied by the original Carib Indians. St. Lucia is more developed, but is breathtaking in its beauty, with high peaks and azure-blue bays dotted with colorful boats. Town and regional maps, color photos, 6 x 9 pbk, 244 pp, $16.99, 1-58843-393-5

THE FLORIDA KEYS & EVERGLADES NATIONAL PARK

4th Edition, Bruce Morris

"... vastly informative, absolutely user-friendly, chock full of information..." – Dr. Susan Cropper

"Practical & easy to use." – *Wilderness Southeast*

Canoe trails, airboat rides, nature hikes, Key West, diving, sailing, fishing. Color.

6 x 9 pbk, 344 pp, $18.99, 1-558843-403-6

PUERTO RICO

4th Edition, Kurt Pitzer

"A quality book that covers all aspects... it's all here & well done." – *The San Diego Tribune*

"... well researched. They include helpful facts... filled with insightful tips." – *Shoestring Traveler*

Crumbling watchtowers and fascinating folklore enchant visitors. Color photos.

6 x 9 pbk, 432 pp, $18.95, 1-558843-116-9

THE VIRGIN ISLANDS

5th Edition, Lynne Sullivan

Comprehensive coverage of both the US and British Virgin Islands, including St. Thomas, St. John, St. Croix, Tortola, Virgin Gorda, Jost Van Dyke, and more. Intriguing historical, ecological, and cultural facts bring the islands and their residents to life, while practical information smoothes the way for a stress-free vacation. Extensive coverage of the islands' protected natural areas both on land and underwater.

6 x 9 pbk, 400 pp, $19.99, 1-55650-907-3

THE YUCATAN, Cancún & Cozumel

3rd Edition, Bruce & June Conord

"This in-depth travel guide opens the doors to our enchanted Yucatán" – Mexico Ministry of Tourism. "A valuable resource." – *Travel & Leisure* magazine

Takes you to places not covered in competing guides. Take to the mountain trails, swim in hidden cenotes, watch the sun rise on a beach near the ancient Maya port of Polé (where the authors celebrated the dawn of the new millennium). Visit Bohemian Playa del Carmen, or history-rich Cozumel.

6 x 9 pbk, 456 pp, $19.99, 1-558843-370-6

TAMPA BAY & FLORIDA'S WEST COAST

3rd Edition, Chelle Koster Walton

Covers all of Tampa Bay/St. Petersburg and north to Withlacoochee State Forest, and south to Sanibel Island, Naples and Everglades National Park. Canoeing the Everglades, fishing on Marco Island, biking in Boca Grande, diving with manatees in Crystal River, sailing along St. Pete Beach, theater-going in Sarasota, shopping the sponge markets of Greek-flavored Tarpon Springs, exploring the history of Tampa's Latin Ybor City - it's all here! Town and regional maps. Fully indexed. Color photos.

6 x 9 pbk, 320 pp, $18.99, 1-58843-350-1

TUSCANY & UMBRIA

Emma Jones

This history-rich region offers some of Italy's classic landscapes – pole-straight cypress trees lining dusty farm roads, rolling hills that stretch as far as the eye can see, fields of vibrant sunflowers, medieval villages perched on rocky spurs above crashing surf. Visit them all with this comprehensive guide that helps you explore the very best places. A largely untouched coastline and protected wild areas only add to the appeal of this top vacation destination. Town and regional maps, color photos, fully indexed.

6 x 9 pbk, 500 pp, $19.99, 1-58843-399-4

SWITZERLAND

Kimberly Rinker

With azure-blue lakes that shine brilliantly against the greenest slopes of the surrounding Alps, its picturesque villages and chic towns are accessible via high-speed trains, though many opt to travel by longboat on some of the country's tranquil waterways. It is one of the world's most advanced industrialized nations, yet its towns and cities are incredibly clean. Part-time Swiss resident Kimberly Rinker has lived and worked here for years. She tells of little-known attractions as well as major tourist draws and everything in-between. Color photos.

6 X 9 pbk, 528 pp, $17.99, 1-58843-369-2

ST. MARTIN & ST. BARTS

Lynne Sullivan

Half-French, half-Dutch, St. Martin offers Orient Bay; duty-free shopping in Philipsburg; Marigot, with chic French boutiques and superb food; and Restaurant Row in Grand Case, with great eateries in charming Creole houses. St. Barts has few buildings higher than one story, no large hotels, memorable food and 22 beautiful beaches along turquoise seas. Lynne Sullivan, author of our best-selling Adventure Guide to the Virgin Islands and several other guides, shows you how to discover and enjoy these islands to the fullest, with island tours, shopping tips, historic sightseeing, watersports and hundreds of places to stay and eat.

6 x 9 pbk, 240 pp, $19.99, 1-58843-348-X

SPAIN

Kelly Lipscomb

A resident of Spain, the author delves into every province and town. He tells of the history and culture, and provides innumerableuseful traveling tips. Everything is explored – the cities, the parks, the islands, the mountains, the foods – plus walking tours, bike trips, sightseeing, hotels, restaurants. Covers the entire country, from Ibiza to Granada, Andalucia, Barcelona, Madrid and Toledo. Town and regional maps, color photos, fully indexed.

6 x 9 pbk, 730 pp, $21.99, 1-58843-398-6

SCOTLAND

Martin Li

The definitive guide to every aspect of Scotland – the legends, the clans, the castles and romantic hotels, the Highland games and, of course, the whisky. This long-time Scotland resident takes us from Edinburgh to Glasgow, Argyll and the Isles, Loch Lomond, the Highlands and to the Outer Isles. Fascinating details on the Loch Ness monster, Shakespeare's "Macbeth" castle, Mary Queen of Scots, the Viking legacy, Burns Night and the royal castles. This book covers it all, and has color photos, maps and index.

6 x 9 pbk, 750 pp, $21.99, 1-58843-406-0

PANAMA

Mother nature has bequeathed Panama with some stunning spots, rich soils and a vast biodiversity. White- and black-sand beaches alternate with mangrove mazes along the coast. Sparkling wild rivers overflowing with trout run through jungle-clad canyons filled with colorful flowers. Mist-crowned Baru Volcano towers above them all. This book explores every region from tip to toe, including the San Blas Islands, offshore Barro Colorado, and urban Panama City, gateway for visitors. Walking tours visit historic forts, gold museums, classic city parks and bustling crafts markets. Special attention is given to the national parks.

6 x 9 pbk, 360 pp, $19.99, 1-58843-368-4

GRENADA, ST. VINCENT & THE GRENADINES

Cindy Kilgore & Alan Moore

Unspoiled islands at the southern end of the Caribbean chain just now being discovered by tourists. St. Vincent, with the oldest botanical garden in the Americas, is dominated by a huge volcano. The Grenadines include Bequia, Mustigue, Mayreau. Grenada, with its pristine reefs, is the source for a third of the world's nutmeg. Full details on accommodations and restaurants, getting around, sightseeing, climate, history and geography.

6 x 9 pbk, 352 pp, $18.99, 1-58843-349-8

GERMANY

Henk Bekker

Bavaria, the Mosel Valley, the Rhine region, the Black Forest, Dresden, Berlin, Hamburg – this highly detailed guide covers every part of the country in depth. The author, a German resident, shows you how to experience the best, through town walks, drives in the countryside and immersing yourself in the entertainment, the sights, the history and culture. Hundreds of hotel and restaurant reviews.

6 x 9 pbk, 550 pp, $19.99, 1-58843-503-2

IRELAND

Tina Neylon

Ireland is steeped in history, tradition and culture, making it one of the most popular vacation destinations worldwide. Its story is told in centuries-old castles (some of which now welcome overnight guests); stone circles strategically placed to shine in the winter solstice moon; and, of course, in its pubs, where local residents gladly share a pint and a tale. Its cities are a treat to explore, with winding streets packed with tiny antique stores. Trips along the coast take you to traditional fishing villages and past some of the world's best golf courses. This book, written by an Ireland native, tells it all. Color photos.

6 x 9 pbk, 624 pp, $21.99, 1-58843-367-6

PARIS & ILE DE FRANCE

Heather Stimmler-Hall

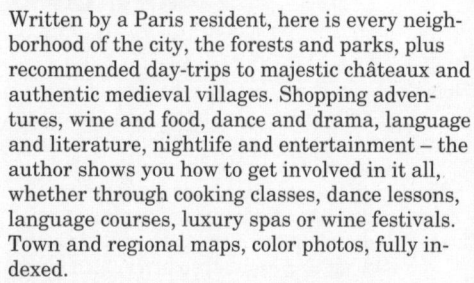

Written by a Paris resident, here is every neighborhood of the city, the forests and parks, plus recommended day-trips to majestic châteaux and authentic medieval villages. Shopping adventures, wine and food, dance and drama, language and literature, nightlife and entertainment – the author shows you how to get involved in it all, whether through cooking classes, dance lessons, language courses, luxury spas or wine festivals. Town and regional maps, color photos, fully indexed.

6 x 9 pbk, 448 pp, $19.99, 1-58843-396-X

MEXICO'S PACIFIC COAST

Vivien Lougheed

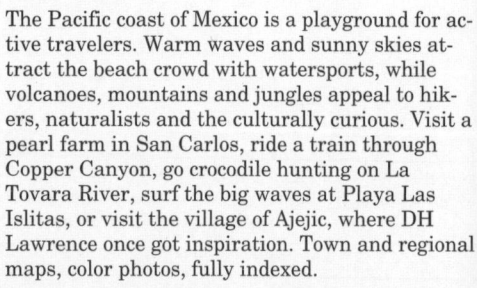

The Pacific coast of Mexico is a playground for active travelers. Warm waves and sunny skies attract the beach crowd with watersports, while volcanoes, mountains and jungles appeal to hikers, naturalists and the culturally curious. Visit a pearl farm in San Carlos, ride a train through Copper Canyon, go crocodile hunting on La Tovara River, surf the big waves at Playa Las Islitas, or visit the village of Ajejic, where DH Lawrence once got inspiration. Town and regional maps, color photos, fully indexed.

6 x 9 pbk, 500 pp, $19.99, 1-58843-395-1

JAMAICA 5th Edition

Paris Permenter & John Bigley

This travel guide walks with the adventurous traveler to the heart of Jamaica, to the miles of sand beaches, to the rugged Blue Mountains, to the country villages that provide a peek at the real Jamaica. The authors focus on the adventures this popular Caribbean island has to offer: scuba diving along coral reefs, biking mountain trails, deep sea fishing, parasailing, windsurfing, horseback riding, and other adventures that range from mild to wild. Special sections include a look at Jamaica's Meet the People program, home visits, local nightspots, festivals, and more. Maps and photos enliven the down-to-earth text.

6 x 9 pbk, 360 pp, $18.99, 1-58843-504-0

NEW ZEALAND

Bette Flagler

Written by a local, this guide covers every region and town, with in-depth information on the Maori culture, the remarkable places to stay and eat, vineyard tours, cooking schools, thermal springs, albatross and whale encounters, scenic drives, and more. Canoe the Whanganui River, ride in a hot air balloon, hike the Waikaremoana Track, explore Whirikana Forest Park, take a glacier tour. There's even a section on how to talk Kiwi English! Color photos, maps and a thorough index.

6 x 9 pbk, 650 pp, $21.99, 1-58843-405-2

All Hunter titles are available at bookstores nationwide or from the publisher. To order direct, send a check for the total of the book(s) ordered plus $3 shipping and handling to Hunter Publishing, 130 Campus Drive, Edison NJ 08818. Secure credit card orders may be made at the Hunter website, where you will also find in-depth descriptions of the hundreds of travel guides we offer.

ORDER FORM

Yes! Send the following *Adventure Guides*:

TITLE	ISBN #	PRICE	QUANTITY	TOTAL
SUBTOTAL				
SHIPPING & HANDLING (United States only) (1-2 books, $3; 3-5 books, $5; 6-10 books, $8)				
ENCLOSED IS MY CHECK FOR				

NAME:	
ADDRESS:	
CITY: STATE: ZIP:	
PHONE:	